A HANDBOOK OF READINGS
IN EDUCATION OF THE DEAF AND
POSTSCHOOL IMPLICATIONS

A HANDBOOK OF READINGS

IN EDUCATION OF THE DEAF AND

POSTSCHOOL IMPLICATIONS

Edited by

IRVING S. FUSFELD

Formerly
Vice President, Gallaudet College
Editor, American Annals of the Deaf
Supervisor of Counseling and Child Guidance
California School for the Deaf, Berkeley

CHARLES C THOMAS • **PUBLISHER**
Springfield • *Illinois* • *U.S.A.*

Published and Distributed Throughout the World by

CHARLES C THOMAS • PUBLISHER

BANNERSTONE HOUSE

301-327 East Lawrence Avenue, Springfield, Illinois, U.S.A.

NATCHEZ PLANTATION HOUSE

735 North Atlantic Boulevard, Fort Lauderdale, Florida, U.S.A.

With THOMAS BOOKS *careful attention is given to all details of manufacturing and design. It is the Publisher's desire to present books that are satisfactory as to their physical qualities and artistic possibilities and appropriate for their particular use.* THOMAS BOOKS *will be true to those laws of quality that assure a good name and good will.*

Printed in the United States of America

BB-14

To
My wife, Dr. Cecile L. Fusfeld, whose patience
provided the opportunity to complete this work

And to
The Children Who Inspire the Thoughts
Which Follow
And the Future to Which Those Children
Aspire

Introduction

A textbook of readings bearing on education of the deaf should be a helpful as well as timely work.

Justification for this observation rests on a number of supporting conditions. First among these is the recent growth of widespread public and general interest in problems of hearing loss. On professional lines many allied disciplines are now actively engaged with these problems, both direct and indirect, covering areas in medicine, psychology, rehabilitation, the guidance sciences, placement offices, social work, general and special education, audiology, electronics, physics, linguistics and communication interest. Converging efforts from these directions have enlisted large numbers of specialized personnel concentrating on programs of research and on points of application reaching all the way into the classrooms of schools for deaf children and ramifying beyond into the ever critical postschool years.

A universal concern that spreads across this array of learned interests relates primarily to a need for orientation in basic background information. What is deafness? It is far more than abbreviation, even closure, of one of the primary senses. As a human quandary it cuts more deeply than that, opening into a baffling complex of many and diverse facets. What are its inevitably accompanying perplexities, each vitally interacting one upon another and so compounding the total problem? It is apparent, then, that a proper approach to an understanding of the field will require touching upon many "ports of call." It is the purpose of this Handbook to aid in this quest, frankly as a guide book. It is its intent, then, to assemble from widely scattered but authoritative sources, information which comprehensively covers a spectrum of the varied aspects of present-day thinking and action in this fascinating yet only partially explored area of special education.

The roster of persons who may find utility in a work of this kind now reaches an imposing number. To begin with, recent national legislation has provided substantial extension of teacher training facilities in education of the deaf, bringing into the scope of this important need a number of the major universities and colleges, thus greatly enhancing the service such centers can render. Accompanying this expansion has been a proliferation of hearing-conservation clinics as well as hospital and medical school audiology departments staffed by specialists in problems of hearing loss. A tremendous new interest in the preschool area in cases of children with impaired hearing is now manifest. A report in a recent issue of *The Volta Review* (September, 1965, pp. 512–524) lists 346 schools and classes for deaf children *under six years* of age in the United States and Canada, in public and private, in residential and day facilities—the latter, in turn, involving teaching, administrative and service personnel, as well as parents. In each of these centers, as in regular special school programs, parent-teacher association activity has waxed strong, adding of course to the numbers closely interested in basic information regarding the phenomenon of hearing impairment and its aftermath implications. In this connection, mention should be made of the growing tendency in this area to arouse wider interest by use of correspondence courses as well as through common public communications channels. A widely aroused interest in the same field has been evident in leadership activity among the adult deaf and among organizations for the hard of hearing.

The account is further amplified when one considers a number of other forces brought to bear significantly in this newly awakened community of interest in the difficulties accompanying the decline or depletion of hearing in childhood. Foremost in this respect has been the benevolent leadership and enlightened support of agencies of government extending chainwise from national sources down through state, county and local jurisdiction. In this particular, the role of the Vocational Rehabilitation Administration and of the U. S. Office of Education has been a constructively stimulating one. Scientific inquiry has been encouraged, made effective by liberal government grants and bolstered by support from private and semi-public foundations and industrial organizations. Much of this has been concentrated in research projects under carefully guarded control conditions, in established university research centers, which has resulted in an enrichment of knowledge within this special field. Numerous conferences, workshops and survey studies, on a national and regional scale, have had added influence. Even church denominational activity has reflected a renewed concern regarding the overlapping problems of deafness. Here then, to serve a sure need for groundwork knowledge by increasing numbers of individuals in specialized related disciplines, this Handbook covering a broad span of data is hopefully offered.

So much for the utility prospect for a textbook of this kind.

It would seem germane to consider the primary accessibility of the material brought together here, or rather lack of accessibility, with respect to ready approach.

Almost every school for children with hearing deficiency maintains a monthly publication which functions as a chronicle of activities of more or less local and current interest. It is, in addition, a vehicle for much valuable information on school policy, classroom practice and general principles of pupil management, source material which should prove particularly useful to those seeking basic orientation in work dealing with hearing impairment. It is frequently also an outlet for papers contributed by staff members and other specialists which directly expound upon problems of close professionally related interest. Often such items reflect background data for the researchist, indeed, are at times reports of research activity. The issues of these journals, fondly known as the Little Paper Family, or the L.P.F., circulate among the schools, and so make possible much interchange of professional thinking.* Frequently, especially meaningful articles will appear as reprints in a number of these school journals, indication of greater-than-local appeal. But the back issues of the L.P.F. are not easily accessible, and it is unlikely a cross-reference file of their contents exists anywhere. With the further rare exception of the libraries of the Volta Bureau and Gallaudet College—both in Washington, D. C.— and of the Royal National Institute for the Deaf in England, this important source of information is lost for permanent study and reference purposes. To illustrate, a recent special number of *The Volta Review* (November, 1963) was given over entirely to a summary review of research activity in problems of hearing loss, an important part of which were lists of reference bibliography. In no instance was the L.P.F. represented among the more than 500 items in these reference lists. To one in close touch with the work of schools for the deaf this omission would seem to be an oversight. This Handbook of Readings aims to avoid that failure. Among its pages will be found many contributions of a professional nature which appeared originally in school papers.

Although excellent reference material is to be found in the current and back volumes of *The Volta Review*, the *American Annals of the Deaf*, the *Teacher of the Deaf* (England), and *The Deaf American* (formerly *The Silent Worker*), the selections included in the present Handbook represent an effort to seek out significant material not appearing in those journals. The same principle applies to the published Proceedings of the Convention of American Instructors of the Deaf, and generally of the Conference of Executives of American Schools for the Deaf, as well as to the few standard textbooks within the same field of interest. In this sense the present volume should serve a supplementing purpose as a supporting source book.

The succession of selections makes claim to a point of special merit, that of recency. Almost all of them appeared in print within the past ten years. In this sense they reflect current thinking and practice, a distillate of both experience and experimental inquiry.

Many of the selections among the readings themselves include documenting and directly related bibliography, thereby obviating the need of repetition in a closing chapter of collected references. The frequency with which certain references are cited will probably indicate something of their special authority.

* "These little papers provide not only training opportunities for little printers, but also provide a dish of often intriguing articles for readers," Fred P. Yates, Jr., *The Virginia Guide*, February, 1965.

The material thus presented is substantial in content, and broadly balanced, espousing no particular brand of school program or theory, but instead providing the student of this area of special education with a practical, foundational orientation and as well a fair insight into the many-sided complex which follows upon a diminished sense of hearing in childhood.

It should be understood the terms "deaf" and "deafness" are here considered in their generic sense. Total irrevocable deprivation of the power to hear is, in fact, an infrequent occurrence. Rather, and far more common, impaired hearing is a phenomenon extending from that zero point all the way to near normality, and hence suggesting almost unlimited diversification in alleviation. Within this latter observation rests a multiplicity of practice in reaching the hearing-impaired individual, and particularly in the preschool and school-age years, encompassing thus a vast variety of educational design.

In that light a measure of understanding is possible regarding the "mystery" of who the deaf child is, the needs made special by his physiological handicap, the sweep and complex nature of the process we are prone to call "education," and finally the adult he is likely to become as he moves toward the problems which assail him and the rehabilitating opportunities open to him as an individual and as a social being.

The panorama of progress in the setting of education is an ever-changing one. Nowhere among the variant phenomena of life is this more apt than when applied to effort in behalf of children subject to impairment of hearing, bearing in mind the adulthood they are to enter. But for the problems always at hand there are no pat answers. No matter what the basic philosophy is, or the practice which it fathers, the fundamental need is for an ever-inquiring, ever-questioning point of view. This then, if it is necessary to pronounce a background theme for this volume of readings, is its purpose.

IRVING S. FUSFELD

Acknowledgment

Acknowledgment is here gratefully made of the help a number of individuals have given in the task of assembling the material for this project. Among these individuals are Thomas J. Dillon, principal in the New Mexico School for the Deaf; Caroline H. Burnes, accomplished librarian of the California School for the Deaf in Berkeley; Helen Myers, on the staff of the high school department of the same school; Frederick C. Schreiber, secretary-treasurer of the National Association of the Deaf; Dr. Elwood A. Stevenson, former superintendent of the California School for the Deaf, Berkeley, and Dr. Pierre Gorman, librarian of the Royal National Institute for the Deaf in London. Equally helpful with clerical assistance has been Rose F. Cuengco of Berkeley, California. Included in the list of those to whom thanks are due are the many heads of schools for the deaf who generously made school publications available. In particular, encouragement by Dr. Hugo F. Schunhoff, superintendent of the California School for the Deaf, Berkeley, and president of the Conference of Executives of American Schools for the Deaf, has helped to lighten the task.

Appreciation is here noted also for the helpful advice of Dr. Harold Geist, of Berkeley, California, and of the editor's sons, Dr. Robert D. Fusfeld, of the Wadsworth Veterans Administration Hospital, Los Angeles, and Dr. Daniel R. Fusfeld, of the University of Michigan.

Finally, permission to reproduce copyrighted papers, those in the main found in professional scientific journals, is gratefully acknowledged, as is also the consent of authors. Effort has been made to indicate in each case proper identification of the original source of publication.

I. S. F.

Contents

	Page
Introduction	vii
Acknowledgment	xi

I. BASIC PRINCIPLES

WHAT I WOULD EXPECT OF A SCHOOL, AND ITS TEACHERS—*W. T. Griffing*	3
FUNDAMENTALS—*Edward L. Scouten*	5

II. SOME SALIENT POINTS IN THE HISTORY OF EDUCATION OF THE DEAF

HISTORY OF THE EDUCATION OF THE DEAF TO 1815—*Byron B. Burnes*	7
HISTORICAL SURVEY OF EDUCATION OF THE DEAF IN THE UNITED STATES—*Harold Ramger*	12

III. ETIOLOGY OF HEARING LOSS IN CHILDREN

THE PROBLEM OF CONGENITAL DEAFNESS—*G. Dekle Taylor*	19
DEAFNESS AND SCHOOL: MIDDLE EAR EFFUSION—*G. O. Proud* and *F. R. Kirchner*	29
HEARING PROBLEMS OF SCHOOL AGE CHILDREN—*John K. Duffy*	33
REGARDING CHANGING TRENDS IN ENROLLMENT OF A SCHOOL FOR DEAF CHILDREN—*Irving S. Fusfeld*	37

IV. EARLY AUDITORY ASSESSMENT

AUDITORY SCREENING OF INFANTS—*Donald R. Caziarc*	40

V. CURRENT TRENDS AND PROBLEMS

DEAFNESS: SOME PRESENT-DAY PROBLEMS—*E. D. D. Dickson*	45
EDUCATIONAL TRENDS—*William Rasburn*	51

VI. PRESCHOOL TRAINING

Page

TRAINING PROGRAM FOR THE EDUCATION OF DEAF INFANTS—*Robert L. McCroskey* 56

THE YOUNG DEAF CHILD AND HIS PROBLEMS—*Adriana Dumitrescu* 62

NURSERY DEPARTMENT IN A RESIDENTIAL SCHOOL—*Sam B. Craig* 66

VII. TYPES OF SCHOOL ORGANIZATION AND PLACEMENT

THE IOWA SCHOOL OFFERS A COMPLETE PROGRAM—*C. Joseph Giangreco* ... 71

PLIGHT OF HARD-OF-HEARING CHILDREN—*Margaret S. Kent* 72

DETROIT DAY SCHOOL FOR DEAF PROGRAM FOR DEAF AND HARD-OF-HEARING CHILDREN—*Harriet Green Kopp* 74

UNITS FOR DEAF CHILDREN—*D. M. C. Dale* 79

THE INTEGRATION OF THE DEAF IN SCHOOLS FOR THE NORMALLY HEARING—*Clarence D. O'Connor* 82

VIII. THE MULTI-SIDED SCHOOL PROGRAM

FROM DISCIPLINE TO SELF-DISCIPLINE—*Melda E. Alber* 86

THE CHILDREN WE TEACH—*Adoracion A. Alvarez* 87

OUR ACADEMIC PROGRAM AND RELATED PROBLEMS—*Alfred J. Lamb* 91

RHYTHM: ITS IMPORTANCE IN THE EDUCATION OF THE DEAF—*Bette Fauth* .. 97

MUSIC IN EDUCATION OF THE DEAF—*Laura Burns* 99

TEACHING SPEECH IN LOWER SCHOOL—*Sarah Harper Abernethy, Sharon Stellwagen, Nancy Keim, Doris Taylor* 101

MANUSCRIPT OR CURSIVE?—*David M. Denton* 103

VISUAL AIDS: AN ENRICHING MEDIUM—*Betty Irgens* 108

THAT THEY MAY GROW—*Frances Wiltse* 111

POTENTIALITIES IN ART EDUCATION FOR THE DEAF—*Rawley A. Silver* 114

BOOK SELECTION FOR A SCHOOL FOR THE DEAF LIBRARY—*George Propp* 120

DORMITORY PROGRAM AT O. S. S. D.—*Keith Pitman* 123

PHYSICAL EDUCATION PROGRAM AT THE TEXAS SCHOOL FOR THE DEAF—*Marian Pharr* 126

IX. LANGUAGE DEVELOPMENT: THE VITAL COMPONENT

LANGUAGE DEVELOPMENT AT THE PRIMARY LEVEL—*Lucile Taylor* 129

HELPING THE DEAF CHILD TOWARD ADEQUATE LANGUAGE AND SPEECH—*Boris V. Morkovin* 133

Page

COMMUNICATION PROBLEMS AT THE INTERMEDIATE LEVEL—*Rev. Lawrence C. Murphy* 136

SOME LANGUAGE TEACHING TECHNIQUES USED WITH THE PRELINGUALLY DEAF—*Martha C. Larsen* 139

THE REVIVAL OF THE ROCHESTER METHOD—*William J. McClure* 142

PROGRAMED INSTRUCTION IN WRITTEN LANGUAGE FOR THE DEAF—*E. Ross Stuckless and Jack W. Birch* 145

LANGUAGE LABORATORY FOR YOUNG DEAF CHILDREN—*Frank B. Withrow* ... 155

X. THE TEACHER FACTOR

WHAT DEAF TEACHERS CAN ACCOMPLISH IN SCHOOLS FOR THE DEAF— *Richard G. Brill* 158

MINIMUM COURSE REQUIREMENTS TO BE INCLUDED IN A PROGRAM FOR PREPARATION OF TEACHERS OF THE DEAF IN CENTERS MEETING THE STANDARDS APPROVED BY THE CONFERENCE OF EXECUTIVES OF AMERICAN SCHOOLS FOR THE DEAF 161

XI. AUDITORY AMPLIFICATION IN SCHOOL PRACTICE

AMPLIFICATION FOR CHILDREN PROFOUNDLY DEAF—*Margaret S. Kent* 163

IN ONE EAR—*Charles DeVinney* 165

MORE ABOUT HEARING AIDS—*Albert C. Esterline* 168

THE FURTHER DESTRUCTION OF PARTIALLY DEAFENED CHILDREN'S HEARING BY THE USE OF POWERFUL HEARING AIDS—*Charles E. Kinney* 170

XII. VOCATIONAL PREPARATION

THE DEAF AND VOCATIONAL CHOICE—*H. W. Hoemann* 176

MEASUREMENT OF THE VOCATIONAL INTERESTS OF THE DEAF BY MEANS OF PICTURES—*Harold Geist* 179

XIII. GUIDANCE SERVICES

GUIDANCE SERVICES AT I. S. D.—*Richard Helton* 181

XIV. ROLE OF THE HOME IN THE EDUCATIVE PROCESS

HEARING HANDICAPPED CHILDREN NEED UNDERSTANDING—*C. Joseph Giangreco* 185

Page

GUIDELINES FOR PARENTS IN PROMOTING VOCABULARY AND LANGUAGE FA-
CILITY—*Margaret S. Kent* 188

LETTERS: THE LIFELINE FROM HOME—*George Propp* and *Mira Jean Kaufmann* 190

A STUDY OF THE EDUCATIONAL ACHIEVEMENT OF DEAF CHILDREN OF DEAF
PARENTS—*Elwood A. Stevenson* 193

XV. THOUGHTS ON A REALISTIC APPRAISAL

SPEECH ALONE IS NOT ENOUGH—*Stahl Butler* 197

AUDIOGRAM—CAN ONLY TELL HALF OF THE STORY—*Richard F. Krug* 198

XVI. DEAFNESS WITH ASSOCIATED DISABILITY

AIDING THE SCHOOLS TOWARD A BETTER DIAGNOSIS—*John F. Font* 204

PROBLEMS ACCOMPANYING CHILDREN WHO ARE DEAF AND MENTALLY RE-
TARDED—*Myron A. Leenhouts* 210

COURT GRANGE 217

MULTIPLE ANOMALIES IN CONGENITALLY DEAF CHILDREN—*Jacob M. Danish,
J. Karetas Tillson* and *Max Levitan* 226

A CLASSROOM PROGRAM FOR AUDITORALLY HANDICAPPED MENTALLY DEFI-
CIENT CHILDREN—*Leon Glovsky* and *Seymour Rigrodsky* 237

USE OF THE "ODDITY PROBLEM" IN TEACHING MENTALLY RETARDED DEAF-
MUTES TO READ: A PILOT PROJECT—*Douglas K. Candland* and *Daniel H.
Conklyn* 248

DEAF-BLIND CHILDREN—THEIR EDUCATIONAL OUTLOOK—*Byron Berhow* 252

XVII. CONSIDERATIONS OF PSYCHOLOGY

PSYCHOLOGICAL AND PSYCHIATRIC IMPLICATIONS OF DEAFNESS—*Helmer R.
Myklebust* 256

ADJUSTMENT PROBLEMS OF THE DEAF CHILD—*Grace Moore Heider* 261

HOW A DEAF CHILD THINKS—*Irving S. Fusfeld* 267

A GUIDE TO PSYCHOLOGICAL TESTS AND TESTING PROCEDURES IN THE EVALUA-
TION OF DEAF AND HARD-OF-HEARING CHILDREN—*McCay Vernon* and
Donald W. Brown 274

PSYCHOLOGICAL ASSESSMENT—*Cornelius P. Goetzinger* 284

WANTED: A MEANINGFUL MENTAL HEALTH PROGRAM. APPLY ANY SCHOOL
FOR THE DEAF—*Taras B. Denis* 299

XVIII. WHAT RESEARCH REVEALS

Page

New Insight Into Lipreading—*Edgar L. Lowell* 306

The Attainments in English and Arithmetic of Secondary School Pupils With Impaired Hearing—*D. C. Wollman* 309

Evaluational Language Processes in the Deaf—*Richard L. Blanton* and *Jum C. Nunnally* 317

Semantic Habits and Cognitive Style Processes in the Deaf—*Richard L. Blanton* and *Jum C. Nunnally* 320

XIX. REHABILITATION BACKGROUND

Special Factors in the Rehabilitation of the Deaf—*John B. Roraback* 330

Establishment of Rehabilitation Unit at the Arizona State School for the Deaf and the Blind—*Thomas G. Tyrrell* 335

Communication Evaluation of the Deaf and Its Implications for Job Placement—*Emil M. Zabell* 338

XX. THE POSTSCHOOL PROSPECT

Occupations of the Deaf—*Stanley K. Bigman* 343

Casework With the Deaf: A Problem in Communication—*Steven K. Chough* 348

"Truly Remarkable People"—*Edgar L. Lowell* 357

A HANDBOOK OF READINGS
IN EDUCATION OF THE DEAF AND
POSTSCHOOL IMPLICATIONS

A class in language development at the California School for the Deaf, Berkeley.

I. Basic Principles

WHAT I WOULD EXPECT OF A SCHOOL, AND ITS TEACHERS*

W. T. GRIFFING

This is a tall order. I say this because everything I put down here can be used against me as a parent, that is, in my high expectations of a school and its teachers, it and they, in turn, can expect even more of me. That is the way it is on general principles.

Now, were I a parent with a child about to embark on an educational and training program that would eventually make or break his life, I would want to take every precaution to assure myself in a convincing manner that I would be making no mistake in his placement at some school. First of all, I would have to be convinced that it was professionally, ethically, and humanly geared to cope with the many problems that this child would encounter through the years.

Its superintendent would have to indoctrinate me. He would have to explain its philosophy of education upon which it rests its cause for education of the deaf. This would tell me a great deal that will be very helpful. Then, I'd like to visit in the homes and places of business of a good many of its graduates and former pupils. I'd want to talk to them as one interested person to another, and I'd want their unqualified endorsement of their school as the one to which to send my child. I'd be keenly interested in how they live, the role they occupy in their communities, how they adjust themselves to life's situations, and the esteem in which they are held by those with whom they both work and play. These people would give me an after-school picture, one that is nearest to my thoughts.

I would be interested in hearing the different systems explained, but I'd be content to let the school select the one that is best suited to the particular needs of my child. After all, I am just a layman; I realize that they know better than I do through experience and training. I also realize that theories can look pretty in print but all too often they fail to hold up when the pressure is greatest. The very fact that I have at last decided on the school is sufficient to put my mind at rest regarding how

* Reprinted with permission from *The Companion*, Minnesota School for the Deaf, Faribault, December, 1964. Dr. Griffing is from the Oklahoma School for the Deaf.

3

the child should be guided throughout his formative years. Still, I'd like to believe these things:

1. That at all times my child would be regarded as a human being, as an individual, with opinions and differences that may irritate at time, yet which should not be killed by impatience or indifference. I'd expect the school to devise a program which will channel all these individual differences in children into a millstream of visual, tactile, olfactory and kinesthetic experiences that can become rich and meaningful.

2. The teachers, of course, were selected by the superintendent on a basis of merit. But I'd like it very much were I sure they were in the school because they were dedicated people, with a genuine affection for the deaf. If this be so, then they were in the teaching field not because of a pay check but because of a desire to serve. These teachers of a school would have to have the knowledge that their work is not based on an 8-to-4 day in a classroom; it would have to encompass the entire revolution of the clock, then extend far after graduation. There is so much learning outside of a classroom, at all hours, that a teacher is literally on call twenty-four hours of the day. If the school made this clear to them at the time they were hired, I'd breathe a lot easier. I don't think any school should have on its roster a teacher who says, "But, I am not paid to do that!" When money is the driving force in a teacher's personality, we can be certain that her charges are going to be short-changed many, many times.

I'd want a school with discipline because that quality is something that will be sorely needed. This involves proper conduct, interest in work, neatness, punctuality, and a flair for handling situations, no matter what, in just the right way.

I'd want the school to probe, to probe deep. I'd want it to be concerned with what was in my child's heart as well as his head. Only a good and a conscientious school can do this in a manner that will win respect and confidence, and build for enduring happiness.

I would not want the school to coddle my child. I'd want him to try to strike out for himself, to learn to get up after some unfortunate experience without too much assistance—just enough to ease the hurt and to strengthen the desire to do better. I'd like to believe the school is rooted in the tradition of truth, no matter how much it might hurt. Truth, taken at tide, can work for the good of all.

This is rather a large order, yet the school I want must be even bigger. It must be rich in wisdom, mellow in its compassion, yet with a certain touch that keeps a child in his world of wanting to belong, to be a part of everything around him. This school would have the gift of opening doors for children, of leading them into areas of splendid newness. This art of adding dimensions to a child's world does not call for anything except doing things more often with them instead of for them or to them. The school would have to invite the children to become fellow adventurers, conspirators, if you will, in its wonderful world of learning.

Its system, whatever it may be, would have to be one that would blow away the dust of drudgery, thus abolishing boredom.

The teachers? Well, I'd expect them to love all children just so much and not more. It should not be too much here and too much there, but an equal distribution of interest and affection. These pupils should not be just in a certain classroom but all in the school.

I'd never want a teacher to call my child stupid, even though that may be the case. She can tell me and I can take it; but not that little one just starting out to try to think, to grasp the unknown. This calls for patience and for tact, yet I'd expect the teacher to excel there simply because she was hired by a good school. A good teacher knows how to deal with situations without losing her temper or by demoralizing a little one by becoming sarcastic about his mentality, something that is in the hands of God.

A teacher should stand ready to give me the facts, without apology or any beating about the bush. She should show me how I am to take up the slack in the learning process while the child is with me at home.

A teacher should never be too busy to listen to a child, no matter what it is that has prompted him to come to her with a comradeship, hoping that she will share his enthusiasm, his disappointment, or his offer of friendship. These little talks do more to cement friendships and to create mutual trust and understanding than a whole year of history facts! These talks are the mind and the heart of a child trying to penetrate a horizon so that they can germinate, and bud, then blossom into flower or fruit.

So, my choice of a school and its teachers does put me pretty much on the spot. In demanding so much, they have every right to expect me to live up to certain standards that might go hard with me at times. But it is this giving and this taking which make a school and its people both good and helpful, and the parents wiser and more grateful for the little things of life which otherwise might have gone unnoticed.

FUNDAMENTALS*

EDWARD L. SCOUTEN

The other day a couple of parents came to the office to find out what the new principal had in mind concerning the education of their deaf child. Be-

* Taken with permission from the column "Scoutin' Around," *The Pelican*, Louisiana State School for the Deaf, Baton Rouge, November, 1962.

cause other parents probably have the same question in mind, it would be practical to set down precisely what we do believe in our business of educating deaf children.

First, however, it must be made clear that merely calling a deaf child "hard of hearing" does not make him hard of hearing. The fact of deafness remains, and with it all of its attendant problems. A frank recognition of the problem of deafness by parents and teachers alike places them in a better position to understand and meet the individual child's special needs and to plan accordingly for his language development, auditory training, and speech work.

To deny the fact of deafness and to veil the problem as being that of a moderate hearing loss which may be alleviated with a hearing aid, lipreading, and speech correction is to deny the deaf child the benefit of an especially developed language foundation upon which his entire future education may be based.

Parents are urged to recognize the deafness of their child for what it is—a state of intellectual isolation caused by an almost impenetrable wall of silence. Because of this wall, all intellectual appeals must be *visible* to the deaf child or else they are wasted. If we wish the deaf child to learn, we must allow him to *see* what we would have him learn. With this thought firmly in mind, we may say:

Our philosophy of education for the deaf child centers upon an implicit faith in the child to reach his maximal achievement through instructional procedures adapted to his specific needs with particular emphasis upon experience framed in visually perceptible English.†

† Scouten, E. L., "The Accelerated Child," Proceedings of the 40th Meeting of the Convention of American Instructors of the Deaf, Salem, Oregon, 335. E. L. Scouten is Principal of the Louisiana School for the Deaf.

II. Some Salient Points in the History of Education of the Deaf

HISTORY OF THE EDUCATION OF THE DEAF TO 1815*

BYRON B. BURNES

Before we begin this brief study of the history of education of the deaf, I must say that I am no historian and I have engaged in very little research on the subject. Such material as I have been able to assemble on short notice I have taken almost entirely from books and periodicals available in the library at the California School for the Deaf, one of the best school libraries in the United States.

I have confined my material mostly to the movements which directly affected the beginning of education of the deaf in America, but the history of the American phase is not included in this paper.

The chief sources of my material have been Arnold's *Education of the Deaf*, Best's *Deafness and the Deaf in the United States*, and numerous volumes of the *American Annals of the Deaf*.

Historians have written that organized efforts to educate the deaf began about 1760, and inspiration for the

* A paper read before a class of teacher trainees at San Francisco State College in October, 1959. It is here reprinted, with consent, as it appeared in *The California News*, California School for the Deaf, Berkeley, April, 1960. Dr. Burnes is from the California School for the Deaf.

effort came from the writings of Girolamo Cardano, a philosopher of Milan, in the sixteenth century. He is sometimes called Jerome Cardan.

In prehistoric times deafness was a baffling affliction and was permitted to remain as such. A writer in the *American Annals of the Deaf* in 1926 said that the Greeks and Romans perhaps had given some thought to the possibility of educating the deaf but Aristotle, the oracle of philosophy, had banned any effort in that direction with the dictum that, "the ear is the organ of education." The dictum was accepted as final, as indicated by this couplet of Lucretius:

To instruct the deaf no art could ever reach, No care improve them and no wisdom teach.

However, there were more or less sporadic efforts to educate the deaf. Dr. Best says that "the earliest instance recorded of instruction to the deaf is that of the Venerable Bede about the year 691, who tells of a deaf person taught to speak or to read the lips, by Bishop John of York . . . he is also said to have had a kind of manual alphabet."

Rodolphus Agricola, a teacher of

7

Greek in Germany in 1442, said he had known a person who had been born deaf, and was therefore dumb, who could express his thoughts in writing. This is said to be the earliest recognition of the fact that the thoughts of the deaf might possibly be made to express themselves without the common medium of speech.

About 1570 a Benedictine monk in Spain, Pedro Ponce de Leon, was given the care of two deaf brothers and a sister. Determined to provide them with a means of communication, he began making them trace the letters of the alphabet and showing them how he pronounced the letters. He then formed words of the letters and showed his pupils the objects indicated by the words. From this beginning the three learned to read and write, and they eventually learned Latin and Greek and some modern foreign languages. They learned physics and astronomy and developed some skill in painting. The reference to de Leon does not say whether his pupils acquired the ability to speak, but the record in the monastery of San Salvador de Oña, where he worked, states that "he obtained a just celebrity throughout the world in instructing deaf-mutes to speak."

In 1748 a Portuguese, Rodriguez Pereira, appeared at the Academy of Science in Paris with a number of deaf pupils he had trained. He was something of a sensation, but he refused to divulge the methods by which he taught the deaf, so he was not heard from again.

Cardano was first to question the Aristotelian dictum. A professor in the University of Milan, Cardano was considered a "universal genius" and his words carried great weight. He wrote that "ideas can be directly associated with written words without the intervention of sound, so the deaf-mute can hear by reading and speak by writing."

Nothing was done to test Cardano's theory until some two hundred years later, when his argument was resurrected and a philosopher in Paris, among others, concluded from the Cardano principle that "it would be as possible to instruct the deaf and dumb by written characters, always accompanied by sensible signs, as to instruct other men by words delivered orally, along with gestures indicative of their significance."

The resurrection of Cardano's theory came along with a general awakening to the need for improvement and change in education. Reformers were changing the thinking of the times. Education had been mostly vocational, but the Reformation brought the sentiment that education should "gain power over Nature," according to Bacon.

It was near the end of the 17th Century that Comenius produced his theories on education which shaped the trend toward modern methods. John Locke rejected the medieval notions of education and contributed to the newer philosophy. With all the study and philosophizing, it was natural that someone would consider handicapped children. Hodgson wrote in a book published in England (*The Deaf and their Problems*) that it was at this time that the "thinkers seized and worried the bone Cardano had thrown down, and got a considerable amount of meat from it."

Several intellectuals attempted to devise a manual alphabet for the deaf. Sir Christopher Wren tried his hand at it, but George Delgarno of Aberdeen is the one best remembered. He invented an alphabet where letters occupied different positions on the hand, and were indicated by touching these positions with a finger of the other hand. He is honored not so much for his manual alphabet as for the study of the deaf his work inspired. In 1680 he published a book on educating the deaf.

With the resurrection of Cardano's theory, efforts to educate the deaf were started or proposed in the eighteenth century in Spain, Italy, Germany, Holland, France, Portugal, England, and Scotland. Books were written on the subject and a few deaf persons were successfully educated. They were members of wealthy families who could afford the services of private tutors.

About 1760, schools were opened, almost simultaneously, by the Abbé de l'Épée in France, Samuel Heinicke in Germany, and Thomas Braidwood in Great Britain, and, according to a writer in the *Annals,* it was then that "the age-long, dark clouds of restriction hovering over the deaf began to lift and drift away."

Charles Michel, Abbé de l'Épée had studied theology but because of disagreement with certain church doctrines he was not admitted to the priesthood until some time later. In the interim he studied law and was admitted to the bar, but he found the "atmosphere wholly uncongenial to his nature." Because of his differences with the church, he was finally forbidden to serve.

By chance he came across two deaf girls in Paris and after unsuccessful efforts to converse with them he decided it was Heaven's will that he should come to the rescue of the deaf and endeavor to deliver them from the darkness of ignorance. He started a school in Paris with funds he had inherited from his father, who had been a noted architect, having constructed the famous palace at Versailles.

The Abbé knew of the Cardano principle quoted by the Paris philosopher and he set to work inventing a system of manual signs by which the deaf could converse. His inspiration came from a book on educating the deaf which had been written by a Spaniard, Don Juan Pablo Bonet, who had studied Pedro Ponce de Leon's experiments. His was the first written work on the education of the deaf. The Abbé could not read Spanish but he found a one-hand manual alphabet diagrammed in the book. He learned this alphabet and proceeded to devise a system of signs. He even learned Spanish so he could read and put to use what Bonet's book said about teaching the deaf.

The sign language the Abbé invented is essentially the same sign language we use today. It had a wonderful effect upon the Abbé's deaf pupils. "It aroused and held their interest because it acted as a quick developer of their intelligence to take in new ideas, new perceptions, and new emotions. Its inspiration directed their steps smoothly toward God; its stimulation carried them easily along the paths of information and knowledge into a new and wonderful world about them; and it promoted their enjoyment and happiness in the social amenities and the recreational exigencies of life. The aura of its glory excited the wonder, admiration, and approval of the scholars and scientists of Paris, and made the Abbé the recipient of general homage."

While the Abbé de l'Épée invented the language of signs and used it in his school, he was not sure it was the best method of educating the deaf until he had explored the oral method. He wrote a course in teaching orally and finally concluded that the manual method "offered the shorter route to practical results, because of its power to give greater clarity, movement, color, and alertness to the expression of ideas and thoughts."

The Archbishop of Bordeaux had been impressed by the work of the Abbé at Paris and established a school at Bordeaux. Roch-Ambroise Cucurron Sicard was selected to head the school. He was Canon of Bordeaux and his chief interest in life was helping "afflicted beings." Preparatory to assuming his duties at the Bordeaux school, Sicard went to Paris to learn the system initiated by the Abbé. He started the school in 1786 but in 1789 the Abbé died and Sicard had shown such promise he was chosen to succeed the Abbé. He carried on the work and attained even greater success and fame,

so his name now ranks with that of the Abbé de l'Épée as one of the great founders of education of the deaf. One of his pupils, Laurent Clerc, later figured in the beginning of education of the deaf in America.

It was Samuel Heinicke of Germany who made the first real effort to teach orally, although he corresponded with the Abbé de l'Épée while planning his oral system. Heinicke began his career as a soldier in Dresden. He was taken prisoner in the Seven Years' War but escaped and went to Jena, where he entered the University and became a qualified teacher. At about the same time the Abbé was beginning his work in Paris, Heinicke started a school for the deaf in Dresden, later moving to Leipzig, where he became director of the "first institution for the deaf and dumb ever established by a civil government." The school was founded in 1778. In 1810 there were five schools in Germany, and by 1850 the number had increased to 80.

The work of the Abbé de l'Épée and Heinicke is of special importance to us because their methods of educating the deaf were the methods which were brought to America. They gave us the manual method and the oral method. Unfortunately, controversy has raged ever since over which method is the better. One author of a book on the deaf began his book with the observation that "The field of education of the deaf is a battleground."

As was noted previously, education of the deaf began in Great Britain at about the same time as in France and Germany. Thomas Braidwood, a native of Scotland, conducted a school of mathematics in Edinburgh, but in 1760 a deaf boy was placed in his school in hopes that he could be taught to write. Braidwood taught the boy to speak and he was so encouraged by the boy's educational development that he decided to devote his life to the education of the deaf. He moved his school to London and enlisted the assistance of his wife and his son, John, who continued the work after his death. Braidwood employed the oral method in his school, but he never revealed the details of his system. At any rate, the oral method remains the chief method of teaching the deaf in Great Britain. Braidwood's reluctance to share his system with others was the reason the American system came from France and Germany, rather than from Great Britain, as will be explained when the American phase is discussed.

The schools in France and Germany were the forerunners of schools in America and, along with those in England, they probably set the pattern for education of the deaf in other countries, although some countries, especially in Africa and Asia, still do not have well established programs for educating the deaf.

The first school in India was established in 1882 by a Catholic missionary, Father Goldsmith.

We have little information on education in Russia, but officials of the Soviet government issued a report in 1930 which stated that prior to the revolution the deaf were absolutely neglected. It boasts that the Soviet regime has effected such vast improvements that the deaf are accepted as the equal of all other citizens. The report says that during the regime of the czar, 96 per cent of the deaf were illiterate but that now, "deafness and deaf-mutism no longer form a hindrance to the filling of even the highest political, administrative, and economic positions in the Republic of the Soviet Union."

Education of the deaf in Italy was begun in 1784 by the Abba Silvestri, who had been trained by de l'Épée. Silvestri used the manual method he had learned in Paris and he added speech teaching, making it a sort of combined system.

About 1800, Denmark established its first school for the deaf, financed by the government. A unique feature of this school was that attendance was compulsory, so Denmark became the first country in the world to make education compulsory for the deaf. Children were required to attend school for an eight-year period, from the age of eight to sixteen.

While the schools in Europe were multiplying and education was expanding, America bgan to feel the need of educational provisions for its deaf children. There were estimated to be about 2,000 deaf children in the United States at that time. In 1815 Thomas H. Gallaudet was sent to Europe to be trained to teach the deaf. This begins the American phase, which can be described on another occasion.

Professor Samuel Porter wrote a history of educational developments which was published in 1853 in a book compiled as a tribute to Gallaudet. He said that in 1815 the "art of deaf-mute instruction had reached the following development:

1. It had demonstrated the fact that the deaf and dumb are naturally equal to other persons in their intellectual faculties, and that by appropriate methods early applied, and wisely and perseveringly pursued, they can be educated.
2. It had, by aid of governmental appropriations, and the contributions of the benevolent, been extended, so as to provide equal opportunity for the rich and the poor.
3. It had ceased to be a mystery, a craft, a speculation pursued for private ends, but was now followed by ingenious men, with a desire to promote the moral and intellectual advancement of the deaf and dumb.
4. It had become, through the publications of experienced and successful teachers, and the establishment of institutions in which there was a succession of teachers, a permanent system, where principles could be studied, and its methods acquired, without the necessity of re-invention, and with all the advantages of the accumulated experience of the past.
5. Its great aim was to impart language, and through its instrumentality, to establish social intercourse among themselves and the rest of the world, and to develop and instruct the minds of pupils by means of speech, or artificial articulation and reading on the lips, natural and methodical signs, the mannal alphabet, writing, pictures, and the art of drawing.
6. The art of deaf-mute instruction, with all its improvements and extension as it existed in Europe in 1815, was unknown in America. A few individuals had been taught to articulate—a few books had been imported—a few isolated experiments had been made—but darkness, profound and palpable, brooded not only over the deaf and dumb mind, but over the whole subject on this continent.

HISTORICAL SURVEY OF EDUCATION OF THE DEAF IN THE UNITED STATES*

HAROLD RAMGER

Earlier Dr. Burnes brought us up-to-date on the development of the education of the deaf in Europe and I shall attempt to carry us forward to the present time. My references are Hodgson's *The Deaf and Their Problems,* Best's *Deafness and the Deaf in the United States,* Boatner's *Voice of the Deaf, A Biography of Edward Miner*

* A paper also presented before a teacher training class at San Francisco State College, supplementing a prior article by Dr. Burnes (see pages 7–12), and reprinted from *The California News,* November, 1960. Harold Ramger is from the California School for the Deaf, Berkeley.

Gallaudet, Frampton and Gall's *Special Education for the Exceptional,* and the *American Annals of the Deaf.* The Best and the Frampton and Gall books have extensive bibliographies.

The first American deaf child to receive a formal education, as far as I can determine, was John Bolling, son of Major Thomas Bolling of Cobbs, Chesterfield County, Virginia. This boy was sent across to the Braidwood School in Edinburgh, Scotland, in 1771. He died soon after his return to his home in Virginia in 1773. His brother and sister, also deaf, attended the same school. It seems that it was not until after 1800 that progress was made in the instruction of deaf children in this country.

Frampton states that Col. William Bolling, hearing brother of the above-mentioned Bolling children, and Francis Green of Boston, father of a deaf boy, tried to establish a school for the deaf in the United States. It seems that Francis Green, because of his Tory leanings, was obliged to leave the country during the revolution. While in England he visited the Braidwood school. He also visited the school in Paris conducted by de l'Épée. When he was able to return to this country, he continued writing on the education of the deaf, and pleading for a school for them in the United States. He estimated there must have been about 500 deaf children in the country at that time. Upon his death in 1809, his dream had not been realized, however.

The Rev. John Stafford worked with a group of deaf children in an almshouse in 1807 in New York. He soon abandoned this effort, but maintained his interest in deaf children so that later he was one of those who helped found the New York School for the Deaf in 1818.

It was Col. Bolling who established the first school for the deaf in this country, and his two children were the first to be formally educated under trained instructors in the United States. He even prevailed upon John Braidwood, the grandson of the founder of the Edinburgh School, to be teacher in the school at Baltimore in 1812. Because of the war with England, it was necessary to secure special permission for Braidwood to remain in this country.

In 1816 Braidwood had to flee to the North for personal reasons and he did not return until 1817. Meanwhile the Rev. John Kirkpatrick of Manchester, Virginia, started another class. There was an agreement that Braidwood was to instruct Kirkpatrick in the art of teaching the deaf. Before long, however, Kirkpatrick broke off relations with Braidwood and carried on the work alone. His school moved, in 1819, to Cumberland County, Virginia. This apparently makes Kirkpatrick the first teacher trained to teach the deaf in this country. It is said that his school did not flourish.

It was at about the same time that Thomas Hopkins Gallaudet became much interested in a little deaf girl, Alice Cogswell, daughter of Dr. Mason Fitch Cogswell, who was a neighbor of the Gallaudet family. After reading some of the writings of the Abbé Sicard, Gallaudet attempted to teach the young girl some simple words and sentences. A group of Dr. Cogswell's friends decided to raise some money and send Gallaudet to Europe to study the methods used in the education of the deaf in England and on the Continent. Gallaudet was twenty-eight years old at the time he sailed for England. His reception there was far from encouraging. The education of the deaf in England was carried on in great secrecy. The proposal made Gallaudet was that he should bind himself to serve three years at a very small salary, after which time he might return to America and engage in the instruction of the deaf.

It so happened that while in England Gallaudet had the good fortune to meet Abbé Sicard, who was then in charge of the Paris school for the deaf established by de l'Épée. The Abbé extended a cordial invitation to Gallaudet to visit the Paris school. After nine months of patient endeavor and frustration, Gallaudet was much encouraged by this friendliness and went at once to France. There he was given every aid possible. He visited classes and was given private lessons. After three months he returned to America, bringing with him a deaf teacher from the school by the name of Laurent Clerc. Clerc was thus the first deaf teacher of the deaf in America. He helped Gallaudet establish the school at Hartford, Connecticut.

While Gallaudet was away, his friends had not been idle. They had succeeded in obtaining an Act of Incorporation from the State of Connecticut for the establishment of a school for the deaf. This was May, 1816. Eventually about $17,000 was raised. Clerc was of help in collecting this amount for he was intelligent and had the ability to meet the public which was in itself proof that the deaf could be educated. April 15, 1817 saw the official opening of the school. The following year Clerc was again successful, this time in an appeal for assistance made to Congress, and 23,000 acres of wild land were given to the new Hartford School as an endowment. This land was eventually sold for more than $300,000.

Thomas Hopkins Gallaudet was head of the Hartford School for a number of years. His position was a difficult one because he was not given full management by the directors. Nevertheless, through his enthusiasm and sincere desire to aid the deaf, Gallaudet was able to firmly establish the free education of the deaf in this country.

As stated earlier, the New York Institution for the Deaf was founded in 1818. The Pennsylvania Institution for the Deaf came into being in 1820. Then, one by one, the other states established residential schools for the deaf, some supported by private funds, some by state funds. Thus a free education became available to deaf children in the United States.

From 1817 to 1867, the first fifty years of free education for the deaf, twenty-four state residential schools were established. All are still in existence. During the latter part of this period a series of events developed in our capital which carry a great deal of significance not only for me, but for many other deaf people from every state of the Union.

In Washington, D. C., in the year 1856, there lived a wealthy man by the name of Amos Kendall. Kendall was a charitable man who gave freely to worthy causes. Into Kendall's life walked a man who pretended to be interested in a philanthropic project to which Kendall quickly made donations. Upon looking further into the matter Kendall discovered that this man, P. H. Skinner, seemed to be an imposter. He had taken possession of a building in Washington and fenced it in like a prison with a high board fence. He had then gone about the city collecting all the deaf and dumb children he could find, adding them to several he had brought from New York City, calling it a school and claiming to be conversant with the methods of instructing deaf-mutes.

In a round-about way Mr. Kendall received a report that conditions in this school were exceedingly miserable and consequently he went to see for himself. Upon investigating he found conditions were even worse than had been reported and, accordingly, he petitioned the Orphan's Court of the District of Columbia and had the indentured children removed and placed under his legal guardianship, obliging himself to support them until a proper institution could be established for their care.

Mr. Kendall went to work with several influential friends and managed to persuade Congress to pass a bill providing for a school to care for his deaf wards. Mr. Kendall was authorized to secure a capable person to serve as superintendent of the newly founded Columbia Institution and he at once corresponded with Mr. Isaac Lewis Peet of the New York School for the Deaf in an attempt to persuade him to take the position. Mr. Peet declined, but in doing so he recommended Edward Miner Gallaudet, one of T. H. Gallaudet's sons, for the position. At that time E. M. Gallaudet was only twenty years of age and a teacher in the Hartford School. His father had died in 1851 when E. M. was fourteen.

Young Edward bravely assumed the position of superintendent and proceeded to develop the new school with an enrollment of twelve pupils eventually to be called The Kendall School for the Deaf, in honor of the original benefactor. Along with this institution came the establishing of the world-famous Gallaudet College, as it is now called, again by Act of Congress in 1864. Edward Miner Gallaudet remained at the head of the Columbia Institution for the Deaf, later changed to Gallaudet College, from 1857 until his resignation in 1910. He died seven years later in 1917.

On the lawn just outside Chapel Hall on the Gallaudet College campus stands a beautiful statue sculptured by Daniel Chester French, the same man who created the wonderful image of Lincoln that graces the Lincoln Memorial in the Nation's capital. This statue on the Gallaudet campus depicts Thomas Hopkins Gallaudet seated in a rather old-fashioned armchair. By his side and leaning against his knee is little Alice Cogswell. On her face there is an adoring and eager expression. She is gazing intently up at her benefactor. Gallaudet has one hand held out with his fingers folded as in the "A" of our manual alphabet. Alice, in a child-like, awkward way, is attempting to imitate him. The statue was commissioned with funds contributed by thousands of deaf people living in every state of the Union and to many of these people, both past and present, it has always conveyed a deep, sentimental message. They feel a debt of gratitude to Thomas Hopkins Gallaudet and his son.

In the next fifty years from 1867 to 1917, all the other residential schools were established, the one in Hawaii in 1914 being the last. In 1954 a second residential school was built at Riverside, California (the first being the one at Berkeley which was established in 1860 and is now celebrating its centennial). Only the states of Delaware, Nevada, and New Hampshire are without state supported schools for the deaf. These states therefore provide funds for sending their deaf children to a neighboring state, or to special public school classes.

The first public dayschool, the Horace Mann School in Boston, was established in 1869. Day classes for the deaf have been formed and disbanded with great frequency. The main cause for concern in connection with day classes is the size of the classes, the spread of ages and ability of the pupils, and the difficulty the teacher must encounter in trying to teach so many children of such varying age and ability. Having gotten away from the one-room country school, we must beware of going back to it in our provision for our deaf children. Such a danger is ever-present in some of the one-room, one-teacher, small-class dayschool setup.

There are not a great many private and denominational schools for the deaf in the United States. Of those that exist, several are conducted by the Catholic Church, and two by the Missouri Lutheran Synod.

For those interested in details, the January issue of the *American Annals of the Deaf* always carries statistics relating to all types of schools for the deaf in this country. The editorial offices of this periodical are at Gallaudet College, Washington, D. C. The *American Annals of the Deaf* first came out in November, 1847, and according to the Reference and Bibliography Division of the Library of Congress, it is the oldest periodical of its kind in the educational field. It was first published at the Hartford School. In 1868 the editorial office was moved to Gallaudet College. One writer states that the education of the deaf has been termed the most completely documented of all special fields of education. This documentation includes 107 years of the *Annals,* proceedings of organizations such as the Convention of American Instructors of the Deaf and the Conference of Executives of American Schools for the Deaf, the *Volta Review,* and a quite considerable and as yet unclassified mass of material reposing in files of the school papers. (Most residential schools publish a school paper.)

The *Volta Review,* mentioned a moment ago, was first published in 1899, when it was called the *Association Review*. It is the official organ of the Alexander Graham Bell Association for the Deaf. From the beginning the editorial office has been at the Volta Bureau in Washington, D. C. Its library is a storehouse of information on matters pertaining to the deaf and their education.

In speaking of Dr. Bell and his work in behalf of the deaf, for he was especially interested in teaching them to speak and read the lips, we might also quote Edward Miner Gallaudet who said, "It is the duty of all institutions for the education of the deaf to provide adequate means of imparting instruction in articulation and lipreading."

Let us consider some aspects of education of the deaf in the United States today. For instance, Frampton records that the average number of preparatory years is 2.6. That is, the number of years spent in school before the deaf child is ready to start the first grade. Then the average number of grades is 10.4, so the average of years spent in school is thirteen. You must remember this is the *average*. There is actually great variation among the different schools.

It is felt that the early education of the deaf child is of paramount importance. It is stated that of the 22,000 children enrolled in schools for the deaf, 1,899 are under 6 years of age. Again, of the 1,802 children on waiting lists, 690 are under 6 years of age. Meeting the need for early education is most difficult. All schools need to make every effort to face the problem and find a solution.

It is further suggested that the primary and elementary levels of education need to be strengthened and improved in order that more of the children attending schools for the deaf will attain high school level. The statistics are that only half of the children leaving school in any one year are graduates having completed the course, the rest are dropouts. Which brings us to the question of teacher training.

Whereas in the beginning nearly all teacher training was in-service, nowa-days we have teacher training centers. Most of them are affiliated with some college or university and earn college credit. This makes for better training. There is, however, such a demand for teachers of the deaf that often teachers with quite inadequate training are employed. Now, more specialized training is required for teachers of the deaf than for those in any other field because the physical handicap of deafness invariably imposes an additional educational handicap. Prospective teachers of the handicapped may bypass the field of education of the deaf for the very reason of this additional discouraging handicap. The size of the classes in schools for the deaf should be much smaller than is possible in public schools for the hearing. Where classes are too large results will be disappointing. This is undoubtedly difficult for persons unfamiliar with the problem to realize. Indeed, educating the public to recognize the problems involved is a most important part of the whole which is the education of the deaf.

There are one or two more things that should be mentioned. One is research. There has been a good deal of research in the field, but there is need of much more. This entails finding ways of testing the hearing, if any, of the deaf child, of estimating the intelligence of the deaf child, of determining, if possible, the best way to approach the problem of educating the deaf child, and many other questions of similar nature.

Finally, speaking of the intelligence of the deaf child, we come to the

newest concern of those in the field
which is that of the multiple-handicapped deaf, and the retarded deaf.
Not that there haven't been those who
have recognized these additional difficulties long ago. Dr. Stevenson of
Berkeley is one who has long been
aware of this. He has continually
sought to bring it to the attention of
those who might work on the problem.
California has several classes for the
mentally retarded deaf child. In the
multiple-handicapped deaf you have
the deaf child who is also afflicted with
cerebral palsy, the deaf-blind, the deaf
child who has been crippled by polio,
and so on. Then, as you may know, it
happens now and again that a hearing
child with a mental handicap, or some
physical handicap other than deafness,
is placed in a school for the deaf when
obviously he or she should not be so
placed.

Let me close on an optimistic note.
The deaf in the United States feel that
they are better off than the deaf in any
other country in the world. The educated adult deaf value their education
highly and are ever alert to keep the
education of the deaf on a high level,
improving continuously insofar as is
possible. As you enter into or continue
with your careers as teachers of the
deaf, we trust that you will keep in
mind and strive to uphold the ideals
formulated by the sincere and dedi-
cate pioneers of whom Dr. Burnes and
I have spoken.

III. Etiology of Hearing Loss in Children

THE PROBLEM OF CONGENITAL DEAFNESS*

G. Dekle Taylor

The mounting interest in disorders of genetic origin stimulated this review of the problem of congenital deafness and what is known about it. It should be of interest to every family doctor as much as to the otolaryngologist.

The study of congenital malformations has today become an urgent human problem involving many diverse fields of learning. The sporadic and incomplete efforts of the past to seek a solution to this growing menace are rapidly being supplanted by worldwide endeavors to promote the development of methods of early detection and treatment of these abnormalities and to stimulate investigation into their causes and the possibility of prevention. The recent First International Conference on Congenital Malformations[1] emphasized the significance of a concerted approach, especially in view of the warning of many of the world's great scientists regarding the possible con-

* A paper read before the Section on Ophthalmology and Otolaryngology, Southern Medical Association, 56th Annual Meeting, Miami Beach, Florida, November 1962, and reprinted with permission from the Southern Medical Journal, January, 1964, pages 1–8. Copyright 1964 by the Southern Medical Association, Birmingham, Alabama. Dr. Taylor is from Jacksonville, Florida.

sequences of radiation. It was pointed out at this conference that whether or not nuclear explosions continue to take place, the radiation from those which have already occurred represents a danger of increasing congenital defects. The urgency of the challenge is thus apparent. There remains the grim necessity to cope with the problem now, as this conference sought to do, by way of prevention if possible, and certainly by way of care that may make life livable for present and future innocent victims of these "errors of nature."

It is now known that congenital defects may occur at all stages of development from the fertilized ovum to the full term of gestation and may run the gamut from total breakdown to local deformity with all kinds of intermediate variations and combinations. The second to the sixth week of gestation constitutes the most vulnerable period. A recent study indicated that because of the remarkable rapidity of cardiac structural development, practically all types of clinically important congenital heart disease are acquired within the first month of fetal life, the most severe cases proving fatal during these early weeks of development. Statistically, then, infants born with congenital heart disease may represent but a small proportion of all instances of congenital heart disease. It is suggested that this study of congenital heart disease may indicate an incidence of intra-uterine disease heretofore unsuspected.[2]

Dramatically, worldwide attention was focused on the problem recently by the discovery of the relationship between thalidomide and phocomelia. Recognition of this association is too recent for studies to be available pertaining to congenital deafness. It is noteworthy, however, that Lenz[3] reported major malformations of the external ear in 14.6 per cent of his series of eighty-two cases of phocomelia in Germany in which the mother had received thalidomide as antepartum medication. Taussig[3] noted the absence of the external ear in some cases, but hearing is usually not grossly impaired. Unilateral facial paralysis, however, is relatively common. In view of the present global interest in congenital malformations, the subject of congenital deafness seems particularly timely. Certainly the otolaryngologist has an important role in the current approach to this problem.

Classification

Deafness may conveniently be designated as total, subtotal and partial. In subtotal deafness there is hearing for sound only without discrimination between speech sounds; in partial deafness, hearing for speech sounds in varying degree.[4]

The factors causing maldevelopment or damage to the conductive and sensorineural mechanism of hearing may be classified as hereditary, prenatal and perinatal. The hereditary factors are due to genetic influences, the prenatal to pathologic influences *in utero* on the developing embryo, and the perinatal to pathologic influences shortly before, at the time of, or soon after birth.

Congenital deafness is present at birth and may be unilateral or bilateral. Hereditary deafness is dependent upon the constitution of the initial cell or cells from which the new life comes into being. It is not always congenital, nor is congenital deafness always hereditary. Otosclerosis is an example of deafness that is hereditary but not congenital. Deafness due to maternal rubella, on the other hand, is congenital but not hereditary. Recessive familial deafness, however, is both congenital and hereditary.

Fortunately, few children born with impaired hearing are totally deaf. Most of them have some defect of the sensorineural mechanism due either to developmental failure during the prenatal period or to damage at or about the time of birth. Relatively few are born deaf because of failure of the conductive mechanism.[5] Congenital deafness, whether hereditary or acquired, is by no means rare. Even histologically, however, differentiation of the two types remains difficult and estimates of the incidence vary widely. In Whetnall's[4] large series of consecutive cases of deafness in young children, 61 per cent were classified as congenital with approximately one third of this number of known hereditary etiology, one third of probable acquired origin, and one third undetermined. In some series, however, the incidence of hereditary deafness is reported to be considerably lower.

Etiologic and Pathologic Factors

TIME FACTOR. To prevent the development of the inner ear, etiologic agents which affect the embryologic development of the hearing mechanism must operate within the first three weeks of fetal life. During that period the otocyst is formed by the budding off of a process from the neural crest. To effect interruption or cessation of development, these agents must operate between the fourth week and the end of the sixth month, at which time the inner ear and sensory end organ have attained full development. Agents causing degeneration of already formed cochlear structures must operate between the second month and birth.

DEFECTS OF THE INNER EAR. Four types of developmental anomalies of the internal ear in order of frequency of occurrence are briefly described:[6] (1) The Scheibe or cochleosaccular type is characterized by malformation of the membranous cochlea with the bony walls of the cochlea normal and the utricle and semicircular ducts intact. (2) In the Mondini-Alexander type, immature development of the vestibule and canals occurs, probably at the sixth or seventh week of gestation, and the cochlea consists of a single-curve, flattened tube representing the basal coil. (3) The Bing-Siebenmann type has a well-formed bony labyrinth, but the membranous labyrinth and sensory end organ are underdeveloped. The sensory end organ is merely a small group of undifferentiated cells, the scala media is collapsed, and Reissner's membrane is in contact with a mound of undifferentiated cells representing an arrested organ of Corti and remains of the tectorial membrane. This type has been associated with retinitis pigmentosa.[4] The Michel type represents the earliest arrest in embryologic development of the inner ear in which there is complete lack of development.

DEFECTS OF THE CONDUCTIVE MECHANISM. Congenital structural defects rarely occur in both the sensorineural and the sound-conducting mechanisms. The sound-conducting system is derived from the branchial apparatus whereas the sensory mechanism is derived from the ectodermal otocyst. Defects of the conductive mechanism depend upon the age in embryonic life at which normal development was arrested and also upon the portion of the branchial apparatus affected. The causative factors are unknown, and there is rarely a family history of such malformations. In the opinion of Henner and Buckingham,[7] minor congenital ossicular anomalies may cause severe conductive hearing loss and probably constitute a type of abnormality more common than has been realized. The ears may be microtic, the canal mildly stenotic, the tympanic membrane dull in appearance and the hammer handle of the malleus chalk-like and avascular.

Malformations of the conductive mechanism may also occur in association with defects of the maxilla. Mandibulofacial dysostosis or Treacher-Collins syndrome is an example.

Microsurgery for otosclerosis has directed attention to the presence of various congenital defects of the sound-conducting mechanism when the auricle, external auditory canal and tympanic membrane are normal. These variations include bony adhesions between the ossicles and the wall of the middle ear cleft, bony union of all three ossicles, absence of the long process of the incus, bony union of the incus and head of the stapes, total absence of the incus, agenesis of the lenticular process of the incus and replacement with a fibrous band, congenital fixation of the footplate of the stapes, and absence of the stapedius muscle and tendon. Even when the tympanic membrane is normal, impaired hearing of a conductive type, either bilateral or unilateral and present since birth or early childhood, should suggest the possibility of middle ear defects. Usually, in a congenital conductive hearing loss the air and bone conduction curves both show a typical flat audiogram through the speech frequencies. A lack of progression aids in differentiating it from otosclerosis. An exploratory tympanotomy is indicated when a hearing loss of the conductive type remains unexplained.

DEGENERATIVE CHANGES SECONDARY TO TOXIC FACTORS. Degenerative changes in the internal ear secondary to toxic factors are believed to be of vascular origin. Hemorrhages and exudates in the scala media, scala vestibuli, scala tympani and vestibule have been demonstrated histologically. A shrunken stria vascularis and absence of demonstrable blood vessels have been noted in some instances. Reduction or absence of endolymph probably results, and collapse of the scala media follows, with Reissner's membrane becoming adherent to the organ of Corti and stria vascularis. Degeneration occurs in the organ of Corti. In congenital syphilis degeneration of sensory epithelium takes place. Deafness associated with kernicterus is probably due to changes in the spiral ganglion or in the cochlear nuclei in the mid-brain secondary to deposits of blood pigments since there is little change in the cochlea.

Pathologic factors such as the virus of rubella may arrest the development of the neural epithelium and the cochlea in deafness of prenatal origin. The degree of damage is greatest soon after conception, diminishing as pregnancy advances. Since the cochlea is affected throughout its length, the hearing tends to be uniform for all frequencies.

The organ of Corti usually suffers damage from genetic factors. The pathologic changes may vary from minor defects in the hair cells to complete absence of the cochlea.

The malfunctioning or maldeveloped eustachian tube associated with defects of the palate may give rise to disease of the middle ear with serous effusion. Also, persistent tubal obstruction and serous effusion without defects of the palate may occur in children who have a narrow head and a narrow contracted nasopharynx.

Hereditary Deafness

Hereditary congenital deafness is of genetic origin and is determined by Mendelian law. It is transmitted in a dominant, recessive, or sex-linked manner, most frequently by a recessive gene. Deaf-mutism is transmitted by a single recessive gene from parent to offspring. The Mendelian principle is adequate to explain hereditary deafness even though the ratio of offspring does not coincide with the theoretical Mendelian ratio. The gene may have passed down through a long line of heterozygous normal persons without the living members of the family having knowledge of deaf ancestors. In families exhibiting hereditary diseases dependent on a recessive gene, the absence of a history of hereditary deafness is not unusual.

Although the usual mode of inheritance is by a recessive gene, nerve deafness may be inherited as a dominant trait. In otosclerosis the usual pattern of inheritance is dominant with reduced penetrance.

RETINITIS PIGMENTOSA. Progressive nerve deafness and mental retardation are associated with retinitis pigmentosa. This type of cerebroretinal degeneration is frequently hereditary. Usually the syndrome is transmitted in a simple recessive, occasionally a dominant and rarely a sex-linked manner.

HEREDITARY NERVE DEAFNESS. A selective degeneration of the cochlear fibers of the eighth cranial nerve probably accounts for progressive hereditary nerve deafness. Beginning insidiously, it may become manifest as early as the sixth year or not until adult life, but it progresses slowly and steadily, and the loss is usually complete by the thirtieth year. Vestibular reactions are normal. Loss is noted in the high frequencies first and the low frequencies last. The family history, the character of the deafness and the absence of other causes form the basis for diagnosis.

Recently a type of deafness, hereditary but not congenital, was described by Dolowitz and Stephens[8] in which the pattern of inheritance was transmitted in an unbroken line from parent to offspring, but was not sex-linked. As expected, the trait appeared in half of the children of the affected parents, indicating a simple autosomal dominant trait. The gene appeared to be fully penetrant. The impaired hearing appears first as a high tone loss in the sixth to tenth year, progresses to the middle or speech tones in the thirties, spreads through this range until about the fiftieth year, and progresses little thereafter, rarely approaching subtotal deafness. The pattern resembles that of presbycusis. These authors thought the defect might be in the organ of Corti, the nerve, or the central nervous system, but probably was in the spiral ganglion.

Hereditary deafness is associated with inborn errors of metabolism. These errors, defined as genetically determined enzymatic defects resulting in metabolic disorders, result from mutation of the genes. The cause of the mutation is unknown, but radiation, nutrition, temperature and atmospheric oxygen have been suggested as possible factors. The mutations are transmitted to future generations, and Hsia[9] thought that mutant genes may account for structural disorders such as occur in congenital defects of the ear, probably by inducing chemical abnormalities early in embryonic development. Albinism, gargoylism (Hurler's syndrome) and cretinism are some of the inborn errors of metabolism associated with deafness.

The Waardenburg syndrome[10] might be classified as an inborn error of metabolism. Occurring in part or as a whole, this symptom complex is characterized by a lateral displacement of the medial canthi of the eyes and shortening of the palpebral fissures, a broadening of the nasal root, hypertrichosis of the medial portion of the eyebrows, a different color of the iris of each eye (heterochromia iridium), a white forelock, other areas of abnormal pigmentation, and in some 20 per cent of the cases deafness. In his study of this syndrome, Fisch[11] noted that in the developing embryo the auditory system and the pigment cells both derive from the neural crest and he assumed that abnormalities of the neural crest may cause deafness and alteration of pigment. The heterochromia is caused by failure in the cervical sympathetic nervous system, which also derives from the neural crest. One or more of the symptoms of the Waardenburg syndrome, exclusive of deafness, may occur in one or more members of each generation for many generations before, unaccountably, a child is born deaf. Although none of the other features of the syndrome may be present, their occurrence in other members of the family serves to identify the deafness with this syndrome and establish it as hereditary.

Prenatal Deafness

For each organ, developing in a definite sequence, there is a period of maximum growth. If during this period metabolism is interrupted or inhibited, the organ will not develop normally and will therefore be rudimentary or defective. The virus of influenza and of rubella, cytomegalic inclusion disease, congenital syphilis and toxoplasmosis may damage the auditory system *in utero*. Mutation of genes may result from roentgenotherapy of the pelvis during pregnancy, and injury of the germ cells by radiation of the gonads before conception may cause defective development of the fetus.

RUBELLA. Since the relationship between rubella (German measles) and congenital defects was first described in 1941, it has been well established that the child of a mother who has rubella in the first trimester of pregnancy may have congenital deafness, congenital cataracts, or congenital heart disease, and may be mentally deficient. Early extremely high estimates of the incidence of such defects have now been reduced to as low as 12 to 15 per cent for the overall risk and 5 to 10 per cent for deafness.[12] As the first trimester of pregnancy advances the risk decreases, the period of vulnerability covering the period of development of the cochlea and rapid development of the organ of Corti. Vascular fragility, leading eventually to abnormalities, has been suggested as a causative factor. A shrunken stria vascularis without demonstrable blood vessels, a collapsed scala media and adherence of Reissner's membrane to the organ of Corti and the stria vascularis have been demonstrated in a five-year-old deaf child whose mother had rubella in pregnancy.

DRUG TOXICITY. For many years it has been known that quinine, the salicylates and alcohol may cause nerve deafness.[13,14] These drugs have a selective action for the auditory apparatus and may injure the cortical center of hearing. Apparently they produce a toxic action on the ganglion cells of the cochlea and the associated nerve fibers. In addition, they may produce changes in the endothelium of the smallest capillaries or a contraction of the blood vessels of the inner ear. Ischemia, lack of nutrition and anoxemia result and are followed by a degenerative atrophy of the ganglion cells in the nerve fibers of the basal whorl of the cochlea. A diminution of the endolymphatic pressure, followed by a collapse of Corti's membrane, may also take place.

Likewise, it is now well established that such drugs as dihydrostreptomycin, streptomycin, neomycin and kanamycin are ototoxic. The recently publicized teratogenic properties of thalidomide serve as a dramatic reminder of the permeability of the placenta to ototoxic drugs and the hazards of administering them during pregnancy.

COMPLICATIONS DURING PREGNANCY. Diseases such as toxemia, nephritis, diabetes and acute poliomyelitis occurring in the mother during pregnancy may cause hemorrhages in the cochlea and the vestibule of the fetal ear involving the endolymph and perilymph. Such hemorrhages have been demonstrated in cases in which pregnancy was terminated because of toxemia in the mother.

Perinatal Deafness

In late fetal life, at birth and shortly thereafter, prematurity, accidental or instrumental birth injury, prolonged difficult labor, anoxia, and kernicterus secondary to erythroblastosis fetalis may be causes of congenital deafness. The bony and membranous labyrinth may suffer injury from a basal skull fracture. Hemorrhages affecting the cortical centers of hearing may occur following tearing of the tentorium cerebelli. The sensorineural mechanism of hearing may be injured by anoxia at birth. Undue pressure on the fetal head and intracranial hemorrhage may result from precipitous delivery with or without the administration of oxytocic drugs. In the perinatal as in the prenatal period, pregnancy complicated by acute poliomyelitis, toxemia, nephritis, diabetes and other diseases in the mother may be detrimental to the fetal ear. The high frequencies are mainly affected, for the damage is in the dorsal cochlear nuclei, particularly the nerve cells transmitting those frequencies. The cochlea is normal.

ERYTHROBLASTOSIS FETALIS. Rh incompatibility has a significant etiologic role in congenital deafness. The Rh positive infant causes the production of Rh antibodies in the Rh negative mother; these antibodies cross the placental barrier and destroy the infant's red blood cells, thereby causing erythroblastosis, which, when severe, may be accompanied by kernicterus. It is estimated that 15 per cent of mothers are Rh negative. Erythroblastosis with kernicterus becomes manifest late in fetal life or soon after birth and may cause bilateral perceptive deafness and other defects, chiefly athetoid spasticity. Unconjugated bilirubin, the toxic factor, does not become elevated until after birth for the maternal circulation controls its metabolism *in utero*. Abnormal levels are produced in the newborn by incompatibility, as in Rh sensitization, ABO incompatibility, sepsis with increased blood destruction, and administration of drugs such as sulfisoxazole (Gantrisin®) and synthetic forms of vitamin K.

The type of hearing loss associated with kernicterus is known as nuclear deafness for the lesion probably occurs in the cranial nuclei. The toxic action of the bilirubin affects the cranial masses traversed by auditory radiations. The degree of impaired hearing varies. If the loss is complete, usually other severe manifestations such as cerebral palsy and mental impairment are present. High frequency deafness is a common residual and in some survivors may be the only one.

Recognition and Management

RECOGNITION. A speech defect or late development of speech frequently is indicative of congenital deafness. The type and severity of the deafness determine the extent of the speech defect. The loss is commonly in the high frequencies. The defective speech is a vowel speech since the child does not hear and is therefore unable to develop the fainter high-pitched consonant sounds. A vowel speech almost completely devoid of consonants is noted early in life, usually during the second year, and indicates a severe sensorineural loss. If there is an abrupt high tone loss, the speech disorder may not be detected until the child enters school. This type of case emphasizes the importance of audiometric screening tests in first grade school children. A diagnostic audiogram should be routine for every child seen by the otolaryngologist.

DIAGNOSIS. The need for prompt recognition of deafness is apparent, and the obstetrician, the generalist and the pediatrician have a major role in early diagnosis. The trend of fitting hearing aids to infants has promoted earlier diagnosis than formerly. Although accurate assessment cannot be made, the physician should perform distraction tests during the first year or two of the infant's life. Zonderman[15] observed that any child who has not developed speech by the age of two needs careful investigation of his hearing. In his study, less than one third of the children were examined before the age of three and only about half before the end of the fourth year.

If the physician suspects deafness, he should refer the child to an otolaryngologist for careful evaluation. He should not discount the mother's opinion if she suspects deafness in her child, for she is seldom mistaken. Instead, he should assume until proved otherwise that the child is deaf and not merely late in developing speech or concentrating too much on what he is doing. In a child with a sensorineural deafness, the auditory canals, tympanic membranes and mastoid x-ray films usually present a normal appearance. The infant in whom deafness is suspected should be referred to a speech and hearing center for complete diagnostic testing.

The testing and evaluation of congenital deafness are time-consuming and require patience, understanding and thoroughness. The otolaryngologist is confronted with the challenge of recognizing a congenitally deaf child early and providing proper training for his development. While there is no treatment, medical or surgical, for sensorineural deafness, ingenious surgical technics are now available for the treatment of conductive deafness in children. They give promise that the child with impaired hearing who has normal cochlear function and a strictly conductive defect can hope for hearing of useful levels. The otolaryngologist should remain the key person always in the counseling of the child with severe deafness, advising and encouraging him at intervals rather than simply referring him to the speech clinic. The parents also need his counsel, guidance and encouragement. The John Tracy Clinic of Los Angeles has much to offer both child and parents.

Prevention and Research

PREVENTION. Although prevention of congenital malformations seems a distant or perhaps unattainable goal, a positive approach is possible. It is estimated that nearly half of the American deaf population marry and most frequently choose mates from the same group. It is particularly important to determine whether or not the prospective deaf parent has hereditary or acquired deafness. The relatively high proportion of genetically determined cases makes it imperative for the otolaryngologist to understand hereditary background factors and to explain the Mendelian law to patients with hereditary deafness who plan marriage with deaf persons or close relatives, whether hearing or deaf. The increased frequency of deafness in consanguineous marriages affords additional indication of the recessive characteristics of the genes, and the tendency of the partners in these marriages to have one or more deaf children is due to the increased likelihood of both related persons carrying the same recessive genes.

Certainly persons contemplating such marriages should know the probabilities of deafness in their progeny and be advised not to marry, or, as a possible alternative, to plan a childless marriage. If intrinsically deaf persons could be persuaded to refrain from marrying near relatives and systematic efforts to integrate rather than isolate the deaf through encouragement of marriages between deaf and nondeaf persons were made, this advice and guidance would contribute substantially to decreasing the incidence of deafness in the population.[16] The otolaryngologist has a unique opportunity to advise the congenitally deaf teenagers and prospective brides and grooms of the importance of proper selection of their mates.

As a preventive measure against fetal abnormalities from maternal rubella, pediatricians today advocate the deliberate exposure of females to the disease before adulthood. Some authorities consider it advisable to administer large doses of gamma globulin to women in the first trimester of pregnancy who are susceptible and who are exposed to rubella.

Ototoxic drugs should not be administered to pregnant patients. The otolaryngologist should endeavor to keep his colleagues in other specialties informed regarding the increasing number of these drugs and the damage they may cause to the fetal ear.

Care in the management of the complications of pregnancy, the prevention of anoxia in the perinatal period, determination of parents' Rh compatibility and immediate replacement transfusion in erythroblastosis fetalis are other measures which contribute to reduction of the incidence of congenital deafness. Further advances in early recognition and prevention will depend on the astuteness of clinical physicians and cooperation among them.

Research. The clinical otolaryngologist has a significant role in the current intensified quest for solutions to the problem of congenital malformations. He can accumulate and contribute a wealth of historical, audiometric and vestibular data on the subject. In addition, he has the opportunity to cooperate with the program of the Temporal Bone Banks Center at the University of Chicago in obtaining histologic specimens for study. He may obtain forms from the Center for parents to fill out and file with the Center after he has impressed upon them the importance of histologic examination of the inner ear of their child. With his encouragement, they will remain interested in the program and, in turn, will educate the child to the importance of willing his temporal bones to this program. His cooperation in making available adequate clinical studies and histologic specimens will be an essential contribution to progress in research in this field.

Summary

The hereditary, prenatal and perinatal aspects of congenital deafness are discussed. The etiologic and pathologic factors are reviewed, the importance of early diagnosis and management is stressed, and a constructive approach to prevention is presented. The role of the otolaryngologist in furthering research is also outlined.

References

1. First International Conference on Congenital Malformations: Papers and Discussions, compiled and edited for the International Medical Congress, Ltd. Lippincott, Philadelphia, 1962.
2. Editorial: The first six weeks. *JAMA, 181:*1071, 1962.
3. Taussig, H. B.: A study of the German outbreak of phocomelia: The Thalidomide syndrome. *JAMA, 180:*1006, 1962.

4. WHETNALL, E. M.: Speech and hearing in severely deaf children. *Proc. 5th Int. Cong. Oto-rhino-laryngology.* Amsterdam, 1955, pp. 710–720.

5. BALLANTYNE, J. C.: *Deafness.* Boston, Little, 1960.

6. ORMEROD, F. C.: The pathology of congenital deafness. *J Laryng, 74*:919, 1960.

7. HENNER, R., and BUCKINGHAM, R. A.: The recognition and surgical treatment of congenital ossicular defects. *Laryngoscope, 66*:526, 1956.

8. DOLOWITZ, D. A., and STEPHENS, F. E.: Hereditary nerve deafness. *Ann Otol, 70*: 851, 1961.

9. HSIA, DAVID YI-YUNG: *Inborn Errors of Metabolism.* Chicago, Year Bk, 1960.

10. WAARDENBURG, P. J.: A new syndrome combining developmental anomalies of the eyelids, eyebrows and nose root with pigmentary defects of the iris and head hair and with congenital deafness. *Amer J Hum Genet, 3*:195, 1951.

11. FISCH, L.: Deafness as a part of an hereditary syndrome. *J Laryng, 73*:355, 1959.

12. SIGURJONSSON, J.: Rubella and congenital deafness. *Amer J Med Sci, 242*:712, 1961.

13. TAYLOR, H. M.: Prenatal medication and its relation to the fetal ear. *Surg Gynec Obstet, 64*:542, 1937.

14. TAYLOR, H. M.: Symposium: Neural mechanism of hearing; nerve deafness of known pathology or etiology; deafness from drugs and chemical poisons. *Laryngoscope, 47*: 692, 1937.

15. ZONDERMAN, B.: The preschool nerve-deaf child, study of etiological factors. *Laryngoscope, 69*:54, 1959.

16. SANK, D., and KALLMANN, F. J.: Genetic and eugenic aspects of early total deafness. *Eugen Quart, 3*:69, 1956.

DEAFNESS AND SCHOOL: MIDDLE EAR EFFUSION*

G. O. PROUD AND F. R. KIRCHNER

The accumulation of fluid within the middle ear cavity ranks second in frequency only to cerumen blockade of the external auditory canal as a cause of hearing loss in children. The apparent increase in the number of patients with this condition probably stems from the following sources: The routine electronic hearing testing of school children and the increased diagnostic prowess of the examining physician. Middle ear effusion is also referred to as secretory otitis media, middle ear catarrh and middle ear hydrops. Senturia *et al.*[1] classified the middle ear fluids into serous, mucopurulent, purulent and mucoid categories; but it is probable that the purulent and mucopurulent types represent varieties of true bacterial otitis media with which the clinician is already on familiar terms. The fluid of the serous variety is sterile. If the disease has persisted for more than a few weeks the mastoid antrum and air cells will, in most instances, be found to contain the same liquid.

The condition is most commonly encountered in the fifth to the eleventh years of life and exhibits no preference for race or sex. The twelve to thirty age group seems to escape as well as individuals over the age of sixty. Its fre-

* A reprint, with permission, from the Editorial Board of *The Journal of the Kansas Medical Society,* Topeka, issue of March, 1963, and by the authors. The authors are from the Department of Otorhinolaryngology, University of Kansas Medical Center.

quency before the age of five remains unknown; since pain and discharge are not amongst its features and minor hearing losses in very young children often escape detection.

Etiology

Eustachian tube obstruction appears to be the common denominator and any situation which leads to it can be counted among the provoking factors. Prolonged postnasal packing, enlarged adenoid, upper respiratory tract infections, allergic rhinitis and choanal polyps and cysts are all abnormalities which can induce tubal block. Benign or malignant nasopharyngeal neoplasms should always be suspected in any subject with middle ear effusion, particularly in the case of the adult.

The child with the cleft palate is very prone to develop it for reasons unknown; but presence of food in the nasopharynx, faulty tubal masculature, extension of oral bacteria to the postnasal space and impingement of speech appliances upon the tubal orifices must remain suspect.

Careless adenoid surgery with inadvertent excision of the torus tubarius leads to tubal stricture and eventual middle ear effusion in a significant number of instances.

The eustachian tube is open only during the acts of chewing, yawning and swallowing, but these brief moments of patency provide an avenue for ventilation of the middle ear cavity and permit an equalization of the air pressure in that cavity with that of the outside world. When tubal obstruction occurs the air in the middle ear space is absorbed by the mucosal blood system, and a relative low pressure appears in the cavity followed by extravasation of fluid into the space. As the fluid pressure increases the liquid finds its way through the aditus ad antrum into the mastoid antrum and, at length, into the mastoid air cells. The barometric pressure changes incited by rapid descent during air flight may also induce effusion of fluid into the middle ear cavity (aerotitis).

Severe body trauma, not necessarily involving direct head injury, mysteriously gives rise to middle ear effusion in an appreciable number of cases. Despite the formidable number of listed causes, however, the immediate factor of guilt remains unknown, in the majority of patients who present with the disease.

Symptoms

Full feeling in the ear, swishing fluid noises, a sensation of speaking with the head in a barrel, increase or decrease in auditory acuity upon assuming the recumbent position and persistent hearing loss are the most frequent complaints. Many youngsters do poorly in school and are relegated to the "dumb-bell section" of the class without cause, for they are actually suffering from this type of hearing loss. An alert, informed teacher may suspect such loss; but the oversized classes of pupils today frequently detract from the harried teacher's acuteness. The child may undergo psychological changes and withdraw from the social group to a position of isolation and ridicule. It should be emphasized that any child who is doing poorly in his studies deserves a thorough audiologic evaluation.

Physical Findings

The eardrum membrane may be dull and thick in appearance, may be lacking in landmarks; or a yellowish discoloration may be apparent. The manubrium of the malleus may appear unduly white. Bubbles may be visible, but a true fluid level is a rare finding. More often than not the tympanic membrane is normal in appearance.[2] The tuning fork will show that air conduction is poorer than bone conduction, but such a subjective response from a child is not to be naively accepted.

The audiometric test will reveal normal bone conduction with depressed air conduction in a flat curve pattern (Fig. 1). The loss for air conduction seldom exceeds the 30 decibel level, and when it does other causes of hearing loss should be suspected.

Clinical Course and Complications

In most instances the condition is self-limited[3] and disappears when the child enters his teens. Some are intermittent and exhibit a hearing loss during one examination and none on a subsequent test. Some are persistent and have existed for years before they come to a physician for management.

Suppression of intellectual development and psychologic changes are the

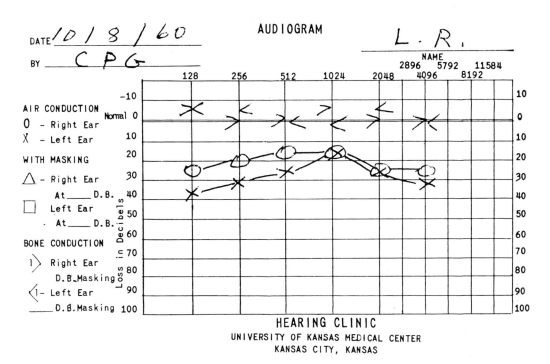

Fig. 1

commonest sequelae. On rare occasions chronic tympanic membrane retraction leads to perforation of the membrane and invasion of the middle ear by epithelium from the tympanic membrane surface and eventual cholesteatomatous destruction of middle and inner ear structures. The latter type of extension leads to its own list of complications.

Treatment

In the adult, a careful nasopharyngeal examination is indicated, and if this space is clear the patient should be re-examined at intervals of six weeks over a period of many months. A cancer of the Fossa of Rosenmueller may lead to effusion long before the tumor itself is visible. Since malignant tumors of the paranasal sinuses may be present, an x-ray of these structures should be ordered.

General systemic measures to prevent and shorten upper respiratory tract infections should be instituted, and allergic disease should be controlled if possible. Obstructing cysts or polyps of the nose or nasopharynx should be removed. Auto-insufflation of the middle ear may be beneficial, and children can be trained to play the game of blowing up a balloon with the nostrils held shut several times each day.

The intermittent type usually persists for six weeks or less, and oral vasoconstrictors may be administered to aid in shrinking the tubal mucosa. Repeated myringotomy is unwise, for it seldom brings permanent relief. It has been suggested that small polyethylene tubes should be placed through the tympanic membrane to afford prolonged drainage of the liquid, but such tubes are hard to maintain in place in the adult and more so in children. Furthermore, the tubes frequently become plugged with the dried fluid and cease to function.

When conservative measures fail the child deserves preferential seating near the front of the classroom if the hearing loss is no greater than 20 to 25 db in the conversational range in both ears. The teacher should be advised of the handicap, and if the defect is unilateral the youngster should be seated with his good ear nearest the instructor.

Too frequent surgical intervention is unwise, not because of resultant damage, but because it is seldom productive of benefit. If the bilateral auditory loss exceeds 20 to 25 db a hearing aid for use during school hours is indicated, and it may be discarded when the child "outgrows" the problem. The patient should be re-examined at least every three months so cholesteatomatous invasion, if it occurs, may be dealt with early and conservatively. At each examination repeat audiometric assessment should be carried out so that the hearing aid may be temporarily or permanently discarded as soon as possible, since the instrument does unfortunately call forth ridicule from fellow students. Although an observant teacher or parent may know when hearing loss exists, a small child, as a rule, does not.

Prevention

Flying in non-pressurized planes is to be avoided especially in the face of acute upper respiratory tract infections or allergic episodes. Adenoidectomy, regardless of the cause for which it is done, should inevitably be carefully performed under indirect visualization with a mirror and safe instruments in order to avoid damage to the nasopharyngeal orifice of the eustachian tube. It must be remembered that the same operation which may bring an end to the problem of middle ear effusion may also be responsible for its genesis. A surgical approach to the correction of tubal stricture has not as yet been devised.

Summary

Middle ear effusion is a very common cause of hearing loss in children. Early detection, treatment and rehabilitative measures are essential to the prevention of the restriction of intellectual development and the introduction of psychologic trauma.

Middle ear effusion is one of the earliest signs of malignant disease of the upper respiratory tract of certain patients.

Conservatism in surgery and treatment, coupled with careful periodic observation, are important measures in the management of the condition. Careful adenoidectomy is essential if one cause of the difficulty is to be eliminated.

References

1. SENTURIA, B. H.; GESSERT, C. F.; CARR, C. D., and BAUMANN, E. S.: Middle ear effusions: Causes and treatments. *Trans Amer Acad Ophthal Otolaryng*, 64 (No. 1): 60–75, 1960.
2. WEHRS, R. E., and PROUD, G. O.: Conductive deafness in children. *Arch Otolaryng (Chicago)*, 67:16–19, 1958.
3. GOETZINGER, C. P.; EMBREY, J. E.; BROOKS, R., and PROUD, G. O.: Auditory assessment of cleft palate adults. *Acta Otolaryng (Stockholm)*, 52:551–557, 1960.

HEARING PROBLEMS OF SCHOOL AGE CHILDREN*

JOHN K. DUFFY

The child with the worried expression on his face as he intently watches as you speak to him may be one of the many children with deficient hearing. So may the child with any of the following characteristics:

He fails to pay attention when casually spoken to.

* Report 5, in Volume 1 of the Maico Audiological Library Series, reprinted by courtesy of Maico Electronics Inc., Minneapolis, Minnesota, and the author. Dr. Duffy is from the Speech and Hearing Center, Brooklyn College, City University of New York.

He gives the wrong answers to simple questions.

He "hears" better when watching the speaker's face.

He is functioning below his potential ability in school.

He often asks the speaker to repeat words or sentences.

He has frequent earaches and running ears.

He has frequent colds.

He has frequent upper respiratory infections like sinusitis and tonsilitis. He has allergies similar to hay fever.

He has become a behavior problem at school and at home.

He fails to articulate correctly certain speech sounds or he omits certain consonant sounds.

He often fails to discriminate between words with similar vowels but different consonants.

He is withdrawn and does not mingle readily with classmates and neighbors.

Today, fortunately, hearing deficiencies which might cause children to exhibit the above symptoms can be detected at a very early age. Prompt and proper medical and surgical care can often restore hearing to normal. Where the hearing loss is irremediable, the early wearing of hearing aids, early speech and hearing training and special educational provisions in the classroom can often help these children to make happy and successful educational and social adjustments.

In America it is inexcusable for a child to be neglected until he manifests the above listed behavior characteristics before his hearing problem is discovered. It is inexcusable because easily portable and relatively inexpensive electronic instruments called "audiometers" are now readily available for measuring the hearing of school children. Also, professional workers such as school nurses, sometimes called "nurse-teachers," speech and hearing therapists or trained technicians are skilled in carrying out procedures for efficiently and accurately testing the hearing of children in order to determine which children fall within the limits of normal hearing acuity and which do not. Normal in this case refers to the child who hears all of the test tones from 250 c.p.s. to 8000 c.p.s. at an intensity level on the audiometer of 15 decibels. Children who do not have normal hearing are thereby "screened out." Careful threshold measurements of hearing are then made on these children and those found to have a hearing loss are referred for medical care. Most children whose hearing cannot be restored by medical or surgical treatment can be helped by hearing aids, speech and hearing training and other special educational provisions. More will be said of this later.

In the hearing conservation programs of some school communities screen testing of hearing is carried out every year on every child. This, of course, is ideal. In other communities screen testing is done only for elementary school children in alternate grades, for example, in the kindergarten, second, fourth and sixth grades. A compromise between these two plans which would be less likely to delay the discovery of a hearing deficient child than the alternate year plan is as follows: screen test yearly all children in the kindergarten, first, second, fourth, sixth, eighth, tenth and twelfth grades; test all children soon after an illness which might affect hearing regardless of the grades they are in or when they were last tested; test any child referred by his teacher and any child newly enrolled in the school. Since younger children are more susceptible to infections and diseases which affect hearing than are older children, screen tests of hearing are most valuable for youngsters in the lower grades. A delay of over a year in discovering the early beginnings of a hearing loss may result in great physical, educational and emotional harm to a child.

There are two methods for conducting screening tests of hearing, the group and individual method. In the former, test tones from a pure-tone audiometer are presented through ten or more sets of headphones to as many children. In the latter, each child is given an individual audiometer test. The group test is less time consuming than the individual test but is, in general, less accurate. However, small groups of from five to ten children, each separated from the other by a partition or screen, can be tested efficiently and accurately. With this method a child responds by raising his hand when he hears the tone or he writes down the number of times short "pulses" of a given tone have been presented. A child cannot be seen by the other children but each child can be seen by the technician administering the test. Such a technique combines the speed of the group method with the accuracy of the individual method. Also, small groups are easier to manage and tend to permit a more quiet testing environment.

The parents of children who are discovered to have a loss of hearing are informed and medical attention is recommended. In some hearing conservation programs otologists are engaged to examine all children discovered to have deficient hearing. These specialists examine the children and when necessary recommend treatment to be carried out by the child's family physician or surgeon.

A graph used to record hearing acuity is called an audiogram or audiograph. The accompanying chart is marked off to show the significance of various levels of hearing deficiency.

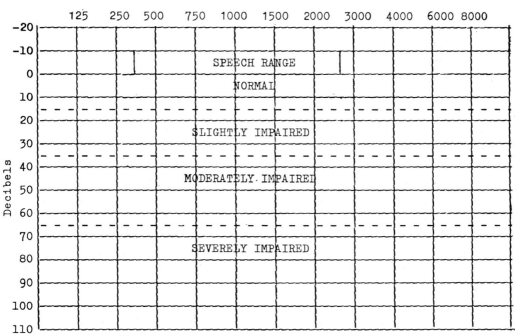

If, between the range of sounds most important for hearing speech, 300 c.p.s. to 3000 c.p.s., a person does not hear the tones until they are greater than 15 decibels but at a level of less than 35 decibels, such a person has some difficulty, although in most cases only slight difficulty, in hearing the normal speech of others. However, if the loss of hearing is between 35 decibels and 65 decibels a person is considered to have a moderate impairment of hearing and will usually benefit appreciably from the use of a hearing aid.

If the loss of hearing is greater than 65 decibels hearing impairment is severe. Although in such cases a hearing aid is usually of great benefit, persons with such a loss of hearing will generally require the additional help in understanding speech which they can receive from watching the lips and facial expressions of those speaking to them.

A person with a hearing loss in excess of 80 decibels may find it very difficult to understand speech even with the use of a powerful hearing aid unless he can obtain considerable additional help from visual and contextual cues. When a child has such a severe loss, he requires intensive language training, speech perception training (training in obtaining meaning from the combined use of auditory and visual cues) and training in the production of intelligible speech. In general, such children receive their education in special classes or schools for the deaf. However, intelligent and well trained children whose impairments are 80 decibels or less, can, and

often do, succeed both academically and socially in the regular school. Since, ultimately, a person must learn to live and work in the world of normal hearing and speaking people, the child who can make this adjustment starting in his early school years is, in general, more likely to succeed in his later associations with normal hearing people than one who has associated with the deaf through most or all of his elementary and junior high school years.

The child with a moderate or severe loss of hearing in the regular school must receive intensive training in language, speech perception and speech through the help of a speech and hearing therapist and must receive special assistance from his classroom teacher and his parents in his academic work. In some schools special classes are provided for the hard-of-hearing child who finds it too difficult to keep up with the work in the regular classroom. Such classes give the child both special educational consideration as well as a good speech and hearing environment.

With modern miniature hearing aids even a child can wear his hearing aid behind one or both ears. If he wears glasses the hearing aid can be in the temple pieces of his glasses. However, for some young children with severe impairment the conventional type hearing aid worn in a pocket or in a halter or harness is usually most satisfactory. For those who have a similar impairment in each ear and who have usable hearing in both ears, binaural hearing aids are being worn to great advantage in increasing numbers. In many instances hearing with both ears aids in localizing the source of sound and in separating the desired signal, speech, from competing background noise. A child who can benefit from binaural hearing aids should be provided with them if at all possible. The help he receives from his hearing aids in hearing the speech of others and in monitoring his own speech will prove to be most beneficial to him in his social and educational life.

Thanks to modern medicine and surgery, modern electronic instruments and the knowledge and skill of specialists in audiology, speech and hearing therapy and special education, the future of the hearing deficient child can become increasingly more promising. We must earnestly see that it does.

REGARDING CHANGING TRENDS IN ENROLLMENT OF A SCHOOL FOR DEAF CHILDREN*

IRVING S. FUSFELD

In a recent number of the *News*, Assist. Supt. Leenhouts presented conclusions of an informative study. This referred to certain trends in the enrollment of the school.† For one thing, it was found, "There has been a continuous indication that an increasingly greater proportion of the student group is congenitally deaf, and that among the adventitiously deaf, the age at onset continues to drop so that the number of students who lose hearing after age six is now negligible." The study revealed further that despite the continued lowering of the age of onset in students enrolled, academic achievement has actually advanced as evidenced by success in qualifying for admission to Gallaudet College, and that this fact seemed more apparent in those who obtained all or nearly all of their training at CSD.

The importance of a study of this kind lies in the challenging suggestions it arouses. Why, for instance, is there this continuing relative increase over the past thirty years in the number of children who on the one hand were born deaf, and as well in the numbers who were deaf either at birth or became so through age six? Speculation concerning this interesting phenomenon centers on a combination of possibilities, especially if there is likelihood similar conditions prevail in other schools for deaf children.

1. A striking achievement of recent decades has been a generally improved standard of living in the population at large, reflected in turn in a lessening of conditions that formerly produced ailments resulting in deafness, and particularly in children. Among the changes may be cited better hygienic and sanitary concepts

* A report printed in *The California News*, California School for the Deaf, Berkeley, December, 1958.

† Leenhouts, M. A., "Etiological Trends Among CSD Graduates Qualified for College," *The California News*, November, 1958.

and practices, greater attention to health education, a better understanding of principles of nutrition and their application to daily living.

2. Improved measures of prevention of, and counteraction against, disease have had important bearing on the incidence of adventitious deafness. Included among such measures has been the use of antiserums and antibiotics, the so-called wonder drugs. For instance, mastoid infection involvement in children was previously a fairly common occurrence, a condition in which the area of the hearing apparatus was highly vulnerable. Today this has largely yielded to treatment by preventatives such as the sulfas, penicillin, and the mycins. This attack upon conditions leading to deafness has had its effect in curbing the incidence of adventitious loss of hearing, and conversely has meant a relative increase in the number of children who are not adventitiously deafened, that is, those in whom deafness is present at birth.

3. A significant item in the movement against injury to hearing in children has been the surge of interest within the past decade in clinical practice as related to hearing pathology. The great increase in the number of speech and hearing centers, and the growth of university sponsored audiology aiming at improved methods of detection and alleviation have meant a frontal attack on hearing impairment in its incipient stages when corrective measures may still be applied. Part of this heightened interest has been the development of more sensitive apparatus in audiometry and electronics in connection with aid to hearing. This also has been reflected in a broadening of provision for special education, including of course deaf children.

4. To the above must be added a new refinement of what is meant by deafness in children. Much too often in the past children have been enrolled in schools for the deaf who really did not belong there. Children in whom lack of response to auditory arousement was only an apparent condition, but whose real difficulty was simply inability to respond by channels of speech, that is, aphasia, found their way into schools for the deaf because frequently there was no other place for them, or because they have been mistaken for deaf children. Far too often children who in reality deviated from average owing to mental difficulty were found in schools for the deaf, again because their response to speech was limited and not because of inability to hear well. Even when severe impairment of hearing was present, the same fact of impaired mentality was really the predominating influence. Occasionally also there would be children who were only psychogenically deaf, that is, who physiologically maintained the power of hearing but because of emotional involvement acted nonresponsive and so were mistakenly classed as deaf. In this broad category of children diagnosed by error as deaf, perhaps because of pronounced speech impairment, could be included cases of brain damage.

Along with these considerations of greater discernment regarding eligibility for admission to schools for the deaf, goes the problem of hard-of-hearing children. With the new impetus to means of detection and programs of therapy has been an obvious increase in the number of classes, and in some cases special schools, for hard-of-hearing children. With this movement on the increase there should be less reason to send such children to schools for the deaf. The latter, if properly organized, serve a need that does not apply in the case of children with only moderate hearing loss.

Since obviously such children do not represent instances of the congenitally deaf, their exclusion from schools for the deaf tends to raise the relative incidence of non-adventitiously deaf children.

5. The closing observation by Mr. Leenhouts that the quality of academic achievement by the student group has advanced, despite the steady lowering of age at onset of deafness, leads to an inescapable conclusion. That is, an educational agency such as the California School for the Deaf serves well the special needs of these children. With a school curriculum that follows closely the standards of public school requirements, and which reaches into the secondary school levels, with development of sound speech and acoustic training, with a well-ordered regime of language teaching as the core for learning, with a vocational department structured along lines of the same efficiency as prevails in the academic department, with a staff of instructors highly and specially trained for the complex task of teaching deaf children, with a corps of alert supervising teachers, with well graded classes that account for both maturity-age and pace of progress, with special classes that provide opportunity, adjustment and remedial guidance where the need exists, with a counseling staff and service to round out the picture of personality and social growth—all of these forces combine to assure the successful consummation of what may be justly called a sound program of education for deaf children.

IV. Early Auditory Assessment

AUDITORY SCREENING OF INFANTS*

Donald R. Caziarc

Many pediatricians, otologists, child psychologists, audiologists, and educators recognize the close relationship between auditory dysfunction and developmental problems in children. Hearing impairment in infants, even that which might be labeled as a slight-to-moderate impairment, may restrict, retard or limit the development of language and speech and contribute to a variety of learning and behavior problems. To detect hearing impairment in infants, physicians and psychologists have depended largely upon observations of growth and developmental changes and upon the parent observations of the infant's responses to gross sounds and auditory stimuli which are common to its environment. Gesell and Amatruda,[1] in their observations of premature infants, wrote that at the fetal age of 30 weeks or more, most premature infants will respond to the sound of a bell, either by positive movements or by immobilization of movement. The same writers

found that there are normal sequences in the development of auditory awareness, although there are individual differences in the time and appearances of these developmental manifestations.

Certain observable signs and symptoms have also been described by Gesell and Amatruda,[2] which may indicate the presence of a moderate to severe auditory dysfunction in an infant. For example, when an infant ceases to vocalize or enjoy listening to its own voice, it is possible that the rewarding aspects of this experience have been lessened due to an auditory impairment. At the age of three months an observable general indifference to sounds and lack of response to the spoken voice may be symptomatic of decreased auditory acuity. Although the infant may respond to loud sounds, such as the slamming of a door or the roar of a jet airplane passing overhead, its lack of response to the human voice and to other pleasant, psychologically rewarding sounds in the immediate environment are the most important clues. Severe deafness can be suspected or inferred in infancy on the basis of these symptomatic observations; however, adequate differential

Reproduced with permission from *California's Health*, California State Department of Public Health, March 1, 1963. D. R. Caziarc is Hearing Conservation Specialist, Bureau of Maternal and Child Health, California State Department of Public Health.

40

diagnosis is imperative lest possible auditory impairment be confused with mental retardation, other neurologic abnormalities, or a manifestation of pediatric psychological problems.

There has existed a need for more accurate methods of determining the presence of partial deafness, the kind of hearing impairment which involves auditory sensitivity to sounds of middle and high frequency, those sounds with a fundamental frequency of 1,000 cycles per second and higher, which often affect the child's language development and speech. Hearing impairments in infants may elude the most discerning observer and not be suspected and diagnosed until the child reaches the age of two years or even later. To these infants and very young children normal conversational speech and many environmental sounds may be muffled. The infants may grow and develop in an environment of distorted sound, and their resultant speech defects and behavior may reflect this auditory distortion.

During the past decade more definitive audiologic tests have been devised which make it possible to measure and evaluate auditory deficits in infants. Psychogalvanic skin resistance (PGSR) audiometric tests and electroencephalographic audiometry are two kinds of objective testing procedures commonly used in audiology clinics. These, and other clinical evaluative tests, are not practical for routine screening of infants. Needed for purposes of identifying infants with even slight auditory impairments have been simple procedures, built around known kinds of responses to familiar auditory stimuli which are commensurate with the developmental patterns of the normal infant.

Normal Auditory Development

The normally developing infant will exhibit a "startle response" or Moro reflex to the loud, sudden sound of a bell, clacker or clap of the hand. This kind of reflexive response is a primitive indication of gross audition. It should not be interpreted as auditory perception. It is a normal overt response which is observable in the full-term and premature infant as soon as the amniotic fluid and debris drain from the tympanic cavity.[3] As the infant develops, usually within six or eight weeks, there is a diminution of this kind of response which accompanies a growing interest in other auditory stimuli, such as soft, quiet voices or squeaky toys and rattles. With normal growth and development, the infant's auditory sensitivity advances rapidly from the stage of gross audition into a period of listening readiness. With listening, repeated auditory stimulation, and developing interest in pleasant environmental sounds, there is a cortical organization of these meaningful stimuli which constitutes the beginning of language acquisition and auditory perception. By the time the infant reaches the age of sixteen weeks, according to Watson and Lowrey,[4] it laughs aloud, smiles spontaneously, and seems to be enjoying its own voice, making it go up very high and then listening. This early vocalization is not to be confused with speech, but it may be interpreted as a kind of intracommunicative phase of oral and aural development.

As the normal infant enters the 40-week zone of growth and development, he may say "mama," "dada" and show other signs of communicative skills. During the ensuing weeks of auditory awareness and communication, there are accompanying physical manifestations of development: The infant sits unaided, attempts to pull himself up, and other general purposeful muscular activities. It is during this development period that the infant responds readily to the human voice in preference to other environmental sounds which may be only momentarily distracting. The infant's ability to receive and respond to a broad range of sounds, such as a well-modulated, soft voice, the sound of a metal spoon drawn gently around the edge of a china cup, and even the sound of voiceless consonants, s-s-s-s and k-k-k-k, provide evidence of his growing interest in meaningful, rewarding sounds and evidence also of his general auditory alertness.

The Ewing Test

The Ewings[5] of Manchester, England, are among the authorities who have investigated auditory acuity in infants and very young children. Although primarily concerned with ascertaining the extent of a hearing problem in infants who were already believed to be handicapped by deafness or who had demonstrated difficulties in communication, the methods used by the Ewings in testing these children have been used by audiologists and teachers of the aurally handicapped throughout the world. The Ewing Test has been incorporated into the well-child conferences in England as a part of routine health supervision of children from nine months to five years of age. The public health nurses are trained in the use of the test either at the University of Manchester or at their local health centers and work under the guidance of physicians who have also been trained in the auditory screening techniques. The test is very simple, and depends upon the child's interest and ability to respond to a variety of test items which provide frequency characteristics of the generally accepted speech range.

Modified Ewing Test Developed

In the United States, as a part of the Collaborative Cerebral Palsy Project at Johns Hopkins University, auditory screening has been included as an ancillary study in an attempt to develop more effective procedures for early detection of hearing impairment in the infants being followed in the study project. The Ewing techniques were modified for this study and used with infants three weeks to 52 weeks of age. High frequency sound stimuli, at a level of 40 decibels, consist of a high-pitched rattle, tissue paper, and *unvoiced consonants*, i.e., s,t,k,p. Speech frequency range sounds were produced with a "middle"-pitched rattle, a cup and metal spoon, and voice. Low frequency sounds selected for the test consisted of the spoken voice, a low-pitched rattle, a xylophone, and a tonette (a flute-like instrument). Other test items covering a broad frequency range of 2,000 to 8,000 cycles per second were a rubber toy "squeaker" (at 50 decibels) and a clacker and doorbell (at 60 decibels). The overall results of the study, as reported by J. B. Hardy and others,[6] indicate that infants can be expected to respond in one or more of fifteen different ways to twelve separate auditory stimuli. On the basis of the study, it has been possible to develop a streamlined screening procedure which has been standardized for infants of eight months of age. The test consists of a few items which are presented at a level of approximately 40 decibels. The primary items are: a soft, pleasant voice for low frequencies; a middle-range rattle for the frequencies essential to speech; and unvoiced consonants, s-s-s and k-k-k, representing the higher frequencies. The intensity level of each item is controlled by the examiner at a prescribed distance from the child's ear.

Applicability to Pediatric Examinations

A recent unpublished report from another study[7] conducted at Baltimore on the follow-up audiologic, otologic, psychologic and neurologic examinations for more than 700 infants who "failed" the auditory screening test, suggests that the procedure is one which should be a part of pediatric examinations and general health supervision in the child health conference. The report clearly indicates that this screening procedure not only identifies the infant with an auditory deficit, but is highly specific in the identification of infants with neurologic or psychologic problems. Children who failed to pass the screening tests were studied further to ascertain the basis for their inadequate responses. In the selected group of children who failed the screening procedures, the correlation between apparent auditory dysfunction and pediatric neurologic examination findings indicated that thirty-four infants out of one hundred who "fail" the screening test show neurologic abnormality. Skilled psychologists who examined these children concluded that sixty out of one hundred infants who fail the screening procedure will be found to have significant psychological problems.

In cooperation with the Baltimore City Health Department, pilot studies have been developed by the Johns Hopkins group which confirm the applicability of this streamlined screening procedure to child health conference examinations. As reported by Dougherty and Cohen,[8] the test procedure proved to be simple, inexpensive, and practical. All testing was conducted in a reasonably quiet (health clinic) room, away from reception rooms and general foot traffic. An effort was made to absorb ambient sound by placing a small carpet on the floor over which the tester would move, and the table on which the test items were placed was covered with a soft blanket or pad. Attention was given to the arrangement of the chairs and table so as to eliminate shadows which might provide visual clues during the test procedures.

The method used in auditory screening of the infants is referred to as the "distraction technique." While the mother holds the infant forward on her lap, the observer, seated directly in front of the mother and infant, attracts the infant's attention with skillful manipulation of colorful toys. At the moment the child's attention is obtained, the tester, moving to the side but out of the infant's peripheral vision, presents the test stimuli. All stimuli are presented in a planned sequence. The effectiveness of the procedure depends upon the skill and agility of the tester and upon the tester's knowledge of the basic principles of the test. There must be constant cooperation between the tester and the observer who work as a team throughout the screening procedure.

If the infant, age thirty-two to fifty-two weeks, does not respond by turning completely toward the side from which the test stimuli are presented, repeated screenings are scheduled. A second and third failure to respond in the manner prescribed for infants of this age group is reason for referral for more definitive testing at a hearing center. The screening procedure requires approximately one and one-half to two minutes.

Conclusion

The modified infant auditory screening procedure appears to be suitable as a part of routine child health supervision at well-child conferences and in the pediatrician's office if it is carried out by carefully selected, trained personnel. The procedure is not one which measures hearing acuity; it is designed to identify those infants who fail to respond to selected auditory stimuli in a manner commensurate with their normal growth and development patterns. Failure to pass the auditory screening tests may suggest the need for further audiologic, otologic, neurologic and psychologic evaluation.

References

1. GESELL, A., and AMATRUDA, C. S.: *Developmental Diagnosis.* New York, HOEBER, 1947, p. 269.
2. *Ibid.,* p. 278.
3. WATSON, E. H., and LOWREY, G. H.: *Growth and Development of Children.* Chicago, Year Bk, 1951, p. 132.
4. *Ibid.,* p. 98.
5. EWING, I. R., and EWING, A. W. G.: *Opportunity and the Deaf Child.* London, University of London, 1947.
6. HARDY, J. B.; HARDY, W. G., and others: Hearing responses and audiologic screening in infants. *J Pediat,* 55:382–390, 1959.
7. HARDY, W. G.; HARDY, J. B.; BRINKER, C. H., and others: Auditory screening of infants. (unpublished).
8. DOUGHERTY, A. L., and COHEN, J. L.: Auditory screening for infants and preschoolers. *Nurs Outlook,* 9:310–312, 1961.

V. Current Trends and Problems

DEAFNESS: SOME PRESENT-DAY PROBLEMS*

Air Vice-Marshal E. D. D. Dickson, c.b., c.b.e., m.d., f.r.c.s.

This thoughtful summary of the state of deafness and work for the deaf today by the Chairman of the Royal National Institute for the Deaf, is based upon a talk he gave to The British Council for Rehabilitation of the Disabled, at Oxford, July 5, 1965.

The human being constructs its world on the basis of messages through the sensorial organs to the brain. One of the main instruments by which impressions from the outer world can reach us is our sense of hearing. Being the sense which enables us to establish contact with our fellows, this "social sense" constitutes the basic brick of the human edifice, and of communication by speech. That is why hearing impairment forms a crucial handicap.

In otological practice—and for a brief moment let me speak as an otologist— any patient with a detectable impairment of hearing may be described as being deaf. I have spent many years seeing and assessing hundreds of individuals with a variety of communication disorders. I have used the increasing number of precision tools for measuring the auditory function and yet I still

* Reprinted, with permission of the Royal National Institute for the Deaf, from *Hearing,* London, England, September, 1965.

find it difficult to give a clear definition of the word "deaf." To some it may conjure up profound impairment. Yet Webster's Dictionary defines it as (i) "wanting, or deprived of the sense of hearing either wholly or in part" (ii) "inability to hear or listen determinedly; inattentive." Medical dictionaries define the term as "lacking the sense of hearing, or not having full powers of hearing" and the most widely used description is "partially deaf." So deafness may be conveniently described as slight, moderate, severe or total. There is no real agreement in all the fields of expertise as to the standards by which these qualifications should be applied.

The practical everyday meaning of deafness is that of being unable to hear and understand the spoken voice. The sociologist and educationist regard deafness from different points of view; the former, in terms of employment and wage earning, the latter, with regard to the problem of schooling. Even if we consider the word "deaf" only as it refers to profound limitation of hearing sensitivity, I still find it difficult to determine the point at which all those this side of the fence are deaf and those on that side are not. The confusion increases when statements are made about the deaf which have nothing to do with hearing sensitivity as, for example, "the deaf are normal and healthy persons" or "the deaf possess highly developed senses and great imaginative powers increased by their faculty of observation," etc.

For the purpose of this article I will confine my observations to severe loss of hearing where the patient cannot hear conversational voice unless considerably amplified, and to total loss of hearing, where the patient is unable to hear the spoken voice, despite maximum amplification. The individuals thus afflicted, will fall approximately within the Grade III of the Educational Classification where hearing is defective and speech and language little developed and the classification suggested by Ministry of Health circular 25 of 1961 (Deaf without Speech, *viz:* deaf and dumb) where no useful hearing is present "and whose normal method of communication is by signs, fingerspelling or writing."

It is impossible to generalize about "the deaf" and if we were to make some form of absolute statement about the deaf—that is, people with profound hearing impairment—it would fall in the following categories: 1. Their auditory system lacks normal sensitivity. 2. If the hearing impairment is acquired before language is learned they will have great difficulty in learning language. 3. If the hearing impairment is acquired before speech is learned the individual will never have normal speech, and if the deafness is acquired later some deteri-

oration in the quality of speech will usually occur.

To understand the behavior of a particular individual with severely limited hearing, we must know (1) the degree of loss of hearing sensitivity; (2) the kind of hearing impairment present; (3) the time of onset of the hearing impairment; (4) the nature and extent of other organic defects present and (5) the education to date.

The pure tone audiometer measures hearing sensitivity and a rough guess at the potential social significance of the loss may be expressed by taking the average of the threshold in the speech range. The speech reception threshold, however, can only be assessed by using speech stimuli and for that speech and language must be reasonably developed. It is obviously not applicable to a child with severe hearing impairment which is congenital or acquired at infancy.

It would perhaps be helpful if we had some clear idea of what is meant by "deaf and dumb" and what are the predisposing causes which bring about the condition. Let me add that a great disinclination exists to attach the label of "dumb" to anyone afflicted with a profound hearing loss. The word dumb conjures up a mental image of mental retardation or, to put it plainly, "dimness" which, of course, is not true. To be dumb, simply means that a person does not possess intelligible speech. As I have stated, these individuals have no useful hearing and their means of communication is by signs, fingerspelling or writing.

It is not always easy to determine

whether any backwardness is the result of the initial pathological or developmental condition which has given rise to the deafness and may have involved not only the peripheral receptive organ (the ear) but the relay stations and the area in the brain where final meaningful interpretation of the sounds takes place. In other words, we must visualize the hearing mechanisms as consisting of an encoding system, a relay and transmission system, and a decoding system. Involvement of any one or more of these systems will have its effect on the hearing function.

When we consider kinds of hearing loss we must realize that the realm of sensory neural hearing impairment is vast and diverse. Studies made in sensory neural losses acquired in adult life suggest major differences which depend upon the site of the lesion—for example, there may be severe difficulties in discrimination between different auditory stimuli, or in following rapid sequences of auditory stimuli, or there may be problems in the storage of and memory for auditory signals. It seems more than likely that injury to or maldevelopment of the embryonic or immature auditory-neural system can produce limited disfunction of the more complex aspects of auditory behavior. In many instances, therefore, it is likely that an impairment to the auditory system incurs much more than just reduction in hearing sensitivity.

The deafness *per se* may cause retardation or arrest of mental development resulting in a limitation of vocabulary and language. It is also possible that even in the absence of deafness the person might have been, in any case, backward.

The deaf—and I mean the profoundly deaf—are those whose sense of hearing is nonfunctional for the ordinary purposes of life. There are two distinct classes based on the time of the loss of hearing: (1) the congenitally deaf; (2) the adventitiously deaf, i.e. those who were born with normal hearing but in whom the sense of hearing became nonfunctional later through illness or accident.

Or, in other words, prenatal or postnatal in onset. I am concerned mainly with the former. The prenatal causes consist of: (1) The hereditary group in whom the perceiving or conducting apparatus fails to develop normally or later degenerates owing to inherited defects of maturation or maintenance. These are the congenitally deaf. (2) The pregnancy group where the perceptive mechanism is maldeveloped, the results of the toxic effects of maternal rubella, rhesus factor, syphilis, etc. (3) The birth group, that is, the period immediately preceding, including and following the birth of the child. The child is exposed during this period to certain hazards, principally toxemias, anoxia and birth injuries.

All these prenatal and perinatal cases have exclusively some involvement of the encoding and, in all probability, of the transmitting and decoding mechanism—a perceptive type of defect. It is this important fact we must appreciate and realize in our efforts to teach a deaf person or child to acquire speech. We have concentrated our efforts too much on what sound, if any, a deaf child or person can appreciate, but we have overlooked that it is the interpretation and translation of such a sound into something meaningful which constitutes success or failure. To appreciate a frequency—its pitch and intensity—does not necessarily mean the ability to discriminate the spoken word. When we plan the habilitation of the deaf it is important to bear in mind some of these essentially fundamental points; they will apply mainly to education and welfare.

Generally speaking, I would say that the legislative provisions in this country are adequate (except possibly in respect of vocational training) but that the application of those provisions encounters some difficulties. In schools and special classes for deaf children there are variations of method and of administrative procedures (which is perhaps to be expected in a country where schools for the deaf have developed throughout a period of more than two hundred years under a variety of auspices). There is nowadays a substantial measure of uniformity in the training of teachers of the deaf, and the differences in schooling which deaf children receive, apart from the inherent differences of boarding and day schools, of town and rural, or of old and new, are probably more apparent than real.

There is one respect in which the services provided may be said to be inadequate. This is in the provision of guidance for deaf children with emotional or social maladjustment. In most audiology clinics the needs of deaf children for psychological care are adequately met, but there is, as yet, no provision for the followup of this treatment by psychiatric social workers specially trained in the work for the deaf. It is because of this inadequacy that the R.N.I.D. is now building a special residential school for severely maladjusted deaf children—the first of its kind, certainly in this country, if not in the world. The children who will come to this new school (it is in Buckinghamshire) will be those who, because of their social and emotional difficulties, cannot easily be educated in ordinary schools for the deaf and partially hearing.

Although there is at present very little knowledge on the best method of educating and rehabilitating such children, it is likely that there will be a very "permissive" atmosphere in the school and much of the education will be through play, outdoor activities, practical methods, etc. Very careful records will be kept so that a store of knowledge will be built up of each child. There will be all the usual electronic apparatus normally found in schools for the deaf and the teachers will probably be a mixture of those trained for the deaf and those with experience of maladjustment. Groups will be kept very small so that some children may receive almost individual attention.

In general, our educational services for the deaf are well organized and well applied but it is often argued that some of the difficulties which young people experience in afterschool life would be diminished if their schooling gave them a better command of written and printed language (with or without speech) and an outlook more adjusted to the realities of modern life.

Education of the deaf has long been a subject of much controversy. Historically, it has developed to a very large extent from the pioneer work of a number of remarkable men and women. It is likely that the next decade will be marked by changes brought about as the result of research and experiment. An investigation was carried out by Professor M. M. Lewis, formerly Professor of Education at Nottingham University, who devoted himself fulltime to the work. The project was designed to illuminate particular aspects of backwardness in the use of language by children with impaired hearing in relation to their linguistic, social and ethical development. The investigation included a study of "fingerspelling and communication by signs." This led to the appointment by the Department of Education and Science, of a committee under the chairmanship of Professor Lewis, to consider the place, if any, of fingerspelling and signing in the education of the deaf. This committee is sitting now and everyone at all concerned with work for the deaf eagerly awaits the findings of that committee.

The difficulties of social adjustment for the adolescent who can hear have received much attention in research programs, and this is especially true of the difficulties arising from the transition from school to work. A deaf child shares these problems but, for him, the process of social adjustment is vastly complicated by his limited powers of communication. That there has been no research in the United Kingdom on the social adjustment of deaf adolescents is surprising, and this gap, I hope, will be bridged by a three-year program of systematic research being undertaken from the University of Manchester. This research, too, is expected to throw useful light on the adequacy of present arrangements for the education of deaf children.

A certain number of deaf adolescents fail to make the transition from the world of school to the outside world satisfactorily and become unsettled and difficult. As a measure toward solving this problem, the R.N.I.D., some two years ago, set up a residential training center (in Devonshire) for difficult deaf young men where they may be given an environment and training which may set them on their feet again. The need for such a center had been apparent for many years to those who worked for the deaf. There were many cases in the past where deaf boys had been so disturbed that they were unlikely to settle down and lead useful lives without special training. This project has been developed in close cooperation with the Ministry of Labor and it is designed to *prevent* young deaf men from getting into trouble.

Within the R.N.I.D. at the present time, the emphasis of discussion and innovation is on adult welfare. Last year the Institute gave £40,000 to found a new College of Deaf Welfare which is now in being and actively participating in a general reconsideration of the training of welfare workers for the deaf alongside the re-orientation of general training for all social workers which the Government set on foot as a result of the Health Visiting and Social Work (Training) Act 1962. The ordinary social worker can cope with the needs of ordinary handicapped people, but only someone practised in modes of communication with the deaf and dumb can penetrate the barrier of their deafness.

The greater part of welfare work for the deaf in the United Kingdom is undertaken by the staffs of the voluntary institutes or societies for the deaf (traditionally called "Missions"). There are about ninety of them, and the majority were founded by Church of England workers in the early and middle nineteenth century for religious and charitable help to the deaf in industrial areas. Over the last hundred years they have been developed to cover the whole country and all religious denominations, and they have taken on an ever expanding range of practical work in addition to their original spiritual ministrations. Before 1940, local institutes for the deaf received no State aid whatsoever, apart from small optional grants from local authorities for specific purposes. They were supported by voluntary gifts or subscriptions, or by income derived from their charitable foundations. By the National Assistance Act, 1948, local Authorities were empowered and, since July 1960, *required* to undertake welfare work for the deaf as part of their services. In very many cases the authorities have appointed the local institutes as their agents for this work and pay regular grants for it to be carried out. Fifteen authorities to date, however, have elected to supply a direct service

and it is possible that more will follow suit. The W.O.D. of the future can, therefore, look for opportunities of employment and service with Local Government instead of only, as in the past, with one or other of the voluntary societies.

Summary

1. It is time that general agreement was reached on the assessment and classification of the hearing impairment present. It should not be beyond the human imagination to assess the magnitude of the handicap. I am not offering any suggestions at this stage how this should and could be done but, if achieved, it will give us some idea of the incidence of various types and degrees of hearing loss and guide us in the management of each case.

2. A better understanding is desirable, by all those working with and for the deaf, of the underlying pathology which has given rise to the loss of hearing and the limitation often imposed on the subject under review. It may help us re-orientate our views in the field of education, welfare and training.

3. The deaf cannot be grouped into cut-and-dried compartments. Each case requires individual assessment by a team with intimate knowledge of the underlying factors concerned.

4. It is essential that any underlying psychological factor should be investigated by a psychologist with experience in the methods of communication with the deaf, *viz:* fingerspelling and sign-

ing. Dr. Eldridge was quite right, in my opinion, in stating in the July *Hearing* that anyone undertaking any work among the deaf should have some knowledge in the field of visual communication.

EDUCATIONAL TRENDS*

WILLIAM RASBURN

The limited space will not allow a comprehensive account of the trends in the educational treatment of the deaf and the problems arising, so the first observation must be in the nature of an apology that whatever follows may do little more than scratch the surface. Also, as I am not well acquainted with the probable readers, I must add a further apology—much of the material may appear elementary and merely a repetition of what readers already know. I must add, too, that whatever I say must be considered as my own opinion and does not necessarily reflect the policy of the National College of Teachers of the Deaf.

Thanks to the efforts of many associations and individuals, more and more publicity has been given through television, the press, etc., to the question of deafness and we have traveled far from the days when the deaf and dumb were classed with idiots and deprived of practically all rights. But we have still far to go before the general public can really understand the problems faced

* A paper appearing in *The Silent Northerner*, Autumn 1964 issue, a publication of The North Regional Association for the Deaf, Manchester, England, and reprinted here by courtesy of the latter organization and the author. The author is from the Royal Schools for the Deaf, Cheshire, England.

by those born with practically no hearing or who are deprived of hearing in the first few months of life. Even today, how often do we hear: "Well, even if he is deaf, he can read"? People cannot be blamed for holding this entirely erroneous idea—how can they know when probably they have not even met a deaf person. It is difficult for anyone, even those who have spent years working with the deaf, fully to appreciate their difficulties and to realize all the difficulties they face. Sometimes I feel that some people who have lost their hearing after having acquired a good command of language find it more difficult to realize the problems than do those who have retained normal hearing.

Very briefly, I will outline the position of the child born so deaf that he cannot hear the sound of voice. Various estimates have been given of the probable vocabulary of a hearing child when he enters school, but it is now considered reasonably certain that 2,000 words is a fair average. By the time he is seven, this number will have increased to 4,000. So, if a child should go deaf at the age of five, he will already have a good knowledge of language and this can be used to explain other language forms which he does not know. In skilful hands he should be able to progress quite rapidly, though not, of course, as quickly as he would have done had he retained his hearing. The profound psychological effect that might be a result of the onset of deafness, though of such vital importance, cannot be more than just mentioned here, but the expression "skilful hands" does take it into account.

The child born with a severe hearing loss is far from being in this position— left to himself he will have no vocabulary, as we know it, by the time he attains the age of five. He will be little better off unless those around him know something of his difficulties and of the special needs due to his deafness. In comparatively recent years parents of deaf children have, in some areas, been able to attend clinics and learn something of the ways by which they can help their children acquire some vocabulary and good habits toward learning. Even in such circumstances the deaf child has a far, far more difficult task than has a hearing child. The more recent approach is to fit a baby with a hearing aid at the earliest possible opportunity and this has been done in many cases in the first year of life. The hope is that the child will hear language and thus learn naturally and it is undoubtedly true that many children can, in fact, do this—perhaps even more than was at first thought. But there are still children whose loss is so great that even the best modern aid cannot help them learn in this normal way. When such children go to school they must try and make up all the lost leeway in addition to learning new language—infinitely more difficult for him than for normal children.

How should we endeavor to help this child? Here of course the vexed question, oralism v. manual raises its ugly head; how much has been, and will be said on this subject! Here I shall content myself with putting forth some of the reasons why the oral method is considered to be worthwhile. Through no fault of his own, a child is born into a community and, to live as full a life as possible, he must, as far as he is able, become an integral part of society. Our society is predominantly a hearing one and has an orthodox method of communication. If it is at all possible every member of the community must be given every opportunity of acquiring some measure of skill in that method of communication which society has developed. Throughout his formative years the child spends his life with family and neighbors who are, in the vast majority of cases, hearing people. His only hope of communication is to use the means they use, even though he can do so only approximately. It is an undoubted fact that even the imperfect speech of deaf children is, in many cases, adequate for communication with their families and friends. Of course they must have something to say and have the language to say it. So far as I know there is no positive evidence that a deaf child can learn more quickly by the manual method than by the oral. Some will cast grave doubts on that statement and point out that the older generation of the deaf, who were taught manually, have a better command of English than have present-day pupils. Have they? Or is it just that the best of those are better than the worst of ours? It would be just as fair an argument to say that nowadays many more pupils obtain G.C.E. etc., than did in the old days. But, say some, how about the big strides made by deaf pupils when they leave school and have the opportunity to learn manually? Could it not be that equally big strides would be made if they stayed on at school? Research has shown that all children—not just the deaf—go through a period, at the age of about fifteen, when their rate of learning slows down and recovers again later. Moreover, these deaf children who learn manually after leaving school are building on foundations already laid.

It seems that this argument could go on forever since all statements on each side are, at bottom, almost entirely matters of opinion. Could it be that here is an avenue where positive controlled research might prove beneficial? Difficulties would certainly arise. Such research would have to be spread over a period of at least ten years, probably much longer; it would be necessary to have two groups of children, as nearly identical as possible in every way: hearing loss, intelligence, home background, etc., and they would have to be taught under similar conditions by teachers of similar ages and similar capabilities. Only the method of teaching should be different. It would, of course, be necessary to find children whose parents would be willing that they should be subjects of the research.

Since the 1944 Act there has been a growing body of expert opinion that handicapped children should be educated along with the normal. This may well be possible in many cases but I hesitate to think it feasible with the majority of deaf children. As has already been pointed out, the rate of progress is essentially very slow so inevitably the deaf child would be far behind the hearing child of the same age. In general, therefore, it is the partially hearing child who is educated in "normal surroundings," and units for such children have been opened in many parts of the country.

There is also the peripatetic service— many authorities appoint teachers of the deaf to help in the education of children with impaired hearing who attend normal schools. This, of course, is only one small facet of the very valuable peripatetic work. This, and the work of teachers in partially hearing units, now form a vital part of the education of the deaf in this country and the concensus of opinion is that any teacher employed there should have some experience in the education of deaf children. And yet, it is not uncommon for authorities to appoint newly qualified teachers to such important posts.

Early Training

It is felt in many circles that mother's presence and family life are primary requisites for the full development of the child. In general, this cannot be denied but with the deaf child the problem arises by the lack of understanding and communication. Some feel that the work which can be done by a trained teacher may outweigh the possible damage caused by the child being away from home. It is necessary to attempt to assess and avoid the greater of the two evils and this assessment is a task of the utmost difficulty.

School Leaving Age

All teachers of the deaf have felt that the length of time needed for the education of their pupils is, of necessity, longer than that given to hearing children. When the school leaving age was raised to fifteen the deaf child lost a year's schooling and when, eventually the school leaving age becomes sixteen he will again have the same length of time in school as does the hearing child. Obviously then, he will suffer even more by comparison and, ideally, he should have *his* leaving age raised.

But when one takes a realistic view the problem of finding a satisfactory job looms large—the deaf leaver is eighteen against the sixteen of the hearing leaver. Some teachers feel that under present economic conditions this age difference might prove detrimental and prevent the deaf from obtaining a suitable and satisfying job. Here again there is room for research and action.

Higher Education

At the moment the Mary Hare Grammar School and Burwood Park School are the only establishments catering specifically for higher academic education though of course there are several other schools where pupils are entered for the G.C.E. examination. The pupils concerned are in the higher strata and as yet little is done for the less able children. One other form of higher ed-

ucation is that at the Talbot House Department of the Royal Schools at Old Trafford. This is not merely a school of industrial training as the boys there do have the advantage of a large degree of social training. I think it should be realized that the trades chosen when the department was first opened were chosen not merely because they were the "traditional" trades of the deaf but, more important, were trades in which there would always be work. This attitude is reflected in the recent closing down of the two trades, tailoring and shoemaking, in which conditions have changed so radically in recent years. It seems to me that there is room for a full investigation of the position and a serious review of the advisability of setting up a similar department with an extension of available courses which the deaf could profitably undertake. Obviously, because of the finance involved, it would be necessary for this to be done on a national level.

The Residential School

General policy has gradually been formulated that the deaf child should be educated in such conditions that he is able to live at home. This is contrary to the opinion of many parents of hearing children who feel that the best education is obtainable at boarding schools. However, it is a fact that the residential schools for the deaf have far fewer pupils than at one time. Many also have day pupils and the vast majority have weekly boarders, pupils who spend four nights at school and three at home.

In some cases children, because of

the position of their homes, must be in a residential school. In some districts "problem" cases are sent to a residential school and also there are children who go to such a school because of home conditions. Gradually, therefore, the problems in residential schools are growing and it appears that the probable standard of attainment must inevitably become lower.

Children with Other Handicaps

Almost four years ago the N.C.T.D. conducted a survey on the Provision for the Deaf Child with Additional Handicaps. One of the suggestions was that 153 pupils might benefit from transfer to a school for Dual or Multiple Handicaps. We have in the country one such school, with a capacity of about thirty boys—no girls, and a similar though larger school for partially hearing pupils. Suitable educational treatment is just as essential for these children as it is for the brightest ones.

Progress in the education of deaf children, in school building and in general outlook has been far from negligible in comparatively recent years but no one concerned with their welfare can rest content. Much work needs to be done, much research is necessary and, above all, the efforts of all the bodies interested in their needs must be intensified and coordinated as far as possible.

VI. Preschool Training

TRAINING PROGRAM FOR THE EDUCATION OF DEAF INFANTS*

ROBERT L. McCROSKEY

Introduction

The term "deaf" does not convey equal meaning to all who hear the word. It should be understood that impairment to hearing exists along a con-

* A report to U. S. Public Health Service, Division of Chronic Diseases, Neurological and Sensory Disease, Service Program, Washington, D. C., October 8, 1962, reproduced here by permission from the author as given in *The School Helper,* Georgia School for the Deaf, Cave Spring, February 1963. In a separate communication, May 5, 1966, Dr. McCroskey advises that work begun at the Atlanta Speech School in January 1964, and possibly elsewhere, outlines as follows: "The program we have developed is almost an exact replication of that which is used in the Netherlands and to the best of our knowledge it was the only program for deaf infants in the United States which takes the work to the home of the child. Other programs usually bring the child and the family to the clinic, or a simulated home, for a brief period of instruction before the family returns to the home community. I have just learned within the last few days that there is some home visitation being done in the State of Tennessee—as a part of the State Department of Health, if I am not mistaken. If this has been done in Tennessee, I would say that this is a reasonable step to be taken. In fact, I expect that this is the way we in Georgia will have to handle our deaf infants if we are to serve those who are located at considerable distances from areas of high population concentration."

It may be noted also that in 1927 the board of directors of the Sarah Fuller Home for Little

tinuum and that there are degrees of deafness. Even in residential schools for the deaf only 3 to 4 per cent of the children are considered to be totally deaf.

The sounds of our environment are almost always complex in nature. Speech is conveyed through sound which is composed of many frequencies. Accurate reception of vocalization requires a listening mechanism which can receive and interpret sound throughout a wide range of frequencies. The auditory system of man can be defective in a variety of ways, each of which will introduce distortion of the original signal, and have effects upon the receptive aspect of communication. When the ear will pass only a limited number of tones, and only these when presented at very high intensity levels, it is felt that the burden of communication falls on the visual and tactual channels.

Limited attempts at utilizing the au-

Deaf Children, now the Sarah Fuller Foundation, instituted a plan of teaching preschool children in their own homes. The Sarah Fuller Service as it was called has since been discontinued.

Dr. McCroskey is in the Division of Teacher Education, Emory University, and is Director of the Department of Speech, Atlanta Speech School, Atlanta, Georgia.

ditory channel reflect the traditional view that while most deaf children do have some residual hearing it is really not usable for the reception of speech nor a reliable means of self-monitoring. Fortunately, interest in the use of the auditory channel with the deaf has persisted through the centuries and there are isolated instances of successful use of residual hearing for the purpose of teaching the identification and discrimination of sounds, words and sentences. More often than not, the end result was applauded but ignored because of the years required and the highly individual nature of the instruction.

With the advent of the electronic hearing aid there was renewed interest in the utilization of residual hearing of deaf persons. At the time of World War II simultaneous efforts toward refining auditory training began in England, Sweden, the United States of America and the Netherlands (Holland).

The method employed at the Instituut Voor Doven (Institute for the Deaf) at St. Michielsgestel, Holland, is of particular interest because a rather formalized home program of speech and language development plus auditory training was begun with infants who were approaching or near the age of one year. Furthermore, a different approach to auditory training with older deaf children was inaugurated. This knowledge, in addition to the conviction that normal deaf children can learn to communicate intelligibly and effectively with their hearing peers, indicated that direct observation and evaluation were the next step. This was accomplished

during the first two weeks of September, 1962, and that which follows is a report of the home training program for deaf infants at the Instituut Voor Doven, St. Michielsgestel, Holland.

History

The Reverend Father A. van Uden is credited with originating and organizing the program which he currently supervises. Dr. B. Tervoort, S. J., appears to have been active in developing the concept that the influence of environmental language is reflected in the prespeech vocalizations of normal hearing infants as early as six to seven months of age. This suggests that the residual hearing of a deaf infant should begin to be utilized just as early as possible.

The first home teacher for the deaf began working in November of 1955. There are now four full-time teachers with the Institute for the Deaf. The first employee had majored in Baby Care and Baby Education prior to receiving training as a teacher of the deaf. While this person appears to have performed successfully, the required educational background for trainees has been changed to that described in the following section.

Educational Requirements for Teachers

A Home Training Teacher (HTT) must have completed college with a major emphasis in Social Casework and be a trained teacher of the deaf. It should be noted that the word "college," as used in The Netherlands, applies to the specialized training a student receives as he begins his eleventh or twelfth year of academic study. The college for Social Casework is a three-year program at a school where only this specialty is taught. Following this, the student is eligible to begin the training as a teacher of the deaf. This is a two-year program which is about divided between academic study and practical experience with all phases of an institutional program for the deaf.

The Academic Program

In general, the course offerings are very much like those required for certification in the United States by the Conference of Executives of American Schools for the Deaf; for example, they must have had course work in the following areas: Audiometry, Language for the Deaf, Speech for the Deaf, Phonetics, Child Psychology, Linguistics, Psychology of the Deaf, Practice Teaching, Psychological Testing, General Psychology and Behavioral Psychology.

Finances

Full pay as a social caseworker is possible during the training to become a teacher of the deaf. Academic work is given on hours and days which keep the schoolday free for full-time observation and assistance to regular teachers. Sixty per cent of the salary is paid by the government.

These teachers of the deaf are paid by the Ministry of Social Work rather than by the Ministry of Education because the latter has no provision for recognizing home instruction.

Professional Certification

The original requirements for certification were established at the Instituut Voor Doven and submitted to the state. At the present time successful completion of a written examination given by the state under the supervision of a state examiner is required. Completion of a training program is prerequisite to taking the examination.

Procedures for the Detection of Deafness

These procedures are not so clearly defined as was thought, based on earlier communication with a representative of the Institute. The primary referral sources are the house physicians of hospitals and otologists. This is facilitated, apparently, by a modified socialized medicine program which allows wide collection of data and serves as a routing agency to refer patients to appropriate specialists. The structure of these services is such that it omits portions of the population. The services are available only to those who earn 8,000.00 Guilder or less per year; there is an automatic 2% wage deduction.

There are many incidental referrals by local doctors, neighbors, etc. This kind of referral is stimulated by a very active publicity campaign through articles published in ladies magazines and newspapers. Special pamphlets are distributed to waiting rooms and offices throughout the country.

Otologists inform the Instituut Voor Doven directly of any child who appears to have impaired hearing. Children who are discovered through other sources are referred to an otologist before the school takes any action. The Instituut's M.D. contacts local doctors for further information (there is a hospital connected with the school).

The detection procedure moves into diagnosis and the dividing line cannot be established clearly. When a child has been referred, and the otological services have been rendered, the HTT begins to visit the home. The HTT begins to assess the child's intellect in terms of developmental and behavioral patterns and is conversant with informal procedures for evaluating hearing. In some instances the audiologist also visits the home.

Eligibility for the Home Training Program

As long as there is evidence of a severe impairment to hearing but exact levels cannot be determined accurately, the child will remain in the program. To be eligible a child must have a hearing level of 90db (re: American Audiometric zero) or worse at 1000 c.p.s. by air conduction, in the better ear. There is also a low-tone factor which seems to be a little flexible, but generally the applicant shall have a 60db hearing level or worse in the low frequencies.

There is no specified lower age limit to be admitted to the program. The up-per limit is set by the fact that four-year-old children are admitted to the regular program at the Instituut.

Observations of Home Training

The following examples are considered to be typical of the procedures followed during the home visits: Child number one was 14 months old and had worn a hearing aid for two months. The Y-cord is routinely employed to give two-ear listening from a single sound source. The parents reported that the child had been silent until the aid was in use; he then began to engage in vocal play. The parents reported that he used some words meaningfully, i.e., mama, papa, da (the equivalent of bye-bye), but these were not heard by the writer. It was observed that the child could imitate simple pitch patterns spoken by the mother. In two months the time of wearing the aid had been increased from five minutes per day to one and one-half hours per day. The original volume setting had been increased, under the HTT's guidance until a level had been achieved which yielded responses. There was general conversation between parents and teacher regarding behavior, stimulation methods, etc. The HTT spent time holding the baby, vocalizing, pointing to objects and naming them, and in general becoming a part of the family.

Child number two was a three-year-old boy. The ease with which these parents handled the child, plus the obvious expectation that he would get information by listening indicated that they believed in the program. He was born in 1959, had been in the program since January of 1961, and had worn an aid for four months at the time of the visit. These visits were the first following summer vacation. As the parents and HTT talked, the HTT provided the boy with various tasks, i.e., stringing beads by colors; formboard of twenty-five common objects; color matching with a pegboard and similar materials. The conversation with the parents centered around such topics as the amount of control that the mother had over the hearing aid and suggestions for making the microphone more accessible. The parents were concerned over the type of school he would go into the following year, one for the hard of hearing or one for the deaf. The audiogram indicated a sensorineural impairment with a 10db per octave drop beginning with a 60db loss at 500 c.p.s. It was the opinion of the observer that the child would probably go to the school for the hard of hearing, although by most standards he could be admitted to a program for the deaf.

Effects

1. Counseling parents on many problems which are not always related to the child with the hearing impairment, but which help the family operate with greater unity and security. They deal with acceptance within the family and within the community or neighborhood. This was considered of primary importance by the visiting teacher.

2. General baby care and recognition of potential health problems. Again, this is not confined to the deaf child.

3. Guide the use of the hearing aid with respect to care and maintenance as well as volume settings and length of use each day.

4. Vocabulary building and comprehension of simple spoken commands. It must be noted that the improvement or correction of speech patterns is never attempted by the HTT. The task is complete when the child is responding to and using meaningful auditory symbols for the purpose of communication.

5. Becoming a part of the family makes it easier for the family and the child when he is admitted to a residential school. He has the security of someone he knows and the parents are reassured by the presence of someone who really knows and loves their child.

6. Create a tie between the child and the school. In the spring preceding entrance into the school in the fall there is one week in which all beginning children are brought to the school for the purpose of medical, ophthalmologic, otologic, psychologic, audiologic and neurologic evaluation. The HTT is the first person the child sees in the spring and in the fall. This teacher also stays with the children during their spring visit.

7. Validation of diagnosis through observation of the child over a period of months and years.

8. Provide knowledge of techniques for language stimulation through example. The parents see the work so often that it becomes a natural part of their relationship with the child. Even the summer vacations allow continued work because the procedures are a part of daily living.

Observed Results of the Home Training Program

The parents of these deaf children do, indeed, know how to work with their children. This was apparent in each home where the infants had been in the program for several months.

It was fortunate that observation took place at the beginning of the school year. It was possible to see the products of the home training as the children began their lives in a residential school.

As the parents arrived with their children, the first person seen by the child was the home teacher. This became more of a happy reunion than a time of separation from parents. The HTT stayed with the children even after they had begun some classroom activities. In only one instance was there trauma connected with the separation and this was occasioned by the fact that the child had had his tonsils removed at the Instituut's Hospital a few months before. The administrators were horrified that such an error had been committed because it was established policy never to operate on a child who was to be enrolled unless there was an emergency. The classrooms were cheerful and well supplied with interesting material, but the center of attraction was a bulletin board on which there were group photographs of each child's family.

From an "academic" standpoint work could begin almost immediately. The children were accustomed to amplification and meaningful use of residual hearing. They were accustomed to brief periods of concentrated effort on vocabulary, language, sense training, etc. They were controllable by virtue of the unified approach to management and behavior problems. The world was meaningful because they had learned many commands and could understand what was required of them even in a strange setting. Their own needs could be expressed because in most instances they entered the program with a limited but useful spoken vocabulary.

The comprehension and expression available to these children gave them a happier start, and certainly a running start, into a very long and difficult program. While much of this contributes to the mental health of the child, there is much to be said for the mental health of the parents and the role this program plays. There were obvious trust and affection on the faces of parents as they greeted their HTT and as they delivered their children into the hands of the school. They had the secure knowledge that here was someone who had been with them from the beginning and knew their child as well as they did. The confidence they felt in the HTT was generalized to the Instituut itself.

Conclusion

A program which provides both education and emotional benefits for parents and children is a significant one.

The singular isolation of the deaf from professional and social intercourse with their hearing peers in the United States of America is testimony to the fact that our education procedures do not equip our deaf for a reasonable share of the job market.

The home training program offers hope that deafness need not continue to be the factor which segregates and limits the hopes of at least 200,000 citizens.

THE YOUNG DEAF CHILD AND HIS PROBLEMS*

ADRIANA DUMITRESCU

The auditory deficiencies of the young deaf child cannot be measured by objective method, but rather estimated on the basis of various tests within the framework of a complex otopsychoneurological and logopedic examination. For that reason the degree of hearing loss can be determined with some certainty only at the school-age level. This accounts for the considerable number of instances where parents are not aware of the presence of an auditory impairment in their children, and especially for the frequency of cases in which parents cling to the illusion of normal hearing in their children.

The most evident and regretful effect that the child's deafness has upon his environment (even though loss of hearing may be but partial) is a marked retardation of development, particularly in the failure to acquire spoken language as a means of social communication. Chiefly from this point of view (without minimizing the therapeutic possibility of hearing rehabilitation), the early detection of an auditory deficiency and the formulation of a plan with corresponding remedial measures are especially important.

For the medical practitioner's activity within the general health area, for

* Reprinted from *Pediatria*, official journal of the Association of Medical Sciences of the People's Republic of Roumania, Vol. 14, No. 1, January–February 1965, 77–81. Translation by the author is gratefully acknowledged.

A. Dumitrescu is Logopedist at the Children's Polyclinic, "30th December" Ward, Bucharest, Roumania.

the many other medical specialists, for the public health nurses' field work, knowledge of some of the young deaf child's characteristics is helpful, first in view of facilitating the early detection of deafness and then for providing information for the parents regarding the various typical problems to which this deficiency gives rise.

If up to one year, contrary to some older opinions, the deaf child is not essentially different from the normal child, in the prelinguistic stage his kinesthetic sensations (muscular and articulatory) being sufficient so that he might learn to resort to simple vocalizations, one cannot say the same thing holds true for the second year of the deaf child's life.

Indeed, up to the very end of his first year, the child, even though he hears neither himself nor those around him, stammers, emits sounds more or less articulated, but without any meaning, within the framework of his playing activities, responding to an instinctive, spontaneous need. He is cooing, gurgling, laughing, he shouts in order to express his desires. This rudimentary mode of expression, prelinguistic, as we call it, is strengthened in other respects by the fact that the adults usually come up to him when he cries, or stroke him and laugh when he babbles, inciting him thus to go on stammering.

But toward the end of the first year, the differences between the normal and the deaf child appear. The normal child begins to repeat a few sounds, consonants and vowels, imitating the words which he hears all the time. In the beginning, difficult words are articulated in faulty manner, but they are being gradually corrected through the comparison that the infant makes between his memory and the better heard word, when the parents, discarding a simulated infantile speech, pronounce each word correctly.

Therefore, while the normal child begins to speak his first words, to his family's delight, the deaf child remains in the babbling stage, and even though his psychomotor development is not affected he often abandons these rudimentary forms of expression in order to express himself more energetically, that is, with the help of gestures. One can observe in the deaf child throughout his second year of life a regressing stammering, accompanying the tendency to express himself through mime and gestures. However, the majority of these children succeed, by imitating complex articulatory movements, in saying two or three words made of double syllables, i.e., *papa*, more rarely, *mama*. But their active vocabulary stops there, if no competent remedial intervention takes place.

These "wordless" children are at the same time without any adequate thinking process. In their world things and actions bear no names. Not only are they incapable of understanding the language of others and so they do not receive the constantly enriching information of their environment, which is transmitted in a natural way to hearing children but, also, they cannot use the language which might express their thoughts, needs, or wishes and thus cannot influence the behavior of others. For that reason the deaf child is handicapped from his tenderest age by his inability to acquire speech and develop his intelligence as well as by a series of behavior disturbances.

The deaf children are mistrustful, wild, inhibited, violent, choleric, they have temper tantrums at the slightest disagreement (especially when the child wishes to make himself understood and fails to do so with his limited means of expression or when he cannot understand when others express themselves).

In order to understand these specific traits of the deaf child's character, let us analyze the permanent feeling of insecurity the child experiences. For instance, when the hearing child does not see around him those close to him (when his mother goes away and disappears from his visual field) he still hears steps. He perceives a mass of familiar noises, indices of the quieting human presence. On the contrary, the young deaf child is at once isolated because in his world of silence he cannot comprehend the outside world, except with the help of his visual and tactile senses so limited in space.

A series of events conveyed to others by forerunning noises affect him by surprise in a most unpleasant way. Consider one example: the deaf child does not hear the approach of persons around him. Their sudden appearance causes him to stare, just as we do when we see someone whom we did not hear coming. The deaf child is subject to such shocks several times a day. This explains why he is mistrustful, fearful and fierce.

The deaf child is passionately fond of whatever he undertakes. He is lost in his playing, keeps himself secluded from people and is vexed by adults interrupting his activity with "It is time for dinner," "It is time for going to bed," "Look out, you are making yourself dirty," and so on. The hearing child always gets an explanation, whereas the deaf child who does not hear the reasons given is under the impression that these are arbitrary interventions, against which he rises in rebellion.

The behavior of the young uneducated deaf child disposes the adult person constantly to interfere, because the child touches everything and is continually spoiling something or another, while these interferences provoke crises of rage in the child.

To these psychic and comportmental abnormalities must be added some motor disturbances of a minor importance. In general, the deaf children have a less developed sense of rhythm, because they are frustrated by the lack of the best teacher in this field, the hearing of recurring cadence of sounds (the speech melody, the musical rhythms, the variations of noises, the whistling of the wind, the barking of dogs, the ringing of bells).

If their sense of visual orientation is well developed, they can compensate for this lack by observing the diversity of movements or if their tactile sense is very keen by perceiving the rhythm of the vibrations. But they seldom may acquire this sense of rhythm to the same degree as do ordinary children, that is, without any remedial training.

The respiration of deaf children is less ample, less put to practical use than that of a child who can speak, shout or sing normally. Their walking may also be impaired when there are labyrinthic lesions, in which case some retardation may occur in the onset of walking, accompanied by a defective movement of swinging the arms. The act of walking may be disharmonious, noisy and marked by dragging steps, due to the fact that a deaf child does not hear the sound of his own steps on the ground. He is, indeed, guided by a series of kinesthetic sensations in trying to maintain his balance, but not in regulating his walk according to that of others. a function which requires auditory control. In the same manner is the young deaf child's social activity impaired, each time that the formation of habits requires the help of hearing. He eats noisily, makes noise in the classroom with his feet, his chair and his toys (the nonsonorous ones).

In the child who is not completely deaf, the disturbances occurring are proportioned to the gravity of his auditory deficiency. The young child affected by a serious hearing loss (around 60 decibels* in the conversational frequencies†) behaves almost exactly as does the child completely deaf. He is incapable of acquiring speech alone. But in the case of a hearing loss of 20–60 decibels, one could in many instances use with success a hearing aid,

* The logarithmic unit of the sound intensity.
† Between 256 and 4,096 cycles per second.

which may greatly help this category of deficient children to acquire a rhythmic and melodious spoken language.

Quite often a hearing loss for speech of 20–40 decibels, creating sometimes serious retardation in speech development, can be detected only quite late by parents, the general practitioners and even by school teachers. The difficulties arising from this slight hearing loss vary according to the two fundamental kinds of hearing impairment, "conduction" deafness and "nerve" or "perception" deafness.

In the first category, the deficient children with a hearing loss of 20–40 decibels by conduction impairment develop without any remedial education, but with some retardation, a spoken language less altered in intonations, rhythm or melody but with specific articulatory defects, especially the substitution of the voiced consonants *B D G V Z* by the corresponding unvoiced ones *P T C F S;* the omission of the final word syllables or sounds, sometimes of the initial ones; the omission of the non-visualized sounds.*

In the second category of perception impairment we find cases which often call for a differential diagnosis for possible feeblemindedness. With these children we are prone to error about their residual auditory capacity because only certain parts of the frequency spectrum are never heard, usually the high frequency components. These children do

* The child omits from the articulation of a word the unheard sounds and those the articulation of which does not entail visible face movements, as with the sounds *C G H*.

not hear the high sounds comprised in this area (like *F–V, S–Z, Th, Sh–J, H*) and though they hear in a distorted and imperfect way even the usual words. So they can neither understand them well, nor can they reproduce them at all, or if they do, the result is a mushy and slurred pattern of talking with various articulatory defects. The hearing impairment of these children is difficult to detect inasmuch as they hear a human voice at 5 or 6 meters and they perceive at a great distance noises of middle frequency (siren, the airplane). So their inability to understand speech and their severe speech defects are considered from the standpoint of mental and not of auditory deficiency.

In conclusion, we must underline the necessity of detecting and diagnosing at an early stage the auditory impairment of the child with a view to permitting him, once the fact of his deafness has been verified, to benefit from a remedial education aiming to prepare him to acquire speech and to prevent the appearance of psychomotor disturbances.

In view of the well-known difficulty of determining the auditory impairment of the young child it is necessary to submit to some complex examinations by a team of specialists (otologist, neurologist, pediatrician, logopedist and psychologist) the children in the preschool age whose manifestations can lead us to suspect such an auditory deficiency. We have in mind first of all children with delayed speech, impaired expressive speech, but also those who show impairment in speech comprehension, and even the children with marked inability to integrate in ordinary life or under environmental conditions such as the day nursery or kindergarten.

References

1. Ewing, I. R., and Ewing, A. W. G.: *Speech and the Deaf Child.* Manchester Univ. Press, 1954.
2. Davis, Hallowell (Ed.): *Hearing and Deafness.* London, Staples, 1956.
3. Kantzer, L.: *L'Enfant Sourd.* Paris, Maloine, 1950.
4. Luchsinger, R., and Arnold, G.: *Lehrbuch der Stimm-und Sprechheilkunde,* second edition. Vienna, Springer-Verlag, 1959.
5. Parrel, G., and Hoffer, H.: *Les Enfants qu'il faut Réadapter: ceux qui entendent mal, ceux qui comprennent mal, ceux qui parlent mal, ceux qui respirent mal.* Paris, Vigot Frères, 1935.
6. Tarneaud, J., and Seeman, M.: *La Voix et la Parole. Étude Clinique et Thérapeutique.* Paris, Maloine, 1950.

NURSERY DEPARTMENT IN A RESIDENTIAL SCHOOL*

Sam B. Craig

The topic given me for this discussion is Preschool Training in a Residential School for the Deaf. It is not my intention to deal with the philosophy of preschool training, the proper age of starting training or the day-to-day program in a preschool but rather to discuss the practical aspects of adding a preschool department to a residential school for deaf children.

We have been operating a preschool department at the Western Pennsylvania School for the Deaf for a number of years and have encountered most of the problems involved in working with very young children in a boarding school situation.

For some years the education of young deaf children between the ages

* A paper presented at a Meeting of the Conference of Executives of American Schools for the Deaf, Jackson, Mississippi, April 5, 1956, and reproduced here by courtesy of Dr. Craig. The author is Superintendent of the Western Pennsylvania School for the Deaf, Pittsburgh.

of two and five years has been carried on with varying degrees of success in both public and private schools and classes. Recently there has been a surge of interest in this phase of our work as evidenced by numerous articles on the subject appearing in publications and by the fact that schools are building units to house preschool children. Even in states where no provision has been made for the education of children under five and six years of age there is considerable interest in the value of this early training program. The question could be asked, "Should a typical residential school undertake the operation of a preschool department when it involves taking very young children as boarding pupils with all the accompanying social, economic and financial problems?"

Let us weigh some of the advantages of preschool training for young deaf children either in residential or day schools. If there is a good nursery school in the vicinity, parents should be advised to take advantage of it if they are sure that they themselves can provide the correct home environment. When the home situation is so involved that proper cooperation with the nursery cannot be carried out or where the distances are too great there should be no hesitancy in advising parents to send their children to a residential school. This places the responsibility of having proper facilities in the residential school.

The Western Pennsylvania School for the Deaf is situated in a densely populated area and serves a wide territory—the western half of a large state. It has most of the problems of a state school and many of the obligations of an urban school. It is located in the center of the area it serves and is accessible by car, train, and bus facilities. Although on the edge of Pittsburgh only twenty of our 380 pupils find it feasible to attend as day pupils. However, fully one half of our boys and girls go to their homes for weekends. Of the twenty who are day pupils only eight are in the preschool department. Frequently pupils who elect to attend as day pupils ask for the privilege of staying as boarding pupils.

When the preschool department at the Western Pennsylvania School for the Deaf was first opened, it was not done primarily to reach the very young children or to expand the school but because it was considered expedient to do so. There was no question as to the value of such training but there was a grave question as to whether it could be done well in a boarding situation.

Within the past ten years there has been a strong upsurge of interest in the hearing-handicapped child in Western Pennsylvania. Prior to that time the Pittsburgh Hearing Society had been active, as well as the DePaul Institute for the Deaf and the Western Pennsylvania School for the Deaf. During the last decade the University of Pittsburgh has added a Department of Audiology located in the Eye and Ear Hospital and Mercy Hospital has established a Hearing Clinic. Both of these agencies are supported by a fine group of otologists. State Rehabilitation Centers have come into existence in Pittsburgh and other areas in the state. The Community Hearing Council of Greater Pittsburgh has been organized and exercises splendid leadership in the field. The departments of special education in the city and county schools have shown an increased interest in the deaf and hard-of-hearing child. A group of parents organized as the Friends of the Hearing Handicapped has become active. Other related organizations have shown interest in the training of the preschool child. A great deal of credit for this accelerated interest in the young hearing-handicapped child should be given to leaders in the Bureau of Special Education of the Department of Public Instruction whose interest and support have been felt in many directions.

As facilities for testing and diagnosis have increased in the Pittsburgh area (in my opinion there are no finer services anywhere), parents have come to this section with their young children for examination and advice. In many cases schooling was recommended at the nursery or preschool age. There were very limited training facilities available. DePaul Institute had been accepting a limited number of very young children. The City Schools had considered setting up classes in the public schools and various organizations considered raising private funds for such classes.

It was at this stage that the Board of Directors of the Western Pennsylvania School for the Deaf decided that it would be wise to set up a preschool department and to admit children as young as three years of age, either as day pupils or boarding pupils. With the pressure of preschool training coming from every direction, The Western Pennsylvania School for the Deaf felt an obligation to establish a nursery school on its campus. We had the facilities and educational organization to continue the child's education from nursery school to graduation without interruption.

We believed that if we could educate the preschool deaf child there would not be the problem of transferring from one school to another at some later time.

Our preschool department was opened five years ago. Today we have an enrollment of 42 children three, four and five years of age. Some of our problems have been (1) meeting the additional financial costs; (2) determining the best means of housing the children; (3) securing suitable teaching personnel. In our particular case the first problem—financing the project—was not an obstacle. The Department of Public In-

struction encouraged the project from the beginning and made no objection to reimbursing the school for children under six at the same rate for those six and older. The cost per child is considerably higher than for primary and elementary school age children. With a general increase in appropriation or higher per capita rate of reimbursement, the additional cost can be absorbed. This is especially true if the department is an integral part of the main school. If it is a separate unit the excessive cost will be more apparent.

Due to the immaturity of the children it is necessary to have twice as many houseparents or nurses as would be needed for children six to nine years of age. In addition to regularly trained teachers of the deaf, other persons, trained in general preschool practices are needed. This, of course, accounts for the major part of the additional cost. Other expenses include special equipment and additional infirmary facilities.

There is a higher rate of absenteeism among the preschool age group than among the older children. They are most susceptible to colds and pick up children's diseases almost from the start of their school careers. Parents are naturally more concerned over the health of their young children and keep them at home or take them home as soon as sickness is discovered. This relieves the school of some nursing and responsibility. However, a certain percentage must be cared for in the school infirmary. Here again, special adjustments have to be made. The average school infirmary is equipped and staffed to care for children six to eighteen years of age who can entertain and care for themselves in many ways. Add several preschool children to the sick list and there is the problem of keeping the children in bed and entertaining them, hence increasing the cost.

The second problem—housing the department—proved to be a more difficult one. Until the project proved to be permanent it was not considered wise to construct or buy a building for its operation. A section of the Primary Building was turned over to the preschool program. This was not ideal but gave us an opportunity to start the project and to observe its progress. Any number of difficulties arose and had to be solved. In spite of careful planning there were times when preschool and primary children were together in play areas and in the dining rooms with considerable confusion and unhappiness. The living habits of the two groups are so different that separate accommodations are almost a necessity. Their sleeping and eating schedules are not the same. Their diet differs. More dining-room supervision is needed. Bath and toilet equipment must be adapted to a younger group. Play equipment must be of a little different nature.

Some schools are solving these problems by building separate preschool units adapted to the preschool child. The American School has a well-planned unit for housing and teaching preschool children which many of us saw during the convention last June. Other schools are either constructing such a unit or have one under consideration. The Western Pennsylvania School has recently acquired an attrac-

tive building which will be adapted to the preschool child and put into operation next fall.

The third problem is staffing the department with qualified teachers. The supply and training of teachers for this level of work are so inadequate that they are coming up for special consideration during this Conference meeting. I do not know how other schools are handling this problem but I suspect they are doing as we did and must continue to do. At the beginning we secured an outstanding teacher of the deaf who had some experience with very young children and asked her to undertake directing the project. At the school's expense, she was given an opportunity to visit other schools throughout the east. This proved to be a good investment for soon she was able to train her own teachers. This director was later succeeded by one of her own trainees who herself visited and studied the work of other schools and spent two summer terms at the John Tracy Clinic in California. One other teacher was sent to the California Clinic. In addition to these teachers who were trained to work with the deaf, two graduates in nursery school education at the Pennsylvania State University were secured to care for the activity program of the children. These two young teachers have taken in-service training for work with hearing-handicapped children. For the present the problem has been met by selecting, training and giving inservice courses to promising individuals.

This summarizes the three major problems—financing, housing and staffing—concerned with starting a pre-school department.

Another question frequently asked is "How are pupils selected for the pre-school or how do they find their way to you?" No particular effort is made by the school to induce parents to enroll their children. The preschool depart-ment is run for those who want to take advantage of it. Because of their age no compulsion could be applied even if it were thought wise to do so. Since the children are under the age of compul-sory education, the regular school placement program does not function. Almost all of our pupils are referred to us by otologists or one of the clinics previously mentioned. A number of our pupils are routed to us through one of two "pre" preschools operating in our area—the Rau Nursery School and the Easter Seal Camp.

The Rau Nursery School, operating under the supervision of the Depart-ment of Audiology of the University of Pittsburgh, has training periods for young deaf children and their parents. It is necessary for the parents to attend and their orientation is considered a valuable part of the training. The Easter Seal Camp is held for two weeks each summer and is for parents with young deaf children. This, too, stresses instruction for the parents. Both proj-ects are highly advertised. Whenever possible, teachers from the Western Pennsylvania School for the Deaf are attached to these preparatory centers to help with the work. They serve to bridge the gap between the two train-ing centers and help the parents to lose their fear of sending children among strangers. As a rule the children are re-ferred to the Western Pennsylvania School at the age of three. There is no particular magic in this age but it does seem to be about the earliest period that a child can be placed in a boarding situation without his mother or an in-dividual nurse.

As I said in the beginning, I have not tried to justify a preschool, to establish the proper age of admission or to dis-cuss the day-to-day program. We were faced with a definite problem and felt we should meet it by providing the services desired by parents and by specialists in the field. I have tried to describe some of our problems and how we have met them. For reasons given and implied in this paper I would rec-ommend that most of you include pre-school training in your programs.

From our own experience, we are convinced that no harm is done the child, that his training for life adjust-ment is greatly advanced and that the parents appreciate the results.

VII. Types of School Organization and Placement

THE IOWA SCHOOL OFFERS A COMPLETE PROGRAM*

C. Joseph Giangreco

This past fall there were inquiries from a few parents as to our feelings in regard to two small day classes which have opened in isolated parts of the state. It caused some parents moments of anxiety and caused much soul searching. Parents had to weigh the pros and cons of the one-room school versus the residential school. The one-room school does keep the child close to home but there are many arguments concerning this type of program and no attempt will be made to list them here. Instead, here is what the residential school has to offer and then parents can easily see why there is a need for the residential type facility:

1. The Iowa School for the Deaf has a goal—to give its students the best education they are capable of achieving. Its curriculum is well balanced with a beginning and an end. It is well graded and in most instances tries to fit the curriculum to the child. In addition to academic learning the Iowa School for the Deaf offers excellent vocational training, training in social living, stresses good moral and ethical standards and emphasizes understanding of the responsibilities of citizenship. These goals are met because of the very nature of the organization of the school: size, personnel, curriculum and special services.

2. Students at the Iowa School for the Deaf are respected and treated the same as children in any good school. While students, they take part and benefit from the same social and recreational activities as their peers in public schools. For example, our students are in an athletic conference which competes against area high schools in football, basketball, track and wrestling. In this healthy competition the students show that they can compete successfully and that they can excel.

3. Further training in the role of living is given through extracurricular activities. The Iowa School for the Deaf is proud of its record in the field. Led by the volunteer efforts of teachers and dormitory personnel, this program includes Scouting, Sub-Teens, Homemakers' Club, Pixies, "I" Club, Trap Shooting Club, Pep Club, Class Organ-

* This statement, reprinted from *The Iowa Hawkeye*, Iowa School for the Deaf, Council Bluffs, January, 1966, outlines well the program in vogue at a typical residential school for deaf children. The author is Superintendent of the Iowa School for the Deaf.

izations, Yearbook, Mardi Gras, Red Cross, Hobby Club and Y-Teens. In many of these organizations the boys and girls are constantly mixing with children in the community and learning to get along with them.

4. The Iowa School for the Deaf offers special services including audiology, psychology and vocational guidance to all its students.

In short, the Iowa School blends its educational and vocational program with personal and social development which gives the child a well-balanced program. The final product of these efforts is an educated, happy, well adjusted adult ready for advanced training, college or work. The success of this program is proven by the excellent progress which Iowa School for the Deaf graduates are making in industry, business, education and other fields. There is a constant demand for our students in many industries.

The one-room school does not and cannot offer a similarly well-rounded program. Throughout our nation the trend in education in general is toward well-organized consolidated school units and away from the one-room country school. A residential school for the deaf is this type of consolidated school. To go to one-room classes for the deaf seems a step backward. Further, if the people who are constantly pushing one-room programs would seriously study the effects of deafness they would learn to understand that students so handicapped require a special approach to education. Education of the hearing impaired belongs in the hands of specially trained personnel working in a well-coordinated program if optimum results are to be attained. The Iowa School for the Deaf meets these standards and is continually striving to improve upon its service of excellence to the hearing impaired and the State of Iowa.

PLIGHT OF HARD-OF-HEARING CHILDREN*

MARGARET S. KENT

We have become increasingly aware of the number of hard-of-hearing children applying for admission to schools for the deaf. We find these children usually from ten to fifteen years of age failing in public school. Most of them have not learned to read or write. Many are socially isolated and often demonstrate marked personality deviation. Rarely do we find them wearing a hearing aid which is in good repair or one which compensates optimally for their loss. In desperation parents turn to the school for the deaf.

An educational conflict arises when these children, who learn language primarily through audition, are edu-

* A reprint from the column, "Educationally Speaking," *The Maryland Bulletin*, Maryland School for the Deaf, Frederick, February, 1966. The author is the Principal of the Maryland School for the Deaf.

cated in an environment with profoundly deaf children who must of necessity learn primarily through vision. Although the hard of hearing and the profoundly deaf child have common language needs which the teacher of the deaf is qualified to meet, the hard-of-hearing child prospers best in a hearing-orientated environment. On the other hand to expect a child with a mild to moderate hearing impairment to progress in classes with normal hearing children *without supportive services* is highly unrealistic. The details of three recent cases illustrate this point.

Case 1: We met Ruth for the first time when she was nine years of age. We found her to be severely hard of hearing with a learning capacity well within normal limits. She had spent three unproductive years in successive first grades with hearing children and had learned to print her name beautifully. She had some spoken language, mainly names of people and things. She was wearing an ear-level hearing aid which provided marginal gain. This was the only type hearing aid she would tolerate so that it would not be noticed by the children in her class. Her comprehension of language was less than that of a three-year-old. She demonstrated marked feelings of inadequacy and was on her way to becoming an educational illiterate.

Case 2: Tommy came to our attention at age thirteen. His hearing impairment was moderately severe and his ability to learn was considered to be average. Although we were able to demonstrate he could understand two-syllable words when amplified with 100 per cent accuracy, he did not wear a hearing aid. He was educationally illiterate. He could read some sentences but could not interpret paragraphs. He had great difficulty composing a sentence but could write a simple sentence from dictation with errors in spelling. School experience consisted of a beginning year in a

class of deaf children, some years in a class with aphasic children, some time in a class with mentally retarded, and finally a few hours a week with a visiting teacher for hearing children. Tutoring was mainly in arithmetic as this was a subject the visiting teacher could cope with when dealing with a language handicap. Tommy was an enterprising thirteen-year-old getting jobs of various kinds in the neighborhood. When we saw him he was saving money to buy a lawnmower for summer work.

Case 3: Jean was a fifteen-year-old when we first saw her. She was in a fifth grade with eleven-year-old hearing children and was not keeping up. Previously she had spent seven years in a program for aphasic children. She only began to wear a hearing aid three years ago. Although speech was fluent it was not readily intelligible by public school standards. Reading and writing language were at a third grade level. Audiometric tests indicated a moderately severe loss with an auditory potential which was just beginning to be utilized. Mental tests indicated a normal capacity to learn. Social adjustment was obviously difficult in a class of younger children.

None of these children had the opportunity to learn with the support the hard-of-hearing child needs. Appropriate amplification and intensive auditory training were not available to them. Under the existing conditions each child ran the risk of educational failure. It would seem to us that this would be a very fruitful area for the attention of directors of special education programs in the public schools. Separate programs which would emphasize language and speech development could in many cases lead to integration into regular classes with hearing children but not until the basic communication skills had been well established. For the severely hard of hearing the school for the deaf may turn out to be the more appropriate placement.

We believe we will continue to see more of these moderately hearing handicapped youngsters knocking at our door as the educational pace accelerates in the public schools. We would urge concentrated efforts be made to meet their specific needs so that they will have the opportunity to realize their potential not as deaf children, nor as aphasic children, nor as the mentally retarded, but as the hard of hearing.

DETROIT DAY SCHOOL FOR DEAF PROGRAM FOR DEAF AND HARD-OF-HEARING CHILDREN*

HARRIET GREEN KOPP

Introduction

Eligibility for pupil enrollment is established through the Day School for Deaf Clinic. Service is offered to all "educationally deaf" children in whom loss of hearing has occurred prior to development of language or speech and who do not have sufficient residual hearing to develop language and speech without educational assistance. These children must manifest sufficient maturity and intelligence to profit from a period of trial instruction.

Referrals are from physicians, social agencies, hospitals, parents, neighbors, university clinics and Detroit Public School Speech Clinics. Admission results from staff evaluation by otologist, audiologist, specialist in language, psychologist and principal.

* In this report Dr. Kopp describes how a corporate city public school system meets its obligation in providing educational facility for children with severely impaired hearing. Even more than this it provides compelling evidence of the highly complex and many-sided concerns of the school program in the case of such children. The author is principal of the school.

Services Available

1. INFANT CLINIC for all eligible children under three years of age. This includes deaf, severely hard of hearing, and children with receptive language disorders who meet criteria of the Admissions Clinic.

2. DIAGNOSTIC TEACHING CLINIC. This includes children between three and five, or those above five who do not meet the maturity or basic intelligence standards for admission into Detroit Public School programs. They are given a trial period of instruction to determine whether they can be assisted to meet these standards and whether they can profit from instruction. They are evaluated periodically during this period of instruction which may continue until the personnel of the Admissions Clinic are satisfied with the educational prognosis.

3. DAY SCHOOL FOR DEAF. This program includes deaf and severely hard-of-hearing children and those with receptive language disorders beyond the age of three. These children meet the

standards for school admission with respect to severity of hearing loss requiring special educational methods and equipment, and sufficient maturity and intelligence to be acceptable to Detroit Public Schools.

4. PROGRAM FOR DEAF TRAINABLES. An experimental program designed to determine whether those children who do not qualify for admission with respect to intelligence and who have the additional handicap of deafness may profit from a program such as is offered to hearing children with similar intellectual deficits. The program provides a teacher of trainable children, and the added service on a .4 basis of a teacher of the deaf, small class size, and the supervisory assistance of School for Deaf Specialists in planning specialized instructional materials, methods and teaching aids.

5. DIAGNOSTIC TEACHING UNIT. This service is provided to meet the needs of children who meet the eligibility criteria of hearing loss and intelligence, but who manifest severe learning problems. Diagnostic teaching services are offered on a small class size basis with intensive training in perceptual skills.

6. TEACHER-COUNSELOR PROGRAM FOR THE HARD OF HEARING AND DEAF. This program serves those children with moderate to severe hearing loss who are capable of attending regular academic classes in public schools if some tutorial assistance is provided. This tutorial assistance may be provided in specific academic subjects, use of residual hearing, lipreading, language and speech. This service is provided at all grade levels from 1st grade through

high school. To date, kindergarten children have been served more effectively by attendance in the program for the hard of hearing at the Day School for Deaf. Severely hard-of-hearing youngsters occasionally are placed in the Teacher-Counselor program prior to 10th grade. However, for the most part, there are no profoundly deaf youngsters included in this program.

7. TEACHER-COUNSELOR PROGRAM FOR THE DEAF. This program serves deaf pupils at the secondary level, 10th, 11th, and 12th grades, who attend Detroit Public Secondary Schools.

8. HEARING AID REPAIR SERVICE. The School for Deaf maintains a hearing aid repair service for hard-of-hearing and deaf children. These services are available to all school age wearers of hearing aids who meet the requirements of the School Social Services Committee for eligibility on the basis of financial need.

Teacher-Counselor Program for the Hard of Hearing—Elementary and Junior High School, Service No. 6 in Program Description

1. PURPOSE. A permanent decentralized educational placement for those hearing-impaired children who can function effectively in classrooms for the hearing, with the addition of some academic tutoring.

A means of providing intensive training for new hearing aid users and for those children who require a brief period of adaptation to their hearing aids, some instruction in lipreading and an intensive period of academic tutoring prior to returning to their own neighborhood schools.

2. ELIGIBILITY. Determined by the the staff of the evaluation clinic at the Day School for Deaf. This consists of an otologist, a psychologist, an audiologist, a specialist in language, with the principal as chairman.

A. *Criteria for eligibility include:* Sufficient use of residual hearing to profit from attendance in classes with hearing children; academic achievement commensurate with the child's educational and intellectual potential; ability to use the hearing aid effectively or to learn to do so within the program.

B. *Referrals:* Children are transferred from the Detroit Day School for Deaf program into the Teacher-Counselor program as soon as they satisfy the eligibility requirements.

Children may be placed directly into the Teacher-Counselor program after evaluation at the Admissions Clinic when they meet criteria for the program.

Children may be transferred from the Teacher-Counselor program to a neighborhood school when they meet the criteria for attendance and successful education at their neighborhood public or parochial school. Follow-up evaluations continue during the period of trial placement in the neighborhood school. Referral is made to the Hearing Conservation Division of the Detroit Speech Correction Department and to the itinerant Speech Correctionist, if necessary. In addition, the Teacher-Counselors follow closely as consul-

tants during the period of adaptation to the school for hearing children.

Periodic re-evaluation is provided whenever requested by Teacher-Counselor, parent or school personnel. This permits re-assignment of children according to educational needs.

Teacher-Counselor Program for the Deaf and Hard of Hearing— Secondary School

1. PURPOSE. To provide secondary school education in a variety of high school programs with placement in a particular program suited to the needs of the individual.

2. ELIGIBILITY. The following qualifications hold for high school enrollment:

All students who have completed the 9th grade at the Detroit Day School for Deaf.

All students who have completed the Special B program at the Detroit Day School for Deaf.

All students who have completed the 9th grade in the Teacher-Counselor program for the hard of hearing.

All students referred from other programs for the deaf and hard of hearing who meet the basic criteria for admission to the specialized program for the deaf and hard of hearing. These criteria include sufficient hearing loss to require the use of amplification; the need for assistance in adapting to methods used in classes for the hearing; some tutorial assistance in specific academic subjects; continued instruction in speech and in use of residual hearing; the need for counseling assistance by a specialist in the education of the deaf; the need for assistance in scheduling of classes.

Students who do not require these services may attend any secondary school, but they do receive a more limited follow-up service during the period of initial adaptation to the school and may receive continued counseling service on a periodic basis. However, only students enrolled in one of the high schools at which service is provided may receive the regularly scheduled tutorial assistance. This decision is a function of the small number of students enrolled in these programs and the inability to provide widely scheduled individualized service. Prior to 1960, an attempt had been made to provide this service in a large number of schools. The dropout ratio attested to the fact that the service was not effective unless numbers of students would be concentrated so that essential services might be provided with sufficient intensity to permit maximal effectiveness.

Dropouts are served by re-evaluation in the Evaluation Clinic and referral to Vocational Rehabilitation or to an appropriate educational or vocational program where such a program exists.

Certification Required for Teachers

All teachers serving in the programs for the deaf and hard of hearing are required to have state certification as teachers of the deaf and hard of hearing.

Teachers who serve in the secondary schools are selected on the basis of previous training to teach at the secondary level. Similarly, teachers who serve at the elementary level are selected because of training at that level.

All teachers who serve in the Teacher-Counselor program have had prior successful experience in teaching deaf and hard-of-hearing children in a day school program.

Areas Serviced

1. ELEMENTARY. Presently, four elementary schools have been selected in various sections of the city. Choice of the school is a function of space available for the Teacher-Counselor and amplification equipment; suitability of space with respect to ambient sound elimination and security of expensive equipment; small class size in the regular grades to provide effective teaching of hearing-handicapped children; willingness of administrative staff to accept a program in the particular school; appropriateness for transportation of children to selected school. The small number of students requiring this service has made it essential to concentrate the services in order to provide for most effective use of teacher time.

As conditions change in school settings, it has been necessary to move the program from one school to another. A major consideration for the selection of a school is that as many of the selected schools as possible provide services for the mentally retarded and for the visually handicapped, since a large number of the hard-of-hearing children served are multiply handicapped.

As for teacher time allocation, each

teacher spends a morning of each school day in one school and the afternoon in another. Students are scheduled with the Teacher-Counselor on the basis of individual need as determined by the Teacher-Counselor, consultation with school personnel and with the Evaluation Clinic. Teacher time is devoted chiefly to tutorial assistance, partially to parent counseling and teacher counseling.

2. SECONDARY SCHOOLS. Junior high school and high schools are selected to provide for particular educational curricula needed by the students, including vocational programs, prevocational training, academic precollege course work, or trade school training. Provision of a job-upgrading program also is required. Availability of space for the Teacher-Counselor and willingness of the administration to accept the program are major considerations. Schools have been selected in various parts of the community, depending upon location of the students to be served so that transportation problems are minimized as much as possible. However, for effective service to be provided, it is essential that student load be concentrated in order that a tutorial program be possible. The schools serviced have changed from time to time as students' needs require and as curriculum changes occur.

In the matter of teacher time allocation, teachers are assigned to the various schools on the basis of the number of students enrolled at the school and the amount of tutorial time required. More students can be grouped for assistance and teacher time can be used

ENROLLMENT SUMMARY 1964–1965

Services	No. of Children Served
Day School for Deaf	245
Diagnostic Teaching Unit (Davison Annex)	12
Infant Clinic	11
Diagnostic Teaching Clinic	27
Trainable Program	14
Teacher-Counselor Program for Hard of Hearing and Deaf	59
Teacher-Counselor Program for Deaf	23
	391

DISTRIBUTION OF TEACHER-COUNSELOR SERVICE

Schools	Staff Personnel	Scheduled Visitations
Elementary	2	46
Junior High	1	7
Secondary High	2	29

DETROIT DAY SCHOOL FOR DEAF STAFF ALLOTMENT

Service	Staff Personnel
Teachers	
Home Room and Team Teachers	35.6
Special Subject	5
Teacher-Counselors for Deaf and Hard of Hearing	4
Trainable Deaf	.4
Specialists	
Language and Curriculum Adaptation	1
Speech and Auditory Training	1
Vocational Education (Added in 1965)	1
Principal	1
Clerks	2
Psychologist	.2
Diagnostic and Infant Clinic	1.6
Teacher Aids (Attendants)	4.5
Research (Wayne State University Contract)	.5
Teacher Training (Coordinator, Student Teachers)	.5

most effectively. Part of the teacher time is allocated to parent counseling and to assistance given to teachers within the school. Scheduling is the re-

sult of consultation by Teacher-Counselor with school authorities and Evaluation Clinic.

UNITS FOR DEAF CHILDREN*

D. M. C. DALE

During the past four years a scheme for teaching deaf children in very close association with those with normal hearing has been given a fairly full trial in New Zealand. The experiment has been extended from the single class of deaf children and their teacher who joined the Clifton Terrace School, Wellington, in 1960, to five other primary schools in the North Island.

The usual pattern is for a small room to be built on to an existing classroom, with a doorway between the two (see the diagram). A group of six or eight deaf children, with a teacher of the deaf, is added to a class of about thirty children with normal hearing.

The deaf children spend roughly half the day with the hearing children. The two groups usually combine for the developmental period (where children choose what they want to do), for reading and mathematics, printing, music, rhythmic work, art, physical education, nature study and class visits. The two teachers work mainly but not ex-

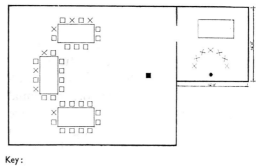

Key:
■ teacher of children with normal hearing
● teacher of deaf children
× places for deaf children
□ places for children with normal hearing

clusively with their own groups. At table-work the deaf children sit, as far as possible, between hearing children, though they do not necessarily do the same tasks.

Subjects for which the deaf children need specialist help, such as speech, language, news sessions, story and, say, the teaching of a new process in mathematics, are taken in the small room.

The combination of a unit for deaf children with a class of hearing children has a number of educational, social and economic advantages. In the first place, more children are able to live in their own homes. Units have been set up in the Hamilton West Primary School, some ninety miles from Auckland. Twenty-one deaf children

* Reproduced with permission from *The Times Educational Supplement*, London, September 3, 1965. Dr. Dale is Senior Lecturer in the Education for the Deaf, London University Institute of Education, and was formerly Head of the School for Deaf Children, Kelston, Auckland, New Zealand.

are now able to live at home and attend school daily rather than come to the school for the deaf as boarders. Two others will board in Hamilton from Monday to Friday and go home each weekend.

Deaf children also become socially more mature through observing the behavior of hearing children of their own age. One class, for example, when taught at the school for the deaf, were still at the baby stage of pushing and quarreling over who was to be first in line when going into school. They stopped doing this almost immediately after arriving at the ordinary school. The deaf children become more "oral." The temptation to use the hands in communication is reduced and there is less gross facial movement when talking than is usual when deaf children are educated in isolation.

What is more, the teacher of the deaf now has an excellent opportunity of observing the behavior, the thoughts and the language of children with normal hearing. I myself heard one five-year-old hearing child playing with blocks say: "I'm going to put my submarine in the dry dock." How many teachers of five-year-old deaf children would think of saying anything as sophisticated as that to them? Mostly we would just say: "Is that your boat?" "What a lovely boat" and so on.

The language teaching is also much easier. When the deaf children see the others speaking and reading and writing, they are stimulated to do the same.

The many chances which the deaf children have of comparing themselves with children with normal hearing is one of the very real advantages of the unit and associate class. The children have an opportunity to adjust themselves to their deafness about twenty times each day. They can learn, for example, that, although they cannot write as much as the hearing children, they can run as fast, they can draw perhaps better, they can build more interesting things, they can do mechanical arithmetic just as well. It is better for them to learn early on what it is like to live in a hearing world with a handicap than to try to make what is a very big adjustment when they finally leave school.

A number of headmasters, doctors and parents have, moreover, made the point that it is good for people without a handicap to learn at first hand about those who do have one.

Another advantage of this system is that when a deaf child is considered ready to return fulltime to an ordinary school, the unit is an excellent place from which to experiment.

The education of deaf children in units would also be very much cheaper than in residential schools. In New Zealand it now costs more than £600 a year to educate a deaf child in a boarding school. The low cost would, moreover, make these units very valuable for underdeveloped countries where it has so far been impossible to do much about educating handicapped children.

The reactions of the deaf children's teachers have been one of the most convincing factors in the decision to extend the scheme. At the outset, almost all the teachers of the deaf and the teachers of the ordinary children were, quite understandably, rather apprehensive. But they have, without exception, become convinced of its merits.

The parents of the deaf children are usually very enthusiastic about these units. They like the idea of their children going to a normal school if possible. Since the classes began, only one parent has complained about the educational or social progress of a child in a unit. These parents were given the option of sending their boy back to the school for the deaf if they wished but, after weighing everything up, they decided to keep him in the unit class.

All the deaf children themselves have seemed very happy in the school for the normally hearing, except one. This boy was a rather tense, nervous child who, although quite intelligent, was a very poor lipreader. He seemed rather bewildered by the large classroom and all the children and so, after a month's trial, we brought him back to a small class in the school for the deaf, where he is much happier.

There can, of course, be disadvantages in this system. The teacher of the deaf is, for example, more isolated from his or her colleagues. We have tried to overcome this by placing fairly experienced teachers in the units; by the junior school supervisor and the principal of the school for the deaf paying frequent visits; by having the teachers over to the school for the deaf for conferences and staff meetings and by keeping them posted with any relevant professional literature. Even so, the isolation is still a disadvantage and we now hope to establish three units in each ordinary primary school, rather

than just the one. Having three units in each school would moreover create a senior position for one teacher in three; it would make supervision by the senior staff of the school for the deaf easier and would allow more team-teaching.

When two teachers are expected to work for more than half the time in the same room, it is imperative that they should get on well together. Although, so far, teachers of very different ages, personalities and teaching styles seem to have worked well together and respected one another's abilities, there will, no doubt, sooner or later be a clash of personalities. This is one of the reasons why the teachers of the deaf have been kept on the staff of the school for deaf children.

There is of course the continuing problem of trying to ensure that the deaf children get as much as possible from lessons taken in the large classroom and from their association with the other children. Experiments so far have suggested that the children in the classes for the deaf should be of the same age and ability; the children in the associate class should be well-adjusted socially and capable of making normal educational progress.

It is quite clear that there are a number of deaf children whom it would be unwise to include in such an integrated scheme—perhaps 30 per cent of the children now enrolled at the school for the deaf. Some are of low intelligence, others have additional physical or psychological problems. They can lead a more sheltered life in the school for the deaf than they could in a big day school. One or two seriously maladjusted deaf children among a group could, what is more, do considerable damage to the normal school's attitude to deaf children in general.

Some children with normal hearing are, of course, much more interested in deaf children than are others. We have had some quite remarkable instances of children (usually girls) befriending deaf children, asking to sit with them and talking carefully to them both in and out of school. We hope soon to do some research on these children. The other children who show no interest at all should also make an interesting study.

The opportunity to mix freely and regularly with children with normal hearing helps some deaf children more than others. The extent of the hearing loss is, of course, an important factor, but even profoundly deaf children have been found to profit very considerably —personality and intelligence seem to be two important factors.

One wonders, more generally, whether this system could not be used with other groups of handicapped children—the blind, for example, or the crippled or cerebral palsied.

Finally, a word of caution. Integrating deaf children into ordinary schools will not make them hear. Many of them will probably remain deaf throughout their lives and will have very serious communication difficulties. Many of them may therefore have to rely on clubs for the deaf for much of their social life and a number of them would be unwise to marry people with normal hearing.

Integration in hearing classes merely helps—just as a hearing aid helps, early training helps, parent guidance helps, a good teacher helps and good teaching equipment helps. The more we can provide all these aids simultaneously, the more the handicap should be minimized to the deaf person and to the general public.

THE INTEGRATION OF THE DEAF IN SCHOOLS FOR THE NORMALLY HEARING*

CLARENCE D. O'CONNOR

Most parents of deaf children at some time or other give serious thought to the possibility of their children attending regular schools with normally hearing children. Members of the staff are frequently asked, "Can my child do this?"

* Reprinted from *Lexington School for the Deaf Parents Newsletter*, June, 1960. The author is Superintendent of the Lexington School for the Deaf, New York.

or "When will my child be ready to do this?" The answers to these questions are complex and call for careful thought. The decision to transfer a very deaf child from the slower-paced special program offered in a school for the deaf to the highly competitive regular program should not be made lightly, for one who is not equal to this challenge might suffer serious emotional damage through the trauma of repeated failure and rejection.

So that we might be better able to counsel parents who might seek our advice concerning this important question, we undertook a study a few years ago of some of the fifty pupils who had transferred from the Lexington School between 1954 and 1957 to public or private classes for the normally hearing. Our primary objectives in this study were to determine the degree of successful or unsuccessful adjustment in integrated programs and the factors influencing success or failure.

Eighteen transfers were finally selected for intensive study. The principal and the teacher in the school each pupil was attending as well as the pupil's parents were interviewed. In addition, each of the eighteen pupils was given the following tests at the school:

Psychometric Test (WISC)

Hearing Test (Standard pure tone audiometry)

Achievement Test (Stanford)

Personality Inventory (Brunschwig)

The tests and the interviews indicated the following concerning the eighteen pupils under study:

1. The Stanford Achievement Tests given to the eighteen pupils showed that they generally divided into two groups as far as achievement is concerned. Twelve in Group A were close to the norm for their age level, being only approximately four months behind regular children on the average. However, six of these twelve were achieving better than average for hearing children. Six in Group B averaged about three and a half years behind children of their particular age level.

2. Both parents and teachers tended to overrate the pupil's academic achievement in comparison to scores obtained on the Stanford tests, the ratings of parents being even more optimistic than the teachers'.

3. Generally, those in Group A had higher IQ's than those in B. The range for nine of the twelve in A was 120–132.

4. Those in Group A generally had more useful hearing than those in Group B, the average speech-range loss for the former being 79 db compared with 85 db for Group B.

5. Parent, teacher and pupil interviews and the Brunschwig personality inventory revealed in general that pupils in Group A were more willful, tenacious, attentive and had outgoing personalities, while those in Group B tend toward being followers and day dreamers, lacking self-confidence and initiative.

6. Those doing best in both groups were with teachers who had adjusted the program to meet the needs of the hearing-handicapped members of the class, such as speaking more slowly, writing more often, arranging for classmate help, and other changes.

7. The presence in the school of a counselor for the hearing-handicapped resulted in higher achievement and better social adjustment for the hearing-handicapped pupils in attendance.

What we learned from our intensive study of these eighteen pupils tended to reinforce the possibilities of deaf children moving through an educational program geared to the normally hearing. These are the following:

1. That, with very few exceptions, children who begin life with an average speech-range hearing loss of 60–70 db or more cannot successfully or comfortably integrate educationally with hearing children at the age of five or six. They need the specialized program of a school for the deaf for a number of years, at least, in order to acquire facility in the use of language, without which they would be hopelessly lost in regular classes.

2. That the percentage of pupils in a school for the deaf who are logical candidates for ultimate educational integration in classes for the hearing is small. The vast majority will need the benefit of the specialized program of the school for the deaf throughout their entire educational career.

3. That no pupil should be transferred to regular classes until he has developed communication ability that will make it possible for him to meet the severe competitive conditions he will experience therein. This means that, in general, he will not be ready for such transfer before the age of eight or nine.

4. That a careful assessment of the following factors that will affect the success of his ultimate integration be made for each pupil for whom a transfer to regular classes is being considered:

HIS AGE. We have found that the majority of our pupils who are ready for integration do not reach this point before the age of eight or nine. If they have been through our nursery and

preschool classes and if all other factors are favorable, they may then be mature enough to meet the challenge of the new regime.

HIS COMMUNICATION ABILITY. At best a hearing-handicapped child moving from a school for the deaf to regular classes will be far behind hearing children in his ability to use and understand language. He should, however, have ability to communicate expressively through speech and writing, and receptively through reading and lipreading supported by the most effective possible use of his residual hearing with sufficient skill to be able to articulate with and become an effectively functioning member of the regular class. If his use of language is not securely established, even within narrow limits when compared to his hearing peers, then he is not ready for transfer. His reading level should be at least at the national norm for his age.

HIS INTELLIGENCE. This is one of the most critical factors for successful integration. Children with marginal ability and a relatively severe hearing loss have little chance of achieving satisfactorily in regular classes. This will be difficult enough for those with better than average ability. Accordingly, he should have an IQ of 110 or over.

HIS PERSONALITY MAKEUP. The hearing-handicapped child frequently must take a lot of emotional buffing-about in regular classes. He must be prepared for repeated even though only temporary failure through not always understanding what is being discussed. He must also be prepared for unintended neglect at times on the part of his teacher or social rejection by his class-mates. The tougher his emotional fiber the more successfully he may override these roadblocks. A timid, sensitive, hearing-handicapped youngster who lacks confidence or does not have the strength to fight back may be emotionally chopped to pieces in an integrated situation to the extent that he may find himself more segregated in the so-called "normal" program than he was in the so-called "abnormal special school segregation" program from which he was "liberated."

THE PROGRAM TO WHICH HE WILL BE TRANSFERRED. The degree to which the staff in the pupil's future regular program is oriented to the special needs of a hearing-handicapped pupil is vastly important. The capacity of a teacher to make simple management adjustments in the pupil's classroom environment and program will affect his entire achievement pattern.

HIS PARENTS. The differential that frequently is the most important factor influencing successful integration is the pupil's parents. How well are they oriented to the problems he will face and to his overall needs?

How much help and guidance can they be relied upon to give their child at home? The answers to these questions are important in arriving at a decision concerning transfer.

GUIDANCE AND FOLLOWUP. Once the decision has been made to transfer a pupil to a regular class, conferences should be set up with the parents and the staff of the school to which he will be transferred. The creation of a favorable educational, social, and emotional climate for the pupil is essential. Similar followup conferences should be arranged after the pupil has been transferred. One final word concerning this question.

As appealing as integration may be to parents who have every right to hope that some day their deaf child might attend his neigborhood school with his hearing brothers and sisters, it might be that such a program is not logical for him. If so, this should be accepted realistically. More than that, if a transfer is tried and the child is not adjusting satisfactorily, parents should have the courage and wisdom to return the child to the school for the deaf. Above all, continue to seek the counsel of those who also love your child and who hold dear to their hearts his happiness and well-being.

VIII. The Multi-sided School Program

FROM DISCIPLINE TO SELF-DISCIPLINE*

Most of the children entering a school for the deaf for the first time are well-trained and reflect the wisdom and resourcefulness of their parents in somehow penetrating the communication barrier of an auditory handicap. They learn to follow the teacher or counselor's instructions, help with little housekeeping chores in school and dormitory, and share their toys and boxes from home.

From time to time, however, a child enters school with a handicap in some ways as severe as deafness—a child who has not known wise discipline. And often the responsibility for this second handicap lies with those who love him most, the members of his own family. Loving parents may do untold damage to a little child by being over-solicitous, overindulgent, too permissive, or inconsistent.

All children find security in a kind but firm adult hand to guide them. The deaf child needs the assurance of an environment he can depend upon even more than a hearing child does because

* Editorial reprinted with permission from *The Iowa Hawkeye,* Iowa School for the Deaf, Council Bluffs, February, 1965. The author is Director of Education, Iowa School for the Deaf.

it is less possible to explain exceptions to the usual pattern of his day. He needs the security of a daily routine, he needs to know exactly what he is allowed to do and what not to do, he needs understanding and love when he makes a mistake, and he needs praise and approval when he does something well.

When a child who has not had the advantage of good discipline enters school, he is not ready for the all-important experience of classroom learning. He may refuse to sit in his chair, to pay attention, to work with educational materials. He may be noisy, take things from desks or cupboards, and annoy or even hurt other children. Such a child cannot profit fully from the best of teachers or the most modern of equipment. His attitudes and behavior patterns must be changed—a time-consuming and sometimes painful process.

Discipline means punishment only in the narrowest sense. A more accurate definition encompasses any constructive means of bringing about behavior conducive to a happy, well-adjusted individual able to get along amicably with other people. Certain other evidences of growth are implied—ability to carry on activities independently, ability to accept responsibilities, and ability to make decisions, all in a degree appropriate to the age of the individual concerned.

As the child grows in stature and maturity, discipline imposed by others should gradually give way to self-discipline. The teenager who maintains good standards of cleanliness and grooming, who accepts responsibility for lessons and other tasks, and who recognizes ethical and moral principles is likely not only to be happy and well liked, but also is establishing traits that will stand him in good stead when he grows into adulthood.

Most of the young men and women who graduate each spring are prepared to be self-reliant, useful citizens, able to work and live in harmony with their associates. The most important lesson they have learned from parents, teachers, and dormitory personnel is self-discipline.

THE CHILDREN WE TEACH*

Adoracion A. Alvarez

Maybe we should start with a common question: "What is a deaf child?" A child who can neither hear nor talk? A child who is difficult to manage?" We often hear these usual responses. This is closely followed by the question, "What is the difference between a deaf child and a child with normal hearing?" I believe there is little difference. I have worked with both of them. They are both children. They share the same toys, the same experiences and the same emotions toward their parents as any other children. We can say that they go to different schools. The deaf child has to be taught by a special method that will meet his needs. But generally speaking, nothing is different socially, spiritually and mentally, a conclusion derived from my experiences with the young deaf children—except their difficulty in language.

A deaf child is like any hearing child in the family. What makes him different from the others is the way he is treated by the people who surround him and the way his childhood is affected by his limited environment. As I have observed, as soon as we find out that the child is deaf, the emotion and attention we give him are quite different from what a hearing child would get. Why? To help him, we may say. He seems to enjoy more privileges than a hearing child. We seem to please him in almost everything he wishes. Why? Is love the real reason for this? We love him so much and would like to protect him, to satisfy him in all his wants. Do we stop him when he does wrong or quiet him when he is noisy? Is this love

* Reprinted with permission from the *North Dakota Banner*, North Dakota School for the Deaf, Devils Lake, May, 1963. The author is a Supervising Teacher in the North Dakota School for the Deaf.

or pity? A deaf child does not need pity. What he needs is help, help and more help.

Protective love is sometimes cruel, unkind—for we are developing a weak and dependent being, who believes that his world is different from that of others. He has nursed in his mind that he should be treated differently from his hearing brothers and sisters, that everybody should yield to his way, that everything he does is right and never wrong. Thus, for every little disappointment he encounters, he can make life miserable for every one. Then, we will jump to the conclusion that a deaf child is emotional, temperamental, rude and stubborn. I believe this will not be true if we get things straightened out at the earliest age of learning before it is too late to expect a change.

Teaching is an honorable profession but educating the deaf is a challenging service to humanity. The teacher must share the challenge with the parents and the child. The child must be equipped with the abilities and strength to meet the challenge of a life behind the glass walls at an early age.

The first grade is a time for learning and growing. We should expect surprises, tears and childish quarrels, teasing and laughter any day or time. Unpleasant situations will happen, but we have to go on with our job and start right where the need arises.

Usually, we start the day with opening exercises that enliven their interests and desire to work. We play some games with words or numbers and exercises that test their speech and lipreading abilities. Or we act out, dramatize some

nursery rhymes to stir their young imagination and spark life into them inside the classroom. (Let me say that it was during this period that our superintendent peeked in and as he glanced at this situation, gave me his German look and commented that I was signing to my pupils. I do not blame him for it looked like it at a glance. I quickly tried to clarify the situation before I was fired. I told him we were dramatizing our new poem for the day in connection with our speech practice.)

Dramatization is one of the most popular and effective methods used to teach language. If hearing children need to dramatize the story to understand and appreciate it, this is even more true for deaf children who need to see, feel and experience the situation before learning can take place. They have always enjoyed these activities and it tickles them to see a star after their names.

Monday is an exceptional day for us. I call our opening exercise "the digging period" for we have to talk about the activities that happened during the weekend. How to put the ideas into words is the most difficult task we face. I try to make them write what news each one would like to tell the class in their own limited vocabulary. To find the words that will express what they really mean to say is a very tough job for them, but this is the only way to discover their needs, to develop their thinking ability and self-expression, if not in speech, in writing. The school should not be a place of silence for them. They cannot grow in their use of language and speech unless we give them opportunity to communicate. My young pupils, like any other youngsters, love to talk about themselves, about a new dress, new shoes, a new toy, a letter or a package from home and of every little thing they possess. I make use of this eagerness to develop their language and speech.

Though I demand speech and lipreading in all subjects, we devote a time every morning for the main purpose of improving their lipreading ability and developing better speech. Teaching speech does not stop at the moment the child learns to say the element. He has to know when it is present and where it is located in a word to be able to say it. And even after he has learned to recognize the sound and is able to say the word, we cannot accept syllabicated speech either. Tapping his hand to make him feel the accented syllable as he sees the marked word on the blackboard or using a drum to show the rhythm will help a great deal in teaching him to say the word better. The speech period may be dull or boring for the child since it takes a long time and requires great effort before a certain element is learned. To keep him interested in it, I try different techniques or exercises to make it as lively as I can. I know that it is really hard work for both child and the teacher.

We make individual booklets where they can draw or cut pictures for their practice words, or collect small toys. For example, a bag of toys for the "r" sound may have a rabbit, a red rose, a car, a marble and other toys with names having either the initial, medial or final "r." Sometimes, we act out the verbs used for our speech drills; for putting everybody into action will help ease the tenseness caused by the hard labor of speech work.

Educators keep on working hard to answer the needs of the deaf and there are many books now that anyone can use for different purposes. I tried different techniques with my class to discover which one is best suited to them, for one may be good for one class but may not work at all in another. However, I believe there is nothing wrong in trying.

Experimentation is the keynote to progress. Nevertheless, let us not judge, calculate or limit the education of a deaf child by means of his speech alone. Speech is not all his education. He should learn everything that any child should learn. In a school like ours, we have to accommodate all kinds of handicapped children—the totally deaf or the hard of hearing as well as the multiple handicapped. We cannot choose our pupils and so all kinds of speech problems and difficulties are to be expected. Some have good speech, others try so hard, though we can hardly understand them and there are still many others who have no speech at all. In this case, I emphasize in the child the power of lipreading and the ability to express himself in writing.

Lipreading, or speechreading, is one of the basic aids to deafness. But it may mean all the difference between success and failure depending upon the user and the speaker. Speech and speechreading may mean nothing at first to a deaf child, just like talking to a newborn baby. But in every way, we have to keep on and be determined to work on it. The time used cannot all be wasted for we even talk to animals and to our pets which, after numerous repetitions, learn to respond to commands, etc.

During the first stage of learning we cannot expect miracles. There may be no understanding at all. But the deaf child needs to acquire skill in speechreading since he cannot hear. And, through constant repetition and exposure to speech every day in his life, we believe that learning for him will not then be so difficult, if he uses his eyes as a part substitute for his ears.

However, I always bear in mind that my desire to teach the child should not overpower his own capacity. That may lead to confusion and disappointment which may result in no desire to learn. But there is one thing I have learned which I believe is very important. There should be definiteness and certainty. Let the child know at the very start of the learning situation who you are, why he is there with you and what you really expect of him. Of course, we don't do this in such a way that will scare the child. Just make him feel that he has a responsibility and that there is a reason for everything we do. It is true we can play while we work or have fun at work, but I try to control the play activity and carry it out to the fulfillment of my purpose. There are times when we need just to work hard to realize our goal. Being honest with them about the results of their work is the best policy. They may try harder next time. I try to make sure that they know and understand what it was they did poorly in this or in that or why they cannot do this and can do that. It is much better

to let them find out for themselves what is wrong and why. In this case, I can be sure that real learning takes place and they are not being "spoon fed" for they can distinguish the difference between right and wrong.

Praise gives my youngsters a lot of encouragement and willingness to contribute more in the class activities. They flourish on praise. But do not praise a child if he does not deserve it for it may ruin his study habits and attitudes. There are times when I have to be as firm as I can to make a child realize that he can not have what somebody else has unless he works for it. This is something we can not buy with money.

I try my best to develop in him all the possibilities that will help him in his struggle for existence—his speech, lipreading and writing abilities—for all these put together will help him a great deal in the daily contacts which enrich life. To make him as independent as early as possible is our main goal. To know himself, his talents and his limits in order to have self-confidence. We can then expect him to develop the attitude of a person with a willing, friendly and happy personality. If I can make him realize that his hearing loss does not change his responsibilities as a human being at all, that he is no different emotionally from the other youngsters in this world then my task of educating the deaf child would seem to have been successful for the most part. Progress may be slow at the beginning but let it so be, for as Emerson wrote: "Progress is the activity of today and the assurance of tomorrow."

OUR ACADEMIC PROGRAM AND RELATED PROBLEMS°

ALFRED J. LAMB

The academic program of the Indiana School for the Deaf is designed to provide for the deaf children of Indiana the same educational opportunities their hearing brothers and sisters have in the public schools. The curriculum offerings are essentially those of the public schools of Indiana. On the strength of these offerings, the qualifications of the staff and the adequacy of the physical plant, this school has been granted a first-class commission by the State Department of Public Instruction for grades 1–12. Students who earn a high school diploma at this school enjoy the same rights and privileges as their hearing contemporaries in the public schools.

Departments

Since the 558 children served by this school range in age from 4 to 20 years, it is obvious that departmentalization is necessary. Perhaps it would be useful at this time to review briefly the makeup and program of each of the educational departments.

Primary Unit

The primary unit is supervised by Miss Sue McKibben. There are fifteen teachers in her department.

° An address presented before the Parent-Teacher-Counselor Organization, Indiana School for the Deaf, Indianapolis, November, 1963, Meeting. Reprinted with permission from *The Hoosier*, same school, December, 1963. The author is Superintendent of the Indiana School for the Deaf.

Childern entering school as beginners go into the primary unit, the most modern academic facility on the campus. The 138 children in this department range from four to eight years of age. The chief academic goal in this department is the development of language skills in speech, speechreading, reading, writing, and use of residual hearing. Normally after three years in this unit a deaf child will be doing first grade work and in some cases be ready to start second grade work.

In general he also will have acquired a certain amount of speech intelligibility, lipreading ability and aptitude for beneficial use of amplification. He is able to write in manuscript and in some cases has converted to cursive writing.

Upper Primary Department

The Upper Primary Department is supervised by Miss Florence Sundstrom. There are eighteen teachers in her department and 166 students.

In the Upper Primary Department the child begins at the level he has reached in the Primary Unit—usually first grade—and continues through fourth grade. Overage beginners and children with special problems make it necessary to provide classes below the first grade level in this department. In first and second grades the child directs his efforts toward mastering of the educational tools—reading, writing, arithmetic—all of which are correlated with language development. Oral communication skills also receive much emphasis at this level.

While subject matter is introduced at the lower levels, it begins to receive greater emphasis in the third and fourth grades. Units in science, geography, history, and other social studies material which require new and expanded vocabulary make these years the most crucial ones for the deaf child. It is at this level that deafness takes its greatest toll, academically speaking. In some schools it is the policy to devote an additional year to the third- and fourth-grade curriculum. This is justified because of the rapidly increasing vocabulary associated with the subject matter. Concepts and abstractions, not mere words, must be learned. For instance in the unit on Indians, the deaf child must learn to deal with such abstract terms as peace, treaty, truce, conflict, the great spirit, etc. A hearing child picks up most of these terms watching TV serials with little or no conscious effort on his part, simply by associating what he hears with what he sees. He has heard these words used so many times in meaningful situations that he cannot help learning their meanings. How is the deaf child to be exposed to these words often enough to acquire knowledge of their use? Arthur I. Gates, a leading authority in reading, has estimated that new words must be met thirty-five or more times to become meaningful to normal hearing children.[1] Imagine, if you can, the task a teacher faces trying to increase her class reading vocabulary by 500 words. Some 20,-000 different exposures would be necessary. Add to this the problem of ten deaf children in a classroom with ten different viewpoints and the possibility of ten different interpretations for each word.

Mathematically it seems impossible for the deaf child to learn to read. But somehow he does acquire some skill in this most important tool of learning.

Intermediate Department

Miss Susan Christian is supervising teacher of the Intermediate Department. There are eighteen teachers and 171 students in this department.

At the intermediate level the curriculum includes the public school 5th to 8th grade subject matter. Reading ability is at a premium—the language problem persists. New concepts must be learned if one is to gain a basic knowledge of U. S. history, geography, science, health, arithmetic, etc. All of these involve increasingly difficult language construction and vocabulary.

While it is not included in the course of study outline, it is in this department that boys begin to study about girls and vice versa. It should be added that this problem also persists throughout the child's educational career. There isn't time to go into the many other psychological problems and their effect on academic progress.

High School Department

The Indiana School for the Deaf has had a high school program since 1942. Until 1958 a single track diploma plan was offered. At that time a four-diploma plan was inaugurated in an effort to provide a more comprehensive high school program. Total high school enrollment is eighty-three. Fifty-three are on a diploma plan and thirty are in a special program leading to a certificate of attendance.

Under the new plan four types of diplomas are offered, each of which is a valid high school diploma meeting all of the state requirements. The type of plan pursued by the graduate is designated on the diploma awarded him on commencement day. Briefly the four types of diplomas are: (1) General, which requires passing marks in seventeen units; (2) Vocational, which requires a "C" average in sixteen units, five of which must be in the vocational area; (3) Regular, which requires a "C" average in seventeen units; (4) Academic, which requires a "B" average in nineteen units.

The typical schedule for a high school student consists of two 45-minute periods of vocational class work, five academic classes, a study period and a thirty-minute activity period. With this broader curriculum offering, students of like abilities tend to group themselves into homogeneous sections in their selection of a diploma plan. This selection is made in consultation with the guidance director, the student and parents. A four-year plan is drawn up on a plan sheet. Both parent and student sign this "contract."

The better students who usually elect to go for the academic diploma must choose the more advanced courses in mathematics, science, English, and literature because the majors and minors required for this plan make this mandatory. These are the best college prospects.

Students who try for the academic diploma but fall short, either because they cannot maintain a "B" average or because they are unable to take the advanced courses, may still earn the regular diploma if they maintain a "C" average.

The general diploma, like the regular diploma, requires fewer units of credit and allows placement of a student in an extra study hall or two if he needs this time. These are the poorest high school students, and our greatest concern because they are borderline cases throughout most of their high school careers.

While the vocational diploma requires one less unit than the general or regular diploma, it requires one more vocational unit, which involves a double period for an entire year. It also requires a "C" average which removes it from the snap course category and makes it a respectable diploma.

It should be mentioned at this point that special programs are provided in every department for students who do not make academic progress commensurate with their age and number of years in school. While these *educationally* retarded children are transferred to the next department with their own age group, the academic work is geared to their level of performance. This eliminates many of the problems which occur when children of various ages, interests and abilities are grouped together. When these children reach high school age they are placed in the certificate section.

The certificate program is basically a two-year program. The academic area includes reading, language, basic math, general business with emphasis on personal affairs, and social studies with emphasis on civil government. Reading courses include material on occupations, current affairs, personal hygiene and other information deemed important to the young adult about to join the working forces. Usually four periods each day are devoted to the academic subjects and the other four to vocational classes on campus or on a work program off campus. This group is the one which needs most assistance in the transition from school to job. Cooperative programs with sheltered workshops and local industry have proved most helpful in some cases.

Educational Lag

In the few minutes remaining, I should like to bring into focus some of the problems our students, your children, face in this world of the hearing.

Automation is rapidly making the high school diploma a must for the youth of today. For this reason much attention is being given the high school dropout problem. Colleges are becoming overcrowded and increasingly selective. Consequently greater emphasis is being put on excellence in academic performance at the high school level. Public junior colleges are growing in number. Advanced placement in high school permits capable hearing students to pursue college subjects while they are still in high school. There are high school students in this city studying calculus and analytic geometry—courses that people of our generation studied as sophomores or juniors in college.

Where does this leave our deaf students in the race for an education and for gainful occupation? On standardized achievement tests our best high school students reach as high as the 70th percentile compared with the general population. That means that they have achieved better than 69 per cent of the regular high school students have. But the average high school student in our school ranks in the 20th percentile. This will never do. Somehow we must improve our record.

There are a number of things we might consider—staff, facilities, curriculum, and the like, but each of these measures up very well. The staff is well-trained, classroom facilities are above average and the curriculum meets the standards set by the State Department of Public Instruction.

The greatest obstacle is the lack of time. The deaf need time to acquire the skills they must have to overcome the handicap of deafness. If they are ever to close the educational gap, they must be given more time in an educational program tailored to their needs.

Educators of the deaf have been saying for hundreds of years that the deaf child cannot be expected to progress at the same rate as his peers with normal hearing. It has also been estimated that the average deaf child is two years educationally retarded when he enters school. If we accept the latter statement alone as true and assume normal progress, an educational program of fourteen years duration would solve the problem of time. A five-year-old beginner would graduate from high school at nineteen. Anyone who has taught the deaf knows that it is incorrect to assume that the estimated two-year lag will remain constant. It is more accurate to expect a slower rate of academic progress. If we assume the annual rate of progress to be six-tenths (.6) of a grade, the deaf five-year-old beginner will require twenty years to complete twelve grades and he will graduate when he is twenty-five. If he is able to achieve at an annual rate of eight-tenths (.8) of a grade, he will graduate in fifteen years at the age of twenty.

These figures should help to pinpoint the time problem. If twelfth grade achievement is set as the standard for a high school diploma and nothing is done to provide additional time for the deaf student's formal education, only the exceptionally bright and the highly motivated will earn high school diplomas. This appears to be the general picture throughout the United States today.

In my opinion the members of this organization, the parents, teachers, and counselors should devote their greatest efforts toward finding ways to buy time to overcome the educational lag.

What Can Be Done?

Let's consider what can be done.

Should there be a hard, fast rule regarding upper-age limit or should the rate of progress determine when a student's educational career is to be ended? Adult education classes are encouraged for the hearing, and nearly everyone is urged to return to school to finish his high school career or to get additional training. Why should the deaf student be denied this same privilege in the

only institution which really knows his learning problems? Forty-five per cent of our graduates take further training elsewhere within three years after they leave school.

Educators of the deaf have constantly complained they do not have enough time with the deaf child to overcome the educational lag. Here again, perhaps, we should look to the public schools. Each year more and more public schools are opening their doors in the summer time. Some are offering full-fledged programs; others are concentrating on remedial work during the summer; others carry on a combination recreational and educational program.

Would it not be good business to operate a school program in the school for the deaf for a period of two months during the summer?* If so, should this be strictly a remedial program? Should it be a program for a select few who show promise (these could be selected very

* According to a subsequent statement in *The Hoosier*, monthly school publication, May 1966, the author's anticipation on this subject was to be realized. The report explained the action in this wise: "For the first time in the history of the Indiana School for the Deaf a summer school session will be conducted. This will be for the junior and senior high school students, grades eight through twelve. This has been made possible by funds granted under Title I of the National Elementary and Secondary Education Act of 1965. The State Department of Public Instruction is responsible for approving and evaluating programs under this act and the Indiana School for the Deaf has received word that its summer project meets the standards set out by the department. A total of $129,000 has been allotted to the school for this program."

[A similar program became effective under parallel auspices in the same summer period at the two state schools for the deaf in California, Berkeley and Riverside.—I. S. F.]

early in their school careers), or should it be open to all? What kind of program would best serve the needs of the deaf child? Should such a program be provided for older students only?

Mr. Roy K. Holcomb, president of this body, sent a questionnaire to all parents in May 1962 regarding summer school.

Slightly more than 50 per cent of the respondents favored some kind of summer school program. Many seem to be reluctant to "give up" their children during the summer. This is natural, but if the proper kind of program were actually offered you parents would have the courage to make a decision that would benefit your child. You were faced with this decision once when you first brought your child to school and I believe you would do it again.

Should we not be investigating more thoroughly the attributes of fingerspelling as a method of communication? It is more rapid than other means of communication for the deaf and just as accurate as the printed word when properly used. From the limited reports we have seen this holds great promise as a means of developing language and promoting achievement in all areas of academic endeavor.

The New Mexico School for the Deaf has employed fingerspelling starting at the beginners level for the past five years. Superintendent Marshall Hester reported on the results of this experiment at the 1963 meeting of the International Congress on Education of the Deaf. Reporting on the achievement scores of students "who had been exposed to simultaneous speech and fingerspelling for up to five years," he

stated, "It appears for the most part that our deaf students age ten, eleven, and twelve are doing better at their present ages than did the college entrance students when they were the same age."[2]

A nationwide study is now getting under way under the direction of Dr. Stephen P. Quigley, associate professor of the University of Illinois. Its purpose is to determine the effect of the use of fingerspelling as a means of communication on such variables as speech proficiency, lipreading, academic achievement—reading—arithmetic—language. This study will match students in schools which use fingerspelling as a means of communication with students in schools which use only oral communication as well as those where the so-called combined method is employed.

The Indiana School has been asked to participate in this study. We should welcome the opportunity to do so. It is only from such well-planned research that we can honestly evaluate the place of fingerspelling in the education of the deaf. Parents and teachers sometimes find it difficult to cast aside resentment toward any form of manualism. We must be objective. If the results of Quigley's study indicate that fingerspelling will facilitate and enhance the education of the deaf child without hampering oral skills, we must have the courage to make necessary adaptations in our educational program. What is educationally sound must be administratively possible.

The program of Captioned Films for the Deaf, a Federal project under the direction of John A. Gough, has been expanded to include development and production of educational materials specifically designed for use in classes for the deaf. Last summer two of our teachers, Mrs. Martha C. Larsen and Miss Mary Belle Grant, participated in the first of a series of workshops under the new program. With eighteen other highly qualified teachers of the deaf from all parts of the United States they initiated the development of educational materials, geared to modern curriculum content which, we believe, will furnish time-saving media helpful in overcoming the educational lag.

Hearing children have all the natural advantages that their sense of hearing gives them plus the advantages of man-made educational tools and facilities such as television, radio, consolidated schools with comprehensive programs, summer schools and so on. If the educational gap between the hearing and the deaf continues to widen, we shall see the day when our deaf youth will enter the working world as second-class citizens. We have a professional and a moral ob-ligation to provide them with the means to acquire at least a high school education.

In his keynote address to the 1963 International Congress on Education of the Deaf, Dr. S. Richard Silverman expressed the needs of our deaf children in a brief, but profound statement, "Our people must learn to learn."[3] As parents and teachers of deaf children we are charged with the responsibility of working together to overcome the educational hurdles of deafness. Our children can "learn to learn."

References

1. GATES, ARTHUR I.: *The Improvement of Reading*. New York, Macmillan, 1959.
2. HESTER, MARSHALL S.: Manual communication. Proceedings of the International Congress on Education of the Deaf, Washington, D. C., June 23–28, 1963.
3. SILVERMAN, S. RICHARD: Education of deaf children—past and prologue. Proceedings of the International Congress on Education of the Deaf, Washington, D. C., June 23–28, 1963.

RHYTHM: ITS IMPORTANCE IN THE EDUCATION OF THE DEAF*

BETTE FAUTH

The advantages of including rhythm in the curriculum for the education of deaf children in this country appeared in papers at meetings of the Convention of American Instructors of the Deaf as early as 1911. No less than twenty-four

* A report from *The California Palms*, California School for the Deaf, Riverside, May 4, 1962. The author is from the Lower School Department of the California School for the Deaf, Riverside.

papers have been presented on this subject at succeeding conventions, all of them extolling the merits of rhythmic training for improving bodily control and coordination, for encouraging self-expression, for stimulating the imagination, for developing the creative processes and for improving the aspects of speech. Some authorities emphasize one area of rhythm work and some another.

Our Lower School favors a comprehensive program to include many phases of rhythmics adapted to the age, interest level and ability of the children. A progression is being developed which is built on the simple foundations laid at the kindergarten level to the more complex and challenging expressions of the child nine years of age. In this way the material presented contains an ever exciting freshness since the work covered in a given year is not repeated a succeeding year although it may be in the same area and seek like results.

The curriculum is based on the following five main divisions: (1) basic rhythms; (2) interpretive music and actions; (3) speech; choral speaking; (4) rhythm band, and (5) dancing.

The subject of basic rhythms is concerned with the child's developing an ability to feel the vibrations of the piano through his fingertips in order to distinguish pitch, intensity and accent to the end that these may be applied to his speech. He learns to differentiate between various tempos which are demonstrated in rhythmic body movements and in speech sounds, phrases and song. There is often a combination of action and speech.

The area of interpretive music and actions is concerned with the child's feeling the piano or the vibration from a record combined with the use of the hearing aid and expressing through actions his interpretation of the music. These expressions include as much of the child's experience as possible such as walking, running, hopping, skipping, jumping, skating, galloping, tiptoeing and swaying. They include pleasant experiences such as falling snow, raindrops falling, bells ringing, nightfall, fairy world of goblins, elves, fairies and giants, the animal world of elephants, lions, ponies, birds, cats, rabbits, the circus, and moods such as happy, sad, sleepy, slow and "dancy." The deaf child's world is further stimulated and enriched by feeling and expressing various kinds of clock movements and gongs, various gaits of horses or ponies, such as ticks and gongs, various toys such as swings, scooters, roller skates, bicycles, and skipping ropes. Out of these creative expressions of the children, poems, songs and dances are developed.

The third category of speech is closely allied with basic rhythms where, in this instance, more concern should be placed on the rhythmic flow of speech rather than articulation. Here one should strive for relaxation, breath control and resonance through the visual, tactile and acoustic combination. As the children improve, they enjoy choral speaking both with and without actions. They are able to learn many of the songs and poems that are taken for granted as a part of every child's heritage.

The rhythm band from its simplest to its most complicated form is thoroughly enjoyed by each level in Lower School. It is sometimes used to fix the rhythm of a song or poem more firmly. It is used as an interlude between verses in song and speech for variety. It is sometimes used for pure enjoyment, an end in itself. In every case, it develops powers of concentration, attention and discipline which are necessary for the deaf child to learn at the earliest possible level. Moreover, it gives the child the joy of performing with a group in the same sense as a member enjoys being part of an orchestra.

In dancing, one of the most valued forms of exercise, we attempt to teach a variety of basic patterns which include the simple skip and hop motions leading to folk and square dancing, simple game dances, simple tap dancing and the most elementary ballet positions and arm movements that these may be incorporated into the children's creative dance expressions.

Lower School children attend rhythm one thirty-minute period a week. There is an attempt made to allot 15 minutes of this time to work at the piano for the purpose of feeling vibrations and for speech development. The remaining time is given to motor activity and creative expressions resulting from the prep-

aration period. Often simple costumes or props such as finger puppets, hats, headbands, scarfs or batons are used to add to the color and enjoyment of the exercise.

The values of rhythm in regard to health, good posture, balance, speech improvement, culture and development of a sense of rhythm in dance are generally accepted. Beyond this, however, it is paramount that the rhythm period be an experience to which the child looks forward with anticipation and enjoyment.

A rhythm program is usually presented for the parents and friends at some time during the year. A presentation entitled "May Fete in Fairyland" was given in the Social Hall May 4 at 1:45. This story in pantomime, speech and dance is a part of the natural outgrowth of our work on seasons and holidays in rhythm classes during the year.

MUSIC IN EDUCATION OF THE DEAF*

Laura Burns

After he became deaf, Beethoven had a practice of clenching one end of a stick between his teeth and resting the stick's other end against his instrument as he played. He was using the stick to conduct the vibrations from the music. With this primitive hearing

* Reproduced with permission from *Music Journal*, November, 1965, Vol. 23, pp. 42 and 68. Mrs. Burns is now with the University of Texas Press. She was formerly with the Texas School for the Deaf, Austin.

aid, he was able to get some concept about the sound of his compositions, and to continue his great career despite the frustration of his handicap.

Today, children who attend special schools for the deaf also touch musical instruments as they are played in order to feel the vibrations. For these children, however, music is something new. Although it is exceptional for one of them to attain more than a rhythm-band level of virtuosity, music nevertheless plays an important part in their education.

The first known use of music in education of the deaf was in 1877. In that year, a drum to march by was found helpful in the military training class at the New York School for the Deaf. (Military training classes for deaf boys were popular in the past because of the supposed disciplinary value of such training, even though deaf men are ineligible for the military service.)

In the early 1900's, the piano and other musical instruments were put into use to help oral training in schools for the deaf. Now, piano, rhythm instruments and phonograph records aid in creating sensitivity to sound in deaf children.

Although "deaf" is a term which to many persons implies a total inability to hear, such a condition is rarely the case. The degree of hearing loss among children attending a special school for the deaf will vary. Most such children will have at least a slight degree of residual hearing, although they cannot function adequately in regular classrooms because of their handicap and usually cannot learn to speak without special training.

Since even the most profoundly deaf person, however, can at least feel vibrations, this ability is made use of in auditory training, in which music is employed. The deaf child attends "rhythm class" and listens to phonograph records, the latter activity usually more beneficial the more hearing he has.

"Rhythm," a somewhat amorphous subject taught at most schools for the deaf, includes lessons in "singing" or chanting in unison as the teacher plays the piano, rhythmic exercises, folk dancing, and rhythmic games, such as London Bridge. Children with some proficiency advance to playing rhythm instruments.

A rhythm class aids the deaf child's speech by giving him an idea of rhythm, accent and fluency, thus helping to counterbalance his tendency as a deaf person to speak in a monotone and more slowly than a person who hears. Such a class also helps coordination, poise and balance, which the deaf child sometimes has more trouble with than does his hearing counterpart, balance being controlled by the semicircular canals in the inner ear. Deaf children often have a shuffling walk since, because of this poor balance, they are reluctant to lift their feet. Games and dances in rhythm class are, in part, an effort to instill more poise and to minimize the shuffles.

One way children begin in such a class is by standing around a grand piano with their hands on the lid. They must first learn to tell when the teacher stops playing, lifting their hands from the lid when she does so.

After a while, the children learn to tell from the piano's vibrations whether the notes played are loud or soft, high or low, and to tell how many chords the teacher plays in succession. They even learn to recognize pieces being played by their rhythms. A descriptive name, rather than the actual title, is usually given these pieces by the teacher. A waltz, for instance, may be known as the "butterfly" piece, and a pizzicato piece, the "rabbit." The children show their recognition of what is being played by imitating the animal.

No great amount of musical talent or training is necessary to be a rhythm teacher, but many schools require a special certificate for teaching the deaf. A Sunday-school pianist's proficiency, plus patience to guide deaf children into a really difficult activity for them —for instance, dancing and singing both at the same time—are the main requirements for a rhythm teacher.

Besides the "live" music in rhythm class, recorded music is also important in the education of deaf children. Group hearing aids bring recorded music to their ears. Unlike individual hearing aids, group aids are all tuned in to only one microphone, instead of picking up all surrounding sounds.

The children sometimes "sing along" with a record. Or sometimes, while they listen, they watch a chart bearing the words to a song sung on the record. When the music stops suddenly, as in a game of Musical Chairs, the teacher selects a student who must try to point out the word on the chart at which the song stopped. Another use of phonograph records is for "Muzak" during other lessons. Children will pick out certain records as particular favorites.

Although the end toward which all these music activities are directed is not primarily the esthetic one, deaf people do indeed learn to enjoy music. Deaf teenagers are as closely attuned as any to fads in popular music, and many deaf persons report much pleasure from touching a musical instrument (the organ, which can be felt from some distance away without even being touched, is a favorite) or even from touching a radio speaker.

The altered perspective on music caused by their handicap has given rise to an unconscious commentary by them on one aspect of the question of the essential unity among the arts. In the sign language that so many deaf people use among themselves, the same gesture which is used to indicate *music*, is also the one which means *poetry*.

TEACHING SPEECH IN LOWER SCHOOL*

Kindergarten

SARAH HARPER ABERNETHY

In kindergarten the child is made aware of speech and its function.

There are four definite objectives in speech work at this level.

* From *The California Palms,* California School for the Deaf, Riverside, April, 1964. The authors are staff members of the Lower School Department, California School for the Deaf, Riverside.

1. To develop in each pupil a voice which as nearly as possible approximates the voice of a hearing child of the same age.
2. To develop the elementary speech sounds.
3. To develop the ability to combine smoothly and fluently the speech sounds.
4. To develop a vocabulary which will enable the child to express his elementary wants and ideas.

When the child becomes aware that he has a voice and has also developed the ability to imitate, babbling ("Bu-bu-bu-bu-bu") is the first exercise used to strengthen and modulate his voice. Later, time is spent in breathing exercises in an effort to develop good breath control, so important in the production of intelligible speech. Daily tongue gymnastics are a necessary factor in developing flexibility and control of the tongue.

The children always use group amplification for the specific speech lessons. In the development of speech sounds the teacher and the child are seated before a large mirror so that the child can easily see both what the teacher does and what he himself does. The child feels the sound vibrations by placing his hand on the teacher's face, thus employing the use of visual and tactile senses as well as the residual hearing.

Later the children are exposed to the printed form of the speech sounds through the use of sandpaper letters. These are used both for speech and speechreading and are given both singly and in combinations.

By constant repetition and use of certain expressions, the children soon learn to say: "hi," "bye-bye," "home" and other words as they are developed.

Second Year

SHARON STELLWAGEN

The second year of speech training combines review, development and the requirement of intelligible spontaneous speech. The speech sounds learned in kindergarten are reviewed and new

and more difficult sounds are developed. Spontaneous use of classroom expressions are expected from each child. Speech drills are practised to facilitate a smooth combining of speech sounds into words. Typical of the many drills used are: combining the consonants with the syllable "um" and a vowel with a consonant, using the consonant both initially and finally.

Many new words are introduced in the course of the year. Parts of the body, numbers, colors, toys, clothing and food are some of the categories concentrated upon. Verbs, nouns and adjectives commonly used to express children's activities and needs are taught. Gradually the children begin to put the words together to form sentences and by the end of the second year are able to speak in one and sometimes two related sentences.

Third Year

NANCY KEIM

During the third year the speech program contains the same expedients as the previous years with additional attention given the esthetic nature of speech. The children are encouraged to think in terms of spoken language, to increase the intelligibility of their speech and the habit of articulating well and to develop further the skills of speech.

The children are held responsible for the elements they have learned and are urged to put this knowledge to work independently in attacking a new word.

Rhythm and accent are given more

concentrated consideration at this level. Economy of motion in articulation is stressed as well as suitable intonation and sequence pattern of activities such as poems, songs and the pledge to the flag.

Colloquial expressions are included for a more natural and well-balanced vocabulary. These are used incidentally in appropriate situations so that the children may get a feeling and sense of their use.

It is hoped that some degree of proficiency is gained with the children depending on their speech in normal living.

Fourth Year

Mrs. Doris Taylor

Speech training during the fourth year in school consists primarily of refining the skills previously developed and introducing those skills necessary for the production of fluent speech.

After the children are able to blend speech sounds into words it is important for them to be able to put these words together into phrases and sentences so that the result will be fluent,

intelligible speech. Much practice in proper phrasing, accent and intonation or inflection needs to be given to accomplish this.

The children need to have a knowledge of where to phrase as well as the ability to control their breath in such a way that the intake of breath coincides with the beginning of a new phrase. This helps to prevent the speech from being choppy and difficult to understand.

The speech of deaf children often has a monotonous quality unless a great deal of training is given to both accent and intonation or inflection. The piano is used as an aid in developing these. The children, by feeling the vibrations of a piano being played, learn to discriminate an accented chord from an unaccented one and a chord of high frequency in contrast to one of low frequency. The knowledge of this is transferred to their own speech production and in time the skill of accenting the proper syllable or syllables of a word and the ability to raise or lower the voice to convey the true meaning of an expression or sentence become meaningful in their effort to produce intelligible speech.

MANUSCRIPT OR CURSIVE?*

David M. Denton

This year marks the end of a three-year experiment in writing at the North

* Reprinted with permission from *The North Carolinian*, North Carolina School for the Deaf, Morganton, January, 1965. The author is Principal of the North Carolina School for the Deaf.

Carolina School for the Deaf. At the beginning of the 1961–62 school year, all beginning, or Preparatory I, classes in this school were started on cursive writing. (In the past, all beginning students had started with the manuscript form.) This project with cursive writing was understood from the very beginning to be an experiment, and any decision as to its permanent use with beginning deaf children would be made at the end of the three-year period on the basis of a study of its apparent results.

The transition from manuscript writing to cursive writing during the third preparatory year was presenting some problems to the teachers as well as to the pupils. This transition was taking place at a time when the teaching of language and language principles needed every extra minute. It was found to be time consuming and frustrating. Since some of the children seemed "ready" and others apparently not, the teacher was faced with the decision of whether to hold back those students who were "ready" or to force the transition upon those who were not. At any rate, it was felt that a great deal of valuable time was lost.

Since the teaching of writing had to be accomplished within a given period of time, it was felt that basic motor skills for writing could be slowly developed from the very beginning, and in sequence with the development of basic language principles, reading and speech. It would seem that the teaching and use of cursive writing would be less apt to interfere with other kinds of learning, and would not interrupt to as great a degree the continuity of language development for the young deaf child. Since manuscript writing, as a language tool, had to be discarded or "unlearned" and cursive writing learned in Preparatory III, the value

of teaching manuscript writing to the beginning student then became of questionable value. One additional reason for this experiment was that writing skills among students at all levels within the school were felt to be not quite "up to par."

Does a five-year-old deaf child have sufficient muscular coordination to learn cursive writing? Will the sloweddown tempo in writing hinder a child's development in language? Since cursive writing is less "akin" to the printed word, will its use retard the young child in reading? These are a few of the questions whose answers could be revealed by this experiment.

An effective and fair evaluation of this project would, of necessity, include the teachers who were directly involved in its completion. All teachers who had a part in this program were given an opportunity to discuss it frankly and openly on the basis of their own experiences, observations, and feelings. Questionnaire forms were completed by this same group of teachers, and in the following paragraphs the questions are listed and the answers summarized in order to have a more nearly complete appraisal. During the three-year period, individual classes and pupils were observed and studied carefully to provide an informal but continuing evaluation.

Results of Questionnaire

1. In your opinion, do five-year-old deaf students have sufficient muscular coordination to learn cursive writing without undue difficulty?

That they can do it, has been demonstrated quite vividly and strongly. All of the teachers agreed that the children have learned this method and apparently learned it quite well. It was felt by some of the teachers that those students who have difficulty with cursive writing would have difficulty as well if started on manuscript writing. In an analysis of the responses by those teachers who felt that the five-year-old deaf child does not have sufficient muscular coordination for cursive writing, it was noted that most of these answers hinted of the fact that, perhaps, we have concentrated on "mastery" or "perfection" too much, at the expense of the development of basic skills. Perhaps we are trying to get words too quickly and should, instead, spend more time in writing exercises and drills before we attempt to get words. In fact, it is the belief of this writer that the success of any writing system depends greatly upon the development of these basic motor skills. The consistent use of proper drills and exercises will insure the gaining of motor coordination much more quickly and effectively than will the same amount of time spent in efforts to write letters and words. The teachers were in agreement that cursive writing is more difficult to teach. This, again, may point to the value of a well understood and consistently used system of writing.

2. In your opinion, does the use of cursive writing retard the children in their ability to read the printed form?

A majority of the teachers felt that it had no adverse effect upon reading. Several teachers felt that there was some difficulty with reading in the very beginning for average to slow children. However, once the connection is seen, there seems to be no difficulty that could be related to the form of writing used. School records will bear out the fact there is no measurable difference in the reading skills of those students, at the same grade levels, started on cursive writing than those started on manuscript.

3. Do you feel there is more time lost in teaching cursive writing to beginning students than is lost in switching from manuscript to cursive writing at a later time?

Most of the responses to this question pointed to this elusive quality called "readiness." More of the teachers felt that if a child was "ready" for cursive writing in Preparatory III, the transition took place rapidly. Other teachers felt there was less time lost in starting the children out with cursive writing since no transition had to be made and that by the time they had reached Preparatory III, they already had this skill and could move ahead with a fuller concentration on other things. The hitch seems to be "the slow child" or the child who is not "ready." The child who is not "ready" for cursive writing in Preparatory I is the same child, it would seem, who is not "ready" for the transition in Preparatory III. Since this child has difficulty with writing, why expose him to two different forms? Would it not be better to spend more time in Preparatory I and II in the development of one skill; a skill that he will use throughout his schooling?

4. Do you feel that the use of cursive

writing in any way helps the young child to understand the nature of combinations, and to see the wholeness of a word better than the manuscript form?

From the observations of most of the teachers involved, the use of cursive writing seems to make no difference in the child's ability to understand combinations. A few of the teachers felt that it would help the child gain a visual impression of a word as a unit. There seem to have been no negative influences concerning combinations resulting from the use of cursive writing.

5. In your opinion, is there any difference in the rate of total language development between those students who began with cursive writing and those who began with manuscript?

All responses, except one, agreed that there was no difference in language development among students started on the two different forms of writing. By the end of Preparatory II, students are up to the course outline. Since they have not been held back, and since they already have, or are developing, cursive writing skills, this seems to be a strong point in favor of continuing this plan.

6. Do you feel that students started on cursive writing develop good penmanship at a faster rate?

The responses to this question were about half and half. Penmanship seems to be related more directly to personality than to the original form of writing used. However, teacher observations make it seem almost conclusive that those students who began with cursive

writing develop writing speed at a faster rate. Perhaps it is still too early to measure the ultimate effect of cursive writing on penmanship.

7. It would seem that since cursive writing is connected and depends more upon flowing movements, it would be easier for the untrained hand to learn than the series of lines, angles, and curves of the manuscript form. (In your opinion, and upon your experience, can this assumption be justified?)

It was felt by most that the children take to manuscript writing more readily than to cursive. Some of the teachers had observed that after writing is begun, cursive seems to be smoother than manuscript. Also, there seems to be less of a tendency to reverse letters when using cursive writing. The negative responses again pointed to the necessity of a good established system with more emphasis on the kinds of drills and practices that will eliminate the tendency to become cramped and rigid, and will help the child develop flowing movements.

Summary and Conclusions

As stated above, it has been demonstrated that five-year-old deaf children can learn cursive writing. From quite careful and continuing observation, it has become evident that there are no ill effects to the students in the areas of language development and reading. (These were the primary points of concern when this program was initiated.) Under the traditional plan, children were changed over (from manuscript to cursive) during the third preparatory year. Since the same level of development can be reached earlier, through the use of cursive writing from the beginning, then it would seem to make good sense educationally, to follow the shorter, more direct route. When facility is considered, manuscript writing is easier to teach, but when long-term goals are considered, it doesn't seem completely worthwhile to develop a skill that will receive limited use, and eventually be discarded.

There is no magic moment of "readiness." Children of the same age vary in their ability to accomplish certain tasks. Where one child may already possess the ability and coordination to do a particular task, another may be ripe for the development, through practice of these same abilities. It is easy to overemphasize the concept of "readiness." This fact has been demonstrated in our public schools with disastrous results. In many places throughout the nation, reading programs are based upon and geared to this theme and yet a shocking number of our children are not reading well.

The negative aspects of cursive writing for young deaf children seem to be directly related to two things. The first of these is a method or system, or the lack thereof. The Palmer Method and other standard methods of teaching cursive writing are dependent upon the development of basic hand and arm skills through drill. These drills are designed to help the child develop the motor coordination lacking in any child. Children do not learn to write well without first learning to make the proper hand and arm movements.

The second thing seeming to increase the difficulty of teaching cursive writing might well be the attempt to get the child to write words too quickly, and without the benefit of previously developed hand skills. Too early attempts at writing whole words seem to encourage cramping and ultimately tension and nervousness in the child. In this respect, perhaps, the teaching of cursive writing moves at a slower pace than that of manuscript writing. The opinion was voiced by a number of teachers that perhaps we are not only requiring the pupils to begin producing words too early, but that we may also be requiring them to write too much. If this overemphasis in writing exists, then it is certainly at the expense of other and more important things.

During the first year of school, when the ground work is being laid in language, reading, speech, speechreading, auditory training, etc., and the child's total educational growth is taking place at a slow rate, the foundation in writing should be developed with the same patience, caution, and understanding that are given to these other forms of learning.

With consideration to all aspects of this project and with deep respect to each individual having a part in it, it is recommended that the North Carolina School for the Deaf continue the use of cursive writing with beginning students.

VISUAL AIDS: AN ENRICHING MEDIUM*

BETTY IRGENS

Have you ever met an educator who did not have a pet method for pounding in the facts? Neither have I. Nearly everyone I know has a "foolproof" theory, and I suppose most people know that I go overboard for visual aids, especially bulletin board displays.

I have always admired the ingenuity of the late industrial engineer and efficiency expert, Frank Bunker Gilbreth, who once taught his dozen children the complete Morse code in a few weeks merely by painting the symbols all over the walls and ceiling of his summer cabin. While such a method may be a little extreme in the classroom, I see no reason why valuable wall space should be taken up by pictures of George Washington, "The Last Days of Pompeii," and American Indians when practically the same pictures can be viewed in the hall, in the library, and in the dormitories. Wall-to-wall bulletin boards above the blackboards should be standard equipment in a schoolroom where deaf pupils must literally visualize their entire education.

The average deaf pupil has a level of interest above his reading level, and I have found that nothing equals pictures to help bridge that gap. No words are required to understand pictures.

For example, in the fifth grade each year we study this magnificently varied

* A reprint from *The North Dakota Banner,* North Dakota School for the Deaf, Devils Lake, March, 1963. The author was an Instructor at the North Dakota School for the Deaf.

country called the United States of America. We usually start with our own state of North Dakota. A whole wall and a half of pictures featuring the shape of the land, the industries, the products, the capitol and other outstanding landmarks are posted, each with short titles. Such pictures are abundant, but not especially eye opening because most of the class has already been to those places.

It is only when we start to swing around the nation that pictures begin to play a star role. To the natives of North Dakota where the land is mostly wide and flat, where most trees are in sheltering windbreaks, where no waves except those of the great wheatfields rise and swell, where Indians, not Negroes, are the minority race, where the cities are far apart and every driver checks his gas gauge when passing a service station, and where the number of factories is negligible, verbal description alone could not explain to them the startling contrasts of the other states. Only pictures can bring into the classroom the snowcapped ranges of the Rocky Mountain states, the beautiful wooded mountains of Washington marred only by the steam of a logging train creeping down the side, and the surf breaking on the rugged shores of the coastlines, the dry vast wastelands of Nevada, the canyons in Arizona, the fertile Mississippi delta, the Negro populated South, the crowded Eastern seaboard, where cities grow out to meet cities and Chicago where miles and miles of factories belch smoke.

What stimulating possibilities present themselves! There are not only pictures of the physical features of the land, but of the industries, the products and the so-called local color that make each state different. Pictures of a miner cutting deep into the side of a mountain of gold, of loggers breaking up a logjam, of salmon fighting up the Columbia River, of the cold fog drifting around a Maine lobster boat, of lighthouses spreading their warning out over the rocky coast, of big cargo ships plowing into harbors, and of children in Utah, just off a school bus, descending the stairs to their homes on the side of a steep canyon above the Snake River. How else can one show these sons of North Dakota farmers that most of the snug little farms in Pennsylvania are not even as large as one of their fathers' wheatfields?

It may be argued that it is not necessary to post pictures when the texts are full of them. That is true of the newer books if one is lucky enough to have them, and even luckier enough to find a text at the interest level of the class which is still easy enough for them to read. In my experience even the best books are read, closed and then returned to the desks. A picture on the wall remains in their line of vision all day long for two or three weeks. As in the case of the Gilbreth children, they were not overly willing to spend their summer "learning" but they could not help themselves. Not only that, but of all the pictures, the ones on the board have been especially singled out for their attention. I always post with each picture a small

card on which is written a short description using as much new vocabulary from their text as possible. All the pictures and cards are arranged as a sort of outline which I read to them at the beginning of each new lesson and refer to often thereafter.

While bulletin board displays are my favorite, I do not disregard other types of visual aids which are just as useful. I use filmstrips occasionally, but prefer my own pictures and titles because then I can select or reject, and arrange my own facts. Most filmstrips are prepared for advanced classes and the depth and extent of their facts only confuse my fifth grade pupils. However, there are a dozen or so new scripts which are excellent for the intermediate grades.

Movies, too, are a wonderful aid, though it has to be admitted that much of the impact is lost on a deaf pupil unless they are captioned. One of the most pleasant boons for the deaf is the program of captioned films under the auspices of the Department of Health, Education, and Welfare in Washington, D. C. Only a deaf person can fully know the tremendous difference it makes.

Even an uncaptioned film can increase their general knowledge. Take for example a recent film shown at this school which showed a girl drinking an envelope of Knox gelatine mixed with orange juice. This sparked the curiosity of my pupils, and upon returning to the classroom, there were many questions. Discussion brought the fact that gelatine is a good source of protein and makes our hair and nails less brittle. Such a fact probably would have been forgotten in the daily flood of learning except for one thing. The next day I brought a package of Knox gelatine to school and mixed each pupil a big glass of protein plus. They manfully downed every last heavy drop and ran to the water cooler to wash down the taste. It will be a long time before that memory will float away.

I use bulletin board displays for history, geography, and for such science lessons as deal with plants and animals. When we study science principles, I prefer actual experiments repeated, not once, but several times. We are fortunate to have at this school an ample science laboratory and a generous science teacher who loans us everything we ask for. Thus, we can play with magnets and prisms, ring bells connected to dry cells, test various things as to conductivity, make water wheels and windmills, melt ice, freeze water, make steam, condense and evaporate water, take the temperature of various liquids, try to pick up mercury, make waves with a tuning fork, push boxes over various surfaces, collect leaves and seeds, and plant beans. Imagine the amazement of one 66-pound lightweight when he discovered he could lift me with a lever! That is something he will never forget!

In reading and in language I have a small file of general pictures at my fingertips. Whenever a word, or an expression, or a situation is difficult to explain, I merely pull out some pictures. We write picture stories once a week and I find that it is a very casual way of introducting new language principles.

On the subject of vocabulary I might also add that our class does a lot of explanatory drawing, especially for nouns. I find it is a more accurate check on

their concepts. For example; take an Indian moccasin. If a pupil defines it as "an Indian shoe" he is perfectly correct, although his answer leaves much to the imagination. But, if he draws a moccasin there is no doubt that he fully understands.

You may wonder where I get all these pictures. Well, I soon learned that good things do not come easily. It took not weeks, not months, but years to build up my modest file, out of the process I have learned where to look. Magazines are my best source, especially *Post*, *Look*, and *Life*. I admit that one magazine which I have not had the privilege of attacking with scissors, but which I think would be very yielding, is *National Geographic*. Until recently the *Post* had many covers which were ideal for picture stories. Another feature that regrettably has been discontinued in the *Post* was the "Face of America" series. Where else could I have obtained such wonderful pictures as a factory making American flags, a peep into Fort Knox and the glittering stacks of gold bars, Bingo Night at a local fire hall, a desolate Indian reservation or a police helicopter checking traffic on a maze of freeways?

I never underestimate advertisements. Thanks to the boys on Madison Avenue, it is possible to clip out and save a complete series of famous men, or landmarks of American history, or natural phenomena, or scenes of cities and countries. Many calendars provide a series, too.

Old, unused textbooks furnish many technical pictures. Anyone can write to the State Department of Commerce and Industry, the State Development

Division, the Division of Publicity, or whatever the state calls its particular department and ask for free brochures. Such departments are usually very cooperative.

Finally, in a squeeze, I impose upon the office picture file or the library file.

But, one of the most inspiring sources of all is my pupils, themselves. If an eleven-year-old boy can voluntarily spare time from his busy daily schedule to clip out a picture or two, what more could a teacher ask?

THAT THEY MAY GROW*

FRANCES WILTSE

What is a sixth grader? We have the usual behavioral patterns of an adolescent group. I have found some of the typical characteristics of this grade to be elfin delights, giggling, emotional instability, tattling, bickering, and learning to get along with and without one another. I am sure that any mother of beinning teenagers will heartily agree on these attributes.

There certainly isn't a dull moment. A sample day may have one child come up and say that he must see the principal right away—I quickly find no other will do—about a cut finger; another may come in crying after recess because she has received a letter saying her brother has a broken leg. Squeals may greet the announcement of a timed arithmetic test, or a sulky boy may claim he is through with girls and must be persuaded back to humanity.

Many objectives are blended into a balance of challenge and pleasurable ac-

tivity with the day's lessons as the tools. There is the building of an *esprit de corps,* the training of leaders, and the rotation of these leaders with academic as well as social goals. The methods that succeed with one class may not work as well with another and this adjustment takes a little while.

Each morning we begin with the Pledge to the Flag. This is followed by a few minutes of news conversation and then we have our English class. Our week's outline has the general following base: On Mondays, we write weekend news on the blackboard in groups of two, promoting two-way conversations. On Tuesdays, we read a story from *Language Stories and Drills,* Book III, by Croker, Jones and Pratt. We answer the given questions or practise asking questions for given answers in the book. This provides good practice in systematic reading or studying. On Wednesdays we develop compositions on the blackboard. I find Dr. Mildred Groht's book on *Natural Language for the Deaf* very rich in motivational techniques for live language and composition development. On Thursdays, we practise re-

* Reprinted with permission from the *North Dakota Banner,* North Dakota School for the Deaf, Devils Lake, December, 1962. The author is a sixth grade teacher at North Dakota School for the Deaf.

medial grammar and drill work. Material for this is gathered from a list of daily errors of the class. Every other Friday we write letters home, write news for the *Banner,* our monthly school paper, or develop compositions.

In this grade, compositions may be partially self corrected. Red pencil marks which underline errors enable each child to study and make changes. It is surprising how often underlined errors are rewritten correctly, and it is also surprising to note the progress made by the end of the year.

The intermediate teacher builds upon the base words and ideas given in the primary department. We have practice with the spellings of root and core words, such as in **to go,** which has spellings of **go, goes, went, going** and **gone.** We work with adverbial endings and with adjective comparisons such as **big, bigger,** and **biggest** as well as the plural spelling of nouns. Establishing the base concepts of spelling departures requires repetition throughout the year and their use in sentences.

This year we made a list of the different forms of the key word said as we went through one story after another. A clue that helps the children with the words placed in this list were **talked, spoke, announced, ordered, cried, explained, repeated,** and **murmured.** Some forms of the word to go were listed in a second column beside the first. Among these were **run, dash, scurry, walk, pass,** and **flash.** The two lists helped with discerning possible word meanings, acting as a pivotal point involving context clues.

In the beginning, vocabulary is learned rather slowly. Minds have become rusty over the summer months. A child must meet a word, ask about it, look it up, understand it and use it. Accordingly, I ask questions about the story using the new words. This builds a fire under any lagging pupil as he cannot answer the question until he understands the word. For a change I am asked questions as to word meanings. The Courtis-Watters *Intermediate Picture Dictionary* is very popular for this age group and makes a splendid gift for your child. The class does not use the nonpicture dictionary well as yet, these skills being improved upon over many months.

Live vocabulary tests include five matching words or matching elliptical sentences taken from the readers; five—true or false; five—choose the right word and five—fill the blanks. The nature of puzzles, as in this varied presentation, is stimulating and gives zest to a lesson.

The class is taught to use imagination with sentences that cannot be taken literally. When **the flowers danced and waved** in the breeze is presented, someone may finally offer the **flowers nodded back and forth** as a more sensible alternative to **flowers actually dancing.** And when we come to: **Totarum felt the side of a rabbit,** the child is sure to think Totarum felt the rabbit itself.

I try as does every teacher to build up sentence comprehension from mere word calling. The symbols of the printed word must be united into an idea. A group of words brought together as in **Mary's heart seemed to leap up into her throat and choke her** are explained with the brief words **was excited** written over it. As the quiet faces show reflections of connected thinking, they are asked why Mary was excited. Perhaps some will remember why, but others may have lost the thread of the story.

When a story presents some difficulties, I sometimes copy two or three key paragraphs on the board. I ask about possible word meanings, similes, and ideas. I ask the whys of a reaction and when answered correctly, dramatize it. The teacher must go hand in hand with the pupil to make the journey of reading a pleasant or dramatic experience.

The children often confuse the spelling of one word with another. The counterpart word asked about is written down for clearer identification and comparison. Recognition then comes readily enough.

I try to instill an interest in reading so that reading will help teach each one. Some in the class are approaching this reading-to-learn level, but most as yet are still learning to read. In reality, reading is taught all day long except for arithmetic and then there are language problems to solve. The content subjects, science, geography, and history are mainly reading lessons with comprehension questions and the **who, when, where, what,** and **why** questions stressed.

With some classes, it is time to utilize more than one basic reader to meet all reader levels. A variety of approaches is used during any one week. Stories are taken up in sequential roundrobin fashion from different readers. On Monday, for instance, a story is read silently from a Basal Book II and a quiz given afterwards. On Tuesday, we use the opaque projector for teacher-pupil translation of a story from a Basal Book III which is projected onto the screen. On Wednesday, each pupil copies part of a more difficult story from a Basal Book IV on the blackboard for teacher-pupil interpretation. Any new word is boxed with brightly colored chalk and its meaning written just above. Idioms or English expressions are also underlined with this chalk when being discussed. I believe in some copy work as it provides atmosphere and to a degree replaces the sort of thing that the children miss hearing. It helps shape the English of a more highly motivated child. On Thursday, story reports are given. These are freely chosen from library book stories. When a good story has been well told, there is a rush after the storytelling to look at the pictures and sometimes to borrow the book. It is here that the fires of inspiration to read are often born and where desire becomes the mother of learning. Reading provides wonderful character training as in the Fairy Shoes which pinch wayward feet, or The Little Pig who found no work was easy and so went happily back to hoeing his garden. Stories of kindness temper rougher instincts when quiet is needed. And each pupil feels personally stronger when he hears that David killed the giant, Goliath. On Friday, a vocabulary test may complete the week's work or we may rewrite a story using the new vocabulary in simple sentences. The variety of presentations during the week has something for everything.

Grade charts on the bulletin board and a class honor roll utilize self-evaluation and arouse self-motivation. When the class exchanges and corrects papers with one another, this builds their confidence and sharpens their perception. Such work is usually followed up and checked.

This year we made some Phrase-O games which are played in the same way as bingo, using phrases on flash-cards instead of numbers. The phrases were taken from a current reading story. It proved a painless way for children to absorb some English phrases through repetition, to read more quickly when timing was stepped up, to read in phrases instead of words, and to cooperate as a unit. The pupils helped make the games. Since the game builds upon fluidity of known expressions, (those taught them), it is unsuccessful with difficult terms.

Letters from home provide important inspiration for our boys and girls, propelling them to work harder. They read and reread these letters until they are frayed and worn. They frequently ask a teacher about the meanings of words and sentences not understood. Parents' encouragement of their child's progress is our most valuable ally.

In closing, let me say that an adolescent must be motivated and sometimes prodded to use his rapidly growing powers. I try to convey a love of work—for no one is prouder than the child himself of accomplishment and honor as he grows his way to gradual maturity.

In conclusion, I believe all teachers share these feelings:

> *And when the time comes, who can say*
> *"I did my share of work today,*
> *Held high the lamp; and drank the cup*
> *Of children's faces looking up?"*

POTENTIALITIES IN ART EDUCATION FOR THE DEAF*

Rawley A. Silver

Education of the deaf centers around the acquisition of language, for without language many kinds of thinking are impossible. The deaf child must learn not only that people, things, and activities can be designated by names, but

* Reproduced with permission from *Eastern Arts Quarterly*, November-December, 1962, Vol. I, No. 2, pp. 30–38. Negatives for the accompanying illustrations supplied by courtesy of Dr. Silver. In her doctoral dissertation she deals further with the same subject, "The Role of Art in Conceptual Thinking, Adjustment, and Aptitudes of Deaf and Aphasic Children," University Microfilms, 300 N. Zeeb Road, Ann Arbor, Michigan. Dr. Silver is from Rye, New York.

that they can be recalled and discussed when they are not physically present.

Although the deaf have the same variations in intellectual capacity as the hearing, they do not have the same opportunities for mental growth because they are deprived of many experiences. While the hearing child often learns new words unconsciously, the deaf must learn them one by one with intense effort. Many different words have the same meaning, and one word can mean many different things. For the deaf, reading comes last.

The ability to understand and use language varies widely among the deaf and seems to be independent of intelligence. Here, a class of sixteen-year-olds translates Latin. There, a boy of the same age is at the fifth grade level academically, although he has an IQ of 157.†

The essential handicap of deafness is not a problem of speech, but the frustration of missing concepts. Since art, as well as language, is a means of communicating concepts, can it do more for the child who is deaf than enrich his school program? Can it serve as an additional avenue of communication? Can it stimulate intellectual growth? Can it ease emotional adjustment?

In search of answers to these questions, an experimental painting class was undertaken at a school for the deaf. Three children with emotional difficulties, selected by the school administration, attended a fifty-minute class once a week for about two months.

Elliot was an attractive ten-year-old boy with an IQ of 89, although a psychological report described him as having average or above average intelligence with a high potential, and "multiple emotional problems obscuring diagnosis and/or receptive aphasia." In the third grade he was described as aggressive and having little concept of right and wrong.

Julia was an eleven-year-old girl who gave the impression of being gentle and reserved. Her IQ was 121 and she was in the sixth grade. It was reported that

† The intelligence of deaf children is often established by nonverbal tests such as the Arthur Point Scale.

she tried to do everything perfectly, was not as popular as she wanted to be, and was sometimes mean to smaller children.

Martin was a well-mannered boy whose appearance suggested that he was about ten. Since records were unavailable, the school accepted a birthdate which gave him an age of fifteen and an IQ of 82. However, the report card from his native country indicated that if he was really fifteen he did not start to school until the age of ten. He was in the sixth grade here and had been exposed to English for about one year. A psychological evaluation stated that "his manner of work is unusually slow . . . figure drawings suggest that he is quite anxious behind a facade of social amiability."

Although she was congenitally deaf and her hearing levels were 81 and 82 decibels, Julia lipread and spoke very well. There was almost no verbal communication with Martin and Elliot. Since the school discouraged manual methods and the instructor was ignorant of them, communication was achieved through demonstration and pantomime. Gestures served concrete ideas. Abstract concepts were sometimes communicated by acting out alternatives. Communication was rarely a problem.

For the first day, a topic was suggested: to show who lived in their homes with them. The instructor communicated it to Elliot and Martin by making a quick sketch of the members of her own family, and inviting them to do the same. No further suggestions for topics were needed, and during the remaining periods the children depicted their own ideas.

Art as Communication

There are qualities of experience that cannot be put into words, but can be articulated in art. A captionless cartoon may be eloquent. Even for the hearing in a literate society, verbal language is not enough. We often say what we don't mean, often are unconscious of what we do mean, but reveal to others, nevertheless, without words or in spite of them. Vision is sometimes more reliable than hearing. Children read facial expressions and gestures. They know what their teacher means regardless of what she says. As the hearing child matures, he depends more and more upon the spoken word; but if hearing is lost in later life, he rediscovers how much he can understand through vision alone.

If language is defined as a system of communication through the use of visual symbols, art qualifies as a language. Its conventional symbols are nonverbal and so universal that they transcend languages and cultures. All over the world in children's art, symbols for the sun, trees, animals, flowers, people, windows, are represented in much the same way. Children draw houses with pitched roofs in Afghanistan where the roofs are flat.

The language of art can never take the place of spoken language. Even written language is a poor substitute. But art has always served to communicate ideas and experiences. It is a language where the handicap of deafness is no impediment. If hearing children sometimes find verbal expression inadequate and need to express ideas in visual form, how much more important might art be to children whose speech is restricted, and how useful to their teachers if they could learn more of what their students think and how they feel through what they depict!

The children in this class spontaneously used pictures to tell what they knew:

Julia's fourth picture was a visual list of outdoor activities—fishing from shore and rowboat, motorboating, waterskiing, swimming, playing ball, jumping rope, bicycling, rollerskating, walking, walking dog, and watching (Fig. 1).

Her fifth picture was a farm scene with grazing cows, farmer, and herself sitting under a tree, reading.

Her sixth picture was a ward with patients in hospital beds eating lunch on trays, and a nurse, Julia, carrying another tray.

Her seventh was an outdoor Christmas scene and her eighth, Christmas indoors with children opening presents under the tree and parents holding hands, watching.

Elliot's second picture was a boat sailing in choppy water; his third, an explicit devil (Fig. 2); his fourth, a butterfly (Fig. 3); his fifth, horses running in a paddock; his sixth and seventh revealed what he knew and observed at a recent puppet show of Jack and the Beanstalk; his ninth, a worm's-eye view

Fig. 1

Fig. 2

Fig. 4

Fig. 3

a large bird provided with water trough and corn bin (Fig. 4).

Art and Intellectual Growth

Art activity requires the exercise of many mental processes. It sharpens awareness and reinforces memory. When Elliot painted his picture of Jack and the Beanstalk, he put his recollections into concrete form. He had to review experiences and clarify impressions.

Art stimulates imagination. Young children relate themselves to the world through fantasy, imagining themselves airplanes, cowboys, lions. The young deaf child cannot verbalize imaginary or vicarious experiences, but he can draw them. He can also invent new processes by experimenting with various materials and techniques.

of a city scene with three identifiable breeds of dogs, fire escapes, street lamps, and the varied shapes of the tops of city buildings.

Martin's third picture revealed observation of how school buses, parked at the curb, look from an upstairs window. The doors, steps, windshield wipers, steering wheel, and people were in perspective. His fifth picture showed his sister and himself looking over a fence at

Martin's fourth picture was the head of a nightmarish creature made with a mixture of paint, crayon, and magic markers (Fig. 5). Elliot's vivid butterfly was painted im-

Fig. 5

mediately after his classmates discovered a small dead moth (Fig. 3).

Art develops reasoning power by requiring organization and the constant exercise of judgment. Evaluation begins with the choice of topic and continues with plans, revisions, and decisions. The art form is a vehicle in which new knowledge can be integrated with what is already known, and perceptions and reactions can be crystallized.

Julia once asked if she might copy a photograph of a group of children singing carols under a lamppost. When she understood that she might use the photograph but not copy it, she had to plan to incorporate it into her own work. The result was a painting of Santa, sleigh, and reindeer in the night sky flying over three houses. In the snow under a street lamp stood her own interpretation of singing children.

Martin's bird picture (Fig. 4) demonstrates organization and the solving of problems. After painting the water from which the bird drinks a blue as deep in tone as the brown of its body, he had walked to the sink to refill his water jar. As he returned, the teacher held up his picture so that he could see it at a distance. He studied it as he slowly approached, and may have noticed that the two colors were almost indistinguishable, because when he returned to the table, he painted white ripples in the water and thus separated the two forms. He did the same when he added wood texture to the fence.

After seeing their pictures at a distance, Elliot added a blue sky above his clouds and Julia decided to texture her hospital floor.

Art and Emotional Adjustment

The world is different for the deaf child and the world treats him differently. Parents often overprotect or reject. Other children often exclude or ridicule. Other people may think him queer or retarded. With all the frustrations which deafness entails, his emotional well-being is often precarious.

While the revelation of a deaf child's knowledge is important, clues to his feelings are hardly less so. Psychology has established the importance of art experience in mental health and uses it in diagnosis and therapy. Paintings and drawings permit the expression of feelings which cannot be verbalized. They provide a socially acceptable channel through which to express emotions, often revealing moods and areas of anxiety.

Elliot's first picture, of his family, included his mother, sister, brother, and himself. Where his father might have stood beside his mother, there was a picture on the wall. The psychological report in his file stated that his father's whereabouts were unknown, and perhaps this picture disclosed an area of his anxiety.

His second picture revealed what he knew about sailing, but little of how he felt.

His third picture was a kind of explosion—a devil with popping eyes, claws, horns and fangs, painted mostly in red with fiery shapes in the background (Fig. 2). His signature, elaborate in size, color and placement, demanded recognition.

During the first three classes, Martin's pictures were executed very slowly in hesitant lines and pale colors—an unfinished family portrait, an unfinished landscape, and the drawing of the buses in a quadrant of his paper. Each time, he indicated that he planned to continue the following week, but when the time came he decided to start anew.

His fourth picture (Fig. 5) was a dramatic contrast—a hideous face in violent colors with fangs and wild eyes. He worked so quickly that, despite time spent mixing colors, he covered the whole paper in one session.

Julia's pictures did not seem to disclose very much of how she felt except for her second, which consisted of tiny figures marching across the bottom of her paper. She seemed to use her pictures as a substitute for words to tell what she knew rather than how she felt.

Art does more than reveal emotions. The expression of unhealthy feelings sometimes serves to banish them. By providing release from emotional tension, art can be integrating and healing. The deaf child seems required to be even more passive in the classroom than the hearing child and his need for the release of being expressive rather than receptive must be greater.

Every child needs recognition, a sense of accomplishment, a feeling that he has some control over his environment, and these are readily provided by the art experience.

At the beginning of the sixth class, Elliot's room teacher said that his behavior had greatly improved. She attributed this to his new status among his classmates because of art.

The day before the classes began, he had to remain behind while the others went to the zoo because his behavior was so unpredictable. Now he was in charge of class lines, keeping the other children in order.

The location of his classroom directly across the hall was significant. On their way to lunch, his classmates, as they formed a line in the hall, admired his pictures extravagantly and escorted him away. One of his friends had been begging to join the art group and the homeroom teacher gave permission one day. His picture was a step-by-step imitation of Elliot's painting.

Martin's last picture, of the bird, was painted in three sessions, one of which lasted for ninety minutes. He had been so intent on his work that he was given permission to remain until the end of the school day.

Julia asked for a great deal of reassurance at first. Should her picture be large or small? Could she make a Hallowe'en picture? What color should she make the skirt? Each time she was asked what she thought, and each time she had an answer. When she made her final seventh and eighth pictures, however, instead of asking for directions, she drew attention to her own decisions.

It is frequently asserted that the deaf lack imagination. Recently, the pictures of twenty deaf children were analyzed and found "so empty of subject matter, of imagery or narrative . . . little planning, organization or care . . . very little involvement and painstaking interest."* Is the lack inherent in the handicap or could it be that the imaginations of these children had not been stimulated? Perhaps it isn't the lack of potential but the lack of opportunity to develop potential.

* Lampard, M. T.: The art work of deaf children. *Amer Ann Deaf, 105*, 419, 1960.

Opportunity seems largely dependent upon whether the art teacher is more interested in the child's personal statement or his artistic skill. Directive teaching, whether "modern" or "old-fashioned," subtle or flagrant, inhibits creativity. It motivates the child through approval and generally produces similar works. It also destroys the opportunity of knowing what a child is like. If he draws cramped figures in a small area of his paper, it is a clue to his adjustment. If we correct his composition, we destroy the clue.

The alternative is not anarchy. Freedom is consistent with responsibility,

and self-expression is consistent with aesthetic merit. The art class can be guided without being controlled.

To the writer the satisfactions of visual expression seem to be intensified in the deaf, and they seem more eager to seize the opportunity for making images, perhaps because their channels of communication are already constricted and concentrated on the visual. If the deaf cannot know the pleasure of conversation, they also have not been distracted by useless talk. Given encouragement and opportunity, they may have a speech to which the rest of us can listen with our eyes.

BOOK SELECTION FOR A SCHOOL FOR THE DEAF LIBRARY*

GEORGE PROPP

No one can question the fact that there is a growing awareness in deaf education for the necessity of improving library services. At the Nebraska School for the Deaf a survey several years ago indicated that our library was one of the weakest segments of our total school program. We have been trying to correct this deficiency and, despite formidable obstacles, have slowly but surely been making some headway.

* A paper written for the Library Services for the Deaf Institute at Gallaudet College, summer 1965, and here reprinted from *The Nebraska Journal,* Nebraska School for the Deaf, Omaha, December 1965. G. Propp was an instructor at the Nebraska School for the Deaf.

I gather from various sources that the problem at the Nebraska School for the Deaf is more or less typical of similar schools. A number of schools for the deaf have recently or within the past few years acquired new library areas and are able to offer expanded services. Acquiring financial resources and space, however, does not end the problem. To make the most of generally limited finances by a wise and careful selection of materials is undoubtedly the most important qualification that a librarian can have.

I am assuming that a selection policy is as much concerned with the quantitative as well as with qualitative aspects. Granted that a library budget is an administrative prerogative over which the librarian has limited control, we must nonetheless assume that the librarian must set up a program and successfully sell it to the school administration. Generally, a school for the deaf should have a library that exceeds the standards set up by the American Library Association. There is a difference of opinion as to the extent to which a deaf library should excel over that of a public school. However, considering the facts that the deaf child is restricted in nonbook material and that the school must provide the material generally provided in the home, no one can justify a deaf library that is less than ALA standards. This means that the minimum annual outlay for new books in even small schools such as ours should be at least $1,500 per year. To achieve the desired expansion and growth it would be reasonable to double this outlay for a period of at least five years. Our library should work toward an immediate goal of 6,000 books as quickly as funds can be made available. Five hundred new titles each year would not seem unreasonable, plus the requisite magazines, selection tools, audio-visual equipment and instructional materials. Federal funds now available make such an outlay quite realistic.

The actual selection of books for the deaf library should include all the stipulations and guidelines used in the selection of books for a regular school library. In addition we have to take into account the peculiar problems of

deafness and the structure and organization of a typical school for the deaf.

The main points upon which a school for the deaf library differs from that of a regular school are as follows:

1. The typical school for the deaf is generally a K-12 setup, frequently beginning with a nursery school.
2. The deaf child has severe retardation in the area of language arts.
3. The interests of the deaf child differ from those of his hearing counterpart. The degree and extent of this difference are subject to argument, but there is no question that it exists.
4. The curriculum needs of the school for the deaf are not the same as those of a public school.

The librarian in a school for the deaf may be tempted to oversimplify the problem of selecting books for the deaf children. The deaf child who can read, like his hearing brothers and sisters, knows what he likes. A librarian who knows what the deaf child likes, however, is not necessarily an authoritative selector of books for him. The librarian for the deaf must attempt to forge a lasting marriage of two incompatible tenets: (1) there are countless books which the deaf child cannot read; (2) there are thousands of books which he must read to achieve the status of an educated adult.

At this point I would also like to point out that the school for the deaf library is more concerned with the development of reading skills than is the public school library. The library is generally regarded as supplement to the reading program. In a school for the deaf the library is, or should be, an integral part of the reading program. This may require further elaboration, but suffice it to say that in selecting books for the deaf reader, the librarian is buying him tools to improve his reading skills.

Below is a list of guidelines we would follow in selecting books and materials for the library at the Nebraska School for the Deaf:

1. Establish a regular policy for library growth; i.e., determine the number of books and amount of material to add each year.

2. Acquire the necessary selection tools.

3. Aim at a balanced collection—balanced in subject areas, grade levels, needs of child as against needs of curriculum, needs of skilled reader versus needs of reader with limited skills, etc.

4. Every book selected should serve a purpose.

5. Determine the needs of the curriculum in each subject and grade area. Seek the help of the teacher in this aspect.

6. Make your objectives clear to the administration and the staff, and energetically seek their cooperation.

7. Basic books should have first priority—basic books according to the general meaning of the term as well as those basic to the needs of the deaf child.

8. Use the resources of the community—public library people, public school resources, university and NEA specialists, etc.

9. If possible, don't buy a book without seeing it.

10. Read the selections if you possibly can.

11. A good book should have good typography, good binding, etc. The best bargain is not necessarily the cheapest book.

12. Book lists for deaf readers should receive careful study, but should not be used as an exclusive guide; opinions vary, and yours may be as good as the so-called authority.

13. Check all purchase recommended lists. State library standards require that a certain proportion of books be from approved lists.

14. Generally the books selected should be:
   a. accurate and interesting
   b. understandable
   c. significant
   d. enriching to the thought of the reader
   e. up-to-date
   f. suitable to the reader
   g. clear in style and format
   h. adequately illustrated
   i. tabled and indexed
   j. durable

15. Keep children and staff aware of all new purchases. Create excitement.

16. Catalog new books and stack them promptly.

17. Gift books are welcomed but must meet the same requisites as new purchases.

18. Duplicate copies are avoided unless there is a proven need.

19. Buy paperbacks for titles read only occasionally, for books in temporary demand, or when no other edition is available.

20. When several editions of the same title are available, be sure you are getting the best one.

21. Give some consideration to works of state authors, books about local events, etc.

22. Selection of periodicals, maps, and visual-aids should receive the same care as the selection of books.

23. Provide some sort of guidance program for readers.

24. Know procedures and the appropriate agencies for obtaining NDEA funds and other forms of assistance.

Above all keep in mind that you are guiding a child toward a love for reading and an awareness of books. Only in the library can the deaf child find a means of satisfying his mental, emotional and activity needs.

DORMITORY PROGRAM AT O.S.S.D.*

KEITH PITMAN

It has been observed that the deaf have much more difficulty in arriving at social and intellectual maturity than do hearing people. The problems involved have been discussed by able people both deaf and hearing for many years. Many have searched for answers to these problems. We at the Oregon State School for the Deaf are also trying to find ways of better preparing our students for life here in school as well as life when they leave this campus.

Perhaps a valid criticism of schools for the deaf is that the students are sheltered too much from experiences and responsibilities which could be made possible to them and would greatly help in preparing them for the role they should play after leaving school. With this thought in mind, among others, we are in the process of trying some ideas which have occurred to us and which we have some reason to believe will help. The future will tell the extent of help to be realized. We are interested in new, helpful and workable ideas.

Last year the counselors in charge of each of the four dormitories with the supervising counselors, school psychologist, assistant superintendent and at times specialists from other departments, began weekly conferences with

the purpose in mind to "plan, implement and maintain an effective program for dormitory living which fosters social and intellectual maturity of the students." Also individual conferences were started involving all the staff in each dormitory to carry on the same purpose and to decide how to handle specific current problems. These conferences require time, but have already proved to be very worthwhile in helping to improve the program.

Underlying and basic to the overall program is the idea that preventative measures are more desirable than remedial measures. An attempt is made to anticipate and discover problems, pressures and strains before they materialize in misconduct. We still have distance to cover.

Children are creatures of action. Their actions often need to be guided rather than left alone or dictated. More leisure time has been scheduled than previously and a reasonable amount of guidance on how to use leisure time is offered. Some leisure is necessary to the wholesome development of the child. Leisure time, if properly used, can easily lead into worthwhile pursuits and keep young people out of trouble at the same time. Wise use of time affects attitude and general outlook and can definitely aid in contentment and bring satisfaction through the development of ingenuity. We believe that the child should learn to entertain himself

* With permission reprinted from *The Oregon Outlook,* Oregon State School for the Deaf, Salem, January, 1965. The author is from the Oregon State School for the Deaf.

and others in a wholesome manner. He should not be constantly entertained (i.e. TV). Leisure-time activities can provide opportunities for the child to learn to know and appreciate the world around him, the value of property, and come to know normal healthy independence. Oftentimes exploring in leisure time leads to choice of vocation. In short, we believe that it is extremely important to know how to use leisure time wisely.

Some of the children who need money for clothing or other essentials find help through the Student Work Fund. This fund is made possible by interested friends who agree with us that it is better for the boy and girl to work for pay rather than be handed money. Many useful tasks are performed daily by the students often without pay on a voluntary basis. But the Student Work Fund is a means of building the concept of financial independence.

Dances are held, some of which are planned in advance and some are impromptu. The students are given opportunity to plan many of their own socials. The homecoming queen is crowned at the time of the homecoming football game. Parents and interested relatives join in the festivities which include the homecoming dance.

Calling Hour is an experiment being made with on-campus-dating. Boys and girls sixteen years of age and in 9th grade or above may make arrangements and visit with each other in one of the social rooms of the girls' dormitory. This is under "semi-supervision" on the part of the dorm staff but is mostly

supervised by the student council. The Calling Hour gives promise of helping the students develop responsibility for acceptable conduct.

The Student Council under the guidance of the Dean of Students has proposed acceptable measures for the governing of some phases of student conduct and has handled discipline problems where infractions occurred involving these measures. The Student Council is a beneficial activity.

Another activity enjoyed by all is swimming, held on Saturday evenings when those who were unable to go home for the weekend have a time of refreshing and relaxing. Being indoors makes it a year-around sport. Quite a number of students are full-fledged lifeguards.

Under the leadership of the Vocational Supervisor and the two physical education instructors a fine intramural sports program is carried on. With a variety of different activities from which to choose, all are able to participate.

An extracurricular activity calendar is compiled for months in advance, which includes weekend outings for Scouts, Saturday trips to the beach or mountains, trips to the zoo for younger students, visits to places of historic and educational interest, sports events and picnics. All Saturdays are soon spoken for. Transportation and food are arranged a few days in advance of the actual date.

Each afternoon between 3:00 and 4:00 P.M. is club time when each student of intermediate age and above is engaged in a club activity of his or her own choosing. Any employee of the school who has a special skill or hobby and who can direct others in learning it may be called upon for that hour to instruct, direct or advise a club. Some of the clubs now active are knitting, flower arranging, cake decorating, upholstery, furniture refinishing, and dramatics.

As the students grow older, privileges and responsibilities are increased commensurate with their age and capabilities. Bedtime is a half hour later for each succeeding age group. Town-going privileges start at a certain age and become more lenient as the students grow older. Special activities and certain jobs (for money) become available to qualified older students, such as the work of assistant counselor.

The term Upper Group designates the oldest group of students in school. These boys and girls are treated differently from the rest of the students in some ways. They will soon be leaving school to take their place as adults in society. For this reason they are given as much freedom, responsibility and opportunity for self-discipline under less supervision as they are able to accept successfully.

Eligibility for entrance into the Upper Groups is based upon age and grade. Application for entrance must be made by the student and approval gained from some twenty faculty and staff members before a student may be admitted. Continued eligibility will be determined by the social maturity, personal conduct, and academic and vocational progress.

Students in the Upper Groups are no longer governed by the rules which apply to the rest of the students but are governed by a common understanding of right and wrong. Punishment is not administered by any and everyone. When any employee of the school may see an Upper Group student involved in what he feels is objectionable conduct, he is required to ask for the student's "conduct card," which each Upper Group student is required to carry at all times. On this card the employee is to write briefly what he observes and to return the card. The reason for writing on the card should be explained at the time. A "conduct report" in more detail, if need be, is to be turned in to the office. Good conduct is also to be similarly recorded. Once a week the Upper Group students bring their cards to the assistant superintendent to be checked. If anything is written on the conduct card it is discussed with the student at that time. He may be issued a warning, reprimand, or commendation. If a serious offense or often repeated offense is under question, the student may be removed from the Upper Group for at least one month. Re-admittance to the Group is gained in much the same way as admittance the first time.

Upper Group boys live in a separate wing of the boys' dormitory where they enjoy considerable freedom and have real opportunity to learn cleanliness, neatness and group living without direct supervision.

Upper Group girls live in apartments in a separate section of the girls' dormitory where they have similar opportunities for learning. Further, their living conditions are under the direct care of the Home Economics Department. In this program the girls, living four to an apartment, are given opportunity to learn home management. Each is issued a "salary" each month in play money. She is to learn to budget, do the "household" buying, cooking, serving, cleaning and to give an account of her management. These tasks are rotated by the four girls periodically so that each may learn every task.

Upper Group boys and girls plan joint socials, money raising campaigns and projects.

By the time the students reach the age of eligibility they almost without exception are very anxious to be members of the Upper Groups. The extra privileges, freedom and prestige no doubt account for this. It is our hope that the future will see an improved program and good results in social and intellectual maturity among all the students. We are confident this will be the case.

PHYSICAL EDUCATION PROGRAM AT THE TEXAS SCHOOL FOR THE DEAF*

MARIAN PHARR

The Texas School is meeting the needs of our young deaf children for planned physical and recreational activity in a program that reaches from the first year of schooling through the junior year. This means that our program is reaching approximately 500 students per year. Fortunately, we are in a position of having an administrative staff which is in harmony with the aims of physical education. We are, therefore, provided with adequate teaching staff, time with the children, and equipment to carry out a well-rounded program.

For example, daily physical education classes of forty to fifty minutes

* A report presented at a meeting of the American Association of Health, Recreation and Physical Education, Dallas, Tex., March 20, 1965, published in *The Lone Star*, Texas School for the Deaf, Austin, April 1, 1965, and here reproduced by permission. The author is Instructor of Physical Education, Texas School for the Deaf.

are a required part of the school day. Because of the large school enrollment, the administration has also provided us with six teachers (three men and three women) to allow a reasonable class load of twenty to twenty-five students per teacher per class hour.

Students between the ages of six and nine are under the direction of one of these teachers who gives the younger ones experiences in learning to get along with each other, experiences in learning to take instructions, and rudiments of low organized games. At age ten, these students transfer to the "big gym" where they are divided among the five remaining instructors into classes for boys and classes for girls. Each of these five teachers has the same teaching schedule which means that we have five physical education classes in progress every class hour. With this arrangement, the class load is reduced so that each teacher is given a greater opportunity for more individual teaching which is so vital for the deaf.

The aims of our classroom teaching are multiple. For one, we place strong emphasis on physical fitness with a program of heavy daily exercise before beginning the day's activity. The girls go a little further with the fitness program and include physical fitness testing three times yearly. We find this encourages greater daily effort because the girls are aiming for better scores with each testing, whereas the boys' incentive lies in the anticipation of varsity sports.

Another phase of classwork is the aim for proficiency in the kind of activity that will give our students a physical, social and mental outlet after they leave the protection of an all-deaf environment for one in which they must find a common ground for integrating with the hearing world. In most instances, individual type sports fit this need. The girls' program emphasizes bowling, tennis, and some recreational type activities such as ping pong, badminton, and dancing in various forms. The boys concentrate on bowling, chess, weight lifting, and ping pong.

Team sports also have an important place in our program and we offer soccer, volleyball, softball, and basketball for both boys and girls. The boys add football.

Up to this point, each teacher has fulfilled the Austin Public Schools requirements for teaching five classes per day plus any extracurricular work. Our students' free time activities take three forms.

First, both boys and girls are offered a full intramural program. In general this is directed, managed and officiated by members of the Boys' Athletic Association for the boys' program and members of the Girls' Athletic Association for the girls' program. Each organization is under the direction of one man and one woman teacher and the program is available for volunteer membership from the freshman level up.

Second is the boys' varsity sports program of football, basketball, and track, each of which is coached by one of the three men teachers.

To balance the boys' varsity schedule, the girls are offered an opportunity to compete for places in the marching Rangerettes, who head the spirit activities for the whole school. This requires proficiency in marching skill and special skills in drumming, twirling, cheerleading, and drum majoring—all an outgrowth of classroom work but continued through the year in free time work after school. This group is under the direction of the third woman teacher.

The entire program has evolved out of a situation close to ideal. We have an administration that is in accord with the aims of physical education, a business office that has been generous in providing our equipment, and facilities and an adequate staff of trained personnel. Our only complaint is the need for teaching space through the winter months in an outgrown gymnasium, but even that is included in the administrative planning for the future building—hopefully before this teacher retires.

On the surface, this is a pretty picture of a near perfect teaching position, but this program has developed to this level only within the last few years through patient planning and just plain salesmanship. Each year, in united effort, our staff tries to establish at least one major improvement in our program. These projects have included:

1. An accreditation of physical education grades to be counted toward the honor roll and graduation credit which we had to "sell" to academic department and administration (meaning that we have a strong enough program to *justify* such a project.)

2. A spirit drive in loyalty and respect for the school which we sold the Rangerettes who in turn sold it to the student body and parents.

3. A project which I'm particularly enthusiastic about at the moment, an effort toward improving the sports vocabulary and language of our girls. After three years preparation, I have just finished an illustrated Sports Diction-ary for girls in one more attempt to give more sports knowledge to our girls. This book is being printed by our Vocational Department and will be off the press within the next few days.

Physical education is a product that each of our staff firmly believes in, but like any other product, it has to be advertised and sold to the parents and administration before any real progress can be made professionally. This means that any PE teacher has to dig for new ideas, keep up with what is new and developing in our profession, and have his aims and goals firmly in mind. Then see to it that these aims, supported by facts, get before the Parent-Teacher Association, the school administration, the school newspaper, and your booster clubs. Then the job of improving the general PE program is half won. The other half, of course, is "merely" hard work, imagination, self improvement, and a willingness to work toward our goals.

IX. Language Development: the Vital Component

LANGUAGE DEVELOPMENT AT THE PRIMARY LEVEL*

LUCILE TAYLOR

Language is a tool used to express man's inner thoughts, his feelings, his experiences. Webster defines language as "any means, vocal or other, of expressing or communicating feeling or thought. . . ."

The infant absorbs ideas from the inflections of the voices around him. As he grows a little older he begins to realize that certain words or expressions mean certain things. He begins to use these words in his spoken language. By trial and error he develops the correct verbal expressions to fit the correct situations. In other words, as he understands or comprehends language, he begins to be able to express his thoughts, his feelings and his experiences by means of spoken language. After several years of hearing spoken language day after day and of using this spoken language, as far as he can, he begins to be able to read, and then to write. The hearing child acquires the ability to

* Reprinted by courtesy of *The Wisconsin Times*, Wisconsin School for the Deaf, Delavan, March, 1964. A paper read before a group of Milwaukee area parents of deaf children. The author is from the Wisconsin School for the Deaf.

read by relating what the word looks like to what it sounds like. From now on, the child, through his formative years on into adulthood, will use language in reading for learning and in reading for pleasure; he will use language in communication with his family, his friends, his teachers, his fellow workers. Through its use depends his ability to lead a happy, well-adjusted and self-sufficient life.

The child who has been deaf from infancy has a marked retardation in all aspects of language. When he has not been able to hear all the spoken language that goes on around him, his desire to express himself, to understand what is going on around him, is thwarted. When we understand this, we can understand the temper tantrums, the sullen behavior, the expressed unhappiness that are often the behavior of some deaf children. Further, the deaf child's ability to understand reading and written language is seriously retarded. Since the natural development of language has been disrupted and delayed by deafness, it is necessary for the child to acquire verbal systems by some other means. And it is there where the education of the deaf is most specialized in techniques.

From the deaf child's beginning year in school until he has completed his last year of formal education, his teachers will work toward the development of the language skills needed in speech, lipreading, social studies, arithmetic, art, in all subject areas. His language teachers will, of necessity, present a great deal of formalized drill on language principles. They will utilize pupil experiences, interests, and needs in order to develop these language principles into natural language that is spontaneous and meaningful.

Most often the deaf child comes to school with no vocabulary at all. During the beginning year of school the deaf child will learn the names of the people he knows, or the objects with which he has contact, and the verbs which he will need to describe his daily experiences. These will not be many in comparison with the experience of a hearing child; however, he must know them well and make them a part of himself before he can go on to the next step. The hearing child has an oral vocabulary of 2500 to 4000 words when he enters school. This gives him a ready reference for learning reading and written language. The average deaf child will learn in his first year in school perhaps only 150 nouns, ten or twelve adjectives, about ten verbs and, as the occasion arises, about ten phrases or words that are described as *where* or *when*. He must have contact with a word at least sixty times before he knows it, or before

he has mastered it. At the same time he is learning to use this vocabulary in meaningful sentences in order to describe his everyday experiences. It takes a deaf child longer to master language principles and to acquire vocabulary, and it takes the skill of a trained teacher to develop the ability of the deaf child to communicate in meaningful sentences.

We use, in our Wisconsin school and classes for the deaf, a visual guide, or aid, to develop correct and natural language structure that is called the Fitzgerald Key. Through the use of the Key, the young deaf child is helped to say and write sentences such as:

I skipped.
I ran.
John fell.
John cried.
I was sorry.
I saw a movie.
I saw a movie yesterday.
I saw a movie downtown yesterday.

A great deal of time passes and a great amount of practice takes place between the time the child can say, lipread, read, and write the first sentence and the last sentence.

As he progresses in the primary department and has need for more complicated sentences with which to express himself, his teachers will develop the Key further. As a rule, because of the need for much repetition, the Key develops quite slowly. During the second year the possessive case and the indirect object are added. At about the child's third year in the primary department he begins to want to use sentences telling *how much, from, for,* and *with,* and so the fifth column of the Key is added. During the next two years, the need will arise for further development of this column, until it is complete, and with its help he can use such sentences as:

> The squirrel took the nuts from the porch.
> Jane bought some oranges for Mrs. Spence.
> Tom went to the doctor's with Mr. Ecker yesterday.
> The basketball team went to Clinton in the school station wagon.
> The Boy Scouts stopped where they had camped before.

Nonlanguage rules will be developed and drilled upon as needed. They are at this level of their schooling, for example:

> How many: What:
> How many: What kind: What:
> How many: What color: What:
> How many: What kind: What color: What:

The teacher will, from the very beginning, encourage the child to use the Key and the nonlanguage rules as a means of correcting his own language. As his visual memory of these rules and as his understanding of the rules increase, he will become more able to do his own correction.

Language teachers will use different approaches in teaching language principles. There is no one correct method for all teachers. One will use one technique, another a different technique, and both are correct as long as they arrive at the same good results. It is not so much the method used as the enthusiasm of the teacher for the method she has chosen

that results in success. However, they all will have to drill and drill on the same things, things that a hearing child hears and absorbs effortlessly from his babyhood, as: *black and white shoes* not *white and black shoes, a red, white and blue flag* not *a white, blue and red flag.* Something that is very important to stress from the very beginning of a deaf child's education is the idea that there is more than one way of saying the same thing, as with the words *immediately, right now, at once.* Also, the idea that there is more than one meaning for many words. As with the word *like,* one may state affection or one may compare. When the teacher of the deaf teaches the meaning of the command "Put out the light," she must be careful that when the child goes home and is told by his mother to "Put out the cat," the child does not extinguish the cat. Further, in order that the deaf child use colorful and idiomatic language, his teachers will have to use formal, prepared lessons to teach expressions such as *run a race, run the electric train,* and sixty other idiomatic uses of the word *run.*

The teacher of the deaf child will make use of any and all experiences the child has in order that he can use these language principles. Another period during his school day is set aside for what is called original language. It is at this time that the child is encouraged to tell and write about his experiences. The teacher will have to lead the child to do this at first. She may use dramatization, picture-drawings, or any method she can conceive to show the child something she did; she will then develop this into a speech, a lipreading, a reading, and a language lesson. Through her performance she will encourage the child to tell, through any means he can, an experience of his own. Or, she may provide an experience for the child, then show the child how to express the action he performed. After much repetition the child will become able to use verbal language to tell of his experiences. Through much emphasis on vocabulary and the language skills he will become able to describe what he did on the playground, what he did after school, what he did over the weekend, about a party he attended, about an assembly program he saw or in which he participated, etc. He learns to write postcards, letters and thank-you notes. The purpose of this, as you can readily see, is to encourage the child's ability to communicate with others about what he saw, what he did, what happened, and how he felt. Teaching communication, then, is the primary object of the teacher of the deaf.

It is hoped, also, that through discussions before and after these experiences, your deaf child will be encouraged to establish good social attitudes and behavior patterns. The disciplines of sharing, of taking turns, of personal hygiene, of care of equipment, of respect for property, or respect for authority, of safety rules, and of the breaking of undesirable habits will be a part of his educational growth.

Do not forget that not all children can travel the academic road at the same rate of speed. Some will progress faster than others; some will at various levels need as much as, or more than, another full school year of presentation and drill in order to be able to use the skills needed before starting the next step. Some deaf children may have other disabilities, such as specific language disorders in addition to the language handicap resulting from deafness. These children may learn little or no symbolic language. They may not progress beyond the stage of using only concrete words. They may be unable to form concepts or get abstract ideas from combinations of words, or abstract words may hinder their progress in language development. These children may have great difficulty with speech, written language, lipreading, reading and fingerspelling.

In spite of all this intensive training, of the willingness of your deaf child's teachers to enter into all aspects, educational and social, of your child's growing years, he will not have reached the educational level of his hearing brother or sister after the same number of years in school. However, if you, his parents, as well as his teachers, can use infinite patience, seize upon any and all methods available to communicate to the child the ideas, the thoughts, the understanding he will need to adjust on a level required for a world made up of both deaf and hearing people, he will be well on his way to becoming a competent and well-adjusted adult.

HELPING THE DEAF CHILD TOWARD ADEQUATE LANGUAGE AND SPEECH*

Boris V. Morkovin

An irreparable loss occurs to a deaf child in the years in which he fails to use language actively and adequately for communicating, learning, reasoning, persuading, and being persuaded. The child's brain has a specified capacity for learning language, a capacity which decreases with the passage of years.

The development of brain-potential depends on the individual's timely and adequate development of language. Scientists know that the solution of the complex problems of our technological era demands that a larger proportion of the population learn the symbols of language at a high level. Yet an important segment of our children—the severely hearing-impaired—is unable to fully utilize its brain-potential because of speech and language deficiency.

The authorities of the English language and members of the Council for Basic Education and of the National Science Foundation strongly emphasize our children's need for better mastery of our native language. In the same

* Reprinted with permission from the *Journal of Rehabilitation*, official publication of the National Rehabilitation Association, May–June, 1963, Vol. 29, No. 3, pp. 12–13. This article was based in part on material from Dr. Morkovin's study, "Research Work of the Moscow Institute of Defectology," which was supported by a National Institutes of Health grant, U. S. Department of Health, Education, and Welfare. An earlier paper on this study appeared in the November–December, 1960, issue of the *Journal of Rehabilitation*. B. V. Morkovin is emeritus professor at the University of Southern California.

spirit President Kennedy appeals to scientists, medical doctors, educators, and school boards to search for a "breakthrough" in the habilitation of handicapped children and for development of American talent in general.

In relation to the deaf and severely hard-of-hearing children, the problem goes far beyond the mere salvage of their talents: it is a question of their mental health and future productive life. Deficient or unintelligible speech and poorly developed language in the critical period of a child's growth and development can result in his social isolation, experiential deprivation, and confusion.

Consequently, these children may become doubly handicapped because of emotional disturbance, blocking of learning, and resultant dependency.

To prevent this, the Moscow Institute of Defectology, since 1953, has been vigorously experimenting to find a method of accelerating language learning by young deaf children. In order to utilize maximal potentialities of the deaf child, the Institute has attempted to find a way to enable him (1) to learn an effective language and to think verbally at an early age, and (2) to develop an immediate and full use of this language in his communication and activities.

The Institute's experimenters criticized the old method of teaching the deaf in Russia, which they called the purely oral method, because these two objectives were not achieved by it. The vocabulary the old method taught to deaf children at first was extremely limited by the sounds which they could pronounce and lipread. This vocabulary was not practical for children's daily use nor fit for their communication.

As a result, outside the classroom the children reverted to a primitive language without words—to signs, mimics, and gestures. The range of the children's experience and contacts was thus greatly narrowed, and their minds were not sufficiently stimulated. These children were not prepared for their school study, and experienced delayed development in comparison to normally hearing children of the same age and mental capacity.

The Institute's experimental group of children, aged three to six, learned during three years of the teaching experiment all the words (more than 2,000) necessary for their communication and activities by means of finger (dactyl) spelling. Step by step these dactyl words were converted by special training into oral language which, at first, the children used simultaneously with dactyl in their conversation. Gradually, as their speech became intelligible and their lipreading fluent, the children dropped their fingerspelling and used it only for difficult new words.

The main emphasis of the experimental method is on the dual necessity of reaching the child's brain by continual direct experience with objects and activities (receiving stimuli, called signals of the first system) and

of enabling immediate translation of this sensory and motor experience into words and verbal thinking (signals of the second system).

Soviet scientists experimentally established that the acquisition of language by children changes their intellectual processes and the structure of their behavior; these findings can be compared with those of Jean Piaget of Switzerland. For the deaf child, an effective language becomes his major mechanism of compensation for deafness. Language systematizes in the child's mind the world around him, and establishes a new relationship for him. Language sharpens and guides his sensory facilities. By way of acquired power of influence, the deaf child is able to fill in contextually the words he misses at first in conversation.

With the concerted effort of teachers, parents, and school personnel, an enriched oral environment is created for the child, and he is strongly motivated to communicate orally both in and out of the classroom. He sees concrete results of using spoken words in his play and activities. His morale is boosted by approval, by rewards, by achieving status as an active participant in common enterprises with the family, by playground experiences, by class performances, recitations, and contests.

It is like being plugged into a stimulating life current. In school the child's oral communication and learning are built upon and closely interwoven with his experience from participation in school activities, projects, excursions, observations of nature and plant- and animal-care, acceptance of responsibilities for various duties in school, talking with visitors and play and work contacts with hearing children and adults.

The teacher organizes these activities, provides needed vocabulary and expressions, helps the child to develop concepts of space, time, cause and effect, numbers, measurement, weight, sense of values, and norms of behavior.

In order to facilitate the deaf child's growth into oral environment, various groups—factories, farms, trade unions, and sport clubs—sponsor individual deaf children. The groups take the children out for different events, arrange trips and vacations, follow their progress, give scholarships, and prepare and slowly introduce the children into jobs for which they are found fitted.

Language is not merely a dictionary collection of words; it is an instrument to organize individual behavior. The development of a child's language and thought is a very complex and prolonged process. It is accompanied by the development of behavior patterns needed for the child's adjustment, and is brought about by his encounters with environment. The development of a child's language and thinking enables him to order and to construct reality. Gradually, a hierarchy of operations for processing information and for coping with circumstances is built into the child's mind.

Experimenters at the Institute use all avenues available to accelerate the deaf child's mastery of language by lipreading, auditory training, and tactual, kinesthetic, and rhythmic techniques. To provide the child with an image of complete words needed in talking and thinking, the experimenters recently added to these techniques a visual-kinesthetic method of fingerspelling which serves as a catalyst for all other techniques.

The words spelled by fingers tie together the fragments of words and sounds the child perceives multisensorily. This eventually gives him an exact knowledge of the phonetic composition of words and of the continuity of words and phrases. The verbalized part of the child's experience (second signal system) is associated in his mind with his activities and communication (first signal system). Dactyl brings words and their sequence and meaning to a focus. It gives the teacher a foundation for further work on phonetic, grammatical, and semantic aspects of the child's language. Dactyl also helps him with early reading and writing; he starts the latter on a typewriter.

On the basis of the child's mastery of sufficient vocabulary and his knowledge of the composition and continuity of words, the teacher—by verbal instructions—is able subsequently to enable the child to (1) concentrate his attention on phonetic and other linguistic details, (2) develop his ability to discriminate and analyze these details, and (3) synthesize the elements of his language and experience.

The analytico-synthetic power of the child's brain is thus put into action, and the child is ready to proceed in his formal education. From the experimental group he enters an elementary school for the deaf, and is adequately prepared to follow its program.

Regardless of which side of the controversy on teaching methods we take, we cannot ignore the effects on the preschool deaf child's language development, which have been shown by experiments. We cannot brush these experiments aside by a statement that there is nothing new in their natural or experiential teaching of language, or that the simultaneous use of fingerspelling is our old Rochester Method.

In the light of these experiments we need to re-examine the role of language and speech development of the young deaf child, and the factors which contribute to this. We need to experiment with these variables ourselves under the conditions imposed upon us by the specific characteristics of the English language.*

* In a communication, dated July 10, 1966, Dr. Morkovin elaborates further regarding his study of language growth in preschool deaf children. His statement follows:

"The paper above was written by me more than four years ago. Since that time, I have spent 63 days in the Soviet Union, studying at first hand the methods and procedures of teaching language to nonverbal deaf children. To satisfy numerous inquiries on the subject, I wish to refer to my monograph, to be published in the fall of 1966 by the Department of Special Education of the University of Southern California. This monograph is the summary of my lecture in the "Series of Distinguished Lectures" in Special Education of USC, given by me on the 29th of June 1966. The title is *The Role of Language in the Development of a Preschool Deaf Child.*

"In this monograph I explain the methods and procedures used in teaching preschool deaf children in the Soviet Union. It will also include my interviews with the parents of deaf children who graduated from the Moscow Kindergarten for the Deaf and my conversation with their deaf children, of the age of 8 (second grade). These children started their communication with fingerspelling and approximate speech. At the present time, they use spontaneous oral communication, resorting to fingerspelling only with difficult words and in new situations."

COMMUNICATION PROBLEMS AT THE INTERMEDIATE LEVEL*

Rev. Lawrence C. Murphy

As the deaf child progresses into the Intermediate Level, i.e., 5th, 6th and 7th grades, the language and communication barrier becomes more pronounced as academic subjects become more concentrated. Here at this level the reading problem, which prevails throughout every aspect of the deaf child's education and extends into his

* A paper read before the Zeta Chapter of Mu Sigma Fraternity, Milwaukee, Wis., January 15, 1964. The author is Director of St. John's School for the Deaf, St. Francis, Wisconsin.

adult life, the vocabulary problem, accentuated by the rapid accumulation of new ideas, new experiences and the verbalization of existing concepts, and the problem of paragraph and sentence meaning loom darker and darker on the deaf child's educational horizon.

In the area of speech, educators of the deaf have devoted much time in working for intelligible speech as well as expressive vocabulary. Particularly at the intermediate level, the deaf child's speech more often than not becomes less understandable and in spite of long, tedious hours of work and study, the final picture sadly falls short of the goal.

A deaf child is encouraged to use speech to the best of his ability. But anyone who has been in this field for any length of time at all, knows that there are the few very good, exceptional pupils who excel academically and also speechwise—there are more on the other end of the scale who are the direct opposite, and the greater majority are those who are getting along well enough in classes for the deaf but who are lost in the world with their hearing peers. This is the danger area where teachers and parents often find themselves believing that the deaf child is like any other child except "that he is deaf" and so they expect him to go along in the mainstream of a cool, calculating world. The deaf child is very clever and usually plays this game of pretense, deceiving his teachers and parents even more than they are deceiving themselves. The deaf child is a great pretender and smilingly nods agreement or disagreement even though he does not have the least idea of what is being spoken to him. He takes his cue from facial expressions and learns early in life that this generally carries him successfully through any situation which may arise. If this deaf child is fortunate enough to be placed in a class where the teacher is alert to the pitfalls open to the deaf child's education and is aware of his expert ability to pretend, he will be placed in a group where he will be able to achieve at his potential, keep-

ing in mind his particular needs. He will be asked to repeat what has been said to him and will be questioned in various ways to determine whether he really understands.

To supplement the education of the deaf child, group hearing aids are used in all classes. The chief role of the hearing aid in the classroom is to assist the child in the acquisition of speech and language. Speech places one in a better position for making friends, earning a living, obtaining results and praying. In other words, speech is the thing which gives one the feeling of "belonging." This kind of speech is what we want for our orally trained deaf child. With very few exceptions, the speech of the intermediate deaf child presents a sad but realistic picture. This child has been wearing the group aid all day long for a number of years and has been watching, listening and repeating, seeing the visual pattern on the lips, having it reinforced with hearing and giving it back in speech. Nevertheless, his speech is often unintelligible and lacking in necessary vocabulary. Every child differs in accomplishments and ample opportunity must be given to have each develop to his potential without becoming discouraged, frustrated and rebellious.

Curriculum is defined as all the experiences which people have while under the direction of the school. This would imply that it includes both classroom and extra-classroom activities. It extends much farther than the courses of study which are part of the curriculum organized for classroom use. Therefore, it is necessary to have the child's ability and limitations well in mind and then plan his instruction around a curriculum which will produce a deaf child who is spiritually, intellectually, emotionally, socially and educationally well developed in order that he may take his place in a hearing world as a useful citizen.

I feel the following points are those which hinder the deaf child from achieving the desired goal mentioned above:

1. Content material becomes so great that a strict oral presentation of vocabulary and sentence and paragraph meaning cannot possibly be acquired except in a few exceptional cases.

2. The time element is not available in which long periods can be spent on speech and lipreading as in the primary classes. Hence, vocabulary acquisition falls far short of the vocabulary which appears in academic subjects.

3. Emotional and behavior problems often arise at this level because a deaf child knows that he is not achieving at a grade level expected for his age and he is often bored at the simple material given to him although he cannot achieve on a higher level.

4. Coming to almost a standstill at the fourth- or fifth-grade achievement, this child when "graduated" from eighth grade can't be expected to achieve at a high school level unless given a watered-down program which he will not be slow in recognizing and, in many cases, resenting.

5. An invisible wall begins to grow thicker between the parent and the child and the teacher and the child because he cannot express himself to those who are closest to him. Therefore, he shuts them out of his life and begins to live in a world of fantasy unless he has deaf friends to whom he can unburden himself in a manner that they will understand.

The above points may seem exaggerated and even cruel but the reality is only too evident in too many deaf children who are in our classes today.

In conclusion, I firmly believe that it is in the hands of us teachers and you parents to help the deaf child avoid these all-too-real obstacles to opening a new world for the child who lives in a silent world.

The provisions for surmounting these obstacles may be summed up as follows:

1. Present content material in keeping with the child's interests and level of achievement. This may require teachers to rewrite or simplify materials in order to maintain a high interest level.

2. Permit the child to use any means of expressing himself adequately whether it is the medium of speech, writing, pantomime, gesturing or fingerspelling. This provides for a basic need of all men—self-expression. If a child is constantly suppressed from expressing himself because of inadequate speech, serious emotional and mental problems may arise which may have consequences which will carry over in later life.

3. Meaningful vocabulary should be presented as fast as the child can assimilate it. The child should be ex-

pected to learn to spell the words correctly as well as learn the definitions and then use this same vocabulary in various ways. For example, use the vocabulary in sentences and then mix up the word order and have the child unscramble the sentence and write it in the proper order. The definitions could be given and the vocabulary presented at random to be matched to the definitions. Children also like to unscramble words and then spell them correctly. Many exercises can be thought up by an ingenious teacher who will keep the children's motivational interest at a high pitch and learning will not only become functional but also fun.

4. Time is at a premium at this level and the teacher should select the courses wisely and give definite allotted time to each so that all areas of content may be covered: reading, original language, grammar usage, mathematics, science, and social studies with vocabulary building along with each subject.

If a child has learned to express himself in some manner, regardless of how, he will find true friends in his teachers and parents. Consequently, he will become that well-adjusted individual we all pray and hope that he will become.

SOME LANGUAGE TEACHING TECHNIQUES USED WITH THE PRELINGUALLY DEAF*

MARTHA C. LARSEN

Language is the outcome of man's ability to hear. It is the golden key which opens the door to the world. Without language an individual exists on the level of preverbal man. Thus, the prelingually deaf child can be compared to the preverbal man. Teaching language to these children is the central problem in any school for the deaf; the greatest challenge any teacher of the deaf is ever likely to encounter.

The hearing child from birth onward

is surrounded by sound. Auditory impressions pour in upon him from all directions. He can't escape them. As an infant he relates gross sounds with their related concepts. Later on he relates word sounds to objects, actions, and feelings. Thus the pattern of language evolves. It is all his just for the hearing.

Tests based on a list of words prepared by Thorndike show that at age five the hearing child has a vocabulary of 2,500 words or more. At age five the average deaf child has no vocabulary—no words at all. He generally has no knowledge of names of things, of words to express actions or ideas, or of language to consider ideas. To obtain an education he must first master the forms

* An address before a Speech and Hearing Section of the Special Education Meeting of a State Teachers' Convention, and here reprinted with permission from *The Hoosier,* Indiana School for the Deaf, Indianapolis, December, 1963. The author is with the Upper Primary Department of the Indiana School for the Deaf.

of communication, starting from scratch at age four or five. This poses one of the major educational problems faced by any individual.

The public in general, and all too often the parents of the deaf child himself, have little notion of the difficulties involved. As far as they can see the child can't talk and there is nothing else the matter with him. Give him a hearing aid and speech lessons and the problem is taken care of. They fail to see that the problem of early profound deafness is language and not speech. Speech is not language. Speech conveys language; it is a means of communication.

Since the preponderate number of our youngsters at the Indiana School for the Deaf are prelingually deaf, our program is geared to fit their needs. Now, where do we begin? We begin right at the beginning, just where all children begin, with single words—simple objects in their surroundings such as ball, shoe, car, and the like; also with simple action verbs such as run, jump, fall, and so on. They learn to associate these words in lipreading, in written form, and by using any remnants of hearing they may have with the appropriate action or object.

Then adjectives of size, color, and number are introduced—a red ball, two apples, a big doll, etc. Right away our pupils begin to encounter trouble. Since they learn nouns first, nouns are the important thing in their minds, so they use them first, resulting in a "a ball red," "apples two," "a doll big." In some languages this is all right, but not in the English language.

Before discussing some of our special techniques, I would like to point out a few more difficulties our acoustically handicapped youngsters must surmount along the language path. Word order in using adjectives of size, number, and color has already been mentioned. There are the multiple meanings of common words. The verb *to run* is a very good example. The boy runs fast, the river runs swiftly, Nixon and Kennedy were running for president, when you are frightened your blood runs cold, your nose runs when you have a cold, you have a run in your stocking and you run out of sugar when you make a cake.

All of us are familiar with our many irregular verbs. Let us take the verb *to be*. There are am, are, is, was and were —all to be remembered and used correctly. In the past tense the final consonant is doubled in some verbs. In others the "y" becomes "i." No rule seems to hold fast. The past tense of *to pet* is petted. The past tense of *to get* is got— not getted. And the verb *to read* is spelled the same in both tenses but pronounced differently.

As if all this isn't enough, we have an interesting variety of plurals. The plural of mouse is mice. The plural of house is houses—not hice. The dog is covered with hair, but when he takes a nap on your sofa he leaves hairs behind him. You eat bacon and eggs although on your plate you may have two eggs and three strips of bacon. You eat corn, but you have corns on your feet.

In spite of all this our deaf pupil is a brave little fellow. If he doesn't know exactly what to say he goes right ahead and says it anyway, and often makes very good sense. Describing her new dress a pupil of mine once referred to the cuff as the sleeve-collar. Not a bad analogy. Another pupil told his teacher he raked leaves until the sun set down and still another boy said that he practised his tracks. He was obviously getting ready for a track meet. Here again we encounter the confusion of multiple meanings. Perhaps it is the youngster's eagerness and willingness to try, and try again, in the face of all the confusing forms and idioms that make us as successful as we are in our language teaching.

As I have already indicated the deaf child has no idea of word order. The problem we face is how a knowledge of language can be imparted to him. The natural channel for acquiring language is through the ear. Since this channel is closed to the deaf child a substitute channel must be provided.

Down through the years more than a dozen systems have been devised and used to teach language to deaf children. No matter what each system was called, all of them dealt with the same basic idea—how to teach word order to deaf children. A great many of these systems have long since been discarded. The main ones still in use in schools for the deaf today are the Barry Five-Slate System, Wing's Symbols, and the Fitzgerald Key which we use in the Indiana School for the Deaf.

I will explain and illustrate two of these methods. The Fitzgerald Key was evolved by Edith Fitzgerald, a congenitally deaf woman. Her idea was that language could not be just memo-

rized. The child must have a guide to find and correct his own mistakes. The Key acts as a sentence pattern guide in much the same way the ear is a guide for the hearing. As I have said, all these methods are intended as substitute channels for the nonfunctioning ear.

Wing's Symbols were devised in 1883 by George Wing, a teacher in the Minnesota School for the Deaf. The symbols consist of letters and numbers representing functions of the different parts of speech. Some of the advantages claimed for this method are that the symbols are simple to learn and easy to remember, that they can be used right on the child's paper without special lines or columns and that they are flexible. Any part of speech can be used anywhere in the sentence and retain its identity by simply placing the appropriate symbol above it.

In addition to these methods used to structure language is a set of four books familiar to almost every teacher of the deaf, the Croker, Jones and Pratt *Language Stories and Drills*. They first appeared in 1920, but in spite of their age are still used in many of our leading schools, including Clarke School for the Deaf in Northampton, Mass., and our own school here in Indiana. These books provide a systematic course of language instruction. The weekly lesson revolves around a story and several drill lessons on new points. The stories are cumulative—each teaching new principles and reviewing old ones. The ingenious teacher is free to enrich and enlarge upon these lessons. In fact they have a sort of "open end" structure which lends itself to enrichment.

In conclusion, I want to add that no matter what the method or system used it is the devoted and dedicated teacher behind the system who determines its final success.

THE REVIVAL OF THE ROCHESTER METHOD*

WILLIAM J. McCLURE

In late February, the superintendent visited the Louisiana School for the Deaf. The purpose of the visit was to observe firsthand the effects of supplementing speech and lipreading with fingerspelling as a medium of communication for deaf children, a procedure now being emphasized at all levels of the Louisiana School from kindergarten or beginning classes upward. The Louisiana School, among others, believes that lipreading alone is not a satisfactory receptive medium for the instruction of deaf children. Lipreading presents to the eyes of the deaf child only a series of "key words" which in themselves do not constitute a complete English sentence. This is much the same criticism which can be leveled at the sign language, so widely used among the deaf themselves. Thus, a deaf child relying solely upon lipreading or upon the sign language will see only the broken patterns of English offered by key words or by signs. As a result, he will tend to imitate in his own language, be it written or spoken, the patterns which he has observed.

* A report reprinted by consent of the author from *The Hoosier,* Indiana School for the Deaf, Indianapolis, April, 1964. Dr. McClure, then Superintendent of that school, is now President of the Florida School for the Deaf and the Blind.

The most widely known exponent of the use of fingerspelling as a supplement to lipreading was Dr. Zenas F. Westervelt, former superintendent of the Rochester (N. Y.) School for the Deaf. He originated this method, later known as the Rochester Method, there in 1878. Edward L. Scouten, principal of the Louisiana School and a former teacher at Rochester, is a thorough student of the Rochester Method. He has for many years been a strong advocate for the revival of this method and has recently put it into effect at the Louisiana School.

The school for the deaf in Rochester has continued to use Dr. Westervelt's method and in recent years three or four additional schools have adopted "The Rochester Method"; however, some have not used the method with the very young deaf child but have commenced supplementing speech and lipreading with fingerspelling at possibly the 3rd, 4th, or 5th year in school. To advocates of the Rochester Method, this is entirely too late as the imperfect patterns of language developed through lipreading and/or out-of-classrooms signs will have been established before the patterns of correct English which can be secured through early use of the Rochester Method. The Louisiana

School is the only one known to be attempting this approach so completely from the beginning classes upward both in and out of the classroom.

The Rochester Method should not be considered a manual method any more than would be writing on the blackboard. According to Dr. James H. Galloway, superintendent of the Rochester School, it is no more manual than oral. It is unique in that it utilizes the manual alphabet and speech simultaneously to develop both the language and the speech of the deaf. Dr. Galloway points out that it lays great stress upon reading, and its effectiveness depends upon (1) the consistent use of English either spelled on the fingers, spoken or written; (2) a strong supporting program of speech and speechreading, and (3) the complete elimination of the language of signs.

Dr. Alexander Graham Bell was undoubtedly the best known supporter of oral instruction of the deaf. He once stated, "I must say that I think that oral teachers are unnecessarily afraid of the manual alphabet. So far as I am concerned I see no objection to any child, deaf or hearing, spelling English words upon his fingers."

At the Louisiana School for the Deaf, teachers, houseparents, the school staff from administration through dietary and domiciliary departments, emphasize the use of fingerspelling to supplement speech and to fill in the broken language patterns visible to deaf children through lipreading. The child continues to read the lips but the gaps which appear in the language patterns of speech as seen by the child are filled

in with the correct grammatical forms which he sees spelled out in English on the hand. Having this opportunity to see English, the deaf child has a greater opportunity to learn it completely and correctly.

Throughout the Louisiana School, one sees cards and slogans encouraging the use of English spoken, written, fingerspelled, as a medium of communication. Among the signs observed were the following:

English is our language, use it.
Poor English is better than no English.
Write, fingerspell, speak.
The deaf child imitates and learns.
What are you teaching him?
Deaf children must see English to learn English.
Signing cheats deaf children of language-learning opportunities.

As one walks about the school, he observes painted signs all over the campus to help the deaf child learn the names or words for what he sees. He sees the word "sidewalk" at frequent intervals on the walkways. As he starts to enter a building, he sees at the top of each rise the word step-step-step. By the iron grating on the sidewalk appears the word "drain." On the playground apparatus appear words such as barrel, slide, swing and so on. On the front of Mr. Scouten's desk is the word desk. Everywhere the deaf child looks, he has the opportunity to acquire a vocabulary which can then be developed into language.

Under this constant emphasis of fingerspelling, the pupils themselves have acquired a pride in their ability to use English. It is now considered a status symbol. The child who does not know the proper word to use in communication feels embarrassment. Complete sentences are used in fingerspelling, writing on the blackboard and in speech. One of the most remarkable results of this emphasis on the use of fingerspelling is the marked decrease in the use of the sign language in the Louisiana School, something which many experienced educators of the deaf would believe impossible in a large residential school where this had been the established out-of-school medium of communication for years.

To develop facility in the simultaneous use of speech and fingerspelling by teachers and staff members not accustomed to, or familiar with, fingerspelling, a member of the faculty has developed a series of lesson plans to develop skill in both receptive and expressive uses of fingerspelling. These use syllable and word drills much as they would be used in the teaching of lipreading skills; i.e., the drill may be on the word or syllable "an"—and the drill may include words such as ban, can, dan, fan, man, nan, pan, ran, tan. Another might be "id"—bid, cid, did, kid, rid, etc.

The same thing is done with prefixes and suffixes—to build up speed and comprehension in use and recognition. This observer had not previously seen such a carefully planned approach to fingerspelling so extensively used with the members of a school staff.

As for classroom results, it was the feeling of the observers that there was a subdued excitement among the teachers. While not all were thoroughly convinced of the advantages of the Rochester Method, the great majority were. They felt language was being taught and used correctly and in much greater quantity and quality than had ever been achieved before at L.S.D. In observing the work of the classes throughout the school, one could not help but feel that this was true. Children who entered the school in September were using complete sentences, fingerspelled and spoken, and were using more complex sentences than are generally expected of children with considerably more educational exposure. As byproducts, one noticed an absence of the hesitancy in writing sentences on the board after they were fingerspelled and spoken. The children had a feeling for the proper word order and the proper spelling of words. Consequently, the written work was both quick and remarkably accurate. There was also a tendency for all of the children to pay attention all of the time to the teacher or to the child reciting. Deaf children in many oral classes where fingerspelling is not used as a supplementary means of communication have a tendency to let their attention wander when they are not receiving the individual and direct attention of the teacher. In most of the classes in the Louisiana School, all of the children were paying attention all of the time even during individual speech instruction. As the teacher spoke and spelled the symbols from the Northampton Charts or spoke words and spelled them simultaneously, all of the children in the class were repeating orally and in fingerspelling what the teacher was saying.

While the experiment is new, the observers had a feeling that there is much to be learned from observation of the carefully planned revival of the Rochester Method as being used at the Louisiana School for the Deaf. Those planning the program for the next meeting of the American Instructors of the Deaf would do well to consider demonstrations and discussions by children and staff members from the Louisiana School.

PROGRAMED INSTRUCTION IN WRITTEN LANGUAGE FOR THE DEAF*

E. Ross Stuckless and Jack W. Birch†

Teachers of deaf children must all be teachers of language. This reflects awareness of the profound effect of auditory deprivation upon expressive and receptive communication. The achievement of linguistic skill by deaf children varies greatly, even under the best teaching. Speech ranges from total unintelligibility through near perfection. Written language shows similar variance. Myklebust (1960) found the deaf to be significantly inferior to the hearing in syntax, sentence length, and abstract thought. On sentence length, considered a valid criterion of written language skill, Myklebust reported the mean sentence length of eleven-year-old deaf children to be 4.98 words and of eleven-year-old hearing children, 12.09 words.

The young deaf child is taught language systematically through one of two approaches. The more common is a highly formalized method, a grammatic approach. The Fitzgerald System, Wing Symbols, and Barry Five Slate, in use for many years, are varieties of a formal method. A second approach, a natural method, simulates normal language development with much less structure than a formal method. Language is taught when the child manifests need for communication. No conclusive research evidence is available supporting one method over the other. Indeed, research on written language and instructional provisions for its development in deaf children is virtually nonexistent.

There has been a recent surge of interest in programed instruction among many educators of the deaf. Two standard sources of information on programing are Lumsdaine and Glaser (1960) and Stolurow (1961). Written language instruction for deaf children is compatible with programing for sev-

* A report appearing in *Exceptional Children*, official publication of The Council for Exceptional Children, Washington, D. C., March 1964, and reprinted here with permission. Portions of this article were presented by Dr. Stuckless at the CEC section program of the annual meeting of the American Association for the Advancement of Science, Philadelphia, Pennsylvania, December, 1962.

† Dr. Stuckless is assistant professor, department of special education and rehabilitation, and Dr. Birch is associate dean, both of the School of Education, University of Pittsburgh, Pennsylvania.

eral reasons: Programed instruction lends itself to a formal method as practised by most teachers of the deaf; it is primarily a visual mode of instruction, appropriate to written language; since it is a visual medium, deaf children are not handicapped by a lack of audition. These values are in addition to those demonstrated for programed instruction in the nonhandicapped population.

A difficulty remains. Because deaf children do not have a strong natural oral language basis on which to build written language, teachers of the deaf use a great deal of pantomime, acting, and other contrived experiences to establish language. Programed instruction permits no such freedom. Another alternative, more useful in programing, is to employ pictorial cues. Falconer (1960) used pictures within a program format to teach a reading vocabulary. Results supported his hypothesis that reading vocabulary could be established in this way.

A program of research in the special education and rehabilitation of the deaf has been initiated at the University of Pittsburgh. This is a report on some aspects of the first investigations in the program, all concerned with the written language of the deaf.

The First Study, A Pilot

The first investigation was a pilot study conducted at the Western Pennsylvania School for the Deaf to determine whether written vocabulary could be established in a manner similar to that employed by Falconer (1960). Another purpose was to determine the most appropriate response mode for optimum learning. Results of the pilot study were positive. The findings led the investigators to the studies reported below concerned with programing as a technique for instructing deaf children in language.

The Second Study, Comparing Programed Instruction and Conventional Instruction

This investigation was conducted at the University of Pittsburgh with the support of a grant under Title VII, NDEA, United States Office of Education. It examined the relative effects of programed instruction and conventional instruction on the acquisition of written language by young deaf children (Birch and Stuckless, 1962, 1963a).

Six schools for the deaf (four residential and two day) participated in the study. Ninety-nine children from thirteen classes constituted the sample. The mean age of these children was 10.3 years. A program was prepared which after revision consisted of 534 frames. Contained within the program were seven verbs, four of which were irregular, three predicate adjectives, three comparative adjectives, four predicate nominatives, and twenty-seven nouns. These five language variables were considered to be appropriate to the population and to constitute approximately one month's formal language instruction to deaf children of normal mental ability and language level.

Preparing the Program

The program was of the linear type, requiring each student to follow the same frame sequence. A vanishing technique was employed, succeeding frames removing cues gradually until only the pictorial cues incorporated into every frame remained. The terminal behavior sought was that a student having received the full instruction should be able to write full descriptive sentences correctly, using the language principles in the program content. Constructed written responses were therefore mandatory.

The program was divided at logical points into twenty units, each unit varying between twenty-four frames and thirty-one frames and comprising a single day's instruction. Review and drills were employed where they seemed indicated. Since the terminal behavior sought was that students be able to write full sentences, 62 per cent of the total frames required full sentence responses.

Since a picture can elicit a wide variety of responses, a means of control was necessary. For instance, a picture of a boy swimming might bring such responses as, "A boy is swimming across the river," "David can do the backstroke," or "The water is much too cold for swimming." A second reason for controlling responses is technical. Programing requires reinforcement. Even the most complex device would be unable to give reinforcement to

such a variety of responses. A set of nonverbal symbols was therefore incorporated into the program as cues. This system utilized what is known as the Fitzgerald Key (Fitzgerald, 1949), used to assist a child in correctly ordering a sentence.

The Fitzgerald Key was developed as part of the Fitzgerald System to assist deaf children in ordering parts of speech and structural units in the English language. The child may first be taught words classified under "who" or "what." (He will in time be taught that words classified under "whose," etc., precede "who" and "what.") The teacher will then proceed to teach the child that the verb (indicated by the symbol $=$), the predicate nominative $(-)$, and the predicate adjective $(\frown)$ follow. The Key is expanded to accommodate the indirect and direct objects, adverbial phrases, and the like. An abbreviated Key might appear as follows:

Who:		What:	Whom:
Whose:	$=$ $=$	( )	Whose:
What:		Whom:	What:

A self-instructional device or teaching machine was specially constructed for the experiment. One window revealed a picture. A written cue and/or Fitzgerald Key symbols were presented in a second window. This cue represented a part of speech or a full sentence. The child observed the pictorial, written, and Key cues and wrote his response in a third window. To verify his responses he tripped a shutter which revealed the correct answer. If in error, he repeated the operation. If correct, he proceeded to the next frame.

The Procedure

Conferences were held with the thirteen teachers of the classes. Manuals were prepared which described the language which they would be asked to teach. No restrictions were placed on the teachers in terms of the conventional methods to be used.

Each class was divided randomly into two approximately equal groups: a control group of forty-seven subjects to be conventionally instructed by the teacher and an experimental group of fifty-two subjects to be program-instructed by the teacher. The two groups in each class were separated for only the formal language period. The control group received a constant forty-five minutes of conventional language instruction daily. The experimental group time was determined by the average amount of time taken to complete each day's program. The experiment lasted twenty school days. Records were maintained by the teachers.

At the conclusion of the experimental period, the ninety-nine subjects of the two groups were tested. The test consisted of writing fifty sentences, large illustrations serving as stimuli. These illustrations had different content from those prepared for the programs.

Findings

The children learned under both experimental and control conditions. The experimental group arrived at the same level of achievement as the control in less than half the time, a difference significant at the one per cent level of confidence. The efficiency of learning by programed instruction was clearly demonstrated. This is particularly noteworthy in light of the fact that the teachers were instructing only one-half the number of children in their usual classes, thus being able to devote more time to each child than under ordinary conditions. The investigation demonstrated that the full sentence response represents an excellent response mode when the explicit object is to teach grammatic constructions. The ten-year-old deaf child was shown to be capable of correcting full sentence responses independently.

Interviews with the thirteen teachers revealed a general enthusiasm for programing and brought forth several suggestions for its improvement. Some teachers remarked that the sequencing of words required in the program had transferred to better word order in the spontaneous language of the children. Vocabulary transferred readily into vernacular language, in the teachers' judgments. Interest of the experimental group remained high, particularly among many of the slow learning children. Negative reactions centered around statements that the language learned through programed instruction was transferring adversely into spontaneous language; that the present progressive tense, for instance, was being used exclusively by some children of the experimental group. The verb "be," as experimental subjects learned to use it, began to be used frequently at inappropriate times, particularly when the verb "have" should have been used.

Such transfer, both positive and negative, has a specific implication for language instruction. Much language requires rote learning. To objects, emotions, and experiences are attached symbols. These symbols collectively may be called vocabulary. Langer (1942) separates symbols and signs by stating that symbols, unlike signs, are attached to their referents quite arbitrarily. The pairing of a symbol with its referent, then, is a task of rote learning. Word order, too, requires rote learning, as those who study foreign languages well know. If only the mechanics of language are programed, then, a significant proportion of the language required for communication is represented.

The general conclusion of this investigation might be summarized as supporting the application of programed instruction to the development of language in young deaf children, a particular strength being in those elements of language requiring rote learning. The task of the teacher of language becomes more specialized, employing programed instruction to establish certain language skills and constructing optimally functional communication from them.

The Third Study, Programed Instruction and the Correction of the Written Language of Deaf Adolescents

While the conclusions of the earlier studies point to the feasibility of programing instruction to establish correct written language in the young deaf child, what of the adolescent and adult deaf in whom language has already been established? Will the errors, sometimes referred to as "deafisms" because of their typical nature, yield also to programing? This question was the basis for an investigation supported by a second grant under Title VII, NDEA, United States Office of Education (Birch and Stuckless, 1963b).

The following excerpt from a composition may serve to illustrate several errors typically made by deaf adolescents. This illustration was selected because it has within it several characteristic errors.

The boys went to ride old car in village. They are name Bobby, Jim and Rudy. Rudy told two boys come on, go the ride old car the around in village.

Many of the errors in the language of the deaf student are errors of rote learning. In the above illustration there was no logical reason for using "went riding" rather than "went to ride." The child must simply learn the rule governing the correct choice. The above paragraph conveys information, but the information is not clear because of the numerous grammatic errors. One may be sure that this student's teachers have taught the correct use of the article, the passive voice, and the preposition. Furthermore, the errors he has made have been corrected many times for him. Yet they remain. They resist extinction.

Mandler (1954) demonstrated that such errors can be reduced by increased practice in the inhibited skill.

Presumably, then, syntax can be corrected through controlled practice, particularly under adequate conditioning conditions. Ferster (1960) investigated the effect of repeated presentations of a program. No additional learning took place when the subject repeated the same program. This program was intended to establish comprehension, however, and it is contended that his results do not hold for rote learning. The use of drills, for example, can lead to improved arithmetic facts. Drills are based on repetition to induce overlearning. With the common errors in written language identified, programs can be established aimed at eradicating them and, further, aimed at substituting correct expressions. Such programs having been developed, can errors be reduced and correct grammar established? Are these errors subject to conditioning, and if so, what will be the effect of repeated presentations of the same program?

Analysis of Errors

Prior to the development of programs for this study, it was necessary to select appropriate program content. Compositions were collected from approximately 500 adolescent deaf students in Connecticut, Ohio, Pennsylvania, Tennessee, and West Virginia. These compositions were analyzed in terms of the frequency with which various parts of speech are used, and an analysis of specific errors was made.

On the basis of these analyses, ten areas were selected for programing. These were: verb tense, verb agreement, "to be" and "to have," verb omis-

sions, auxiliary verbs, infinitives, articles, prepositions, conjunctions, and noun number.

Instructional Material

Ten programs were developed around the ten grammatic errors identified in the preliminary study. Grammar rules, intelligible to deaf students, were prepared. For instance, for verb tense the rule was stated that "all verbs show time." Several such rules were formulated to guide the student in the application of the correct tense. The programs were then prepared utilizing these rules and providing many examples. Deaf adolescents were selected from the Pittsburgh area for a total of 200 trial sittings. The programs were twice revised as a result of information gained at these sittings. These programs were linear in design, requiring elliptical responses. Length of the programs after revision varied from forty to sixty-seven frames.

A sample of five frames taken from one such program follows. In this instance, those verbs which were observed most frequently to be in error were incorporated in the program. As several frames appear on each page, written instructions in the book advise the student that he is to work *across* the book, *not down* the page. He is directed to write the missing word or words on a sheet of lined paper, then turn the page of the book and read the correct answer. After checking his answer, he proceeds to the next question, which is adjacent to the answer for the preceding question. When he has completed the first frame appearing on each page of the book, he returns to page one and completes the second frame on each page. This procedure is followed until he has completed all six frames appearing on each page.

RULE 5

41. We know that *most* words end with *"ed"* in the *past* tense, but some words in the past tense do *not* end with "ed." *Some* words are made differently in the *past* tense.

42. | Past | Present | Future |
|------|---------|--------|
| "went" | "go" | "will go" are verb tenses. |
| "got" | "get" | "will get" are verb tenses. |

Write the verbs in the *past tense:*
I (*go*) to the movies last night.
Mary (*get*) a new sweater for her birthday.

42. went
got

43. | Past | Present | Future |
|------|---------|--------|
| "saw" | "see" | "will see" |
| "left" | "leave" | "will leave" |

Write the verbs in the *past tense:*
We (*see*) an exciting game last week.
The boys (*leave*) their house early in the morning.

43. saw
left

44. | Past | Present | Future |
|------|---------|--------|
| "came" | "come" | "will come" |
| "rode" | "ride" | "will ride" |

Write the verbs in the *past tense:*
My friends (*come*) to visit me yesterday.
I (*ride*) a big white horse last summer.

44. came
rode

45. | Past | Present | Future |
|------|---------|--------|
| "ate" | "eat" | "will eat" |
| "ran" | "run" | "will run" |

Write the verbs in the *past tense:*
I (*eat*) bacon and eggs for breakfast.
John (*run*) to see his friends.

Two forms of each program were constructed. These two forms differed in one way only. One form presented first the rule, then examples; the other form presented examples followed by the rule. Experimental use of the ten former programs and the ten latter programs was intended to provide data on the relative influence of the deductive and the inductive method in programed instruction.

Population and Procedure

A total of seven schools participated in the experimental phase of this investigation. Residential and day schools in Connecticut, Michigan, New Jersey, Ohio and Pennsylvania were represented. Students of three schools served as a control group totalling 105 subjects. Students of two schools served as a first experimental group of fifty-seven subjects, and students of the two remaining schools served as a second experimental group of fifty-two subjects. The mean age of the 214 subjects was 17.0 years, and mean hearing impairment in the speech range was seventy-eight decibels.

The first experimental group received two different programs each week for a period of five weeks. On Mondays the subjects wrote compositions. When possible, those programs which were assigned to the subjects followed directly from errors noted in the compositions; for example, the program on articles was assigned to a subject who omitted an article unless that program had already been assigned during a preceding week. Subjects in this group were taught conventionally over a full six-month experimental period. The programed instruction during the first five weeks was additional to conventional instruction.

The second experimental group received programed instruction at the rate of two programs each week for a full six-month period. On Mondays compositions were written. The first two grammatic errors for which programs had been developed were underlined by the teacher, and these two programs assigned to the subject. It is conceivable that a given subject might receive the same program each week for up to six months. As with the first experimental group, conventional language instruction was given in addition to programed instruction for the full six-month period.

The control group was taught conventionally over the six-month period, and no restrictions were placed upon the teacher as to methods of instruction other than that programed instruction not be employed.

Two independent criteria were used to compare the performance of the three groups over the six-month period. A grammar test was developed which consisted of seventy items. All of the items were concerned with errors covered by the ten programs. A scoring procedure for assessing compositions by direct inspection was also developed. This procedure permitted actually counting and classifying grammatic errors and yielded a composition score. A score of twenty indicated twenty grammatic errors per one hundred words in a composition. The three groups were all administered the grammar test at the beginning of the six-month period, after five weeks, and at the end of the experimental period. Each group was also required to write a composition (the

choice of theme being left to each subject) at the same three periods. Thus, each subject was assigned grammar test scores and composition scores.

Findings

The two criteria were tested for reliability. The coefficient of stability for the grammar score over a five-week period was .89 and for the composition score, .57. The low coefficient of stability for the composition score probably resulted from the fact that the content of the compositions was not controlled. For example, a student might write a letter at the beginning of the six-month period and follow this five weeks later with a composition on a relatively abstract theme. The coefficient of correlation between grammar test scores and composition scores was —.60, the negative relationship due to the fact that a high composition score indicated many grammatic errors in a composition.

EFFECT OF SINGLE PRESENTATION OF PROGRAMS. Two three-part analyses of variance were conducted on the gains of the first experimental group over a five-week period during which time each program was presented once. No significant improvement was noted by either criterion (grammar test score and composition score).

EFFECT OF REPEATED PRESENTATION OF PROGRAMS. The performance of the second experimental group, that group in which a given program had been repeated as many times as indicated over a six-month period, was compared with the performances of the first experimental group and the control group. Two independent analyses of covariance were conducted, the covariates being the grammar test scores and the composition scores at the beginning of the six-month period. Mean grammar test scores and composition scores at the end of the six-month period were adjusted and the adjusted scores for the three groups compared. The group receiving repeated presentation of programs when indicated scored significantly higher than the other two groups on the grammar test ($F = 7.76$, $p < .01$). The two groups receiving programed instruction (single and repeated instruction) were significantly superior to the group receiving conventional instruction alone on the criterion of composition scores ($F = 3.31$, $p < .05$). No significant difference on the criterion of composition scores was found between the two experimental treatments, however.

The analysis based on grammar test scores reveals superiority of the repeated presentation of programs, while the analysis based on composition scores indicates only that programed instruction contributes more favorably to improved grammar than conventional instruction alone. No significant difference was found between the effectiveness of deductive (rule followed by example) and inductive (example followed by rule) forms of the programs.

Considerable additional information was produced from application of the scoring procedure which yielded the composition score. It was found, for example, that the three most common grammatic errors involved the incorrect tense of verbs, omission of the article, and errors in the singular and plural forms of common nouns. Approximately ten per cent of the compositions could not be analyzed because of their unintelligibility, and 33 per cent of the errors could not be discretely classified.

Implications of These Studies

This group of investigations has concentrated on written language. The implications drawn are:

1. That young deaf children can be taught the mechanics of written language by means of programed instruction and that these mechanics, notably word order, basic vocabulary, and other elements of language requiring rote learning, can be more quickly and efficiently taught by program than by conventional instruction.

2. That the grammar of adolescent deaf students can be significantly improved by the utilization of programs constructed around specific areas of difficulty to deaf students, particularly when students are systematically and repeatedly presented with programs when the same errors recur.

3. That language can be taught more effectively to young deaf children than to adolescents when errors tend to strongly resist extinction.

4. That programed instruction by teacher is by no means a substitute for conventional instruction by teacher but a complement of it. In its present stage, it clearly needs professional teacher supervision. Without the systematic control by the teacher, programed instruction might actually interfere with language already correctly established. On the other hand, the well articulated use of programed instruction can serve

to strengthen the language of deaf children.

5. That teachers of the deaf are receptive to the use of programed language materials as a beneficial adjunct to instruction.

The methods of instruction of deaf children have not changed markedly in many years. The reason is obvious. Superior methods, if they exist, have not come forward to replace those now in use. Programing is not represented as a new method but as an efficient technique of maximizing the effectiveness of these methods and as a supplement to them. The severe language deficit of the deaf child requires that all the tools which can serve the teacher be employed.

The task ahead is first to examine closely the language curricula developed in programs for the deaf, separating elements which lend themselves to programing. There should follow a unified effort to develop programs. This will require the resources of many persons skilled in the language instruction of the deaf, of programers, and particularly of educational institutions directly concerned with deaf children.

Finally, while the focus of these studies has been on the deaf, they may hold implications for all language disabled persons, for the mentally retarded, and for other groups of exceptional children. Programed instruction does hold the promise of contributing substantially to more effective written communication for deaf persons.

References

1. BIRCH, J., and STUCKLESS, R.: The development and evaluation of programed language instruction for children with auditory impairments. University of Pittsburgh, 1962. (U. S. Office of Education, Project No. 773.)
2. ————: Programing instruction in written language for deaf children. *Amer Ann Deaf*, 108:317, 1963a.
3. ————: Programed instruction and the correction of the written language of adolescent deaf students. University of Pittsburgh, 1963b. (U. S. Office of Education, Grant No. 7–48–1110, 188.)
4. FALCONER, G. A.: Teaching machines for the deaf. *Volta Rev*, 62:59, 1960.
5. FERSTER, C.: The role of review material in continuous programing with teaching machines. Indianapolis, Indiana University Medical School, 1960. (U. S. Office of Education, Project No. 355.)
6. FITZGERALD, E.: *Straight Language for the Deaf*. Washington, Volta Bureau, 1949.
7. LANGER, S.: *Philosophy in a New Key*. Cambridge, Harvard Univ. Press, 1942.
8. LUMSDAINE, A., and GLASER, R. (Editors): *Teaching Machines and Programed Learning. A Source Book*. Washington, Department of Audio-Visual Instruction, National Education Association, 1960.
9. MANDLER, G.: Transfer of training as a function of degree of response over learning. *J Exp Psychol*, 47:411, 1954.
10. MYKLEBUST, H. R.: *The Psychology of Deafness: Sensory Deprivation, Learning, and Adjustment*. New York, Grune, 1960.
11. STOLUROW, L.: *Teaching by Machine*. Cooperative Research Monograph, No. 6, 1961.
12. THOMPSON, W.: An analysis of errors in written composition by deaf children. *Amer Ann Deaf*, 81:95, 1936.

LANGUAGE LABORATORY FOR YOUNG DEAF CHILDREN*

FRANK B. WITHROW

It has been an established concept that the deaf child who has frequent opportunities to use his speech and speechreading in meaningful situations develops greater proficiency in these areas. Quigley and Frisina† found in a study of day and residential pupils that the day pupils had significantly better speech and speechreading abilities than residential pupils.

They attributed this to the practice effect or oralness of the environment of the dayschool children. Another significant finding was that the day pupils of deaf parents, while not doing so well in speechreading, did do significantly better in a test of fingerspelling ability and vocabulary. Again, they attribute the results to the use of fingerspelling in the home environment. The better vocabulary shown by this group can be attributed to the richer language environment or the practice effect of their everyday life.

The Quigley and Frisina study assumes that the more contact the deaf child has with language practice, re-

* An outline, prepared by Dr. Withrow, of an experimental program of language development using a systematic application of audio-visual aids to reinforce the classroom teacher's program. A report in *The Illinois Advance*, Illinois School for the Deaf, Jacksonville, November, 1964. Dr. Withrow, then Director of Research and Clinical Services, Illinois School for the Deaf, is now with the U. S. Office of Education in the same capacity.

† Quigley, S., and Frisina, D.R.: Institutionalization and Psycho-Educational Development of Deaf Children. Washington, Council for Exceptional Children, 1961.

gardless of the mode of his communication, the more proficient he will be in language.

An age-old problem in the education of deaf children is how to increase their total communication contact. This is obviously evidenced in the current increase in interest of education of the very young deaf child.

Even an early start, however, does not give the deaf child sufficient contact with language to develop a natural free flow of language.

A language lab for the deaf child can bridge in part the communication gap of the deaf child. It can use both visual and auditory stimuli in a response oriented program. The child receives a corrected response immediately following his own.

Such a language lab has been developed which will extend communication opportunities for hearing impaired children by adapting a highly structured language program to teaching machines programed through audio-visual aids. Additional contact in lipreading and auditory training is given in the classroom, and can be extended to the dormitory and the home.

The use of 8 mm cartridge-loaded movies, and the use of tape recordings, in conjunction with slide projections, give the child an opportunity for a variety of receptive communication experiences.

In this first phase of our program, we are preparing and studying the use of a structured language program using this language lab. Our immediate purposes are (1) to prepare audio-visual material for the use of acoustic training for vocabulary and language building, and (2) to prepare audio-visual material for the use of vocabulary and language building in lipreading. This program is used in the following manner:

1. The teacher develops the vocabulary and language skills with the children. Colored pictures illustrating the vocabulary or language concept are available to the teacher.

2. After the vocabulary or a language concept is developed by the teacher, it is reviewed and reinforced in the movies; thus, the child practises lipreading.

3. After the material has been developed by the teacher, and reviewed in lipreading in the movies, it is reviewed on the tape recordings and the slide projector.

Half of the class uses the language lab while the teacher does developmental work with the other half of the class. About every twenty minutes the class changes and those gaining practice in the language lab work on new material with the teacher.

During the school year, 1964–65, six classrooms were equipped with three teaching booths each. Three of these classes are at the Illinois School for the Deaf. The other three classes are at the Dallas Pilot Institute for the Deaf in Texas. The choice of a residential school and a dayschool population for this initial work was made so that we would have a variety of teaching situations.

The scope of the work includes the in-

troduction of a vocabulary of some three hundred basic nouns, and work with prepositions, verbs, adjectives, and numbers. The language has been chosen on the basis that it will be functional for the child in his environment.

There are thirty filmstrips and tapes and sixty five-minute single concept movies for use with nouns. Six strips and tapes will be provided for practice on the question forms: "What is this?", "What do you see?", and "Who is this?" Twelve single-concept movies will be made using these questions and sentence forms. Ten filmstrips and tapes will be provided for practice on the following prepositions: *In, on, under, between, by* and *over.*

Twenty single-concept movies will be produced for this part of the language development. Ten filmstrips and tapes and twenty single-concept movies will provide practice on color concepts. Ten strips and tapes plus twenty single-concept movies will provide practice on number concepts. Eight strips and ten tapes and sixteen single-concept movies will provide practice on the present progressive verb tense. Ten film strips, twenty tapes and twenty single-concept movies will provide practice on descriptive stories which will include a summary of all of the previous concepts presented.

In addition to the filmstrips and movies, 1,000 illustrations of language concepts will be prepared for this study. The teacher will use 7″ × 10″ cards in her initial introduction to the language principles desired. The teacher will continue to use such conventional devices of teaching these language concepts as she has in the past . . . action work and other techniques that are common in the classroom teaching of deaf children.

The language laboratory is designed to provide a basic vocabulary and frees the teacher to develop on her own initiative many meaningful situations where this language and vocabulary can be reinforced in daily living.

This project is sponsored by Captioned Films for the Deaf and the Research Unit of the Illinois School for the Deaf.

X. The Teacher Factor

WHAT DEAF TEACHERS CAN ACCOMPLISH IN SCHOOLS FOR THE DEAF*

RICHARD G. BRILL

Probably every head of a school for the deaf from time to time receives a letter from either a college counselor or rehabilitation counselor about a student who has recently lost or is losing his hearing. The letter usually expresses the idea that because this person has now lost his hearing, he should be advised to work in a school for the deaf and, more particularly, go into teaching deaf children. The letter frequently asks about opportunities for such deaf people in schools for the deaf.

Policies and philosophy may vary somewhat, but I believe my views are those of the large majority of heads of schools for the deaf. First of all, however, it would be well to look at the actual employment situation for deaf teachers. According to the January 1962 *American Annals of the Deaf,* during the 1961–62 school year 503 deaf teachers were employed in schools and classes for the deaf in the United States. This represents 12 per cent of the total of

* Reproduced by permission from *Rehabilitation Record,* a publication of the Vocational Rehabilitation Administration, U. S. Department of Health, Education, and Welfare, July–August 1963. Dr. Brill is Superintendent of the California School for the Deaf at Riverside.

4,309 teachers employed in these classes. However, a closer look at the figures shows that 488 of these deaf teachers were in public residential schools and classes for the deaf, and only fifteen were employed in all the public day-schools and classes, denominational and private schools and classes, and the special schools and classes for the multiple handicapped deaf children. Thus the real employment possibilities for deaf teachers are in the public residential schools.

An analysis of these *Annals* figures shows that the 503 deaf teachers listed for 1962 include both deaf and hard-of-hearing teachers and both academic and vocational teachers, and that there are about 250 academic deaf teachers and sixty-five academic hard-of-hearing teachers in our schools, with the balance being vocational teachers. It is interesting to note that the number of both deaf and of hard-of-hearing persons who teach academic subjects has been consistently greater over the past several years than the number who are vocational teachers.

The position of a teacher in the school for the deaf should be analyzed. The most important handicap of deaf children is the lack of language. Consequently, every academic teacher of the deaf must know how to teach language to deaf children who had no concept of the meaning of words or of what language was before they started their schooling. To do this it is essential to have had appropriate course work and practice teaching with deaf children.

Another important part of teaching the deaf is to teach speech and lipreading. For such work the factor of normal hearing is quite important for two reasons. A person with a hearing impairment will usually have abnormal speech because he cannot hear his own speech to monitor it. The teacher must have excellent speech himself because he must demonstrate the proper speech formations to his pupils. In addition, he must have normal hearing to be able to know when his pupil is speaking correctly and to be able to analyze his errors.

Another function of the teacher in the higher grades is to teach such subjects as social studies, mathematics, and science. Still another function in any good school is to act as a counselor to children. This is not limited to vocational counseling, but includes being a counselor in personal and social areas as well.

The question of communication methods in a school for the deaf enters into the type of teacher a school will probably employ. A school that insists on using exclusively oral methods of teaching probably will not employ a deaf teacher because he cannot teach speech or lipreading, and oral schools do not allow manual communication. For this reason

virtually no deaf teachers are employed in day-schools in the United States or in private schools because these schools are almost exclusively committed to the oral system.

The Deaf Teacher

What kind of people, then, are the deaf teachers in the residential schools? Generally they are, first of all, excellent teachers who have had the opportunity to learn methods of teaching language to deaf children and to do practice teaching in classes of deaf children. Practically the only place in the United States where such training is available to deaf teachers is at Gallaudet College, with the practice teaching being carried on in the Kendall School on the campus of the college in Washington, D. C.

A deaf teacher in a school for the deaf almost always uses manual communication. This means that the deaf teacher is teaching a subject in a rotating system, or perhaps teaching a single class which has proven to be nonreceptive to learning through oral communication. With the knowledge of good teaching skills, a deaf teacher can teach deaf children as well as any other person if he can communicate manually.

In many schools for the deaf, even when they have hearing teachers who are excellent in manual communication—perhaps because they are the children of deaf parents—the deaf children tend to go to the deaf teacher with their problems. This is because the pupil knows the deaf person can understand him through manual communication, and he also knows that this deaf person has gone through the same experiences and attended the same kind of school that he is attending. Such deaf teachers are an inspiring example to deaf children in school. But this is so only when the teacher has been through the same kind of school the deaf child is attending.

This means that the individual who had normal hearing as a child and who attended regular school for normal children and then later lost his hearing has no real understanding, through experience, of the problems of the child in a school for the deaf. This is also true of the person who may have been deafened earlier in life but who attended regular classes with hearing children.

Approximately 90 per cent of the children in residential schools for the deaf today are prelingually deaf. A person who has had normal hearing for a long time before losing it has no real concept of the problems of the deaf person who has never understood language. Also, one who loses his hearing later on in life and who has never associated with deaf people usually has no knowledge of manual communication. Thus such a person really has nothing to offer a school for the deaf.

He cannot teach speech or lipreading because he is deaf. He cannot easily communicate with deaf children because he does not understand manual communication well. He is not an example to these deaf children because he did not have his hearing loss at birth or in early childhood as they did. He has never attended the kind of school that these children are attending. In addition, in attending a college other than

Gallaudet, he has had no opportunity to take methodology courses in teaching the deaf or do practice teaching of deaf children. Colleges that prepare hearing teachers of the deaf do not admit deaf teachers to these courses because they cannot take the speech, speechreading, or audiometry courses.

For all of these reasons the person who loses his hearing later on in life or who spends most of his student days in schools for normal hearing children should not be encouraged to become a teacher of the deaf in a school for the deaf. There are many other kinds of work he can do where hearing is not an important factor. Mere loss of hearing by itself does not qualify a person to teach others who have lost their hearing.

Important Qualifications

There is an important place for the deaf teacher in schools for the deaf, but deafness *per se* is not the qualification. In addition to appropriate personality traits for teaching, the following qualifications are important for the deaf teacher:

1. He should have been deaf from an early age if the deafness is to be considered an advantage in understanding the problems of deaf children.

2. He should be fluent at manual communication as a result of having used this means of communication most of his life.

3. He should have attended a public residential school for the deaf or Gallaudet College so that he can be an example to the children he will teach in residential schools.

4. He should have had formal preparation to teach language and content subjects to deaf children, and he should have had supervised observation and practice teaching in graded classes of deaf children.

MINIMUM COURSE REQUIREMENTS TO BE INCLUDED IN A PROGRAM FOR PREPARATION OF TEACHERS OF THE DEAF IN CENTERS MEETING THE STANDARDS APPROVED BY THE CONFERENCE OF EXECUTIVES OF AMERICAN SCHOOLS FOR THE DEAF*

Following are the minimum course requirements that are to be included in a teacher preparation program for those training centers to be approved by the Conference of Executives of American Schools for the Deaf. Suggested minimum and maximum semester hours of credit are indicated for each course. It is recognized that course content rather than course title is the guide.

	Sem Hrs	
	Min	Max
A. *The Teaching of Speech to the Deaf*	4	6

This course should include a study of the principles and techniques used in developing the formation of English sounds by the analytical method and also the introduction of speech by the whole-word method. Some time should be devoted to the correction of speech defects in the hard of hearing, but the major emphasis should be placed on the development of speech in the preprimary and school-age deaf child. It is essential that demonstrations and practice with deaf

* The provisions here described represent revised requirements as drawn up by the Teacher Training and Certification Committee of the Conference of Executives of American Schools for the Deaf, and which it was empowered to make by the latter body meeting in Colorado Springs, Colo., July 1, 1959. (See Report of the Proceedings of the 39th Meeting of the Convention of American Instructors of the Deaf, U. S. Government Printing Office, Washington, D. C., 288, 1960).

children under expert supervision be an integral part of this course. The course should include special consideration of the speech problems of the deaf child with multiple handicaps.

B. *The Teaching of Language to the Deaf*	4	6

This course should include a study of the principles and techniques of teaching language to the preprimary and school-age deaf child. The student should become familiar with the leading systems of teaching language to the deaf and should become familiar with the step-by-step development of at least one language system. The material in *Outline of Language for Deaf Children* by Edith M. Buell or the *Language Outline* prepared by a committee of teachers at the Central Institute for the Deaf or similar material should form the basis of this course. The course should include consideration of the language problems of deaf children with multiple handicaps.

C. *Methods of Teaching Elementary School Subjects to the Deaf*	4	6

This course should include principles and methods of teaching reading to deaf children in the lower and higher grades. Methods of teaching subjects such as arithmetic, social studies, and science should be considered in this course. Particular emphasis should be placed on methodology in the intermediate and advanced grades. This course should also include consideration and use of visual aids in classes for the deaf.

D. *Methods of Teaching Speechreading*
   (Lipreading) to the Deaf and
   the Hard of Hearing   2   3
   The various principles and techniques
   of teaching speechreading should be
   studied. Familiarity with such methods as the Nitchie, Jena, Kinzie,
   Müller-Walle and others, and research pertaining to lipreading should
   be a part of this course.

E. *History, Education, and Guidance*
   of the Deaf   2   3
   This course should cover the history
   of the education of the deaf and the
   evaluation of the place of the deaf
   in the community from social, economic, and political viewpoints from
   ancient times to the present. The
   course should help the student become familiar with the bibliographic
   source materials in the field on the
   education and welfare of the deaf.
   Research studies related to the psychology of the deaf, social adjustment
   of the deaf, and studies related to
   the learning problems of the deaf
   should be considered. The student
   should become familiar with the place
   of the adult deaf in today's society.

F. *Auditory and Speech Mechanisms*   2   3
   This course should include a study
   of the anatomy, physiology, and
   pathology of the speech and hearing
   mechanisms.

G. *Hearing Tests and Auditory*
   Training   2   3
   The techniques and interpretation of
   pure tone hearing tests and an introduction to speech audiometry should
   be included in this course. Audiogram
   interpretation and at least ten air and
   bone conduction tests should be completed on children of varying ages
   who are in schools or classes for the
   deaf. The students should be introduced to several types of amplification
   systems used in schools and classes
   for the deaf.
   In auditory training, the student
   should learn the techniques and principles of auditory training with spe-

cial reference to such programs in
schools and classes for the deaf.

H. *Observation and Student*
   Teaching   6   10
   Facilities for observation of classroom
   procedures and student teaching
   should be sufficiently extensive so
   that the deaf pupils are well graded.
   This implies at least six classes at
   different grade levels, including preprimary if possible. The student
   should be required to do at least
   some practice teaching under direct
   supervision on several grade levels,
   in order that he might have an understanding of the overall educational
   problems of the deaf child.
   Preprimary classes include preschool,
   nursery, kindergarten, and prenursery
   classes.

                                  Min   Max
   Total Semester Hours   26   40

The above minimum course requirements presuppose that the student has
had work in the area of Education, pref-
erably a major in Elementary Education. The student should have had, or
should be taking concurrently, a course
in Child Growth and Development, and
a course in the Psychology or Education
of the Exceptional Child.

Upon request, training centers established in the future will be evaluated by
a subcommittee of one or more members
of the Conference of Executives appointed by the Chairman of the Teacher
Training and Certification Committee.
The criteria listed in the first section will
be used for evaluation of new training
centers until such time as these requirements are changed by majority
vote of the members of the Conference
of Executives.

XI. Auditory Amplification in School Practice

AMPLIFICATION FOR CHILDREN PROFOUNDLY DEAF[*]

MARGARET S. KENT

Parents sometimes question why we recommend amplification for children whose hearing may be classified as profoundly deaf. Knowing that this may be a question which others might find interesting, we would like to cover some of the reasons we think the use of an individual hearing aid appropriate in gain for the profound loss as well as the opportunity to benefit from group amplification in the classroom is frequently recommended.

The benefits of amplification can be viewed from a mere awareness of sound to subtle auditory tasks of discriminating the fine differences between vowels and consonants. An awareness of sound means that the child simply knows when sound is present and when it is not. This experience may be of limited significance to audition but it may make a large contribution to the psychological well-being of the child by establishing auditory contact with the environment. The child is aware every time the teacher makes sounds into the microphone. We have found that our deafest youngsters wearing hearing aids in the classroom attend to the teacher longer and are less distractible than when they are not using amplification. This shows up dramatically when we have a breakdown in the equipment. The children are disappointed and the teacher usually remarks that their attention span is shorter, and that they are more restless.

In viewing a hearing loss we look at the audiogram in two ways. We see it vertically as a decibel loss and horizontally or across the range of sounds from low to high frequencies. We have found that the child who responds to frequencies out to 4000 c.p.s. will receive substantial help since this area covers most of the vowels and consonants in conversation. The child with a loss as great as eighty to ninety decibels but with an extended range can usually make good use of auditory clues. It has also been found that the child who can monitor his own voice, that is, hear himself, learns to speak with less difficulty than if he cannot hear himself. We need to remember that speech is not an isolated activity but one which is integrated into the language process and makes a large contribution to memory and recall. We

[*] A report in the column, "Educationally Speaking," *The Maryland Bulletin*, Maryland School for the Deaf, Frederick, February, 1963.

163

can say that amplification improves the memory not only for words but for larger units, phrases and sentences.

The child who relies entirely on vision is psychologically different from the child who is able to combine vision and audition. There are three sensory avenues for learning open to a deaf child—the sense of vision, the sense of touch, and the sense of hearing to a greater or lesser degree. The eyes are the primary sensory avenue for the profoundly deaf child with the tactile and auditory senses making a supplementary contribution. It can be shown in this way:

$$\text{Vision} \qquad \frac{\text{Audition}}{\text{Taction}}$$

We are saying here that the profoundly deaf child is primarily visually oriented, with the tactile or sensitivity to vibration along with some degree of audition making a limited but important contribution to the information received through the eyes.

With our present audiological equipment we have been able to demonstrate these reactions in children for ourselves. With reliable audiograms and careful hearing aid adjustment we can say to what extent we can expect amplification to help a particular child. We have seen very shy, inhibited children become more outgoing, happy children when all aspects of this type of adjustment are in their proper perspective.

In a recent analysis of the hearing loss of our school population we found that nearly two thirds had a decibel loss which can be benefited by the use of a hearing aid. When we consider the range of frequency response or look across the audiogram we found that over two thirds of our population had sufficient range for discrimination of speech sounds by audition. This can make a significant contribution to the reinforcement of speech and language.

Another question which may arise in the minds of parents concerns the amount of time given to auditory training possibly at the expense of reading and writing. In the main, there is no conflict, any more than the use of glasses takes time away from learning to read. The hearing aid, as in the case of glasses, adds a dimension to learning. The teacher proceeds with the multisensory approach. The child sees the printed form, hears it spoken or is aware to some degree of some of the components, is able to hear his own vocal response as well as see his own written responses. All this adds up to a vivid and more lasting impression than if it were done by vision alone.

The outcome of this type of training helps to break down some of the isolation of profound deafness. It improves the opportunity for more intelligible speech, broader understanding of language and improved lipreading simply because it adds a critical dimension to learning.

IN ONE EAR . . .*

CHARLES DeVINNEY

I

The general public, and quite often the parents, do not fully understand just what results to expect when a hearing aid is placed on a deaf child. There are many factors that have to be considered when evaluating the benefits of amplification; the most important one being that the average aid is engineered and manufactured for the use of the individual who loses some of his hearing in adulthood, and not for the early cases of deafness.

The deafened person has established normal speech and hearing patterns through auditory experiences with perfect or near perfect hearing. The deaf child, or child with a hearing loss, has not established these normal patterns. Most aids are designed to amplify the areas most necessary to maintain these patterns. In this respect they do an excellent job. It is in the field of developing speech and hearing that problems arise. The normal ear has a frequency range from approximately 45 cycles to 15,000 cycles per second. The most essential speech elements fall in the 500 to 4,000 cycle area. However there are elements in speech above and below these frequencies. The develop-

ment of perfect speech and understanding depends on hearing these additional sounds connected with speech. Once this understanding has been established it can be maintained through the use of amplification, even though the 500 to 4,000 cycle area is drastically reduced.

The deaf child presents a different problem. He has never heard perfectly, or has lost his hearing before normal patterns were established. His audiogram may show responses to all frequencies, but the level is so low that most sounds do not reach him. The hearing aid, nothing more than a miniature public address system, is not capable of reproducing all of the essential range. Roughly speaking a hearing aid will amplify from approximately 750 to 2,500 cycles. Because the ear is completely sealed by the ear mold, the wearer hears only the sounds reproduced by the aid. With the distortion inherent in all amplifiers, plus the reduction in hearing range, development of speech and understanding becomes a critical and long range problem. The severity of the problem depends on the amount and type of loss, and upon the individual child.

In solving this problem it is important to recognize the value of the hearing aid, and also to understand its limitations. Some of these important factors will be covered in the discussion which follows.

---

* A series of discussions, on the relative utility to be obtained from use of hearing aids, in *The Washingtonian*, Washington State School for the Deaf, Vancouver, November and December, 1961, and January, 1962. The author is Supervisor of the Audio-Visual Program, Washington State School for the Deaf.

II

In the preceding section some of the limitations of an individual hearing aid were outlined. Here we will attempt to explain what to expect from the use of an aid.

First of all the results will depend on the amount of loss, the individual child and the type of damage. The child with enough residual hearing to develop some speech and a reasonably good language pattern unaided will naturally receive the greatest benefit from an aid. The area of loss between 40 and 60 decibels is considered to be the area of greatest benefit. As the loss decreases below 40 decibels, need for amplification becomes less. As it increases above 60 decibels, the objective use of amplification decreases. The need is still there, but the child finds it increasingly difficult to project himself into a hearing situation.

The child in the 40 to 60 decibel range should be able to hear and understand speech in most situations. As the aid is worn over the years, this understanding should improve. As sound is both physically and psychologically disturbing, it is important that a beginning period of adjustment be allowed when first wearing an aid. Very few perceptive deaf individuals are able to wear an aid for long periods of time when first beginning. Tolerance must be built gradually and over a period of time. Since the hearing aid amplifies both foreground and background sounds equally, extremely noisy environments can be painful and disturbing. Situations where sudden or prolonged loud noises will occur should be avoided when first starting to use an aid. Over a period of time tolerance will be built to handle some of these situations. However, it is the rare individual who can ever learn to tolerate an aid in all situations.

In general it can be said that the child in the 40 to 60 decibel range should be able to use a hearing aid objectively and that this ability will improve over years of use. Definite auditory training periods should be utilized to enhance this usage. Because of the limited frequency response of the aid, all speech will not be understood. However, amplified hearing combined with lipreading should produce 90 to 100 per cent understanding. Ability to hear and understand will be reduced drastically in direct ratio of the distance to the source of the sound. Don't expect your child to understand speech from the kitchen to the bedroom. Some may, most won't.

Individuals with a loss greater than 60 decibels find an aid helpful in structuring their environment, and as a direct assist in lipreading. This area requires the greatest amount of auditory training and the most understanding. In most cases amplification serves as a crutch but will not enable them "to run the hundred yard dash." Single words will be understood, but connected speech becomes a meaningless jumble unless sight is also used. It is important to remember that speech will improve in most cases. Hearing themselves talk produces better rhythm, more pleasing voice quality and better breath control. Research has also revealed that lipreading can be taught faster and retained for a longer period of time when amplification is used in instruction. The success of this program is again dependent on the severity of the loss.

In general you can expect a child with a greater than 60 decibel loss to understand some words, but not connected speech. Lipreading ability should improve when combined with amplification. Speech will have better tonal quality. Interaction with their environment will be greater. Pleasurable sources of sound will become an important part of living.

All of the above factors can vary according to the individual and the type of loss. Some of these will be discussed below.

III

Hitherto the discussion has been concerned with the actual physical fitting and wearing of the individual hearing aid. Very often we find students that none of the factors discussed will fit. Children with identical audiograms frequently will react to amplification in directly opposite manner. Logically there are two explanations for this, the psychological factors involved and the nature of the actual nerve damage.

Psychologically, hearing has been defined as, "The ability to reach around a corner or into the dark and feel a sound." Hearing is an environment, an actual physical area of our living. Deafness or silence also becomes an environment. The most traumatic part of suddenly becoming deaf is the change from our noisy world to the dead, eerie, absolute silence of the deaf. However, to the person born deaf this is the natural state of being. The desire must be built to change this environment to the noisy, sometimes distracting, world of sound. The problem of adjustment to this change becomes an individual matter. All facets of our personality and abilities are built on individual differences. The ability to adjust to sudden and dramatic changes varies from person to person. For this reason we find all levels of acceptance of amplification, from use 100 per cent of the time to refusal to wear an aid at all. This isn't just limited to the deaf. We all know deafened individuals who economically and socially would be greatly helped with a hearing aid. Yet psychologically they refuse to be helped. Some deaf youngsters are the same. The desire to hear can be developed in many of these cases; in a small percentage amplification is never accepted.

When we talk of the type of nerve damage we enter an almost unknown world. Too many times we assume that all that is necessary to restore hearing is to amplify sound to near normal level. Actually we know very little about what the damaged nerve really transmits. Is it distorted sound? Is it meaningful? Is it just a jumble of sensations? Apparently the above is true in some cases. Very often we find children with good residual hearing who accept and want amplification, yet the use of this hearing is practically nil, while classmates with the same or less hearing use and understand amplified sounds. The most logical explanation seems to be that the damaged nerves are transmitting distorted impulses.

MORE ABOUT HEARING AIDS*

ALBERT C. ESTERLINE

It might be well to talk a little more about hearing aids for the benefit of parents.

In the first place, a hearing aid does not do for hearing what eyeglasses do for seeing. If a person has difficulty seeing and he gets glasses with the proper correction he sees what any person with normal vision sees. This is not true of a hearing aid because of the makeup of sound and especially speech sounds. Speech is made up of high and low pitched sounds, soft and loud sounds, and any number of combinations of these. A hearing aid takes all of these sounds and makes them louder. Many people have hearing losses of such a nature that they are unable to hear some sounds regardless of how loud they are; so, making sounds louder isn't the whole answer. Some sounds are so soft that if they were to be made loud enough through a hearing aid for a person with a hearing loss to hear, the louder sounds would be unbearable. In the word "cat," for example, the "k" sound for the letter "c" and the "t" are very soft sounds compared to the vowel sound for the "a." Hearing aids are built and can be ad-

justed to a certain extent to take care of some of these extremes but to a very limited extent.

A hearing aid cannot tell the difference between speech sounds and unimportant sounds such as footsteps, coughs or a falling book; so, it makes all sounds louder including the unimportant sounds. These "unimportant" sounds should not really be called unimportant because they can be very important as warnings or in helping a "deaf" person to be more aware of what is going on around him. In fact some people wear hearing aids mainly for this purpose and get very little if any help from them for speech. The point is that a person wearing an aid has to *learn* to unscramble the sounds that he gets through an aid.

The important idea is that even though a hearing aid is far from perfect in helping a severely hard-of-hearing or a "deaf" person to hear, it is still a great help.

A child in school with training, practice and help can learn to change or understand the sounds that he gets through his aid as meaningful words and sentences that are needed in a world of sound. These sound clues combined with speechreading give much more understanding than speechreading alone, thus improving the amount

* From "The School Corner" in *The Companion,* Minnesota School for the Deaf, Faribault, February, 1966. The author is Principal of the Minnesota School for the Deaf.

and quality of education a hearing-impaired child can get.

Second, to get the maximum benefit from a hearing aid it should be worn at all times. There are, of course, exceptions. Football players don't leave their aids on, nor are aids worn during swimming. These are rather extreme examples and quite obvious, but they were given for that reason. When children reach for their hearing aids in the mornings (no, they don't wear them to bed) as adults do for their glasses, we can be sure they are benefiting from them. To get children to this point takes a lot of work, effort and encouragement on the part of houseparents, teachers and others at school and *a lot of support and cooperation from home.* Help your child to make his hearing aid as much a part of himself as his clothing and you will be doing him a lifelong favor. Be sure he wears it all the time!

Getting the child's cooperation in some instances to wear the aid can present problems in the same way that getting a child's cooperation in any matter can. Firmness works well with some children and not with others; whereas, rewards and encouragement work with some and not others. *Forcing a child to wear an aid against his will may result in a permanent feeling against wearing an aid.*

Third, a hearing aid needs care. The earmold should be kept clean. It can be washed in warm soapy water and rinsed with clean warm water . . . neither hot nor cold. A pipe cleaner is good to clean out the opening in the mold.

Be sure the mold is dry inside before it is put back on the receiver so water won't get into the receiver or the ear. Shake it and blow through it, or run a pipe cleaner through it.

Earmolds have to be replaced from time to time. As a child grows his ear also grows and the earmold is too small permitting feedback, which is the squeal that is sometimes heard when the volume is turned up.

Batteries should be taken out of an aid at night or when it is not in use. A leaking battery can ruin a hearing aid.

Cords have to be replaced when they break, and oftentimes the break is invisible. If a person wiggles the cord, intermittent sound will sometimes get through when the broken wires make contact.

A good carrier is probably the best safeguard against damage to a hearing aid, especially for younger children. It can be worn under a dress or shirt, or for everyday use it is often more convenient to have it worn over the clothes, especially for the very young.

In spite of all the precautions that anyone can take there are going to be broken aids, broken or lost receivers and earmolds, just as there are wrecked cars, broken bones and misplaced glasses. And, just as some people seem to be accident prone, some children more than others seem to have more trouble with their hearing aids. However, people don't stop driving cars, stay in bed for fear of an accident, or go without glasses because of past troubles and, neither should a child be denied the benefit of a hearing aid because of an accident. Imagine not replacing the car, not setting the broken bone, or not getting new glasses to save money! It might well be a lot more foolish not to keep a hearing aid in good working condition for a child whose education may heavily depend on it.

Hearing aids are important . . . only when they are worn!

THE FURTHER DESTRUCTION OF PARTIALLY DEAFENED CHILDREN'S HEARING BY THE USE OF POWERFUL HEARING AIDS*

CHARLES E. KINNEY, M.D.

At the beginning, it is thought best to point out that this report is based on clinical otological observations and not on laboratory experiments. Although the use of binaural hearing aids in certain types of cases will be condemned, this report is not intended to (1) question the fact that for the recognition and interpretation of speech there is both a binaural summation and a binaural integration, or (2) question the fact that in certain cases the use of binaural amplification is the only answer. The personal experience of an eminent past president of this Society is proof of this last statement.

It would seem that the first published inference of binaural summation was by Seebeck[1] in 1846. In 1943, your present essayist[2] reported that children with a bilateral hearing loss could not hear pure tones binaurally any better than by monaural testing of the better ear but that this same individual could

hear and analyze speech much better binaurally than he could in his better ear alone.

Since 1936, it has been the writer's privilege to supervise the Hearing Conservation Program in the Cleveland, Ohio, Public and Parochial Schools. At the present time, these two school systems have a student enrollment of over 200,000. During these years, many changes in procedures have been instituted. In 1938, there was started a procedure which over these years has proven to be the real core of this program. This was the establishment of a central otological diagnostic clinic for all children with a suspected hearing impairment. This clinic is located in our Alexander Graham Bell School which is the oldest public (supported by school tax funds) school for the education of deaf children in the United States. This school was started in 1893 and has been in continuous operation on the same site ever since then.

At this clinic, we attempt to diagnose the presence or absence of a hearing loss in these referred children. Of those positive cases, we try to establish the degree of loss, its potential remediability, its

* Read before the Annual Meeting of the American Otological Society, May 26–27, 1961, Lake Placid, N. Y. Reprinted from *Annals of Otology, Rhinology and Laryngology*, September, 1961, Vol. 70, No. 3, page 828, Copyright, 1961, Annals Publishing Company. Dr. Kinney is from Cleveland, Ohio.

etiology and then make appropriate recommendations. This is accomplished by (1) having at least one parent present; (2) obtaining a complete otological history including the dates and severity of all prior illnesses; (3) making a complete ear, nose and throat examination, and (4) making a pure tone threshold audiometric test. When necessary in order to confirm or make an etiological diagnosis some of these children are subjected to bone conduction audiometry and speech audiometry or both.

Since 1938, we have records on more than 8800 children. Of this number about 2000 have had more than one test and about 800 have had at least four tests. In 1953, Dr. H. L. Williams asked me to report before a Triological Society meeting an analysis of this rather large series of hearing tests on these children. In this report,[3] it was stated in referring to sixteen cases of progressive sensorineural hearing loss that "the progress was not noted until a wearable hearing aid had been put on these children and in every instance the increased loss was more marked in the ear in which the hearing aid was used." From 1953 to the present time many writers with international reputations have reported on noise induced hearing loss in some industrial workers whose hearing had been normal before exposure to sustained high noise levels. The fact that this can happen is disputed by no one although some of the important problems are still unsolved. One of these problems is the matter of "susceptibility." During the years from 1953 to 1956, your essayist had many personal discussions with experts in the field of acoustic trauma. In these discussions, the question of hearing aid trauma was brought up and every time this possibility was deprecated. It was only natural to assume that my 1953 observations had been in error and for several years it was forgotten. Last year a rather exhaustive search of the American literature on this subject was made. It was found that in 1957, Silverman[4] stated, "The evidence from the relations of hearing loss to noise exposure suggests the possibility of damage to an ear exposed to the level of sound pressure generated by a hearing aid." Maybe other American writers have mentioned this possibility but none was found.

From the years of about 1955 to 1959, American hearing aid manufacturers were vying with one another to produce hearing aids that were smaller, more disguisable, more powerful and with greater fidelity. Now one prominent manufacturer claims that they produce a small aid with five transistors and two transformers which has a fidelity range of up to 4200 cycles with a maximum acoustic gain of 80 decibels and a power output of up to 146 decibels. This writer questions the last of these three claims but the fact that most of these aids are now very powerful is without question.

About two years ago, there was started the idea of fitting children of between the ages of two and twelve years with binaural hearing aids[5] of one of these powerful makes. An earpiece was molded to fit each ear and a metal spring bar went over the top of the head to hold these two earpieces tightly in the ear canals. A hearing aid microphone and amplifier were attached to each side of this metal headpiece in order that this small aid would be just superior to and behind the upper part of each auricle. It is presumed that such an arrangement was devised in order to make it more likely to stay in place and also to decrease the likelihood of feedback. We have observed that it fulfills the latter point, even when such powerful aids are turned up to maximum capacity. It would be most interesting to try to ascertain if the sound pressure within an ear canal of a subject wearing an aid by this method is increased over the maximum pressure in the same ear canal when the aid is worn in the more conventional manner. It is logical to assume that this method itself might increase the ear canal sound pressure. As far as can be ascertained this investigation has never been done. At no place can one find that the development of this kind of amplification was done under otological supervision or approval. It is claimed by the proponents of such hearing aid fittings that "speech intelligibility can be increased by fourfold." This has never been proven on the basis of speech audiometry by use of spondee words and it is impossible of attainment from a neurophysiological viewpoint.

Keys,[6] Hirsh,[7] Bocca,[8] and Bergman[9] have reported on the probable advantages of binaural hearing aid amplification over monaural amplification. In none of these reports is there anything like the four times better results previously mentioned. As a matter of fact, the inferences in some of these reports are not borne out by their own figures. On the other hand, DiCarlo and Brown[10] found that binaural amplification actually reduced the speech reception threshold in their series of cases.

In consideration of the education of the totally or subtotally deafened child one can find no fault with the use of binaural amplification of even very high intensity. It is a matter of nothing to lose and the possibility of some gain.

During the past two years, we have been privileged to make some repeat hearing tests on partially deafened children who had been wearing these powerful hearing aids of both the monaural and binaural type. This stimulated me to start another study to see if there may not have been some merit in the observations first reported in 1953. In October 1960, a communication was received from Dr. Rejakjar,[11] director of the Hearing Rehabilitation Center in Odense, Denmark. In this paper, he confirmed my observations of 1953. He also refers to papers of Gromov[12] and Dunajvitser[13] who have been making similar observations in Russia. This lent stimulus to my project and herewith is reported my findings.

The files on every one of the previously mentioned 8800 children were examined individually.

The following criteria were used in selecting certain records for further study:

1. The child must have been wearing a hearing aid for at least one year.

2. There must have been at least one pure tone threshold hearing test on this child prior to the use of the hearing aid.

3. There must have been at least two similar tests after six months' use of the aid.

4. The diagnosis of the etiology of the hearing loss must have been fundamentally of a sensorineural type.

(To otologists it is not necessary to stipulate the points in making such a diagnosis but to others it may be well to so stipulate.)

(a) There was no history of purulent discharge from either ear.

(b) Visual examination of the eardrums showed that both were normal.

(c) There was no clinical or visual evidence of obstruction in the nasopharynx.

(d) Approximately 38 per cent of the selected records showed that bone conduction testing had been done and this testing confirmed the diagnosis as one of perception loss.

(e) Approximately 10 per cent of the selected records showed that speech testing had been done and the discrimination score confirmed the diagnosis.

5. Each record must show that the child had normal or nearly normal speech. *Therefore the development of speech in these children was of no importance.*

Criterion 2 meant that six years of age was the minimum age of the first examination of these selected records. Actually sixteen years of age was the oldest of any of these cases. Approximately half were boys and half girls. Because of these criteria seven of the sixteen cases referred to in the 1953 report have not been included in this report.

Because of the desirability of having some sort of control in this study, these records were divided into two groups. The first group which I choose to call my control group were those children who had been studied according to the mentioned criteria from 1938 through 1958. During these years, the aids used were less powerful and always used monaurally. Of the 178 selected cases, 146 were in this control group. The remaining fifty-two cases that had been selected according to the previously mentioned criteria were cases that had been studied during 1959 and 1960.

Of the 126 cases in the control group, five showed an increased loss of an average of 10 db in the speech range in the used ear. Eight showed an increased loss of an average of 20 db in the used ear. This means that 10.3 per cent of these 126 showed a further loss of hearing in the ear in which the aid had been used. Four cases (3.2 per cent of the total) showed an appreciable loss in the ear which had not been used but in all four of these cases the loss was more pronounced in the used ear. One hundred nine cases (86.5 per cent of the total) showed no change in their hearing level.

Of the fifty-two cases in the latter group, 39 used their aid in one ear only. Of these thirty-nine, nineteen (48.8 per cent) showed an increased loss of an average of 20 db in the used ear. Only one of these nineteen showed an increased loss in both ears and in this case the loss was more pronounced in the used ear. In this latter group of fifty-two, thirteen had been using a binaural aid as described previously. Of these thirteen cases, nine (69.2 per cent) showed an average increased loss of 25 db in both ears.

Critical Analysis

You will note that the use of the word "permanent" has been avoided in considering these increased losses. No one can rightfully talk about these cases as having had a permanent increased loss any more than one should talk about permanent increased hearing after any of the operations performed with such an object in mind. However, it should be pointed out that in criterion 3 in the selection of these records there must have been at least two hearing tests following the use of the aid for six months. In no case did the second or further tests show improved hearing. The averages used were the averages of the last test in each case.

One could logically ask "In how many of these cases would there have been an increased loss if a hearing aid had not been used?" The answer to that question is not easy. During these twenty-three years and in this series of over 8800 cases the number of partially sensorineural deafened children with an average loss of 40 db or more in the better ear who have not used a hearing aid was insignificant.

Because the same examiner examined all of these 178 selected cases and by using the same general methods, it is felt that division of the control group from the other group is perfectly fair. The only difference between these two groups of 126 and fifty-two was the power output of the aids being used. It would have been very helpful to have

had records as to the hours per week that these aids were worn and to what intensity they were turned to. This was not recorded. However, it is honestly felt that with respect to these two variables there was no significant difference between the earlier and the latter group.

A start has been made to try to study these 178 cases from an etiological viewpoint. This will take a tremendous amount of mathematical evaluation on a basis of probabilities and possibilities (so-called chi-squaring). As otologists, you will realize that the etiological diagnosis of such cases is presumptive in the majority of instances. In those cases, in which such a diagnosis was made, they were classified as hereditary, post-meningitic, measles virus, mumps virus, erythroblastosis fetalis, toxicity of mothers during the second and third month pregnancy, birth anoxemia and cerebral palsy. It is my opinion that of these etiological diagnoses, the one case that is least likely to have hearing aid trauma is the hereditary case.

My personal feelings as a result of this study are:

1. In sensorineural partially-deafened children, no hearing aid of more than 40 db gain should be used in spite of the fact that a more powerful aid may possibly give better speech hearing (spondee score) improvement at the first fitting.

2. The use of binaural amplification in such children should be condemned.

3. Children between the ages of five and sixteen years who wear a hearing aid should have their hearing evaluated by an otologist at least every six months.

References

1. SEEBECK, A.: Beitrage zur psychologie des gehör und gesichtssinnes. *Pogg Ann, 68:* 449, 1846.
2. KINNEY, C. E.: Interpretation of hearing tests. *Laryngoscope, 53:*223–231, 1943.
3. KINNEY, C. E.: Hearing impairments in children. *Laryngoscope, 63:*220–226, 1953.
4. SILVERMAN, S. R.: Education of the deaf. *Handbook of Speech Pathology.* New York, Appleton, 1957, p. 412.
5. BENDER, R. E., and WIIG, E.: Binaural hearing aids for young children. Volta Bureau. Reprint No. 732.
6. KEYS, J. W.: Binaural versus monaural hearing. *J Acoust Soc Amer, 19:*629–631, 1946.
7. HIRSH, I. J.: Binaural hearing aids—A review of some experiments. *J Speech Hearing Dis, 15:*114–123, 1950.
8. BOCCA, E.: Binaural hearing: Another approach. *Laryngoscope, 65:*1164–1171, 1955.
9. BERGMAN, M.: Binaural hearing means better hearing. *Hearing Dealer, 6:*10–12, 1956.
10. DiCARLO, L. M., and BROWN, J. W.: The effectiveness of binaural hearing for adults with hearing impairments. *J Aud Res, 1:*35–76, 1960.
11. MILLER, T. T., and REJSKJAR, C.: Injury to hearing through hearing aid treatment (Acoustic Trauma). Fifth Cong. of Internat. Soc. of Audiol., Bonn, Germany, 1960.
12. GROMOV, P. N.: Effect of prolonged use of hearing aids on hearing. *Vest Otorinolaring,* 14,3:93, 1952.
13. DUNAJVITSER, B. I.: Effect of prolonged application of hearing aids on hearing acuity. *Vest Otorinolaring, 15,* 5:12–18, 1953. Russian AS IS Ref. No. 12.

Additional References

MARKLE, D. M., and ABER, W.: A clinical evaluation of monaural and binaural hearing aids. *Arch Otolaryng (Chicago),* 67:606–608, 1958.
HEDGECOCK, L. D., and SHEETS, B. V.: A comparison of monaural and binaural hearing aids for listening to speech. *Arch Otolaryng (Chicago),* 68:624–629, 1958.
WRIGHT, H. N., and CARHART, R.: The efficiency of binaural listening among the hearing-impaired. *Arch Otolaryng (Chicago),* 72:789–797, 1960.
JERGER, J., and DIRKS, D.: Binaural hearing aids. An enigma. *J Acoust Soc Amer,* 33:537–538, 1961.

XII. Vocational Preparation

THE DEAF AND VOCATIONAL CHOICE*

H. W. HOEMANN

The vocational choices of people who are deaf are unfortunately and often unnecessarily restricted. A large measure of this limitation is intrinsic. A deaf person is not likely to become a piano tuner or an audiologist. Occupations which require hearing, intelligible speech, or fluent language present obvious barriers to employment for profoundly deaf persons. This is understandable.

Moreover, there are factors related to deafness which tend to create vocational problems. Three such factors have received considerable attention from psychologists: (1) lack of information on the world of work; (2) lack of insight regarding interests and abilities, and (3) personality problems which may accompany the handicap of deafness. Such deficiencies, to the extent that they exist, certainly have significant implications for both the choice of vocation and vocational adjustment.

There is a further limitation imposed upon the deaf from without. It lies outside their handicap and beyond their control. It resides in the culture of their time and place, and it is perpetuated even by those who wish to help them. It imposes upon them too low a ceiling on what the deaf can do and too narrow a room in which they can do anything. This is unnecessary.

Even the factors related to deafness which limit vocational choices could be mitigated by a conscientious effort on the part of those who serve the deaf professionally. If it is true that young deaf people are too uninformed about job opportunities within their capacity to make a free and intelligent choice of vocation without guidance, then more could be done while the deaf child is still in school to acquaint him with jobs and with working people. If young deaf people depend too much on counselors and aptitude tests to tell them as if by magic what their interests are, then they need earlier and stronger encouragement to develop a wide range of interests and to have the courage of their convictions when some of them emerge as dominant. And if personality problems do sometimes accompany the handicap of deafness, then more atten-

* Reprinted from *Rehabilitation Record*, official publication of the U. S. Vocational Rehabilitation Administration, Department of Health, Education, and Welfare, Washington, D. C., September–October, 1965. The author is pastor of the Lutheran Church of the Deaf, Silver Spring, Maryland.

tion could be given to the personality development and the mental health of deaf school children.

Certainly a more concerted effort could be made to acquaint deaf children in school with jobs and with working adults, especially deaf adults. Too often classroom instruction on jobs deals with job stereotypes. Young deaf children learn to identify a picture of a policeman or a fireman. But how many deaf children ever become policemen or firemen? And if the picture is more relevant, a baker perhaps, the child still does not learn much about the job itself, how much a baker earns, what kind of hours he works, where he learned his trade, or how he obtained his job. Even a field trip to the bakery is usually designed to stimulate the use of original language about the trip, to teach related vocabulary or perhaps to let the children see how bread is made. Such a trip is not generally planned to introduce the children to the various job classifications which one might find in a bakery.

Many children are never home when their father comes home from work. Most deaf children have only a vague idea of what their father does at work. They do not usually know much about the jobs of their uncles or cousins or aunts. If they attend a residential school, most of the adult deaf people with whom they come in frequent contact are members of the school staff in one capacity or another. If they attend day classes for the deaf in a public school, they may never get to know any adult deaf people at all! How in the unique world of schools for the deaf will a child ever develop an image of himself as a deaf adult working? It is hardly surprising that young deaf people are judged as not interested in making a vocational choice in preparing for one until a choice is forced upon them by termination of their formal education.

An *effective* guidance program should be available to deaf pupils everywhere, whether they attend a residential school, a dayschool, or day classes. Such a guidance program should take into consideration the fact that deafness will present an information barrier to the pupil and will insulate him from many experiences with jobs and with working people.

A second critical need is related to the existing programs and facilities for the vocational training of deaf individuals. This point was made repeatedly at the National Workshop on Improved Opportunities for the Deaf held in Knoxville, Tenn., Oct. 18–22, 1964. Additional facilities are desperately needed. The National Technical Institute for the Deaf, for which provision has now been made by Congress, will serve as a partial answer to that need. But for the large number of deaf people who will not be able to attend this new school, there is still more that could be done by way of regional facilities and by facilities designed not only for the highly gifted but also for the average and for the pupil who is below average in academic achievement. Existing facilities could undoubtedly be used more intensively and more imaginatively. (Although if deaf people are integrated with other handicapped persons, the special problems in language and communication which are unique to deafness will have to be recognized.) But additional facilities are needed, and with them a better transitional arrangement for deaf pupils from one type of school to another.

A third factor in the limitation of vocational choices of the deaf lies in the way in which they get their jobs. Too many young deaf people are simply graduated into an occupation which they happen to have learned at school, invited by no better attraction than the fact that other deaf people are already earning a living at it. The concentration of large numbers of deaf people in the printing trades, for example, suggests that many deaf people drift into an occupation that is traditionally appropriate for them rather than venture into uncharted vocational waters. In those communities where one company has gained a reputation for hiring the deaf, a high percentage of the deaf population in that community will be found on the payroll, a kind of "one-crop economy" for the deaf. More diversification in employment opportunities will have to be developed. The elimination of many semiskilled jobs by automation should place a high priority on the effort to broaden the offerings placed before the deaf and from which they must choose a vocation.

At the present time, not only the deaf but also their vocational counselors often follow the path of least resistance that leads to a job. The true capacities of the individual are given less weight than the more practical consideration of what is available. Even if the counselor is conscientious enough to try to appraise his client's real potential, the instruments which he must use to measure that potential are inexact and perhaps even invalid. Meanwhile a closure is a successful placement and a successful placement is a closure. The identity principle for arithmetic works also for the rehabilitation process. Perhaps we need a new word for "placement." Too often that is exactly what it is. It ought also to be a vocation.

The term *vocation* comes from a Latin word which means "calling." The job which a person assumes is one to which he has been called. In choosing a vocation, the individual answers a call to perform a special contribution to society. To allow a deaf person to wander into an occupation to which he feels no call is to deprive him of the opportunity to answer one. Inadequate vocational guidance, inappropriate vocational training, and a lack of respect for the true potential of the deaf client will diminish the call to a whisper and reduce the prospect of performing a legitimate and needed service to just getting a job and getting paid. "Vocational placement" is a contradiction in terms.

Every time a guidance counselor steers a deaf client toward a job that is beneath his capacity, he is lowering the ceiling for him, forcing him to stand less straight and less tall. The counselor may have the best of intentions. He may wish to spare the client the anguish that awaits him at a difficult task. He wants to set realistic goals. And so a potential research chemist becomes a laboratory technician because it is a "related occupation." And a potential accountant becomes a bookkeeper because it is an "attainable goal." (We have words for our rationalizations.) But one gets from people pretty much what one expects. Teachers know this, and good teachers challenge their pupils to rise to their potential. Rehabilitation counselors ought also to know this. Low expectations produce a mediocre performance. Even more pointedly, it is not helpful to the deaf to pave their path to success with condescension. We should never aim low in order to succeed. Nor is it appropriate in a Great Society to expect less of a person than he is able to contribute.

While society is revising its opinion of what the deaf person can do, it can simultaneously strive for a more sophisticated understanding of what deafness is. So long as the general public harbors an attitude toward the deaf that is uninformed, mildly superstitious, and unaccepting of either the person or the handicap, this will pose insurmountable barriers to satisfactory attainment by the deaf. When an employer would prefer not to hire a deaf person because of the extra time required for communication or because of the risk of error over a misunderstanding, the chances of employment for the deaf are immediately diminished. When an entire community regards the deaf as appropriate objects of sympathy or charity from a distance—it is difficult to imagine how a deaf person within the community could ever become a contributing member of it.

This article has explored three areas in which more could be done than is being done to improve the vocational opportunities available to the deaf. These areas are: (1) the education of the deaf, academic, prevocational and vocational, including an emphasis on vocational guidance and mental health; (2) the vocational rehabilitation process and counseling of the deaf, especially the problems associated with the evaluation of the client's potential and with his appropriate placement, and (3) the public image of the deaf and its effect on their employability.

This certainly does not exhaust the subject. It merely introduces it. One entire phase of the question has not even been touched, that is the deaf person himself and the attitudes which he brings to the limitations imposed upon his choices of vocation. One thing is certain. We must give every individual an opportunity to swim against the stream to reach that portion of the river where the waters are at least more refreshing if not more serene.

MEASUREMENT OF THE VOCATIONAL INTERESTS OF THE DEAF BY MEANS OF PICTURES

HAROLD GEIST*

Because of the difficulty associated with measuring interests of the deaf by

* The author is a certified psychologist from Berkeley, California.

existing psychological instruments, a new test virtually eliminating verbal material known as the Geist Picture Interest Inventory, Deaf Form, Male

(GPII:D:M) was devised as the result of a research grant awarded by the Vocational Rehabilitation Administration, U. S. Department of Health, Education, and Welfare. This instrument published by Western Psychological Services, P. O. Box 775, Beverly Hills, California, uses pictures instead of words in the assessment of vocational interest. It has been shown to be of utility to counselors of the deaf in the residential schools, public schools, state vocational rehabilitation agencies and many other installations where deaf people are counseled for vocational guidance. The standardization was done at most of the residential schools in the United States, classes for the deaf in the public schools, public and private vocational rehabilitation agencies. Validity studies were carried out on a large sample of adult deaf and the instrument has been shown to have great promise in not only assessing interests of the deaf but also getting at reasons why they chose the occupations they did.

A summary of the validity of the test on approximately 900 employed adult deaf males is given in a report by Geist in "Occupational Interest Profiles of the Deaf," in *Personnel and Guidance Journal*, September 1962, pp. 50–55. That report describes the experimental design by which the test was constructed and provides supporting data in tables of T-scores for the differentiated occupational groups, as well as tabulation of a scale of P-levels of significance for all the occupational groups. An arresting conclusion was that the interest profiles of deaf men appear to be little different from those of hearing persons in the same occupational categories. Research workers in this hitherto overlooked area should find here incentive for fruitful study.

The findings of this research project, including the Picture Interest Test itself, were impressive enough to warrant nomination in 1962 by the American Personnel and Guidance Association as one of the outstanding pieces of research completed in its field.

XIII. Guidance Services

GUIDANCE SERVICES AT I. S. D.*

RICHARD HELTON

There are many different ways to classify guidance services. I will classify them here into six broad services.

The primary purpose of guidance services is to assist each individual to know and accept himself in such a way that he may attain more purposeful directions in his life.

Since guidance infers helping an individual know himself and to plan in the light of that knowledge, it is necessary to find out as much about the individual as it is possible to know. One of the guidance services that helps us determine this is the testing service. A new student entering high school is given a mental abilities test, a general achievement test, and a reading test. Each year after entry into high school he is given a general achievement test and a reading achievement test to determine his progress for the year. Once during high school the student is given a manual dexterity test. If an individual has very definite potential in a certain field he may be given a special aptitude test.

Last year the teachers of the high school and the teachers of grade 8 administered 170 achievement tests. I administered ninety-eight achievement tests, 156 reading tests, sixty-one mental abilities tests, and forty-two dexterity tests.

A second guidance service that helps the individual know himself is the individual inventory. This consists of putting down on paper, everything pertaining to himself: his age, family information, work experience, educational plans, vocational plans, all past subjects and grades, test scores and his likes and dislikes. The reason that it is put on paper is that the information on the inventory can be readily compared, at any time, with the requirements necessary for the individual to attain his future goals.

I would like to present a few statistics from the individual inventories of our high school students.

Almost 70 per cent of the high school students know their mother's occupation and over 60 per cent know the extent of her education. Only about 40

* A talk given at a meeting of the Parent-Teacher-Counselor Organization of the Indiana School for the Deaf, April 1, 1966, and reprinted from *The Hoosier*, monthly publication of the same school, May, 1966. The author is Guidance Director at the Indiana School for the Deaf.

per cent of the students know their father's occupation and one half know the extent of his education.

In 1964 less than one fourth of the students had jobs in the summer. No girls worked that year. The jobs held by boys in the summer of 1964 were: Farmers, car washers, gas station attendants, lawn mowers, painters, veterinary helper, stock boy, ice carrier, city park maintenance worker, timber cutter, construction worker, and lifeguard. In the summer of 1965, 30 per cent of the students had employment. Only two girls had employment—one was a cook's helper at a summer camp and the other girl picked cherries in Michigan. The jobs held by boys were the same as in 1964 with the addition of golf caddy, upholsterer's helper, janitor, camp counselor, odd-jobs man, dishwashers, carpenter, tin plater, silo construction worker, printer, rose potter, caterer's helper, and a worker at Crossroads Rehabilitation Center.

Thirty-seven per cent of the students do not want any more schooling, 23 per cent are undecided, 34 per cent want to go to college, and 5 per cent (all boys) want to go to trade school.

Almost two thirds of the students do not know what work they want to do after their schooling is completed. Of the boys that say they do know what they want to do, the greatest number indicate printing, highway worker, and factory worker. Other jobs indicated by boys are upholsterer, undertaker, pro-basketball player, carpenter, engineer, designer, janitor, shoe repairman, and construction worker. The girls want to be teachers, key punch operators, fac-

tory workers, housewives, and typists.

The favorite academic subjects of our high school students are (in order of times mentioned): math, English, reading, history, geography, and science. Two students say that they like all academic subjects and two say they do not like any academic subject. The vocational subjects liked in order of number of times mentioned are: printing, typing, general shop, clothing and metal shop. Three per cent of the students say that they like all of their vocational subjects, and 13 per cent say that they like none of their vocational subjects.

Only about one third of the students have hobbies. The most popular hobbies are stamp collecting, coin collecting, and sports.

In their choice of reading, 15 per cent say they like mystery stories, 15 per cent like all kinds of reading, 14 per cent prefer love stories, and 18 per cent say they do not like to read at all.

Forty per cent of the students indicate that their favorite activity in summer is swimming. Other activities the students like include travel, basketball, and working.

A third guidance service is counseling. Through individual interviews the student is assisted in resolving problems, establishing realistic goals, and planning a course of action.

The number of individual interviews fluctuates considerably from year to year. The least number of interviews (184) were recorded in 1956–1957. The most interviews (569), were recorded last year. The interviews usually pertain to:

Self study and vocational planning.
Educational placement.
Assistance with government forms.
Future training.
Prospective employment.
Personal problems.

Through the years, counseling with parents has increased. In 1955–56 there were no interviews with parents. (It was my first year and I guess the parents thought I would not know very much anyway.) Last year there were sixty-one interviews with parents. These interviews pertained to:

Student progress.
Preparation for college.
Financial assistance for college.
Advanced placement in high school.
Educational placement of the student.
Working permits.

A fourth guidance service is that of providing information. Throughout the year information is supplied to students, staff members, parents, prospective employers, officials of other schools and agencies, and the Office of Vocational Rehabilitation.

Information requested by or supplied to the student is usually educational or occupational in nature. This information may be the requirements of graduation, the cost of a year at college, the average hourly wage of automobile production workers or questions that may be asked in an employment interview.

Miss Irene Hodock, our librarian, has assumed responsibility for providing educational and occupational books. We have many new books in our library that have a high interest level, and a low vocabulary level. These books have been well received by the students.

A fifth service is vocational placement. The school has provided only limited services in this area. Limited time and financial resources make it it necessary to confine this service to those contacts made at the school. Each year I receive several calls from prospective employers wanting workers. Most of these calls are for printers or office workers. If I can match a former student or a student leaving school with the job, I do so. If not, I contact Mr. Myers of the Vocational Rehabilitation Division and give him the information on the job and the requirements of the person desired. Since Vocational Rehabilitation is statewide, they have a good opportunity to serve all of our former students.

This year I have had twenty-five calls for offset printers and pressmen, ten calls for bookkeepers, typists, and other office workers, one or two calls for metal-lathe operators and shoe repairmen, and two for dishwashers.

The last service I wish to talk about is the followup service. I try to keep a continuous follow-up of our students. The school staff has been very cooperative in passing on information they have about the doings and whereabouts of our students.

Every five or six years an organized followup is made. Questionnaires are mailed to each former student. In 1959 a study was made of the classes of 1954–58. At that time 83 per cent of those who answered the questionnaire were working. There were forty-five different occupations represented. The job stability of the group was very good and the salaries were comparable to those of the hearing. Most of the occupations were in the skilled and semiskilled trades. Almost 40 per cent of the group had obtained further schooling. Twenty-one per cent had attended a trade school, 17 per cent college, 3 per cent night school, and 3 per cent had gone to business college.

At the present time a study is being made of the classes 1954–65. A quick glance through the returns seems to indicate about the same results as the previous study. The employment rate seems to be near 90 per cent, which is better than the former study. The 10 per cent unemployment rate of our students is much greater than the present 2.3 per cent for the State of Indiana or the 4.0 per cent for the nation as a whole.

There are twice as many girls unemployed as there are boys unemployed.

What will happen in the next ten years? It has been predicted that the labor market will be flooded with 1.5 million more workers each year. Teen-agers and young adults will make up over 700,000 of this number. White collar workers will increase. State and local government jobs will increase by one third. Service workers will increase by 25 per cent. Finance, real estate, transportation, public utilities, retail trade, and construction will increase 12–15 per cent. Manufacturing jobs will increase only 5 per cent. The printing and publishing industry will undergo a tremendous change with newer methods and automated machines playing a larger role than in any other industry.

At present over half of our students find employment in manufacturing industries and over one third of the boys find employment in the printing industry. In the light of the above predictions it appears that our students will have to grow up faster. They will have to learn faster and go to school longer in order to compete for jobs with higher qualifications. Our students will have to be mentally and emotionally prepared to retrain themselves possibly two or three times in their lifetime in order to keep up with the changing occupational structure of the labor market.

XIV. Role of the Home in the Educative Process

HEARING HANDICAPPED CHILDREN NEED UNDERSTANDING*

C. Joseph Giangreco

One of the less desirable duties among the responsibilities of administrators of schools for the hearing handicapped are those times when parents come to discuss the difficulties of their family relationships due to the presence of a hearing handicapped child in their midst. Anyone who is the parent of a handicapped child knows that there are innumerable problems and ideas that must be oriented in the parents' mind when the news of the handicap of the child is first announced to them. After the initial shock and attempt at orientation are over, the realities of the situation are faced. One of the first things any parents probably hear is that they should treat the deaf child the same as any other child. This is almost a universal statement in all literature written for parents. With the best of intentions, people involved in this field of endeavor may have minimized the differences of a hearing handicapped child to such a degree that the inevitable special problems surprise and

* Reprinted with permission from *The Iowa Hawkeye,* Iowa School for the Deaf, Council Bluffs, October, 1963. The author is Superintendent of the Iowa School for the Deaf.

frighten us to such an extent that the parent-child relationship soon deteriorates and there exists an unseen barrier in the family. In an attempt (and an honest one, too) to treat the child the same as hearing offspring, the parent soon finds that the results are different. The deaf child doesn't seem to care. The deaf child strays away from the family group. These are what an administrator hears all too often. Other parents wait patiently for their child to suddenly come home from school and be a part of the family, and when he doesn't it is such a bitter disappointment that only bits and pieces of an inadequate relationship can be picked up. The situation "puzzle" always has too many pieces.

After one has been the sounding board for many of the parents in a residential school, the desire to study the situation more closely has resulted in some observations and findings that may be of interest to others.

Initially, there are several basic facts that should be considered. The parent of any atypical child may be inclined to be overzealous and show a special eagerness that may put some sort of unnatural quality into the parent's personality. Parents often admit being anxious or concerned about deafness. This may or may not be sporadic, but it appears especially in times of stress of the child. Oftentimes the problem is confused because it is not easy to establish whether the child's difficulty is due to age, or his handicap. Often, everyone forgets that all children can be exasperating, demanding and remarkably unlovable at times, and on the other hand, all parents feel harried and overburdened some of the time. Parents react with guilt to a momentary, or sometimes more permanent, dislike of the child, and wonder if they have some kind of hidden or not-so-hidden negative feelings about the child. Finally, in any family there are differences in temperament, talents and interests, regardless of what the parents are like.

With these ideas in mind, let me re-emphasize a statement made earlier that in our eagerness to soothe over the initial anguish of learning that a child is deaf, the parents are all too often told to treat him as if he has no problems—"treat him just like the other children in the family." This is no doubt done with the best of intentions, but it seems to me that this is the beginning of the downfall of the parent-child relationship. It is misleading and actually countenances a falsehood to say first that the child doesn't hear well and then turn around and tell the parent to assume there is nothing wrong with him. It is because of this initial direction that we then have

parents unprepared for the special problem and the later shock and surprise and general inability to cope with the situations which arise. *Deafness does make the child different.* If he was not different parents would not have reason to seek medical and educational help. Although he requires the same love and care that any child needs, there is need for special consideration by all in the family circle if the child is to continue in good standing in his family relationships.

Dr. Helmer R. Myklebust, in research at Northwestern University, points out that deafness affects the whole organism. He claims that not only is hearing affected, but vision, balance, taste, smell, maturation, and educational development are all altered because of a hearing problem. And, even further, Myklebust states that it causes differences in perception. Knowing these things from research, one cannot say that this child with hearing problems should be treated the same as a hearing child. It is a disservice to the child to do so. This does not mean the deaf child should be set apart as peculiar. It is rather simply recognizing his problem for what it is.

What, then, are some suggestions that can help parents enjoy a better relationship with their hearing handicapped children?

1. Tender, loving care is essential. Love and affection go far in cementing a bond of family unity. Dr. M. C. Hill says, "The vitamin of love is the greatest single thing we can give our children. Those who were blessed with the

vitamin of love when they were young will mature into well-adjusted adults."

2. Talk to the child, but remember that your child's speechreading vocabulary is not so large as your speaking vocabulary, so choose your words with care. Be willing to visit with your child patiently so that he really knows and understands not only what you are saying, but the "how and why" as well. Take time for casual, as well as necessary conversation.

3. Make it clear what you demand of your child. Hearing children require much repetition for learning and the hearing-handicapped child needs much repetition too. Because you must speak directly to your hearing-handicapped child, it will seem that the repetition is more excessive than it is to hearing children. Also, the hearing handicapped can understand what you want done more clearly if you can take time to *show* what you want.

4. Try not to compare maturation of your children. Research shows that lack of hearing tends to slow down maturation, so don't expect the same rate from the child who doesn't hear so well as from his hearing brothers and sisters.

5. Unless the hearing-handicapped child is unusually bright, there will be an educational lag. Some authorities say there is a gap of three to seven years between hearing children and hearing-handicapped children. Be cognizant of this fact and realize that there will be differences in the school situation.

6. The deaf child also tends to be slower in social development. Schools are making every effort to help the child by providing social situations for the children's development. This is an area where the home can provide many possibilities for growth.

7. Make sure the child is aware of his responsibilities as an integral part of the family and his home. He should not be the privileged weekend, month-end, or vacation guest. Chores and privileges commensurate with his age and abilities are an important part of building a feeling of belonging to the family group.

8. Pay attention to the child's interests. Admire the results of his creativity, or give time to learn of something the child wants to share with you, whether great or small.

9. Meals and bedtime are times for family closeness and pleasure.

10. Religious training should be started early. It may be a difficult area of understanding, but simple understanding is possible and necessary for the nurture of the child.

11. Parents should show that they are a source of strength.

12. Patience, friendliness, politeness, and consideration of each other are family virtues which make parent-child relationships satisfactory to all. Consciousness of these traits should be uppermost in families with a hearing-handicapped child.

In conclusion, remember that the *deaf child should not be treated like any other child, but rather, treat him with an understanding of his deafness.* This new concept, which requires compensation and education on the part of the parent, is well worth the effort. Like all worthwhile endeavors, rearing a hearing-handicapped child has its challenges, and it also has many satisfactions. All the joys of parenthood can be realized if the parental outlook consists of a realistic understanding of the organism that is the child with a hearing handicap.

References

1. HILL, MINER C.: The greatest thing you can give your child. Chicago, *Family Weekly*, April 28, 1963.
2. MYKLEBUST, HELMER R.: Towards a better understanding of the deaf child. Proceedings, Conference of Executives of American Schools for the Deaf, 32nd Meeting, Northwestern University, Evanston, Illinois, April, 1960.

GUIDELINES FOR PARENTS IN PROMOTING VOCABULARY AND LANGUAGE FACILITY*

MARGARET S. KENT

When school begins in September we frequently note that many deaf children have forgotten some of the vocabulary and language facility they had when they went home in June. We have attributed some of this forgetting to the lack of language experience during the summer vacation. Deaf children enjoy their summer experiences but unless someone takes special care to help them put these experiences into words they remain nonverbal in the child's mind. This summer we are encouraging parents to take advantage of the many opportunities to enrich their child's language understanding and to help him use language appropriately.

Here are some language activities you and your deaf child might engage in during the summer:

* This outline, appearing in the column, "Educationally Speaking," in *The Maryland Bulletin*, Maryland School for the Deaf, Frederick, February, 1963, illustrates the effort the school may make in the case of deaf children by reaching into the home along lines of guidance.

Reading and Writing

For Younger Children

1. Use picture dictionary freely in the home to get meanings across.
2. Have a blackboard available in kitchen, family room, or bedroom for drawing and writing. Encourage the child to write words. Later encourage him to write sentences.
3. Help the child verbalize his experience. This means that the parent gives him the words he needs to express an idea. Remember the ideas must be the child's so that the meaning is clear to him.
4. Read stories with your child. You can begin by talking about the pictures. Later you can name objects, and people in the story. You can tell a simplified version of the story somewhat later. Eventually you can read the text of the story with your child, discussing the meanings as you go along.

For Older Children

1. Get books from the public library. Supervise the selection so the book fits your child's reading level.
2. Read the story yourself so that you can

discuss it with your child. Be sure he gets the meaning of the story. Help him to understand it.

3. Use every opportunity to help your child learn the meaning of new words. New words come up in conversation, in books, etc.

4. See that your child does more than look at pictures in books, magazines, and newspapers. Encourage him to read items and discuss them with him.

5. Keep a record of books read during the summer.

6. Encourage your child to write letters to friends and relatives. Give him help when he asks for it. This is one of the best ways for the deaf child to practise language.

7. Help your child keep a diary on a vacation trip, or an unusual experience. Help him with the new words and expressions.

8. Make a scrapbook on something of interest—animals, flowers, a trip, etc.

9. Help your child write short summaries of stories he has read. Help him organize his thoughts into complete sentences.

10. Remember that when a deaf child can express himself clearly in writing you can be sure he understands language.

Listening and Talking

For Younger Children

1. If your child has a hearing aid be sure that it is in good working order and that he gets the benefit of it every day.

2. Encourage your child to listen to television and radio while wearing his aid.

3. Listen to recordings of songs with the words written on paper.

4. Use the hearing aid to improve lipreading. Even little clues make lipreading easier.

5. If your child can monitor his own voice while he is wearing the hearing aid, use it to improve his speech. Repeat the word, phrase, or sentence for him. Then help him to say it.

6. Help your child practise the polite things to say in the proper situation, at the table, greeting people, etc.

7. Help him to know the names of the things around him, his toys, clothing, food. Help him to use them in an appropriate sentence.

For Older Children

1. If your child has a hearing aid be sure he wears it as much as possible and that it is kept in good working order.

2. Encourage him to listen to television and radio while wearing his hearing aid.

3. Listen to recordings of songs with the words written on paper.

4. The hearing aid will make lipreading easier. Use it when talking to hearing people.

5. Help your child practise the polite things to say to other people.

6. Encourage him to ask for things at the table, in a store, or a restaurant.

7. If he can monitor his own voice when he is wearing his hearing aid, help him to speak more clearly. Speak the word or sentence for him and have him repeat it after you.

8. If your child's speech and language development are not adequate for his everyday needs, use fingerspelling (manual alphabet) with speech to make language more readily understood.

These language activities should be carried on in as positive a manner as possible. That is, they should be free from frustrating and negative feelings. If they are kept pleasant, your child will want to continue them. Learning to understand and use language is a long-term process for every deaf child. The continued efforts of parents as well as teachers are needed to achieve this goal.

LETTERS: THE LIFELINE FROM HOME*

GEORGE PROPP AND MIRA JEAN KAUFMANN

Who among us does not enjoy receiving mail, particularly mail from our friends and loved ones? To the child in a residential school for the deaf mail call is the most important moment of the day. A letter from home lets the child know that he is being remembered. Being informed of events happening at home lets him know that he belongs, that he is a segment in that most important of all social circles, the family.

Receiving letters is important, but it is much more desirable to have mail that means something to the child. The purpose of this article is to emphasize that writing as a duty is not adequate, and that writing to a deaf child requires a special effort on the part of the parents. The letter must reach the child where he lives; the letter from home must communicate the love of the family to the child and constantly reinforce the bonds of home. There is, we feel, a very significant distinction between a letter from home and a communication.

As much as the typical residential school tries to provide a homelike atmosphere, we can at best imitate it, and we have neither the wish, ability, nor desire to sever or depress the bonds of home. In spite of the best we can do, the school, as a home, is and should

always be second best. The school encourages strong bonds with the child's family, but the problem of maintaining and strengthening these bonds is largely up to the family.

It is well worth the effort to put some thought into the art of writing letters that really reach the heart of the child. We are brought to mind of a case where a deaf child in the upper grades brought a letter to her teacher with the following notation: "Show this to Mrs. X. (a teacher) and she'll explain it to you." This particular letter was probably better than no letter at all, but it is hardly what you would call a satisfactory communication between parent and child. It seems strange to us that parents who resent anyone's usurping their sole right to spank their child would deliver an even more vital message via an interpreter.

Following are some suggestions for improving the lifeline of communication from home. These suggestions are important to all ages of deaf children, but their application will vary with the age and maturity of the deaf child.

Keep the sentence structure of your letters simple and uncomplicated and use words and expressions that are well within the scope of the child's understanding. The age of the child should determine the degree of simplicity. The young deaf child has a very limited vocabulary and is unable to follow long, complicated sentence structure. The child's ability to read letters does not

* A staff paper appearing in *The Nebraska Journal*, Nebraska School for the Deaf, Omaha, February, 1965. The authors were instructors at the Nebraska School for the Deaf.

greatly exceed his skill in writing, so, using the child's own letters as a language pattern for your writing style is perhaps the simplest solution. To illustrate:

> Mr. Jones, a business acquaintance of your father's, had to get rid of two stray kittens that were staying around the place, and he asked your father if he wanted them. We finally agreed that we would take them and keep them here.

> We have two new kittens. One is black and the other one is white. They are cute. They love to play. You can play with them when you come home.

We cannot argue with the fact that the former of the two statements above is superior English, but for the average deaf child in the lower grades the latter example carries a great deal more appeal, and it is going to make him anticipate his next visit home.

Brevity is desirable. This is not always easy. A simple, concise, understandable letter dealing with one or two ideas, in addition to the routine greeting, is better than a letter that rambles on for several pages telling of things which have no meaning for the child. Long complicated explanations that require assistance in translation make the letter a frustrating rather than a fulfilling experience. The deaf child wants to learn things simply and directly in the language in which he thinks; his own unimpaired imagination will fill in the details.

Letters should be concerned with news of the family, the home life, the friends and relatives of the child, possible plans for the immediate future and things within the knowledge and experience of the child. Mention of pets and farm animals carries considerable impact. All members of the family should participate in letterwriting.

Keep the letters cheerful. Try not to worry a child with problems over which he has no control. His adjustment at school will be hampered by the burden of carrying problems from home. Of course, as the child gets older and develops maturity, it is a mistake of equal magnitude to deny him the responsibility of participating in family decisions.

Write often. Letters should come at least once a week. Several short letters are better than one long one. Writing regularly is as important as writing often. A child who expects a letter every Tuesday and gets it is secure in the knowledge that everything is all right at home. For students weekending at home, a letter in midweek will remind the child that his family is thinking of him. Furthermore, this child needs the attention he receives from his peers when he has a letter to show in class. Even students who commute home daily get a lift from an occasional letter.

Encourage relatives, friends and playmates to write letters to your deaf child. Post cards from cousins in distant places are worth much more to the deaf child than the cost of sending them. Knowledge and information on these cards can often be shared, and thus multiplied, with the child's classmates.

Bear in mind that letters are only one means of communicating with your deaf child. Don't overlook the fact that there are other means of good communication which can be used to substitute for a letter or supplement it. A single stick of gum enclosed in a letter is a very powerful message of parental affection. Pictures, newspaper clippings, cartoons, drawings, schoolwork of brothers and sisters, or any reference to a previously shared experience will greatly improve a letter as a means of keeping in touch with your deaf child.

As the child gets older the letter writing technique will need to be changed to adapt to his language and reading growth and to his rapidly expanding environment. For example, one should not oversimplify language in letters for the older students. As a matter of fact, a letter is perhaps the most successful means of introducing new vocabulary and idiomatic expressions. With the older students the problem of sharing interests is perhaps as great as meeting the student on his language level.

Communications with home should be a two-way street. As soon as possible the deaf child should be encouraged to write independently of the regular classroom letters. Although the school generally provides writing material, it is well to supply the child with stationery of his own. Also see to it that the child is provided with postage stamps; a surprisingly large number of letters which are written are never mailed because the student lacks a stamp. Writing letters is one of the most important opportunities the child has for utilizing the language he learns in school. For most deaf students, the

ability to express themselves in good English after they leave school is directly proportional to the number of letters they write during their schooldays.

A final suggestion, one that strengthens the child's intellectual development at the same time it strengthens the bonds of home, is that parents should be on the lookout for the many inexpensive items available that provide hours of fun and learning experience for the child. The children enjoy and need books. Many valuable stories can be found in inexpensive bindings. Also available are color books, stickem books, dot-to-dot drawing books, cut-out or press-out books, color dictionaries, etc. Also, a box of crayons or a set of colored pencils will make a big hit. For the older children similar materials are available on an ascending scale of difficulty to match their ability. Books encouraging special interests are perhaps the best bargain. Don't forget that for the older students a subscription of the hometown newspaper would be well worthwhile.

We have from time to time been impressed with the pains that some parents have taken to communicate, really communicate, with their deaf children. It reminds us continually of the old adage, "Where there is a will, there is a way." The letters are not intended to serve as models for writing to your own child, but are simply intended to illustrate the fact that, knowing your own child, you should be able to meet him, with some effort, at his level of language and interests.

A STUDY OF THE EDUCATIONAL ACHIEVEMENT OF DEAF CHILDREN OF DEAF PARENTS*

Elwood A. Stevenson

We have always felt that a survey of the educational progress and achievement of deaf children of deaf parents as compared to that of the average deaf child of hearing parents would be most interesting as well as revealing and enlightening. From experience and personal contact and knowledge, we have always taken the position that, things being equal, the deaf child of deaf parents seemed to be stronger and more efficient in his school accomplishment than his schoolmate of hearing parents. There are others who hold this same view, although there are some who feel that the deaf child with deaf parents suffers a severe additional handicap. There is no doubt that the public considers it hopeless and often pathetic when deaf parents' offspring are deaf. However, those of us who have been in the field for many years and are in the position to associate with the deaf in general, thus being able to meet the various types of deaf persons and to make comparisons, honestly feel that, educationally, to have deaf parents is not a handicap but actually is a great asset. To prove this point, this particular study was made at the School for the Deaf at Berkeley, California. It is hoped that other schools will make similar surveys so as to make the study stronger and more conclusive. One may say that this study made at Berkeley cannot be considered as conclusive because of the small and limited number under study. However, it has revealed many interesting points, and strongly substantiates our feeling over the years. The findings make it imperative that several other schools for the deaf should make this study. We plan to write to the superintendents of at least fifteen other schools hoping that each will take time to make this study and compare their findings with ours.

It must be assumed that in a study of this kind there is room for honest error, but not sufficient to affect the final results. The records at the school in Berkeley were very carefully studied and covered a period of forty-seven years, beginning in 1914 and extending through 1961. These were listed and rechecked twice. Fortunately, we know practically all the students considered, thus making the findings more definite and reliable. Each deaf child of deaf parents was paired off with a deaf child of hearing parents of about the same age, of the same sex wherever possible, and entering school at the same time. For example, in listing the child of deaf parents, we entered the next following deaf student of hearing parents of the same age and sex. The progress of each was carefully noted

* A reprint, by consent, from *The California News*, California School for the Deaf, Berkeley, November, 1964. The author was formerly Superintendent of the California School for the Deaf.

and a check of the educational achievement and comparison made through the period spent at the school. Those who did not remain in school for sufficient time for fair comparison or for other obvious reasons were omitted from the study. Some students in both groups under study did not enter as beginning children but had entered later after attending another school for a short time. Wherever possible the deaf parents of the deaf children were studied as to their scholastic abilities and general intelligence. In a majority of the cases, where there was strong intelligence found in the parents, it followed that the children, likewise, showed strong ability. By the same token, where the parents were limited mentally and educationally, the offspring were, likewise, limited and did not fare so well in school. There were only three cases where the parents showed very limited education but where the children were very strong students and were graduates of Gallaudet College. The study brought out two very interesting points. One, the deaf children of deaf parents came mainly from urban areas, whereas the majority of the other children came largely from the rural areas. Number two, the deaf parents were engaged predominantly in the printing trades.

During the period of 1914–1961, there were 134 deaf children of deaf parents. As to sex, this number was surprisingly evenly divided—sixty-eight girls and sixty-six boys. A deaf child of deaf parents who was poor scholastically was found to be extremely poor. However, of the 134 only fourteen were found to be weaker, educationally, than the children of hearing parents with whom they were compared, which is only 10 per cent and which is remarkably low. This would mean that 90 per cent were better students and attained a higher educational level than the children of hearing parents. It is very interesting and very indicative to find that the deaf children of deaf parents invariably possessed a very strong command of language, a factor that should call for further study. This could be very revealing and might prove the crux of our problem in educating the deaf.

Of the 134 deaf children of deaf parents, thirty-one have succeeded in going to Gallaudet College and twenty who are at present still in school will succeed in going to college. Those twenty pupils show very clearly that each possesses the potential necessary for college entrance. We know them personally and have checked their school records and have made comparisons. Percentagewise, this means that 38 per cent of the 134 are of high educational achievement. There were seventeen other students of the 134 whose educational achievement was equal to or better than the level required for college entrance, but for one reason or another decided not to go to college. All in all, this is a far better showing of achievement than that indicated by all the other students of hearing parents, congenitally or adventitiously deaf. It would be safe to say that during this period (1914–1961), of all students enrolled, by rough estimate, only just less than one out of every ten children of hearing parents succeeded in going to college as compared to the 38 per cent who were deaf children of deaf parents.

It is of great importance to any deaf child and his initial progress in school that he be emotionally stable and that he adjust to his school life as early as possible. It means so much to him to have the feeling of security and of "belonging." Likewise, he is aided greatly if he comes with some means of communication, especially that of language. However, it is understood that the deaf child of hearing parents enters school at 5½ years of age with none of these essentials. In fact, the opposite is generally true. He is usually emotionally upset and even, in many cases, disturbed. He feels uncertain and insecure. He is very much "alone" in this new environment and does not feel in any way that he "belongs." He begins his school career very much "handicapped." It is commonly said that it takes at least the first six months of his first year to help him to settle down and to adjust before any teaching can be done. The deaf child of deaf parents, on the other hand, enters school with no such "handicap." He has felt "secure" long before he came to school. He felt that he "belonged." He developed a means of communication early in life long before it was time for him to attend school. In the majority of cases, he comes to school with some foundation of language communication. He has established somewhat of a "bridge." He possesses advantages over his other classmates from the very first day of school. We feel that it is because of these factors that the deaf child of deaf parents, things being equal,

is a far better student than his average classmate and is able to obtain a stronger and more satisfying education. It should be concluded that far from being "handicapped" in having deaf parents as many think, he is truly "blessed" and more fortunate in his long struggle for a sound education.

It might be well to mention that of the several students who were sent to Riverside in 1953, a few have been checked and in most instances have gone to college. All in all, the study is strong and sufficient enough to support the findings already indicated and should more than justify a further study by several other schools.

The fact that the average deaf child of deaf parents enjoys a means of communication and understanding with his parents and his environment long before he enters school should be thought provoking and a challenge to the profession. "How does he secure this early communication with his deaf parents?" one may ask. Simply through his natural means of expression—pantomime, signs, and fingerspelling are a part of the answer. As has been said before, many of these children possess the understanding of the daily actions and needs of everyday life long before they are placed in school. They know their own names, the names of members of their family, and the word values of most of their environment. In fact, many possess use and comprehension of ordinary daily conversation of their age level before age five and one-half years. There is no denying that this proves to be a great asset and advantage in their early foundation for an education. One can appreciate the importance and meaning of this when it is realized that it takes the other deaf children of hearing parents at least a year or two to reach that same level.[†]

[†] In a continuation of this study, Dr. Stevenson included additional pairings to bring them up to and including the year 1964, covering thus a total of 50 years. With this extended period, a total of some 2,200 pupils had attended the school. This made the number of pairings 158 instead of the original 134. The additions, however, made little change in the percentages previously noted. If anything, the main pattern appeared more deeply etched.—I. S. F.

Regardless of present day philosophies in the education of the deaf and the long-standing misunderstanding by many of the use and value of fingerspelling, an unadulterated and non-prejudiced study should be made of the very early use of fingerspelling in the formal education of deaf children. We feel that its adoption will answer the greatest problem we have, namely, the teaching of language and of reading to our deaf children.

XV. Thoughts on a Realistic Appraisal

SPEECH ALONE IS NOT ENOUGH*

Stahl Butler

Professional workers easily understand the strong desire of parents for speech instruction for their deaf children. It is perhaps natural that some should go to extremes and become almost fanatical in their emphasis on the importance of speech.

To combat such misinformation and lack of information, teachers and administrators need to give more time and effort to parent education.

Occasionally, uninformed parents seem to think that speech involves the total education of a child. Apparently they assume that other aspects of child development are tied closely to and carried on by speech, including vocabulary and language development, ability to read, speechreading, skills in other academic subjects, personality development and character training.

Really, this choice by uninformed parents is like the choice of an uninformed purchaser of a used car who, without careful consideration, buys the best looking chassis on the used car lot and gives no thought to the condition of the other parts of the complicated machine.

Perhaps visibility is involved. The uninformed parent does not see the child's deafness. He cannot look at the child's lack of information and lack of mental growth. One cannot view the poverty of vocabulary and the absence of a natural language pattern. All the parents see is that the child doesn't talk as other children do and they want him to be like other children! Hence the emphasis on speech.

To resist what I think to be a natural over-emphasis of speech, we should be sure that parents understand the following points:

1. It is important that a typically deaf child, as far as possible, be taught speech and lipreading so that he can communicate orally with the inner circle of his associates and be able to make light, obvious conversation with the hearing world. The extent to which this objective can be emphasized without materially reducing other educational achievements is extremely important.

2. It is extremely important that a deaf child develop a vocabulary, a language pattern, an ability to express himself in words, and an ability to read, whether he can speak well or not.

3. It is extremely important that each individual be developed to his highest poten-

* Reprinted, by courtesy of the author, from *Michigan Hearing*, East Lansing, Spring, 1963. The author is Executive Director of the Michigan Association for Better Hearing, East Lansing.

tial so that the public can see beyond the deafness and recognize and appreciate an educated and cultured individual, whether he can speak well or not.

4. For the deaf individual, it is highly important that he have verbal and academic skills sufficient to make him confident that he can compensate for his inability to hear.

5. An individual's happiness being the most important objective of all, it goes without saying that there should be opportunity for personality growth, character development, social adjustment, vocational training, and job placement.

AUDIOGRAM—CAN ONLY TELL HALF OF THE STORY*

RICHARD F. KRUG

My purpose is not to review with you exciting new research, nor is it my purpose to discuss interesting theories related to audiology. Instead, I propose to present to you, as briefly as possible, several pleas. Most often, we as professional people are so wrapped up in our own professional journals looking to research to answer some of our many vexing problems, that we fail to look at our fellow workers, our patients, and the parents of handicapped children as human beings with certain basic feelings, abilities, and limitations. The plea I make to you as professional workers in the field of speech and hearing disorders deals exclusively with the feelings, abilities, and limitations of both the child with whom you may be working, and the feelings, abilities, and limitations of the professional persons providing the training and guidance.

My first plea will be made on behalf

* A paper originally given at the annual meeting of the Texas Speech and Hearing Association in San Antonio in the fall of 1962 and published in *The Lone Star*, Texas School for the Deaf, Austin, November 15, 1962. It is here reproduced by courtesy of the author and *The Lone Star*. The author is Associate Professor of Speech, University of Colorado.

of the speech therapist, and will be based upon many discussions with speech therapists working with acoustically handicapped children.

My second plea is made on behalf of the teacher of the deaf, based upon the problems confronting the teacher who has the responsibility to educate the deaf child.

My third plea will be made on behalf of the acoustically handicapped child who is, initially, a victim of circumstances with regard to his acoustic handicap. Unfortunately, the child is often found to be additionally handicapped by the results of unsound professional advice.

My fourth plea is on behalf of the parents of acoustically handicapped children, and is based upon contacts with parents over the course of years.

To prevent as much misunderstanding as possible, the group of acoustically handicapped children will be further defined.

When I speak of the deaf, I mean those individuals who have a hearing loss so severe it precludes learning our language through hearing. Further, the loss is so severe it prevents the individuals from obtaining an education through aural communication either with or without a hearing aid.

When I speak of the hard of hearing, I mean those individuals who, either with or without a hearing aid, can learn to communicate orally through their residual hearing.

The deafened are those who have learned, through audition, to communicate orally, but who have incurred a hearing loss so severe that now the reception of oral communication is impossible through hearing.

To whom are the pleas directed? The pleas are directed to the person I will call a consultant (or Mr. C.). I shall use the term consultant to include all persons who confer with parents and provide them with educational management or guidance of acoustically handicapped children. In some instances, it may be an audiologist or a medical doctor; in others a teacher of the deaf, speech therapist, nurse, director of special education, clinic director, or the classroom teacher who is interested in handicapped children. My concern is not with the title of the position, but rather with the activity of the individual. So, if you confer with parents regarding the educational placement and management of an acoustically handicapped child, the following pleas are aimed directly at you.

If the analysis of discussions with speech therapists is correct, the plea of *the speech therapist* to the consultant can be summarized something like this.

Please don't send me a child without language. My training has been geared to re-educating the speech of those with defective but usually near adequate communication skills. My training has been based upon working with children who have developed their communication skills through hearing—imperfect though the hearing be.

Please don't send me a deaf child to educate. Even though I may have had course work in speech development for the deaf, language development for the deaf, and special materials and techniques for the deaf, I do not operate in a classroom situation and therefore cannot devote the amount of time it takes to train a deaf child.

I am trained to deal with the oral aspects of the child's developing language system. I am not expected to initiate such development in the deaf child. Nor am I expected to teach him to read and to write. Furthermore, I am not expected to teach the deaf child the academic subject material taught in the elementary schools. And all of these things the deaf child must have . . . and they must come through specialized instruction. Don't send me a deaf child, for his major problem is not one of lack of speech but, more importantly, a problem of having no language . . . and speech and language are not the same thing.

As a speech therapist, I implore of you, Mr. Consultant, do not send to me the acoustically handicapped child with the expectation of having him develop adequate communication skills. For when you refer a deaf child to me alone, two things most often happen: First, you present to me a task with which I cannot possibly deal on an outpatient basis . . . and sometimes, the task almost completely overwhelms me. Secondly, by sending the deaf child to me you are preventing him from obtaining training from persons better equipped than I to manage him. Better equipped in terms of the amount of time they are expected to spend with the child; better equipped in terms of training, and better equipped in terms of teaching materials and special classroom equipment.

The above plea on behalf of the speech therapist, I feel, is a rather accurate summary of the feelings which have been expressed to me by speech therapists themselves.

Speech therapists are not the only group of individuals pleading for realistic educational and therapeutic guidance for children. *Teachers of the deaf* join, and their pleading can be summarized in the following manner. For *they* say:

Please don't send to my classroom a hard-of-hearing child who has a good command of language. My training has been geared to learning how to train and educate the child who exhibits no communication skills other than informal and nonconventional gestures. To send to me a hard-of-hearing child with language skills already developed is to present me with real problems. First, you are asking me to engage in two completely different types of classroom training situations. One geared to the needs of the hard-of-hearing child, and the other geared to the needs of the deaf child. Second, you are asking me to devote much of my time to help a child who already has developed, through hearing, an adequate system of communication . . . and this time is so desperately needed by the deaf child with little or no verbal communication.

Mr. Consultant, please do send to me the young child who has failed to develop oral communication, and upon whom you have now placed a hearing aid. Please do send to me the young child who has no oral communication and who, with a new hearing aid, may now be classified audiometrically as hard of hearing. Please send to me these childern, for operationally, they are still deaf, and they need help to develop a language system and oral communication.

Please, Mr. Consultant, consider the child's present facility in oral communication as more important than the residual hearing loss as evaluated while wearing a hearing aid. It may be true that with the hearing aid the child is now able to hear the speech of others to a greater degree . . . but also recognize, Mr. Consultant, that today he has no language or speech. And the hearing aid will not, overnight, allow the development of speech . . . and for several reasons. Not all acoustically handicapped children want to hear. We have to teach the deaf child that this intrusion of new sounds into his world of silence can have meaning. We have to teach him that the apparent confusion of unwanted sounds can become meaningful and that understanding the source and intent of sound will allow him to operate more effectively in his environment. Language and speech, Mr. Consultant, do not develop in two hours or two days, or within two weeks after a child is exposed to amplified sound. With deaf children, results are usually evident only after a year or two of continuous exposure and training.

Please, Mr. Consultant, send me the deaf child as early as possible: wishful thinking is a heartbreaking substitute for practical training. Time is short, and the task is great . . . so let me start early with the deaf child, and let the speech therapist start early with the hard-of-hearing child.

The plea of the speech therapist and the plea of the teacher of the deaf can be easily heard, for the members of both groups are, for the most part, quite vocal, but the plea of *the child with a severe hearing loss* is not clearly audible. There is, nonetheless, a real plea, and if I may transmit *this* plea to you, it would be much like this:

Above all, Mr. Consultant, don't indulge in unrealistic hopes and wishful thinking. Look at the facts.

Please disagree with my parents when it is evident they fail to understand the significance and ramifications of my hearing loss. Disagree with my parents, Mr. C., and speak up for me . . . for I cannot speak for myself. Don't let my parents sacrifice my chance for maximum achievement simply because they fail to understand what a hearing loss means. Don't feel as if you have done enough when you have only talked to my parents, because your real job is to change their unrealistic attitudes toward me and my handicap.

Please don't compromise, Mr. C., don't settle for second best when discussing my education and training with my parents. Inform them in no uncertain terms of what you know is best for me. I know the final decisions are up to

my parents . . . but please do your best to influence them . . . for my sake. Remember, Mr. C., in the countless millions of years this world has been in existence, you and I live only once . . . and for a fleeting short time. What time and effort and opportunity are lost to me now, are lost forever . . . never to be regained. And since I am handicapped, I can't afford to waste or lose a single hour of my precious childhood.

I am a deaf child, Mr. C., so won't you try to impress upon my parents the importance of a system of communication? I want to tell my parents about things I see and do and feel. I need a means of conveying this information to them. Some of my deaf friends are proficient at lipreading . . . but I may not be so fortunate. Some can develop intelligible speech . . . but perhaps I am not one of these. I implore of you, Mr. C., if I fail in my attempt to develop intelligible oral communication, convince my parents to accept manual communication as a tool for my education. For I shall never forgive you for sentencing me to solitary confinement within myself if you fail to provide for me a means of escape through some method of communicating.

Another thing I ask of you, Mr. C. Please impress upon my parents the importance of a hearing aid even though I am deaf. I know I can't understand speech through hearing alone even though it is highly amplified by a hearing aid. But I do find that when I combine even the faintest auditory cues with my lipreading skill, I am better able to receive oral communication.

A final thing I ask of you, Mr. C., try

to stop my parents from wasting precious money, effort and time. Sometimes they run from pillar to post, looking for a miracle to make me hear. I don't know what they expect to find . . . but I do know that I resent everyone pushing and probing, and peering and squirting and blowing into my ears and mouth . . . and rubbing and exercising, and twisting and jerking everything from my head to my toes. Not only have I become resentful . . . I have become hateful of any place or anything that resembles a clinic or doctor's office . . . and I am fearful of anyone who even looks as if he were about to pounce upon my ears.

In short, Mr. C., I am a human being . . . with feelings, abilities and limitations, and since I am a deaf child, I cannot speak on my own behalf . . . I need your help.

The most difficult task is to state briefly *the plea of the parent* of an acoustically handicapped child. If review of parent attitudes and comments can serve as a reliable index, the plea of the parent can be summarized in this manner:

Please, Mr. Consultant, be honest with me. Base your suggestions and recommendations for the training and education of my child upon fact . . . and not upon prejudice. Look at the facts you and your professional associates have accumulated, and then interpret them to me in a manner I can understand.

Please help me to become a parent who understands the implications and ramifications of a hearing loss. Keep after me . . . for sometimes I resist

your ideas . . . resist change . . . but I secretly and sometimes openly express a wish for things to be different. Tell me what limitations are imposed upon my child because of his hearing loss. Tell me how our family can learn to communicate more easily with our deaf child.

Please don't feel afraid to step on my toes . . . sometimes I need to be jolted . . . and to be honest, Mr. C., I began seriously thinking about the many things you said only after your forceful comments and accurate observations hit me squarely between the eyes.

I want you to call a spade, a spade, Mr. Consultant, but don't be discourteous. Don't be cold, aloof or cruel to me simply to satisfy your own personal needs or ego. I have enough trouble as it is. I need facts and truths . . . and I also need someone in whom I find understanding for the many problems and questions facing me as my child grows. While it is true I shall lean heavily upon you during the early years of my child's training and education, you will find that I too can grow in knowledge and understanding. And then someday I shall be in a position of helping you in your work with parents who have only recently discovered that their young child is deaf.

Clearly point out to me, Mr. C., the way I must go to provide the finest educational opportunities available for my acoustically handicapped child. I may not be able to make all the necessary adjustment because of other family obligations . . . but I have a right to know what is best.

In conclusion, Mr. Consultant, if you

are honest with me, help me become an understanding parent, and point out to me the proper path and goals for my acoustically handicapped child. I shall be eternally grateful to you for your help . . . for in the entire world there are only a few people who have a real interest in my child . . . and you are one of them.

"Well now," you may ask, "what does all this add up to?" Reading between the lines of the pleas of the speech therapist, the teacher of the deaf, the acoustically handicapped child, and the parent, it is clear that we must be cognizant of many things when advising parents in the management of their child. Not only must we be cognizant of the clinical or audiological aspects of the hearing loss, but in addition we must pay close attention to the practical or performance aspects of the individual.

For instance, to consider only the audiometric results fails to acknowledge the effects of: (1) the age of onset; (2) the home influence whether it be adverse or advantageous to development of communication skills; (3) the degree to which a child utilizes his residual hearing; (4) the efficiency of oral communication in meeting daily requirements, and (5) the individual's past training and specialized education.

Recommendations based only upon observation of the child's apparent inability to make use of sound lets the door wide open for a failure to understand the actual cause of failure to develop a system of oral communication. Certainly, assuming that a child is deaf solely upon the basis of his failure to develop language skills is ignoring the well established concept of differential diagnosis.

In short, audiological test results are only half the story. The actual performance of the child and referral to the proper professional person for training is the other half. Parent counseling based solely upon the audiogram, or child management based only upon informal observation of the child, is simply wishful thinking on the part of the consultant. Unsound, inappropriate recommendations by the professional can be viewed by the parent as a breach of faith, and by the child as sheer robbery of his potential.

XVI. Deafness with Associated Disability

AIDING THE SCHOOLS TOWARD A BETTER DIAGNOSIS*

JOHN F. FONT

While the origin of language remains a mystery, and while there are a number of theories regarding the process by which language is acquired by the child, we can, without letting ourselves get carried too far away with theoretical considerations, make a number of statements regarding observed phenomena. That is, we can talk about what we see happening without getting into the controversial issues regarding why that something is happening.

What are some of the statements that we can make? Let us list a few:

1. The system of symbols which go to making language is peculiar to man alone. He alone was able to create this system; he alone can perpetuate it.

2. The acquisition of language is a learned process. The degree to which man can utilize these linguistic symbols rests with the appropriate harmony of a number of identifiable and critical variables. These can be seen as subdivisions of his organic condition as well as nonorganic or psychic state.

*An address given at the seventh annual conference of the New York State Association of Educators of the Deaf in Rome, N. Y., October 1962, and here reprinted from *The Register*, New York State School for the Deaf, Rome, N. Y., March–April, 1963. The author is with the Division of Speech Pathology and Audiology, School of Medicine, Stanford University.

3. All things considered equal, language and speech develop systematically and with order.

4. Language can be present without speech. This exists in special cases which we will discuss later on.

5. Language can be considered to be a system of common symbols used for the purpose of communicating. We will limit the symbols to those which are spoken and we will add further qualifications that these symbols must be able to identify objects, feelings, ideas, the past, the present, and the future, etc.

6. While language is peculiar to man there are those who (a) Never learn language, or (b) Learn it imperfectly, or (c) Learn it and lose it either totally or in part.

Now that we have made some broad general statements regarding language, let us amplify some of these. I mentioned just a while ago that the degree to which man can learn and utilize verbal symbols depended upon the harmony of a number of variables. First, there are organic or physical variables. These include the cortex of the brain and the cranial nerves, the spinal cord, muscular development, biochemical, physiologic and endocrine homeostasis, as well as an adequate sensorium or receptorium.

Secondly, one must consider the environmental conditions under which language acquisition takes place and

204

in addition, the psychological composition of the individual language. Myklebust[1] has listed the conditions under which normal language develops as requiring the integrity of the central nervous system and the peripheral nervous system, as well as psychological integrity. Essentially, we are talking about the channels through which certain events are received by an organism, assimilated, synthesized and stored and finally released by that organism. Kirk and McCarthy[2] have recently organized a model of psycholinguistic behavior that was developed by Osgood.[3] They have called the input events decoding and the output events encoding. These events are then organized centrally according to various levels which account for degrees of linguistic behavior. Before I leave this general area, I would like to sum it up simply by stating that for the language process to occur, the organism must be physically and psychologically healthy.

I indicated earlier in my third point that language and speech develop along rather orderly lines. Not only does this order imply temporal relationships, but it also implies time predictions. For example, a child's receptive language exceeds his expressive capacity for a number of years. The child's earliest language experience is auditory and it is through this modality that he will eventually come to imitate his own vocalizations or expressions and, later, to imitate those of others. Language development proceeds from the simple to the complex. Within certain limits, it is possible to predict the

sequence of occurrence of the parts of speech as well as the individual components of speech. Not only are the sequences predictable, the time at which each should occur is also predictable. It is possible, therefore, for a language or speech pathologist to assess where a child is according to how well he approaches accepted values or norms for speech development. Again, let me repeat that we are dealing with the hypothetical "normal" child, and that in any assessment of a child we must allow for a certain amount of deviation from a norm value.

I mentioned in my fourth point, that language may exist without speech. I indicated too, that this situation exists in special cases. I refer specifically in the first observation to several things:

1. The young child who has not yet developed expressive speech possesses receptive language to a limited degree.
2. The deaf child learns a form of subsymbolic language by which he can internalize many of his concrete experiences. Yet, he has little speech.

A case with a severe aphasic disturbance may exhibit a great deal of stereotyped repetitive and serial speech and may yet have a linguistic disturbance severe enough so that he cannot decode or encode linguistic events through any modality.

A mentally retarded child may possess speech and yet have very limited ability in terms of language concepts. His limitations can be seen in terms of breadth of vocabulary, level of linguistic complexity, speech sound acquisition and so forth.

However, I do not want, at this point, to go any further with this subject since to do it any justice would require a great deal more time than we have. Let us turn our attention then to the conditions under which language acquisition is prevented, or impeded or reversed. Language and speech can be delayed as a function of brain damage, mental retardation, deafness and emotional disturbance. We are all familiar with these categories and you have heard just now several discussions expanding some of these areas. But the problems in the schools are similar to the problems in the clinics; that is, what has caused this child to be linguistically retarded. Further, do several of these problems exist in one child and, finally, how does one parcel out the amount of say emotional disturbance in an emotionally disturbed deaf child; or the amount of retardation in a brain damaged mentally retarded child? I believe that if anyone knew the answers to this problem, there would have been little point in having this panel. This point is that, in many cases, the clinical "hunch" or intuition or insight is providing the basis for much of the diagnostic work that goes on today. I don't mean to say that there is no structure to an evaluation and that someone merely sits and observes a child and finally makes a "pronouncement." Not at all. What I am suggesting is, that our clinical tools are as yet quite unsophisticated and can lead us only a part of the way toward a clinical diagnosis or impression or understanding of the nonverbal child. Further, there are constellations of behaviors, which viewed as behaviors alone can be found among children in each of the above categories. I might add at this point that a number of linguistic dis-

turbances have been reported among congenitally blind children, particularly those with retrolental fibroplasia, which resemble the language characteristics of emotionally disturbed children and brain-damaged children. An excellent discussion of the characteristics of these children can be found in a book entitled *Psychopathology of Communication* edited by Hoch and Zubin.[4] With this and other pieces of evidence in the literature regarding language and blindness we might do well to heed Dorothea McCarthy's[5] advice to perhaps spend a little less time among normal children and to begin developing some well controlled studies among children in whom there has been a breakdown of the language process.

Let me get back to the clinical "hunches" that I mentioned earlier. Many of the children that we see in clinics and some of the children that you find coming to the schools for the deaf defy a singular category of disturbance. To begin to attempt to differentiate among several disturbances within a single child is today a rather risky undertaking and one for which there is little accumulated evidence. Therefore, let me suggest to you a rough procedure or outline that you might find useful in going about the job of evaluating a nonverbal child. I shall develop this outline only as a first step for the school teacher since I am assuming that certain other procedures will be taken over by the psychologist, the audiologist and other specialists. The outline I suggest divides itself into two parts.

1. History interpretation
2. Behavioral observation

A third part, clinical testing, will be left to the specialists who will also be utilizing information from the two items just mentioned to aid them in interpreting their tests.

History Interpretation

One looks specifically here for pre-natal, or postnatal problems which may be associated with brain damage. One will look specifically at the history of pregnancies in the mother, the con-ditions of the pregnancy with the particular child in question, Rh prob-lems, toxic diseases before the 3rd month, prematurity, labor difficulties suspected cerebral injuries, convulsions, meningitis, encephalitis, mumps, whoop-ing cough and so forth. You are all aware, I'm sure, of the number of con-ditions which have been found to be related with brain damage, sensori-neural hearing losses and auditory per-ceptual problems. While I don't mean to labor this point here, I am merely trying to point out a logical first step. To attempt to understand a child in-dependent of his history makes as much sense as trying to describe a child only on the basis of his history. Also, one should look for the absence or presence of convulsions without fever, cerebral injury with unconscious-ness and any history of drug therapy. One should determine whether any neurological studies have been done and the reports should be obtained for a review of the neurological findings. In many cases children are enrolled in schools and the schools lack informa-tion about the child which may be of value in helping to understand the child. A complete history of the child is indispensable. It should be noted that while the presence of brain dam-age need not reflect an associated lan-guage disturbance, neither does a neg-ative history indicate that brain dam-age is not present. Lubic[6] points out that abnormal EEG's can be observed among persons with no language prob-lems and with no other neurological signs. He cautions that EEG findings "must be evaluated in light of the clini-cal picture."

We next want to review in the case history the child's developmental se-quences. A number of scales are avail-able for use as guides which include the Gesell Scale, the Vineland and the Cattell. Many of the items can be de-termined from the history, but many will have to be evaluated with the child himself. The stress here would be on motor skills, self-help skills, and nonverbal associative and imitative tasks.

Further, we would want to have some idea of this child's relationship with par-ents, siblings and peers. We would want information as to his early abilities to integrate his environment, his reactions to frustration, his modes of behavior, observations concerning his visual and auditory skills. We would look for any history of intense or unusual fears, re-jection of strangers or close relatives, smiling and laughing, hyperactivity, withdrawal, temper tantrums or rage, behavior, rocking and unprovoked cry-ing or other intense emotional reactions.

Finally, one would review carefully, the speech and language history, if any. When did vocalizations cease? Were any meaningful words ever learned? Was there an abrupt change? Was this change accompanied by any significant physical or environmental event? Did the child ever use gestures or other signs? Did he respond to gestures? How well did the child use other sense modalities? Does the child have any appropriate language or speech now? How has he responded to pictures and to objects? How appropriately does he utilize these pictures or manipulate these objects? Does the child vocalize and, if so, is there anything unusual about his voice?

Finally, also, one would want to make critical comments on the basis of observation of the child's behavior in the school environment as well as in the cottage or home environment. In particular we will be looking for information regarding:

Consistency of response to sound or voice
Use of speech or language or gestures
Self-help skills
Appropriate use of environmental objects
Imitative behavior
Attention
Bodily activity, motor coordination, handedness
Ability to operate within limits
Attention to facial expression or response to facial expression
Relationship to others
Echolalia
Distractibility and disinhibition

We could include more items here but I believe these are sufficiently representative.

After the teacher has reviewed the entire history and made a number of personal observations of the child, she should consult with the psychologist or audiologist either for further testing or for a review of their findings.

I would suggest to you that in some cases, after a very thorough review of all the available information including test results, you may feel somewhat more secure in identifying the basic problem. It is likely in many instances that this may not be the case, and you will not be any closer to the child's basic problem than when you began. If you sent him to some experts you would likely receive conflicting reports and have as many interpretations as there are "experts." I suspect that in these cases the "experts" are partially right and partially wrong. However, I don't mean to belittle the "experts" since each views the child within an entirely different framework, at a different moment in time, under diverse conditions, and for varying lengths of time.

It is my firm belief that we are passing out of the "era of the diagnostician" and I think this is good. More and more we read in the literature and hear from the "authorities" themselves that they are incapable, with many of these severely linguistically disturbed children, to produce a diagnostic label. More and more we see children, when they do not present relatively clear diagnostic pictures, being exposed to language training which is not based on a "method" peculiar to a specific type of language disability. This type of training, however, depends upon great flexibility on the part of the teacher who must be able to abandon fruitless efforts and to explore with the child those procedures which will be most realistic and appropriate. What happens in this kind of situation is that, with time and close observation, we can begin to categorize children, not so much in terms of pathology, but in terms of their educability. This is not a new concept and we hear it usually referred to as "diagnostic teaching." It is my firm belief that we learn more about a child after a year or two of working with him than we know after an hour or two of "evaluating him."

Therefore, if I were to make a recommendation to you as teachers of the deaf who are concerned about the child who comes to you and does not "behave" as a deaf child, it would be to worry less about his diagnostic category and be more concerned about the number of ways that you might approach this child. Your legitimate concern, of course, is that, as teachers of the deaf, you are perplexed when you are confronted with children that may represent many things other than deafness and whose admission to the scohol was on the basis of limited or no response to sound and the lack of language and speech development. Your problem is a real one and will likely continue as long as our methods of assessment remain as relatively crude as they are. On the other hand, I'm wondering if we couldn't conceive of an expanded role for schools for the deaf. Such a role would include a division within the existing structures where the emphasis would be on working with children with undifferentiated language problems. This would relieve the teachers of the deaf of the responsibility of handling these special problems, and, equally important, it would provide the time necessary for continuous observation and appraisal of these children. The research potential would be unlimited and such a program could function as a kind of "language laboratory."

I'm not sure if I have answered anything for you or told you anything that you don't already know. I suspect, however, that when it comes to "Aiding the Schools Toward a Better Diagnosis" our thinking must be, at least at this time, away from brief interviews and observations, and very much toward systems of "diagnostic teaching."

References

1. MYKLEBUST, H. R.: *Auditory Disorders in Children.* New York, Grune, 1954.
2. KIRK, S., and McCARTHY, J.: *Illinois Test of Psycholinguistic Ability,* Experimental Edition. Institute for Research on Exceptional Children. Urbana, U. of Ill.
3. OSGOOD, C. E.: A behavioristic analysis; in *Contemporary Approaches to Cognition.* Cambridge, Harvard, 1957.
4. KEELER, W. R.: Autistic patterns and defective communication in blind children with retrolental fibroplasia; in *Psychopathology of Communication,* P. H. Hoch and J. Zubin (Eds.). New York, Grune, 1958.
5. McCARTHY, D.: Language development; in *Language Development and Language Disorders: A Compendium of Lectures.* Nancy Wood Monographs of the Society for Research in Child Development (25). Yellow Springs, Antioch, 1960.
6. LUBIC, L. G.: A neurologist discusses the evaluation of a nonverbal child; in *Language Development and Language Disor-*

ders: *A Compendium of Lectures.* Nancy Wood Monographs of the Society for Research in Child Development (25, No. 3). Yellow Springs, Antioch, 1960.

PROBLEMS ACCOMPANYING CHILDREN WHO ARE DEAF AND MENTALLY RETARDED*

Myron A. Leenhouts

The faculty of hearing is undeniably the most significant and important avenue for gaining knowledge and for developing communication skills. We learn to speak because we hear; we learn the pattern of our language through hearing that pattern repeatedly; hearing offers the constant avenue of reception to our environment whether it be the sounds of the wind, rain, birds, a siren, a beautiful song, or the conversations of parents and friends, or the more profound (we hope) lectures, discussions, and explanations that our ears readily receive during those years of our formal education. Hearing is voluntary and involuntary and proffers a veritable continuous bombardment of information to the receiver.

When this avenue of reception is completely closed, the resulting deprivation is almost too smothering to contemplate. It is no wonder then that for the child who is deaf—either at birth or before language and speech are well established—the matter of gaining knowledge and an education is tremendously difficult. Instead of the flood of information hearing affords, for the deaf child reception of information must be obtained by conscious effort and through visual means, and consequently the quantity as well as accuracy of reception is lessened.

A few prelingually deaf individuals become well educated in spite of this overpowering handicap. They are the fortunate ones who possess some or all of the following conditions: (1) an exceptionally high IQ; (2) intelligent parents who established communication with their child in infancy, and/or (3) the opportunity for a great deal of individual tutoring during and beyond formal education.

Obviously, there are comparatively few such fortunate deaf individuals who are able to attain an education comparable to their hearing contemporaries. The far greater majority—even those with average or better than average IQ—are doing very well to maintain an educational lag of no more than three grades. In other words, if a deaf student with average or better than average IQ—at sixteen years of age, and ten years in school—can do 7th grade work we can consider his achievement quite praiseworthy for a *deaf* child. This being so, we must ac-

* A paper presented at the Central Coastal Region III Meeting of the American Association on Mental Deficiency, Palo Alto, Cal., April 4, 1964, and reproduced here with consent of the author from *The California News,* California School for the Deaf, Berkeley, October, 1964. The author is Assistant Superintendent for Instruction, California School for the Deaf.

cept the premise that, in considering the IQ of deaf children, the performance potential is depressed by approximately 15 to 20 points. Our experience proves that this premise is especially fitting in the instance of deaf children with an IQ of 100 or below. In other words, a deaf child with an IQ of 95 compares in *achievement potential* with the hearing child with an IQ of 75.

The really serious problem, then, is the deaf child who has an IQ below average. As pointed out in the preface above, deafness, in itself, is the greatest of all obstacles to securing knowledge and an education. Therefore, when low mentality is superimposed upon deafness, the chances for educational attainment are lessened in almost geometric proportions.

With this as prelude, let us get down to cases and talk about the problems which accompany the enrollment of of mentally retarded deaf children in our school at Berkeley and in schools and classes for deaf children generally.

First, a few statistics: we have at the Berkeley School for the Deaf 480 students; 93 per cent or 446 of these children are prelingually deaf, having either been born deaf (74%), or having lost hearing before speech and language patterns were established (19%). These figures are impressively significant when you consider that 93 per cent of our students have been completely or nearly completely deprived of that most important avenue of reception . . . *hearing.*

As further statistics, data were gathered that confirm our experience that deafness *does* depress the opportunity for gaining knowledge. Regarding categories of learning potential, our school's student population was compared with the national norms for hearing children. The percentage distribution follows:

	Students at C.S.D.	Hearing Students
Above Average	12%	20%
Average	45%	60%
Slow Learners	32%	18%
Retarded (Educable)	10%	2%

It appears then, that in our school 42 per cent of our students will have an educational lag of considerably more than three grades, and 10 per cent will be little more than trainable.

Our greatest concern in a residential school for the deaf lies with the final 10 per cent, those who are in the severely retarded group, achievement-wise, even though intelligence tests may show an actual IQ range of 70 to 80. Several problems immediately accompany the enrollment of these children with low capacity: (1) class placement; (2) an appropriately revised program; (3) adept teachers; (4) social adjustment to residential living, and (5) the inordinate amount of time spent by personnel in the continuing evaluation process.

First, regarding *class placement,* there is always a wide age range among the new enrollees who are mentally slow. In classifying them, therefore, one is faced with the alternative of placing them with other children approximately their own age but with superior ability; or of forming a heterogeneous age group, all with approximately the same limitations. Either way, the results are far from ideal. In the first instance, the one or two retarded children in an average class require an excessive amount of the teacher time and attention, thereby distracting from the fair progress of the majority: and in the second instance the teacher is required to conduct practically an individual program for each pupil, and is faced with the inevitable problems accompanying the fact that the remaining children, not being given her direct attention, can not work independently.

A second problem connected with the enrollment of retarded deaf children is the matter of an appropriately modified course of study, both academic and vocational. These programs must be modified in scope of content as well as in method of presentation; and in the matter of vocational placement, the retarded students must generally be limited to very simply routine type training that will require hardly any verbal instructions or complex related trade language. We have noted that there is not a really significant correlation between retardation and ability to master a skill, but there is a definite relationship between the language limitations of a retarded student and his ability to pursue many of the normal trades generally open to the deaf. Consequently, it becomes necessary to compose an academic course of study especially geared to the retarded child, and also to provide outlets in the vocational program suited to his limitations. During the past several years, committees of teachers and supervising teachers have initiated courses of study for retarded children—one for lower grades and one for the upper grades. They emphasized two basic principles of learning: (1) concept building through experience, and (2) memorization through repetition. These courses have been quite effective.

The matter of securing the proper type of teacher for retarded children is a third problem. Teaching normally intelligent deaf children requires tremendous patience and ingenuity as we know. This requirement is many times compounded in teaching retarded children. The teacher must be infinitely patient, must be able to invent many special devices for concept building, must be an artist, must be completely versatile in communication skills, and should be somewhat of a gymnast, since occasionally it may become necessary to stand on his head to affect a point of illustration. Our experience convinces us that the deaf teacher who possesses these qualities is usually most effective with retarded children. However, it should be emphasized that the fact of being deaf alone is not a qualification. Some deaf teachers possess none of the really important qualities necessary for the job, and many, who are aware of their qualification shortcomings, wisely avoid teaching retarded children. However, the capable deaf teacher, with the proper sympathy and devotion, can accomplish a great deal. He exercises the principles of simplicity of presentation, and of repetition; he is sympathetic to the pupil's personal needs and emotions; he is quick to discover the child's plateau of understanding; he can readily establish the manual communication facility usually so necessary for these children; he may exercise his talent for pantomime, and use this along with other devices to promote concept understanding. The writer must quickly add that the hearing teacher, with these qualifications, can also do an outstanding job.

Probably the most serious problem connected with the enrollment of retarded children is the matter of their adjustment and integration to residential living. The retarded child is generally a serious misfit in the school family; he is the "sick chick" who gets pecked at and picked on by the other chicks, and may well be the scapegoat for the group whenever trouble occurs. He requires an inordinate amount of the dormitory counselor's attention both in the matter of being protected from abuse, and also of being trained in the physical routines of personal care. In addition, it is very difficult to explain regulations, and their whys and wherefore to the retarded pupil, and consequently he may make serious infractions of rules in innocence and ignorance—but *in the presence* of the other children. Immediately there arises the problem of proper and just correction, while simultaneously maintaining group morale. Another very serious problem arises when the retarded student reaches adolescence. With this group, there are more social privileges and more freedom from campus restrictions. The retarded student who is physically mature but uninhibited because of mental immaturity is obviously a continuous worry to school administration, school personnel, and parents.

Because of the deficiencies—both educational and social—which retarded children present, various members of the school staff must spend an inordinate proportion of their time in their behalf, and consequently the great majority of the student body, who have the ability to progress normally, are relatively neglected. The counselor, the teacher, the supervising teacher, the dean, the principal, the psychologist and the superintendent— everyone concerned finds himself excessively involved. A disproportionate amount of supervision is required; frequent staff meetings are necessary to determine the child's current status or to discuss some immediate difficulty; repeated written reports are needed to insure a complete and valid record of evaluation; frequent retests and psychological consultations are required; and often the supervising teacher and the dean must assume the role of "baby sitter" when the teacher or counselor feels that insulation is best accomplished by temporary isolation.

From the foregoing, one can hardly mistake the fact that the writer takes a rather dim view of having the mentally retarded deaf children enrolled in a residential school for the deaf. The matter of training these children in a non-residential situation is difficult enough, but when the factor of twenty-four-hours-a-day social adjustment and integration is added, the situation becomes a really serious problem. Yet, strangely enough, in spite of the very obvious disadvantages of the residential factors, there is a universal tendency to consider the residential school for the deaf *the* appropriate facility for the deaf child with multiple handicaps, including the mentally retarded deaf. Somehow the feeling has gained ground that when at other facilities such children make little effective progress along lines of language, communication ability, and general academic advance, the thing to do is for them to learn a trade. Where? At the residential school for the deaf, of course. But here too the problem remains a sensitive one, for the supervising teacher in the vocational area, bearing in mind the nature of the complex equipment in the shops and the fact that the program calls for language and reasonable skill in arithmetic as well as manual skill, finds the mentally retarded pupil unable to cope with requirements. This is often further complicated by the insistence of parents that their child take up a trade beyond his natural competence. All of this further emphasizes the fact that the residential school for the deaf is not necessarily the magic panacea for the mentally retarded deaf child. In many instances, pre-enrollment evaluation indicates mental retardation so severe that the child's application for admission must be rejected. In other instances, the child may be accepted on a trial basis, but later dismissed because of complete incompetence academically and socially. When the child is not admitted or must be withdrawn after a trial period, the reaction of the parents is usually resistance, bitterness, and recrimination, and then comes the inevitable question: "What now for my child?" In California we are fortunate

in having a partially satisfactory answer to this question. We are able to suggest to the parents that they investigate the possibility of enrolling their child in one of three State Hospitals (Sonoma, Porterville, or Pacific) where classes are provided for the Point II deaf child. However, at this point another problem arises with regard to the mentally retarded deaf children who, by objective tests earn an IQ of 70 to 80, but who after trial enrollment in our school for the deaf, show that they cannot cope with, or benefit from the school's program and social routine. Careful and thoughtful staffing results in the conviction that these children's retention is more harmful than helpful to themselves, and so dismissal is recommended. From our viewpoint these children's best interests would be met in a program such as that offered at our state hospitals for the mentally retarded. However, here we meet the problem head on. The child's 70 or 80 IQ is "too high" for eligibility there, and so his application must be rejected or acceptance must be postponed for a long time. The result is that the child is suspended in no-man's-land. He is unable to function in a regular school or class for the deaf, yet his apparent potential excludes him from the state hospital program. There is, at present, at least, no intermediate facility for this child. But, more on this thought later.

But as for the deaf child who is eligible for the state hospital program the suggestion that he be enrolled there is often resisted by the parents who attach a dreadful stigma to committing their child to a hospital for mentally retarded. In at least 60 per cent of the cases, it becomes impossible to convince the parents that these special services are unique and definitely would serve their child's best interests. Instead, these parents begin an anxious and desperate search for some alternate facility for their child, and more often than not this search brings them back to the residential school armed with some amateur's supporting statement that: "The residential school for the deaf is the only appropriate agency for this child." It is at such times that we appreciate the authority and finality of decision which the school psychologist and the eligibility committee wield.

Were it possible to remove the stigma associated with the state hospital, and thus experience ready parent acceptance to the suggestion of placing their retarded child in the special program, California would be approaching the ultimate in its services to these children. At present approximately one hundred Point II deaf children are enrolled in classes at Sonoma, Porterville, and Pacific State Hospitals. This is considerably less than one half the number of children who would be eligible. In the main, the programs at these three agencies are creditable, and although a few weaknesses exist, the service offered is many times better than any alternate facility now available. Deaf teachers man the basic teaching staff for these programs, and the children are taught manual communication skills, the simple vocabulary of basic everyday language, the very elementary three R's and some

form of simple routine work training which might later lead to semi-independent employment. A very important part of the program is the emphasis placed on developing social maturity and improving interpersonal relationships.

Although the state hospital programs are now very good, suggestions for improved services indicate that the three separate programs might be combined into one. This would make for much more homogeneous grouping; it might justify having a separate dormitory facility for the deaf youngsters who could then be under the supervision of trained personnel and thus eliminate one of the strongest oppositions to commitment on the part of parents. Also it is indicated that there be more provisions for vocational training so that those capable may have a better chance for employment when they "graduate." Finally, it is suggested that some means may be devised to get parents of prospective pupils to visit the hospital and see for themselves the opportunities for training and for happiness the program offers.

In order to insure an effective and continuous evaluation of children who are in the program at the Sonoma State Hospital, personnel from our school arrange to visit once or twice each year. During these visits, we observe the children and re-examine any whose current status may be in doubt. If re-examination indicates the child's performance may now show promise of fitting into our program at Berkeley, a transfer is arranged. The fact is thus emphasized that the potential of these children as well as their educational placement is not considered static and irrevocable.

What about the plans for the future services to the mentally retarded as well as other multiply handicapped deaf children of California? Because of the more accelerated activity in differential diagnosis, and the consequent discovery of an astounding number of atypical children, our state along with most others has become very conscious of the need for special services to the handicapped. Within the state department of education there is a deputy superintendent in charge of special schools and services, and under him is a chief of the bureau of special education who is concerned with the programs in the public schools. During the past several years many new services to handicapped children have been inaugurated and many more expanded. And, through conferences both at local and state level, the continuing concern for improved services is evidenced. In the field of the education of the deaf, our particular concern has been the proper disposition and training services to the deaf child who is mentally retarded or atypical in other ways. We have gained the sympathetic ear of our state department officials regarding the serious problems which accompany the enrollment of atypical children in our regular schools. We are in agreement that the ideal facility for these children would be a separate unit on the campus of a residential school for the deaf. The advantages of such a facility are obvious:

1. It could be a resource to which parents could and most likely would turn in their natural bewilderment upon learning, through diagnostic tests, that their child does deviate from the normal, and cannot benefit from regular school placement.

2. It could relieve the community of the dilemma of providing the proper care and training of such children, and should therefore be highly desirable to community agencies.

3. It could assure properly trained and appropriately specialized personnel essential for an effective diagnostic, therapeutic and training program.

4. It could provide a maximal opportunity for adjustment and rehabilitation, and in favorable instances, for the eventual acceptance in a regular school program for deaf children.

5. It could relieve all present educational facilities for deaf children in the state of the present enrollment pressures, permitting them to concentrate on the functions for which they are intended, and thus would make possible a more effective service for both the normal deaf children and those who experience multiple handicaps.

A recent state survey has found that there are approximately 700 multiply handicapped deaf children in California, and of this number a large proportion are now being denied *any* kind of public school training. Although much effort has already been made to secure the appropriate facility for these neglected deaf children, results thus far are discouraging. It behooves everyone who is concerned with, and sympathetic to the plight of, these children to add his active and determined support to the proposition that California shall no longer postpone this *most urgent* unmet need to potentially useful citizens, who, if they remain ignored, will be forever dependent.

COURT GRANGE*

RESIDENTIAL TRAINING CENTER FOR DEAF YOUTHS: THE ROYAL NATIONAL INSTITUTE FOR THE DEAF,
ABBOTSKERSWELL, DEVON, ENGLAND

The Problem

Court Grange has been established by the Royal National Institute for the Deaf as a training establishment for maladjusted deaf youths between the ages of sixteen and twenty-four. The need for such a center has been felt for some years by local authorities, welfare workers for the deaf and others having in their care deaf boys who are so disturbed in various ways that they are unlikely to settle down and lead useful lives without specialized training in surroundings away from their local environment.

Without training, it is possible that these youths will find themselves on the wrong side of the law, when they must be dealt with by the due process of the courts which may have great difficulty in helping them because of the added complications of the disability of deafness. Court Grange will take any deaf boy with behavior problems or emotional difficulties, but not those who need long-term hospital treatment for any illness or physical disability, or those who are in need of specialized psychiatric treatment within the confines of a mental hospital.

The aim is to try to inculcate in the young deaf men who come to Court Grange the will to lead a full, happy

* A publication of the Royal National Institute for the Deaf, reproduced by courtesy of the administrative office of that organization, 105 Gower Street, London W.C.I.

and industrious life and to fit them to do so. To achieve this end, a number of methods of training are being used. It is envisaged that a number of those coming will have suffered broken, unhappy or unsatisfactory homes, and so the first essential is for them to be introduced to a happy, contented environment.

The Training

The training envisaged is intended to give self-confidence and an acceptance of the world as it is, and to assist the deaf lad in accepting and learning to live with his disability.

It is important that some provision is made for the practice of casework. It is hoped that during the youth's stay, the staff, under the direction of the warden (whose training in social science has included a course on casework principles and practice) will be able to come to grips with the difficulties which are besetting each lad and help him to resolve them and, where necessary, in conjunction with the welfare officer for the deaf in his home area bring about a better relationship with his own home.

Many of the lads who come have inconsistent or bad work records. This may be through the lad himself, his inability to stick to a job, to wrong placing in work or to lack of knowledge of the job he is doing and the lack of someone there to help him—all again aggravated by his personal problems and his deafness. The efforts of the staff through training in various trade skills are directed to inculcate good work habits.

Some boys will need prolonged trade training within Court Grange; a few, who do not show any aptitude or interest in the courses which can be run on the premises, may be accommodated in small businesses in the Court Grange area where they can learn some job satisfactorily; a further few may have had sufficient trade training which they have not used particularly wisely in the past, but may be found employment in that trade in the area with selected employers. By all means, the lads, during their rehabilitation period, can be cushioned against the difficulties they have come up against in the past in their work. This does not mean that no responsibility is expected from the lads toward their work, but it does mean that when all is not going well, discussion can take place and the best solution regarding their continuing or changing their work can be taken.

Facilities must be provided for lads to have certain games available and, important in a place like Court Grange, the provision of a youth club. Lads can then be encouraged to exchange visits with those of other clubs on a purely social basis. Evening classes in hobbies are important as they help to encourage a lad to occupy his leisure time to some advantage.

Another side of recreation is the arranging of outings to places of interest, works, historical sites, and so on. It has been found that lads belittle these outings before they happen, but quite often become engrossed when the outing is taking place.

The Domestic Side

The warden and his assistants are the chief workers in the training of the lad, but this also devolves on the domestic staff. The matron sets the tone of the whole establishment and the strength of her influence cannot be underestimated. Her staff cope with all the domestic arrangements. Lads can help, and are encouraged to take their part in doing some of the chores, but their trade training means they are occupied all day and consequently can only do some of the work essential if Court Grange is to be kept in first-class condition.

Objectives

It is of little use stating that the aim of training must be to try to inculcate in lads the will to lead a full, happy and industrious life and to fit them to do so, unless this statement is amplified in relation to those expected to reside at Court Grange. Some of the following may appear rather banal, but they are, nevertheless, important:

1. Training in cleanliness, tidiness, care of clothing, good manners and socially acceptable general behavior. So many of the lads who come are boorish and ill mannered, untidy and often dirty in their habits; to make them more acceptable to live in any society, these traits must be eradicated and the lads persuaded to accept a higher standard.

2. Training in specified trades, in regular work habits and a proper attitude toward work. It is appalling to read in reports the ap-

parent irresponsibility that a lot of young men have toward work; they lack the skill to undertake any but the most menial tasks, they lack any loyalty to employers, or even to their fellow workmates. We provide courses at Court Grange on which most lads will be placed after the initial period of residence, during which time the staff will be assessing their capabilities. Most courses will be for eighteen months to two years.

3. Training in the careful spending of money. Pocket money here is, of necessity, limited, but when the lads are earning by encouraging them to save and to buy clothing and other essentials for themselves, we hope that they will develop good habits with regard to the use of their wages in the future.

Leisure

All boys automatically become members of the youth club which has its own special clubroom. A great number of activities take place under its auspices, including camping, canoeing and hiking, and visits to and from other clubs for games, tournaments and social activities.

Facilities are provided for learning and playing football, badminton, basketball, padder tennis, swimming, gymnastics, cricket and tennis in the gymnasium or on the field adjacent to the house. Of indoor games, we have billiards, table tennis, darts, draughts, chess and dominoes and others.

In the hobbies classes we include the following: gymnastics, mime and amateur theatricals, basketwork, rugmaking, woodwork, model aeroplane making, lampshade making, model making, painting and drawing, and perhaps later, pottery. Tuition can also be provided for boys who wish to improve their general education.

Religion

It is most important, too, to care for the spiritual well-being of all those who live at Court Grange, and to help them to resolve the many inner conflicts to which adolescents are prone. The chapel is always open and all encouragement is given for the lads to practise the religion of their choice. On so many documents where a religion has to be stated, one often finds the word "nominal" in brackets after the religion named. Adolescents are at the age when they question the beliefs of their parents and family, where they are not prepared for blind acceptance. By putting them in touch and keeping them in touch with the clergy or ministers of their stated religion, and by the example of the staff at all times, we hope to help them through the uncertainties with which they are faced to a maturer outlook, bringing with it, we hope, membership of their chosen church.

Sociability

In general, we try to make a lad more socially acceptable to the public at large and in doing so, to his family in particular. Excuses can be made for the adolescent kicking against the rules, and reasons can be given for such behavior, but in the end we are driven back to the fact that the rules are still there. Gradually, we encourage our lads to accept this fact and to abide by them.

It has been said that adolescence is like the god Janus, with one face in the old year and the other in the new. Our young men are advancing toward manhood, but can still at times behave like children, and spoiled children at that. We try to help them through this difficult period. For the deaf it is often a more difficult time than for the ordinary lad. We must be tolerant with them, but seek all the time to draw them nearer to the adult world.

Conclusion

While the reasons for their inability to adjust can be recognized by a trained social worker, our lads must not dwell on the past too much. It is a mistake to encourage them to think of themselves as so different from everyone else that they either become freaks or too precious. The society in which we live demands adherence to certain basic rules from anyone seeking to live in it, but through lack of training during their childhood, aggravated by being unable to hear, they have not learned these basic rules. Our lads must learn these rules and adherence to them as quickly as they can. When they have done this they will find themselves more socially acceptable to their fellow men and will have no reason to return to their anti-social behavior, or to resort to law-breaking activities.

Realization of what is required is the first essential and, following this, the will and determination to change. Miracles rarely happen and the process of learning or re-learning is a slow and often painful one with many regressions to the old style of behavior. But to the trained observer, if our work is being carried on properly, imperceptible changes are noticed and these add up

to quite a substantial alteration in character when viewed at the end of a lad's stay with us. That a young man has left does not mean that the work is over. A great deal still needs to be done by us, if he is remaining in this area, or by his parents and the deaf welfare worker in his home town if he returns there. Between us we must carry on the work in the outside world, helping the lad to relate what he has learned at Court Grange to his own particular circumstances.

Because of these special problems and the services needed to help, progress will be slow and the cost high in comparison to schemes for hearing persons. This is a scheme for the deaf (i.e., those who are born with little or no hearing and are unable to communicate readily with their fellows) and also for those who have become deaf to such an extent that they also cannot fit into ordinary life.

[*In his Second Annual Report, 1964–1965, from which the following excerpts are here reproduced, the Warden of Court Grange, D. C. Vincent, elaborates further upon the policy and practices involved in the program.—* I. S. F.]

Probably the most important development has been recognition of the trade training by the Ministry of Labor. After negotiations extending over a long period Court Grange became a recognized training center on October 1st, 1964.

From the point of view of the R.N.I.D. and the staff at Court Grange there has been a clarification of the scope of the training. After a period of experiment it is established now that the necessary training can be divided into four parts:

I. Social training
II. Trade training
III. Education and welfare
IV. Adventure training

Each trainee accepts that these are the lines his training will follow during the time he is with us. The stress varies from trainee to trainee and also from month to month depending upon the need of each trainee at a particular time. But we do not consider that training is complete until at least the first three have been dealt with satisfactorily.

It is becoming more and more obvious with the type of boy we are getting that three years is the normal period for completion of training. Firstly, there is the initial period of settling down which can take anything from one month to six and, after the actual central period of solid training, there is the final period where we must be sure that not only does a trainee know his job, but is also socially adjusted to a sufficient extent to carry it out in an industrial setting.

One of the most important factors is that the trainee shall arrive at the point where he wants to get on with his training because he has come to see its value to him.

Advisory Panel

The panel° has met at bimonthly intervals throughout the year. One of their prime tasks is the selection of

° Comprising the advisory panel of nine members are the director-general of the Royal National

trainees, and the value of the work they are doing is showing itself in the excellence of the recent intakes selected from the batch of applications. The interest shown by all the panel members is most gratifying both to the warden and the staff.

Trainees

The training given presupposes that a boy will be able to earn his own living on leaving us and that we are not a sheltered workshop or a "home" in the sense in which this word is usually used in welfare circles.

April 1, 1964, twenty boys were in training. Since then thirteen more have come to us. Of these thirty-three, ten have been discharged during the year for the following reasons:

Requiring prolonged mental treatment and adjudged not to be able to benefit from training   6
To go to a sheltered workshop   1
Sent by the Court on a wrong premise   1
Prevented from continuing by parent   1
Refused to accept training after 12 months trial   1

It is not always possible to judge the mental state of a trainee beforehand, besides which there are dormant mental conditions which manifest themselves in adolescence. All trainees for whom it is considered necessary are subjected to exhaustive psychiatric examination at

Institute for the Deaf; a member of the Council of that organization; the headmaster of a school for the deaf; a consulting otologist; a consulting psychiatrist; a university lecturer in sociology; the regional officer of the Ministry of Labor; the principal of the British College for Welfare Officers to the Deaf; and the warden.—I. S. F.

Tone Vale Hospital, near Taunton, and if they can benefit are given treatment. Only after prolonged discussion and trial is their discharge from Court Grange recommended. In the case of the six boys concerned who were so discharged this year two were so mentally subnormal as to be adjudged incapable of work and indeed really incapable of living satisfactorily outside a mental hospital; the other four were so mentally disturbed as to be a danger not only to other people but to themselves.

If a trainee is sent by a court, and the Home Office will, in certain cases, agree to be responsible for payment for up to one year, then it is important that some arrangement is made with another authority, generally a department of the appropriate county or borough council for the fees to be guaranteed beyond this year, so that training will not be interrupted or curtailed.

At all times it is necessary for the sponsoring authority to ensure that the trainee is aware of the type of place to which he is coming; that he knows and understands the form the training will take (and that he will be required to take part in all its facets); the probable length of his stay; and the position regarding holidays and pocket money. It is amazing the odd notions which some of our new entrants have when they come. I do not believe this should be left to the staff here to cope with after the boy's arrival. He feels cheated and quite an appreciable amount of time has been lost with trainees when the facts have not been made clear to them.

The time is coming when the first trainees will be leaving us and we shall be watching the results. It is as important for us to plan their leaving with them, their parents, the welfare officer and the Ministry of Labor as it is for us to train them. They will still need support and guidance and a joint effort by all the agencies involved is necessary to see that the trainee's feet are firmly placed on the correct rung of the ladder.

I. Social Training

The importance of training the boys socially cannot be overstressed. If they fail because they are unable to become socially acceptable both to live with and work with others all our other training counts for nothing.

We have reached the point where we have established a routine of behavior which is accepted by most of the boys. Our new entrants are quickly absorbed into the routine without too much trouble. At all times, though, the staff must be making a conscious effort to see that behavior does not deteriorate. If it is allowed to do so, further deterioration follows quickly.

If a boy finds difficulty in conforming it is important to find out the reason for the nonconformity, and to try, with patience and understanding, to bring about a change. With all of our trainees it is not sufficient, because of their disability, to know what is being said to them, but also that they should understand what is being said. Even using all methods of communication the one does not always follow the other.

There are very few infringements of

the few rules we have and what damage is now done, apart from very occasional outbursts of temper on the part of a disturbed trainee, is through thoughtlessness rather than the desire to do damage.

Occasionally we have a boy who finds it difficult to be honest and one of our present trainees has no sense of honor with other trainees' property or indeed any feeling of guilt or contrition when he is discovered.

Most of the boys are developing a sense of occasion now and are reacting well in this direction. We understand from parents that their behavior during holidays has improved and they present less of a problem than they did in the past.

Among themselves they are exhibiting more tolerance, more friendship and they have more ability to get on with each other than they had. Occasionally there are outbursts, but they are by no means so frequent as they were and boys are managing to overcome their loss of temper more quickly.

In appearance there have been great changes with a lot of them. Washing, care of clothes, and of their personal appearance are becoming good habits with them.

During the past year we have been quite pleased with this all-around general improvement in social behavior and social awareness. They are finding it easier to have a place in the hearing world in consequence—the various outings we have, the intermingling in the youth club we have on the premises, the way in which they can accept other groups of people who come to Court

Grange (the working party of Quakers, Scouts, Newton Abbot Repertory Company) and the manner in which they can integrate with others at camps and youth hostels all serve to illustrate this point.

II. Trade Training

The following occupational lines are contained in the current vocational training program: (1) horticulture and agriculture; (2) painting and decorating; (3) carpentry, and (4) kitchen work.

After considerable thought and discussion with the Ministry of Labor Training Center personnel, it does appear that courses which would commend themselves, if Court Grange is enlarged, are those connected with the building industry. I would suggest that bricklaying be given the first consideration.

III. Education and Welfare

It has become increasingly obvious that most of our trainees need some extra formal education to help them to cope both with their trade courses and with the job of living in the world outside. Most of the boys have some mathematics, dealing largely with measurement and money, some English, to help them understand the written word, forms, etc., and some general knowledge instruction each week. Television programs are used quite a bit where they fit into this scheme of education and we are also making some of our own aids to teaching.

The Local Education Authority is still cooperating with us in providing three teachers for evening classes. All these instructors have changed since last year and, although their methods are different from those of their predecessors, they seem to be achieving as good results.

The Keep Fit class is still compulsory, since we feel that all the boys can benefit from a short period of formal physical exercise each week.

The Craft class covers as large a variety of subjects as we can accommodate and boys, particularly the less able, welcome the diversity.

The Art class while running on more formal lines still has plenty of diversity within the scope of "Art" as a subject and the boys are encouraged to express themselves in all kinds of art forms.

Our painting and decorating instructor also takes a weekly class in model-making with the less able.

At the moment, as so many of the boys have bicycles, a police officer attends fortnightly and is taking a series of classes in cycling proficiency. We are conscious of the difficulties our boys have in using cycles on the road and feel that it is important to give them as much tuition as possible in the care of their machines and proper conduct on the road. Unfortunately, it has not yet been possible to start the photography class.

As far as welfare is concerned, it is of the greatest importance to keep alive to problems boys may have, some of which concern their relationship within or outside Court Grange with their families or with others they meet. If a trainee has such worries it is bound to have an adverse effect upon his training. Boys are more willing to discuss difficulties they have and at least to consider advice that is given. That a boy can do this and then make his own decision is some measure of his maturity.

IV. Adventure Training

As our experiment has gained momentum the value of this training becomes more and more evident. So many of our trainees have the view that this type of activity must of necessity be denied them because of their deafness, or they feel that even though they would like to take part they would not be wanted.

We have made a number of experiments in this field and are certain now that Adventure Training is as necessary a part of our training as the other three sections. Our activities have ranged through rock-climbing, camping, hosteling, canoeing and hiking and have involved most of the trainees we have. Most of them are reveling in these pursuits and are asking for more. Their value cannot be underestimated and, not only from the pleasure the boys obviously get, but from the self-reliance and independence the experience can give them.

Recreation

All the usual games are being played. A feature of our progress is that many boys are able to play games with each other without constant recourse to the staff. Consequently, more of them are happy to play games more often. We hope to have a games marathon annually where the overall winner holds a cup for a year and receives, as well, a medal to keep.

Swimming has been taken seriously by some of the boys during the winter and they have been regular visitors to Torquay Indoor Baths. As soon as the weather improves we shall start teaching our nonswimmers in our own pool.

Regular film shows are still held at fortnightly intervals.

The youth club, consisting of our trainees together with some boys and girls from the village, meets weekly. It is still in its infancy but we hope that this will be another useful point of contact with those who are not handicapped.

With all this activity the television set has few regular adherents. It is noticeable, though, that our few older trainees do require a less concentrated approach to this kind of activity. They are more inclined to feel that after a day's work they have finished.

The usual parties for both boys, staff and their relations have been held in the summer on an outing, on Guy Fawkes night and at Christmas at a dinner and later at the pantomime. The boys mix happily on these occasions and do not appear to be at all apart from the rest of those attending.

Religion

Services are still held in the chapel every Sunday morning and in recent months there has been 100 per cent attendance. Occasionally, at Harvest and Christmas we join with parishioners at the village church.

Six boys are attending weekly confirmation classes where instruction is being given by the vicar. He is now able to conduct parts of his service in the chapel in sign language by himself. We have valued his continued interest throughout the past year.

Health and Medical Matters

The sick bay has hardly been used during the past year—except for visitors staying overnight. It is fast becoming a "white elephant." Boys have regular weight and height checks, and dental checks and those wearing glasses are also checked periodically.

All the boys have attended Musgrove Park Hospital for otological examination and the seven who can benefit from hearing aids have them. It is, however, difficult to get one or two of them to use their aids consistently.

MULTIPLE ANOMALIES IN CONGENITALLY DEAF CHILDREN*

Jacob M. Danish, J. Karetas Tillson, and Max Levitan†

Introduction

Genetic etiology is recognized as the commonest determinable cause of perceptive deafness in children (Johnsen, 1954). However, infection and injury, both during embryonic development and after birth, also play a prominent part in the etiology of deafness. It would be interesting to know the relative frequency of deafness from various causes and whether these different causes produce deafness in similar ways. In this paper an approach to this question will be made by studying a deaf population and determining whether deafness of different etiology is accompanied by different associated anomalies.

Interest in congenital deafness is not limited to the specialty of otology. Because visceral defects may be associated, this anomaly is worthy of study by other branches of medicine. The presence of any congenital anomaly in any patient justifies search for other coexistent abnormalities. This has been demonstrated in studies of congenital

anorectal anomalies, for instance, by Mayo and Rice (1950), who reported associated anomalies in 51.8 per cent of males and 36.3 per cent of females, and by Ladd and Gross (1934), who found "other anomalies" in 26 per cent of 162 patients, some with as many as seven or eight. The importance of the associated anomaly was indicated by the fact that in twelve cases the other anomaly was serious enough to be responsible for the death of the patient. In another discussion of the same subject, Baldi and Bigardi (1960) assert that associated malformations may influence the treatment and prognosis of the primary disorder. Similarly, associated abnormalities may influence the treatment, education, and vocational adjustment of the congenitally deaf.

Search of the literature disclosed that deafness was mentioned in association with the following:

1. Keratitis (Cogan's syndrome) (Eisenstein and Taubenhaus, 1958)
2. Lenticular abnormalities (Sohar, 1954)
3. Juvenile Optic Atrophy (Leber's Disease) (Gates, 1946, page 221)
4. Retinitis Pigmentosa (Gates, 1946, pages 78, 210)
5. Waardenburg's Syndrome (Waardenburg, 1951)
6. Mental retardation (Pearson, 1912)
7. Endemic goiter (Johnsen, 1958)
8. Non-endemic goiter (Pendred's Syndrome) (Pendred, 1896)
9. Nodular Goiter and Thyroid Carcinoma (Elman, 1958)
10. Friederich's Ataxia (Gates, 1946, page 205)

* Reproduced by courtesy of the authors and of *Eugenics Quarterly*, official publication of the American Eugenics Society Inc., New York, March 1963, Vol. 10, No. 1.

† Dr. Danish is clinical associate professor of medicine, Woman's Medical College of Pennsylvania. Mrs. Tillson, third-year medical student, Woman's Medical College of Pennsylvania, participated in the study under USPHS grant FG667. Dr. Levitan, whose part in this research was supported by National Science Foundation grant G-12384, is professor of anatomy and medical genetics at Woman's Medical College.

11. Myoclonus (Gates, 1946, page 996)
12. Huntington's Chorea (Gates, 1946, page 1017)
13. Subcortical Encephalopathy (Gates, 1946, page 1035)
14. Osteogenesis Imperfecta (Gates, 1946, page 765)
15. Osteopetrosis (Nelson, 1959)
16. Osteitis Deformans (Paget's Disease) (Morrison, 1938)
17. Laurence-Moon-Biedl Syndrome (Gates 1946, page 771)
18. Neurofibromatosis (Gates, 1946, page 1053)
19. Wilson's Disease (Everberg, 1957)
20. Periodic Peritonitis (Mamou and Cattan, 1952)
21. Pulmonary Stenosis (Lewis *et al.,* 1958)
22. Prolongation of QT Interval, Syncope, and Sudden Death (Jervel and Lange-Nielsen, 1957; Levine and Woodworth, 1958)
23. Hereditary Interstitial Pyelonephritis (Perkoff *et al.,* 1951)
24. Hereditary Nephropathy (Hereditary Hematuria) (Sturtz and Burke, 1956; Reyersbach and Butler, 1954)
25. Ectodermal Dysplasia (Marshall, 1958)
26. Syndrome of Retinal Degeneration, Obesity, and Diabetes Mellitus (Alstrom *et al.,* 1959)
27. Certain trisomic syndromes (Patau *et al.,* 1960; Edwards *et al.,* 1960).

Since it is difficult to evaluate the hearing status of the very young or the mentally retarded, this list may be incomplete.

Deafness may be fortuitous in some of these conditions and frequent in others. It is encountered more or less regularly in such syndromes as Waardenburg's, hereditary nephropathy, hereditary interstitial pyelonephritis, and the cited trisomic syndromes. In the first mentioned, variations of incidence are

ascribed to differences in penetrance (Waardenburg, 1951). Deafness also occurs commonly in association with retinitis pigmentosa and osteogenesis imperfecta. In other congenital or hereditary abnormalities listed above, it has been reported sporadically. The present study was undertaken to determine whether conclusions could be drawn concerning the prevalence of associated abnormalities in the congenitally deaf as compared with other types of deafness. In addition, unusual incidence of particular anomalies was looked for which might reveal a predilection of other anomalies toward deafness. These associations, if found, might indicate genetic or ontogenetic association.

Methods

We reviewed the preadmission health reports and infirmary records of the pupils in residence at the Pennsylvania School for the Deaf during the school year 1960–61. Ages ranged from four to twenty years. Information concerning other cases of deafness in the family and the parents' report of the cause of deafness was usually included. The latter was of varying reliability. In most cases the parents' statement was based on a physician's evaluation; in others, however, this was the parents' judgment. The headmaster of the school and the infirmary nurse are intimately acquainted with each pupil and were helpful in completing and correcting deficient histories.

On the basis of the above-mentioned written and verbal reports, the 499 avail-

TABLE I

CLASSIFICATION* OF CHARTS OF 499 STU-
DENTS IN RESIDENCE AT PENNYSLVANIA
SCHOOL FOR THE DEAF IN 1961

	No. in Classes	% of Classified Charts
1. Acquired deafness	145	31.0
2. Congenital, nonhereditary deafness	82	17.6
3. Congenital, hereditary deafness	240	51.4
a. Probable 115		
b. Presumptive 125		
Total classified	467	100.0
Not classified	32	
Total charts reviewed	499	

* As explained in text.

able charts were classified as shown in Table I. Thirty-two were deleted because of insufficient data upon which to base classification or because they were cases of auditory agnosia and auditory aphasia, which are not strictly deafness. The rest were divided into three categories following the scheme of Van Egmond (1954):

1. Acquired deafness
2. Congenital, nonhereditary deafness
3. Congenital, apparently hereditary deafness.

All children who suffered an illness or accident to which their doctors or parents ascribed the hearing defect are included in category 1, despite the fact that in many cases these incidents occurred at an age when already existing deafness would have been difficult to recognize. In other cases the child was known to have been able to hear and speak prior to the loss of hearing so that the causal relationship was more convincing. Because of insufficient data, no attempt was made to uncover delayed onset hereditary deafness, some cases of which may be included here.

Erythroblastosis, kernicterus, maternal rubella and other viral diseases in pregnancy, birth trauma, and prematurity were accepted as etiological factors when reported as having occurred. These cases were placed in our second category: congenital, nonhereditary deafness. Note that heredity played an indirect role in many of these, those ascribed to erythroblastosis and maternal diabetes, for example.

The remainder were placed in the third group. These were children who were never known to have been able to hear, who had no history of an illness or accident which might have caused their deafness, and whose histories did not mention suspected prenatal or neonatal deafness-inducing factors.

The probability of a hereditary factor is strengthened where a close family history of deafness exists (Close, 1961). Class 3 was therefore subdivided into "probable" and "presumptive." "Probable" indicated deafness in the family of the affected; "presumptive," no mention of deafness in the family.

Results and Discussion

The reported causes of "acquired" deafness are listed in Table II. Of the 145 children in this group, meningitis was the most common assumed cause of the deafness (54 cases). It is of interest that measles was as important as otitis in producing defective hearing (12

TABLE II
REPORTED CAUSES IN 145 CASES OF ACQUIRED DEAFNESS

	Number		
	Age at Detection of Deafness		*Aft.*
Reported Etiology	*Unknown*	*1st yr.*	*1st yr.*
Bronchitis			1
Tracheitis		1	
Croup		1	
Virus		1	1
"Colds"		1	1
Influenza		1	
Otitis		7	5
Pneumonia		5	2
Rheumatic fever			1
Varicella		5	3
Scarlet fever		2	
Measles		5	7
Pertussis		3	1
Mumps		1	1
Encephalitis	1	2	1
Meningitis		22	32
Peritonitis			1
Unspecified febrile illness		3	
Concussion		2	
"Fall"		2	3
Auto accident		1	
"Injury"			1
Cerebral hemorrhage		1	
"Illness"			1
Unknown cause	1	4	11
Total	2	70	73

TABLE III
INCIDENCE OF DEFECTS IN CHILDREN WITH ACQUIRED DEAFNESS

Defect	*Number*
"Poor Vision"	2
Strabismus	3
Hyperopia and/or hyperopic astigmatism	8
Hyperopia and strabismus	1
Hyperopia and possible brain damage	1
Hyperopic astigmatism and flat feet	1
Myopia	1
Epilepsy	2
Petit mal	1
Mental retardation	1
Cerebral palsy	2
Apraxia	1
Narcolepsy?	1
Apical Gr I systolic murmur	1
I.V. septal defect, possible pulmonic stenosis	1
Soft blowing mitral systolic murmur	1
Loud rumbling mitral systolic murmur	1
"Heart condition" and hernia	1
Albuminuria	1
Hernia—umbilical	1
inguinal	1
Recurrent swelling of parotid glands	1
Pyloric stenosis	1
Bronchiectasis and emphysema	1
Pes planus	2
Osteochondrodystrophy	1
Abnormal gait, short, blunt fingers	1
No. with at least one additional defect	40
No. with no defects other than deafness	105
Total	145

cases each). Table III shows the associated abnormalities in these children. Forty, or 27.6 per cent, were reported to have additional abnormalities, including five (3.4%) who had more than one defect besides the deafness.

Table IV is a breakdown of the eighty-two cases of congenital, but probably nonhereditary, deafness and other defects present. Deafness was not an isolated defect except in the group of subjects prenatally exposed to maternal measles (7 cases) and miscellaneous maternal illnesses (5 cases). Among these twelve there was only one child with another defect besides deafness,

TABLE IV
REPORTED ETIOLOGICAL FACTORS AND OTHER DEFECTS FOUND IN 82 CASES
OF NONHEREDITARY CONGENITAL DEAFNESS

Etiological Factor	Other Defects Present	No. of Cases
Rh incompatibility (25 cases)	Cerebral palsy	11
	Cerebral palsy and mental retardation	1
	Hemiplegia	1
	Mental retardation	1
	Retrolental fibroplasia	1
	Divergent strabismus (esophoria)	1
	Hyperopia	1
	Inguinal herniae	2
	Cryptorchidism	1
	Valvular defects (one noted as murmur)	2
	No defects	3
Neonatal jaundice (4 cases)	Cerebral palsy	1
	Strabismus	1
	No defect	2
Prematurity (17 cases)	Retrolental fibroplasia	1
	Myopia	2
	Hyperopia and chorioretinal atrophy	1
	Hyperopic astigmatism OS, blindness OD	1
	Hypospadias, albuminuria	1
	Agnosia	1
	Ataxia	1
	Cerebral palsy	1
	No defect	8
Birth injury (10 cases)	Cerebral palsy	5
	EEG abnormality and hyperopic astigmatism	1
	Esophoria and hyperopia	1
	Heart murmur, pes planus, astigmatism	1
	Left hemiplegia	1
	No defect	1
Maternal rubella (14 cases)	Mental retardation	1
	Possible patent foramen ovale	1
	Patent ductus arteriosus and congenital hip dislocation	1
	Hypospadias, cryptorchidism	1
	Hyperopic astigmatism	1
	Dwarfism or progeria	1
	No defects	8
Maternal measles (7 cases)	Hyperopic astigmatism	1
	No defect	6
	(One developed otosclerosis at age 10)	
Other maternal illness		
Maternal toxic goiter	No defect	1
Maternal streptomycin treatment	No defect	1
Maternal diabetes	No defect	1
Unspecified maternal illness	No defect	2

and this was hyperopic astigmatism in a child whose mother had measles during pregnancy. Not included was a child who developed otosclerosis at the age of ten. The prevalence of multiple defects in the remainder of this group was striking, cerebral palsy occurring in twelve of the twenty-five cases of Rh incompatibility, in five of the ten cases of birth injury, and one each in neonatal jaundice and prematurity. This array of defects is not surprising in this class of deafness, since the noxious factors are known not to be specific for any single organ system.

Table V shows the defects found among the 240 children in group 3. It will be noted that 50.4 per cent had at least one defect in addition to deafness. This is almost twice the frequency among the children with acquired deafness. Also noteworthy is the fact that many of the children in group 3 had defects involving several body systems. Thus thirty-nine (16.2%) of these children had multiple defects, whereas only five (3.4%) of the 145 children in category 1 had more than one defect besides deafness.

Our detailed results were not submit-

TABLE V

ASSOCIATED DEFECTS IN 240 CHILDREN WITH CONGENITAL HEREDITARY
HEARING DEFECT

	Probable*	Presumptive*
Cataract		2
Cataract, microphthalmia, hernia		1
Defective vision		1
Defective vision and cryptorchidism		1
Defective vision and abnormal gait		1
Macular degeneration	1	
"Loss of vision"		2
Hyperopia and/or hyperopic astigmatism (H & HA)	19	9
H & HA and strabismus	2	
H & HA and strabismus and ptosis of lids	1	
Hyperopia, anemia, purpura	1	
Hyperopia and retinitis pigmentosa	1	1
Hyperopia and pes planus		1
Hyperopic astigmatism and petit mal		1
Hyperopic astigmatism and sarcoid		1
Hyperopic astigmatism and hirsutism		1
Hyperopic astigmatism and obesity		1
Hyperopic astigmatism and epicanthus		2
Hyperopic astigmatism, pronated feet, tight heel cords, scoliosis		1
Myopia	1	1
Myopia, albuminuria, petit mal		1
Myopic astigmatism, otosclerosis		1
Strabismus	2	4
Retinitis pigmentosa	2	1
Retinitis pigmentosa and aphakia		1
Retinitis pigmentosa and hernia		1
Bitemporal pallor of discs	1	

(*Continued page 232*)

TABLE V—*Continued*

	Probable*	Presumptive*
Lacrimal duct surgery	1	
Epicanthus, scoliosis and proteinuria		1
Epilepsy, grand mal	1	1
Mental retardation	3	2
Frequent headaches	1	
"Cerebral palsy"		1
Aphasia and dyslexia		1
Cerebral palsy and apahsia		1
Albuminuria	2	1
Hydrocele	1	
Hydrocele and hernia	1	
Hydrocele and varicocele		1
"Anomaly of GU tract" (surgical correction)	1	
Cryptorchidism	2	
Cryptorchidism and hernia	1	
Cryptorchidism, abnormal gait, obesity		1
Hernia	2	
Atresia of auditory canals, hernia and mental retardation		1
Atresia of auditory canal and branchial cyst		1
To and fro murmur, mottled retinae		1
Murmur and palpable thyroid		1
Systolic murmur		2
Machinery murmur		1
Heart surgery for congenital defect		1
Patent ductus arteriosus, mental defect, and petit mal		1
I.V. conduction defect and hyperopia		1
"Heart condition"		1
Anemia		2
Recurrent swelling of parotid gland	1	
Hemangioma (skin)	1	
Tight lingual frenum	1	
Nasal polyp		1
Right azygos lobe	1	
Pes planus	1	
Wry neck		1
Micrognathia		1
Cleft palate and spina bifida		1
Fainting spells		2
Waardenburg's syndrome	2	2
Cases with at least one associated defect	54	67
Cases without additional defects	61	58
Total cases in subsample	115	125

* "Probable" indicates presence of deafness in family history; "presumptive" indicates genetic deafness is presumed (see text), even though familial history of deafness is lacking.

dromes; in fact, some cases of congenital deafness, even without other defects, may be incomplete expressions or "formesfrustes" of such entities.

Multiple defects may be explained in various ways. They may be accounted for by pleiomorphism of single genes, multiple abnormal genes, gross chromosomal abnormality, variations in gene expressivity, or interaction between environmental and genetic influence. When any of these mechanisms are involved in early differentiation, many derivative structures may be affected, thereby giving rise to multiple defects, possibly involving diverse organ systems (Corner, 1960).

This study shows that, just as in many types of environmentally induced deafness, there is an association between genetic mechanisms producing deafness and the production of defects of other systems, and it suggests that an ontogenetic relationship exists among these defects. The further study of deaf children, by increasing the sample and strengthening its statistical validity, should define more accurately which of the conditions are regularly related, which occasional or fortuitous. Recognition of relationships among congenital defects would be useful to physicians and to those engaged in the training of congenitally handicapped children, as well as to geneticists and embryologists. The problem is an interdisciplinary one, meriting the cooperation of pediatrician, otologist, internist, geneticist and other specialists. To resolve it requires a program which could include:

1. Accurate determination of type of hearing loss.

2. Investigation of pedigree and establishment of hereditary basis.
3. Study of individuals to detect presence of associated inherited defects.
4. Chromosomal studies.

Summary

The medical records of 499 students in the Pennsylvania School for the Deaf were reviewed to determine the incidence of congenital anomalies. Information in these records permitted separation of the children into three groups: acquired deafness; congenital, nonhereditary deafness; and congenital, apparently hereditary deafness.

There was a greater incidence of associated defects in those with congenital deafness as compared with those whose deafness followed postnatal illness or injury. In the former, multiple defects were also more frequent. Differences in the types of anomalies appeared when congenital deafness was separated into hereditary and nonhereditary causes.

Acknowledgments

We gratefully acknowledge the assistance and interest of Mr. John G. Nace, headmaster, and Mrs. Paul Bane, nurse, at the Pennsylvania School for the Deaf.

References

1. ALSTROM, C. H.; HALLGREN, B.; NILLSON, L. B., and ASLANDER, H.: Retinal degeneration combined with obesity, diabetes mellitus and neurogenous deafness. *Acta Psychiat Scand,* 34: supp. 129, 1959.

2. BALDI, H., and BIGARDI, D.: Associated malformations in patients with congenital anorectal atresia or stenosis. *Minerva Pediat, 12*(40):1203, 1960.

3. CLOSE, P.: Heredity and productivity in families of institutionalized deaf. *Eugen Quart, 8*(1):34, 1961.

4. CORNER, B.: *Prematurity.* Springfield, Thomas, 1960, pp. 298–9.

5. EDWARDS, J. H.; HAMDEN, D. G.; CAMERON, A. H.; GROSSE, V. M., and WOLFE, O. H.: A new trisomic syndrome. *Lancet, 1*:787, 1960.

6. EISENSTEIN, B., and TAUBENHAUS, M.: Cogan's syndrome (interstitial keratitis and bilateral deafness). *New Eng J Med, 258*:1074, 1958.

7. ELMAN, D. S.: Familial association of nerve deafness with nodular goiter and thyroid carcinoma. *New Eng J Med, 259:* 219, 1958.

8. EVERBERG, G.: Familial study with otologic, neurologic and ophthalmologic aspects-unilateral deafness, speech defect, dyslexia, petit mal, aphasia (Kramer-Pollnow syndrome?), astigmatism (amblyopia), disseminated sclerosis and goiter. *Acta Psychiat, Scand, 32*:307, 1957.

9. GATES, R.: *Human Genetics.* New York, Macmillan, 1946.

10. JERVAL, A., and LANGE-NIELSEN, F.: Congenital deaf-mutism, functional heart disease with prolongation of the QT interval and sudden death. *Amer Heart J, 54*:59, 1957.

11. Johnsen, S.: Clinical aspects of hightone perceptive deafness in children. *Acta Oto-Laryngol, 44*:25, 1954.

12. ———: Familial deafness and goiter in persons with low serum level of PBI. *Acta Otolaryng Supp, 140*:168–182, 1958.

13. LADD, W. E., and GROSS, R. E.: Congenital malformations of anus and rectum. *Amer J Surg, 23*:167, 1934.

14. LEVINE, S. A., and WOODWORTH, C. R.: Congenital deaf-mutism, prolonged QT interval, syncopal attacks and sudden death. *New Eng J Med, 259*:412, 1958.

15. LEWIS, S. M.; SONNENBLICK, B. P.; GILBERT, L., and BIBER, D.: Familial pulmonary stenosis and deaf-mutism; clinical and genetic considerations. *Amer Heart J, 55*:458, 1958.

16. MAMOU, H., and CATTAN, R.: La maladie periodique (sur 14 cas personnels dont 8 compliqués de nephropathie). *Semaine Hop. Paris, 28*:1062, 1952.

17. MARSHALL, D.: Ectodermal dysplasia: Report of a kindred with ocular abnormalities and hearing defect. *Amer J Ophthalmol, 45*:143 (Supplement), 1958.

18. MAYO, C. W., and RICE, R. G.: Anorectal anomalies. *Surgery, 27*:485, 1950.

19. MORRISON, W. W.: *Disease of the Nose, Throat and Ear.* Philadelphia, Saunders, 1938, p. 613.

20. NELSON, W. E. (Editor): *Textbook of Pediatrics,* Philadelphia, Saunders, 1959, p. 1240.

21. PATAU, K.; THERMAN, E.; SMITH, D. W.; INHORN, S. L., and WAGNER, H. P.: Multiple congenital anomaly caused by an extra autosome. *Lancet, 1*:790, 1960.

22. PEARSON, K.: *Treasury of Human Inheritance,* Vol. 1. London, Dulau, 1912.

23. PENDRED, V.: Deafmutism and goiter. *Lancet, 2*:532, 1896.

24. PERKOFF, G. T.; STEVENS, F. E.; DOLOWITZ, D. A., and TYLER, F. H.: Clinical study of hereditary interstitial pyelonephritis. *AMA Arch Intern Med, 88*:191, 1951.

25. REYERSBACH, G. C., and BUTLER, A. M.: Congenital hereditary hematuria. *New Eng J Med, 251*:377, 1954.

26. SOHAR, E.: Heredo-familial syndrome characterized by renal disease, inner ear deafness and ocular changes. *Harefuah, 47:* 161, 1954.

27. Sturtz, G. S., and Burke, E. C.: Hereditary hematuria, nephropathy and deafness. *New Eng J Med, 254*:1123, 1956.

28. VAN EGMOND, A. A. J.: Congenital deafness. *J Laryng, 68*:429, 1954.

29. WAARDENBURG, P. J.: A new syndrome combining developmental anomalies of the eyelids, eyebrows and nose root with pigmentary defects of the iris and head hair and with congenital deafness. *Amer J Hum Genet, 3*:195, 1951.

A CLASSROOM PROGRAM FOR AUDITORALLY HANDICAPPED MENTALLY DEFICIENT CHILDREN*

Leon Glovsky and Seymour Rigrodsky

Abstract

Although a number of studies have been published reporting audiometric evaluations of mentally retarded populations, the literature describing the educational programs of deaf and mentally retarded individuals is practically nonexistent. Many state and private facilities have become increasingly aware of the special needs of the multiple handicapped mentally retarded child. Recognizing this need The Training School at Vineland initiated a special class for auditorally impaired mentally retarded children. The main objective of this class was to provide structured learning situations stressing increasing awareness of visual and verbal communication. It was believed that homogeneous grouping would result in improved behavior, more flexible social functioning and improved communication attitudes.

Six children were enrolled in this class. Each child chosen for the study group had a hearing loss, and extremely limited language. The age range was from 11–17 years. Mental age as measured by psychological test performance ranged from six years six months to seven years and six months.

Lesson plans for the class evolved from a basic unit plan dealing with the association of familiar objects, The Training School environment, clothing, body parts, etc. Word presentations for each lesson were chosen because of visibility; readily identified and recognized through the use of objects and pictures, and familiarity to the children. The class day was arranged to provide attention to eye contact, review and introduction and review of new words, and individualized instruction in speechreading and auditory training. This paper will describe the program in detail as well as point out the areas of improvement and failure.

* Reprinted, with permission from *The Training School Bulletin,* American Institute for Mental Studies, Vineland, N. J., Vol. 60, No. 2, August, 1963. L. Glovsky is Senior Speech Pathologist, The Training School Unit, American Institute for Mental Studies at Vineland, New Jersey. S. Rigrodsky is Professor of Speech and Hearing at the University of Connecticut.

Introduction

There is increasing interest in the study of speech and language development of mentally retarded children. Various investigators studying mentally retarded populations have discussed such aspects of language development as word acquisition, sentence growth and speech sound development (Karlin and Kennedy, 1936; Strazzulla, 1954). Other studies have reported on the incidence of defective speech as well as the incidence of hearing loss, (Schlanger and Gottsleben, 1957; Sirkin and Lyons, 1941). In recent years several studies have appeared which have discussed therapy programs specifically designed for mentally retarded individuals, (Rigrodsky and Steer, 1961; Schneider and Vallon, 1955). However, literature describing the communication difficulties of auditorally impaired mentally retarded children is practically nonexistent and relatively little has been published concerning the teaching of language and lipreading to these children, (Johnson and Farrell, 1957).

Those experimental studies reported

by Heider and Heider (1940), O'Neill (1951) and Pintner (1921) were concerned with the relationship between lipreading ability and the factors of intelligence, perceptual skills, educational achievement and personal adjustment. Pintner found that all correlations between speech and measurement of non-verbal intelligence were zero. Pintner also found that in the advanced groups, speechreading and intelligence also gave a zero correlation. Goda (1959) investigated the chief language skills of adolescent pupils at a residential school for the deaf. Four language skills were measured: writing, speaking, lipreading, and reading. The conclusions drawn were: (1) because of consistent inter-relations of the language skills, the prediction may be made that the deaf child who is superior in one will generally be superior in all of the skills, and the deaf child who is inferior in one will generally be inferior in all the skills; (2) the quantitative and qualitative aspects of expressive language appear to be related; the child who uses a relatively larger number of words in his speaking and writing will generally express himself with relatively longer and more complex sentences. Simmons (1959), studying factors related to lipreading ability in a group of adults for whom lipreading had been recommended, found that there was no significant correlation between lipreading ability and IQ. It is interesting to note that there was a significant relationship between the Digit-Symbol subtest of the Wechsler-Bellevue Intelligence Scale and the two types of lipreading techniques utilized in this paper. These

series of studies, although dealing with lipreading ability and intelligence, do not speak of the mentally retarded deaf child.

This paper will describe the procedures utilized in a special class for auditorally handicapped mentally retarded children.* The major purpose for the establishment of the class was to develop and promote greater awareness to auditory and visual communication on the part of the individuals enrolled in this program. Attempts were made to create and modify existing lipreading and language training techniques to make them applicable to mentally retarded individuals.

The following is a summary of the latest psychological tests administered: The results, comments by the psychologist and etiological classification; social age and social quotient, personality; type of educational program; audiometric results and comments concerning speech and language abilities.

Subjects

L.R.: This 11-year-8-month boy is functioning at the moderately retarded range of intelligence. Such tests as the Arthur Point Scale of Performance (MA 5-1, IQ 44), Nebraska Test of Learning (Learning age 7-1, Established IQ 61), Leiter International Performance Scale (MA 6-0, IQ 52), Draw-A-Person (MA 5-3, IQ 45) were administered. The psychologist stated, "Relative strengths were found in form perception, awareness of the environment and simple manipulative tasks with blocks. Weaknesses were noted on

---

* This special lipreading and language class is being conducted at The Training School by the Speech and Hearing Division in cooperation with the Education Division.

tasks requiring fine discrimination (visual), social awareness and immediate memory." On the Vineland Social Maturity Scale, he received an SA of 7.6 and SQ of 65. Relationships with peers and adults have been satisfactory to excellent. Acuity of L.R.'s hearing was assessed by means of psychogalvanic skin resistance audiometry. The results indicated a severe bilateral sensorineural impairment. Etiology: unknown. Since the age of three this boy has attended schools for the deaf with little accomplishment in the way of communication. Little spontaneous language. A personal sign or gesture language. Able to produce some sounds and words following auditory amplification. Dif-

ficulty in receiving oral language. Cannot differentiate between written symbols. He is presently enrolled in an intermediate school program where his performance has been satisfactory.

C.F.: The most recent psychological testing places this 17-year-10-month boy in the range of moderate retardation. On the Nebraska Test of Learning Aptitude he received an MA of 7–6, IQ 50, Cornell-Coxe Performance Ability Scale MA 7–2, IQ 46, Ammons Full Range Picture Vocabulary Test MA 5–0, IQ 34, Draw-A-Person Test MA 7–0, IQ 52. It is reported "he performs relatively well on the items involving simple reasoning and awareness of his environment.

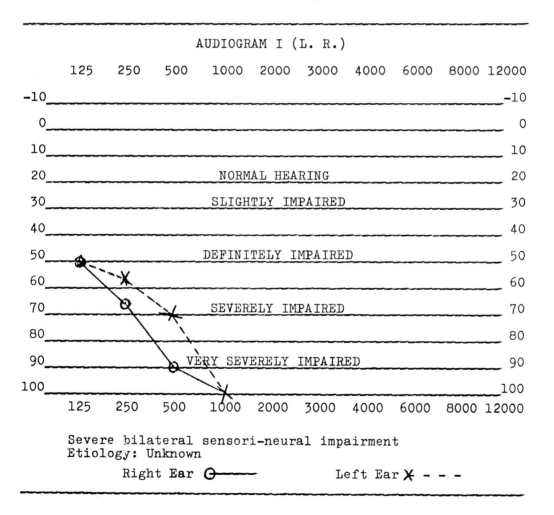

AUDIOGRAM I (L. R.)

Severe bilateral sensori-neural impairment
Etiology: Unknown

Right Ear Ɵ———   Left Ear X - - -

AUDIOGRAM II (C. F.)

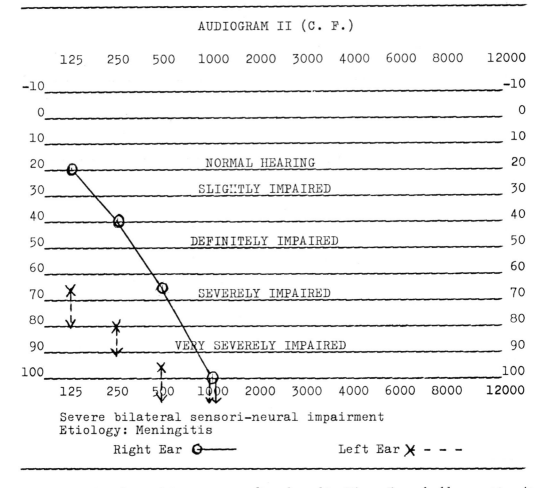

Severe bilateral sensori-neural impairment
Etiology: Meningitis

Right Ear ⊖——　　　　　　　　　Left Ear ✗ – – –

Difficulty with tasks involving motor coordination." No significant personality disorder. Etiology: meningitis. He has received an SA of 7–8 and SQ of 43 on the Vineland Social Maturity Scale. He is cooperative with fellow students and all adults. Hearing examination: PGSR audiometry revealed a severe bilateral sensorineural impairment. Able to recognize pictures and written symbols. Can follow instructions through gestures. Uses some gestures for communication. Can discriminate between 3 to 4 isolated stimuli. He is in a prevocational program, working part time at the garage and the farm, in the vegetable producing areas and in landscaping.

E.L.: Present obtained results on the Nebraska Test of Learning Aptitude indicates that this 15-year-7-month-old youngster is functioning within the range of moderate retardation. Etiology: Meningitis. He obtained an MA of 6–6 and an IQ of 44. Best results obtained on the items involving practical judgment, memory for visually presented number, and identification of similarities. Always friendly and cooperative with peers and adults. No indications of aggressive or hostile behavior. On a PGSR evaluation it was found that E. L. has a severe bilateral sensorineural loss. No usable oral language. Very little gesture used for communication. Can discriminate between 3 or 4 common environmental objects. Engaged in an educational program of wood and metal shop, occupational therapy, manual training, physical edu-

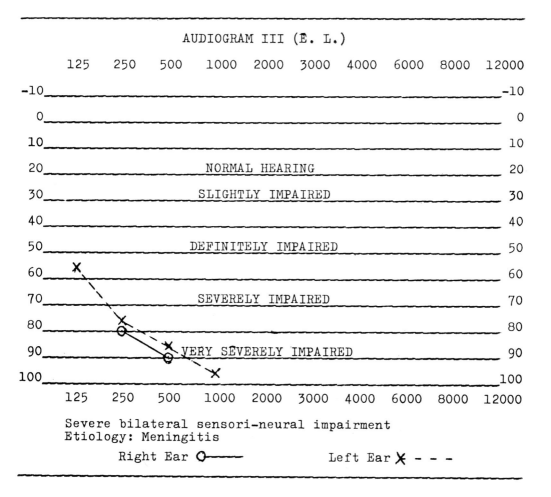

AUDIOGRAM III (E. L.)

Severe bilateral sensori-neural impairment
Etiology: Meningitis

Right Ear O⎯⎯⎯   Left Ear X - - -

cation and academics. Academically, progress has been negligible.

W.D.: W. D. is functioning in the moderately retarded range of intelligence. Etiology: Prenatal infection and trauma. He is 16-years-11-months-old and has received an MA of 5–3 and an IQ of 33 on the Draw-A-Person. On the Nebraska Test of Learning Aptitude he obtained a learning aptitude of 6–5. MA 5–6, an IQ of 42 were recorded for the Leiter International Performance Scale. Weaknesses observed in patterned visual-motor reproduction, some manipulative tasks and simple reasoning. Strengths are in the areas of pictorial associations and the ability to comprehend simple pictorial analogies. Difficulty shifting from one concept to

another. On the Vineland Social Maturity Scale, W. D. has received an SA of 7–0 and an SQ of 41. Friendly toward other peers and adults in his cottage. No reports of any behavior disturbance and a study of his hearing was assessed by means of psychogalvanic skin resistance audiometry. The results of this test would indicate a severe bilateral sensorineural hearing loss. Language communication through gestures. Some sounds and words but completely unintelligible. Able to differentiate between some pictures and a few written symbols. He is in a prevocational education program. Is a messenger boy and works on the farm and does landscaping.

G.G.: Has been in various schools for the deaf since the age of six. Reports from other

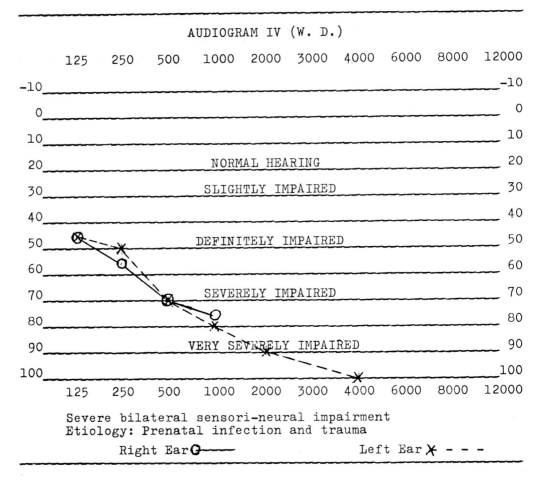

AUDIOGRAM IV (W. D.)

Severe bilateral sensori-neural impairment
Etiology: Prenatal infection and trauma

Right Ear O——   Left Ear ✕ - - -

institutions have indicated that G. G. is functioning in the low dull-normal range intellectually with capacity to function in upper range and a capacity for visual conceptual learning. Visual-motor and motor learning appeared to be more retarded. On the WISC she obtained an IQ of 38 (performance part) estimated MA 4–9. There was no evidence of the reported dull-normal potential. In the Education Department she is enrolled in a primary class. Likes to participate with her peers. Friendly toward adults. Etiology: Unknown. Hearing assessed by means of psychogalvanic skin resistance. Results of testing indicated a bilateral sensorineural loss of moderate degree with perhaps a slight superimposed conductive element on the left side. Uses words which

are understandable. Can readily identify pictures and write the correct corresponding symbol.

S.K.: S. K. is currently functioning within the moderately retarded range of intelligence. On the Nebraska Test of Learning Aptitude he received an MA of 6–9 and an IQ of 42. Chronologically he is 16 years 10 months. The Leiter International Performance Scale revealed an MA of 6–0 and an IQ of 46. There was no pattern of strengths and weaknesses present on either of the tests. He responded only to those tasks which had some personal appeal. Others he simply ignored. There was no obvious reaction to praise or encouragement. Etiology: Prenatal infection associated with maternal rubella. Severe personality disorder. On the Vineland

TABLE I
SUBJECTS IN EXPERIMENTAL CLASS

Subjects	Etiology	Intellectual Level	Chrono-logical Age	Mental Age	IQ	Type of Hearing Loss
L.R.	Unknown	Moderately Retarded	11–8	7–1	61	Severe bilateral sensori-neural impairment
C.F.	Meningitis	Moderately Retarded	17–10	7–6	50	Severe bilateral sensori-neural impairment
E.L.	Meningitis	Moderately Retarded	15–7	6–6	44	Severe bilateral sensori-neural impairment
G.G.	Unknown	Mildly Retarded	11–0	4–9	38	Bilateral sensorineural impairment of moderate degree. Slight superimposed conductive element on left side
S.K.	Maternal rubella	Moderately Retarded	16–10	6–9	42	Severe bilateral sensori-neural impairment
W.D.	Prenatal infection trauma	Moderately Retarded	16–11	5–7	42	Severe bilateral sensori-neural impairment

Social Maturity Scale S. K. received an SA of 4–7 and an SQ of 28. He is withdrawn but co-operative at times with peers and adults. He has recently been placed in an occupational therapy as well as a woodworking class under the Education Department. Psychogalvanic skin resistance audiometry revealed a moderate to severe bilateral sensorineural hearing loss. No language or communicative system.

Experimental Class

Prior to the start of the experimental class, September, 1960, lesson plans were drawn up, primarily evolving from a basic unit plan. Unit plans were planned from items concerned with The Training School environment, clothing, body parts, food, everyday social activities and objects which are of common usage to these children during their everyday experiences. Word presentations for each lesson were chosen because of: (1) visibility on the lips; (2) could be readily identified and recognized through the use of objects and pictures, and (3) familiarity to the children.

An appropriate distribution of class-room time seemed important to hold the complete attention of each child in the class. The forty-five-minute class sessions were divided into fifteen-minute periods. The following is an active distribution of class time:

I. First 15 minute period
  A. Eye contact
    1. With complete group
    2. With individual child

II. Second 15 minute period
  A. Review and introduction of new words
    1. Through pictures
    2. Lipreading
    3. Written symbol
III. Last 15 minute period
  A. Individualized instruction
    1. At child's seat
      a. Lipreading and writing of words
    2. Child sent to board
      a. To choose correct picture after lip-reading teacher's lips
      b. Write the word on the board
      c. Student attempts to say the word
      d. Choose the correct written symbol among other words

In all methods visual aids were employed. The children were required to match a picture of the word to the written form of the word. Words were repeated after the teacher said it and then children matched the object or picture to the written form of the word. The following is an example of the steps which were used in each unit plan for the teaching of specific words.

In the clothing unit the word "pants" would be taught:

1. Teacher would prepare a poster with the picture of a pair of pants.
2. Another poster would have the word "pants" printed and written on it.
3. A third poster has both the picture and the word printed and written on it.
4. The first poster was presented to the class.
5. Each child was given a magazine, scissors, mucilage and paper. The child goes through the magazine looking for a picture of pants.
6. He cuts the picture out of the magazine and pastes it on the paper.
7. The printed and written word is presented.
8. Word "pants" was written beneath the picture.
9. The object, a real pair of pants, is now presented.

10. The word "pants" is written on the board by the teacher.
11. For the first time the teacher utters the word "pants," attempting to utilize a normal conversational line of production.
12. Each child then attempted to repeat the word "pants." (Any vocalization or lip movement is accepted).
13. Words and pictures which have previously been worked on are presented. The child now has to match the word "pants" with the correct picture.
14. Teacher writes word on board, children copy the word and say it.
15. Children repeat the word after watching the teacher say it and then match the object or picture to the written form of the word.
16. The child now has complete eye contact with the teacher. The teacher says the word, the child will then repeat the word and identify the object.
17. Now that word being taught has a concrete meaning, a carrier phrase is introduced to add meaning to the word.

The carrier phrase which was taught for the word "pants" is: "Put on." The complete phrase was uttered as a pantomime demonstration was performed. Pants are actually put on over clothing by the teacher and by each child. During this action period the phrase is said, "Put on pants." Each child will lipread and repeat the phrase to the best of his ability. Other carrier phrases which have been used are: "I eat, I sleep, He is, I drink, I am," etc.

Phrases and sentences of 3–6 words were taught in this same manner for words from all units. Some sentences which the children can now lipread and attach a meaningful purpose to are, "I eat pie," "I sleep in a bed," "My cottage is——," "He is a big man," "I am a small boy," "I drink milk," "I wash my hands and face." These sentences were also taught through the use of matching main words:

Big	Boy
Eat	Milk
Small	Bed
Drink	Man
Sleep	Pie

When the children were first enrolled in the experimental class, they appeared apathetic toward communication with little awareness of speech (their own and others.) Communication contact was difficult to establish, since most of the children reacted by withdrawal or other negative behavior. Initial attempts to have the children attend to visual stimuli were met with failure. Visual attention was almost nonexistent, responses were poor to almost all types of stimuli. Initial eye contact between teacher and student could not be held for more than three or four seconds, at which time the student would look away or just stare into space. It was felt that too much emphasis was placed on eye contact. It was decided that this technique of direct eye contact training needed to be modified.

Participation by the group was felt to be essential as a prerequisite for eye contact. Each child was given an oak tag with his first name printed as well as written on it. Through the use of gestures and lipreading, the recognition of the individual's first name was taught. Once each child could copy, write and recognize (written and through lipreading) his own name, work was started on the identification of the names of the other children in

the class. Each child came to the front of the room with his name tag, showed the tag to the class, the teacher would say the name and each child would then write the name in his own notebook and the name would then be written on the board. When it was felt that each child could lipread his classmates' names they were "tested." The teacher would lipread a child's name and the child being tested would then point to the correctly named classmate. If the response was incorrect, then the name would be written on the board, and the child would then point to his classmate. The child was then asked to lipread the name again. At this time, four of the children can lipread and identify correctly all the names of their classmates.

Since these children are in an institutionalized setting, it was felt that each child should be familiar with his immediate environment. A walking tour of the Training School grounds was conducted, encompassing all the cottages (in which the children live), the school buildings and various administration buildings. The complete tour was comparable to three class sessions. During each session, specific cottages were visited. Notebooks and pencils were carried by each child plus a complete floor sketch of the Training School. Names of buildings were omitted from the plan, but there was appropriate space allotted for the child to write the correct name of the building. At the entrance to each building is a sign giving the name of the building. The purpose was to have the child associate, by lipreading and by the printed and written symbols, every building on the grounds of the Training School. Upon returning to the classroom, the teacher would lipread the names of the various buildings. Only one child received a perfect score. The others could identify only three or four names while some could identify only one. During each session, there was a review of the words learned in previous sessions.

During the first few weeks of the program many problems were encountered. The biggest handicap which had to be overcome was in finding lipreading technique. As the class progressed, it was learned that overemphasis was not a benefit but a hindrance in the teaching of lipreading to retarded children. Exaggeration of lips only confused the children. Normal lip movement accompanied with some use of gesture was to be much more satisfactory and successful. Voice was used throughout the session, so that those children with residual hearing could benefit by receiving some sound signal. When voice was incorporated with lipreading, there was a tendency for the children to "listen harder," and a tendency on the teacher's part not to overemphasize but use normal inflectional patterns and lip movements.

In addition to the daily classroom sessions of forty-five minutes, there was a fifteen-minute period of individual auditory training which each child attended at least three times a week. During these auditory training periods the speech audiometer was used advantageously for the purpose of increasing an awareness of sound. There was a

complete review of the words used in class. Each word was presented through lipreading techniques and then spoken into the speech audiometer by the therapist. Both methods were used simultaneously. These sessions have proved to be a means of stimulation, motivation and as additional training media for these multi-handicapped children. At a later date auditory units will be placed in the classroom for direct teaching benefits.

Seating arrangement of the class was found to be unsatisfactory. Chairs and desks were arranged in four rows with two children in a row, the taller children in the back.* Visibility of teacher's lips and the blackboard was reduced for the children sitting in the back row. Rearrangement of seating plan was deemed necessary—a semicircular arrangement was found to be more conducive for the presentation of material and each child now had a direct view of the teacher's lips. Lighting facilities in the room were used more advantageously with the seats arranged in this manner.

Distractions from the outside as well as internal classroom distractions proved to be a problem. Pictures, objects and charts which had no relationship to the unit word being taught were removed. Blinds were placed on the windows to reduce the distractions coming in from the street. Occasional temper outbursts and other behavior disturbances proved to be distractions in themselves. Some would not partici-

* When the class was started, it comprised six children. Two children were added to the group following their enrollment in the Training School.

pate with the group, one boy would get out of his chair, walk to the door and leave the room, another would pound on his desk and stamp his feet. Giggling and laughing inappropriately were characteristic of another child.

Another problem which became evident after these children learned the words, was how to incorporate them effectively into everyday usage. Lists of learned words are sent to teachers, The Training School Hospital, psychologists and most important the child's house or cottage parents. These words are used as often as possible to give meaning to the everyday activities of these children.

Currently there are no formal tests which can be used to measure reliably and validly the lipreading ability of mentally retarded subjects. The procedures described were utilized on a trial-and-error basis and did not represent any attempt by the authors to institute experimental methods. The class was created in order to meet an urgent clinical situation that existed at the Training School. The authors recognized the need for controlled research programs in this area, however it is hoped that teachers of similarly handicapped children will find the following information stimulating and useful.

Two hundred and fifty words have been presented to the children in this experimental class. Of the eight children, there is only one who is able to identify through lipreading almost all these words. Most words must be presented at least twice until completely comprehended. He will then write the word. Children, who at the start of the experimental class could not identify one word, can now choose the correct word wanted (through lipreading) point to its written symbol, or choose the correct corresponding picture or object. One child, who seemed to have a personal language, is now able to comprehend only the most visible words on the lips.

There was much confusion between words which start with homophonous sounds. This child had trouble distinguishing between the words "man" and "bed" in isolation. Recognition was at a higher level when carrier phrases and gestures were used. A boy, who at the start of the class was very hyperactive and inattentive, can now focus his attention on the teacher for the complete period of forty-five minutes. He is able to lipread many of the words with a carryover of complete meaning. Only one child was unable to identify any words regardless of stimuli. At the start of the experimental class in September, 1960, this child would not sit in his seat, hold a pencil, or do any type of constructive work. There has been a lessening of hyperactivity to such an extent that he will allow teacher to place a pencil in his hand and trace words, or write words while the teacher guides his hand. This child has also been placed in a prevocational program.

It is felt that if this class continues, methods to test the lipreading ability of the mentally retarded deaf should be investigated. Classroom and therapy techniques other than those used in this experimental class should be tried. It is the opinion of the authors that this class should continue since the results have been promising. Other institutions should seriously investigate the possibility of initiating such programs.

Summary

This paper has described a communication oriented program for a group of auditorally handicapped mentally retarded children. Lipreading and other language techniques were modified for presentation to these severely handicapped children. Group and individual reactions were reported.

References

1. GODA, SIDNEY: Language skills of profoundly deaf adolescent children. *J Speech Hearing Res, 2:* Dec. 1959.
2. HEIDER, F. K., and HEIDER, G. M.: Studies in the psychology of the deaf. *Psychol Monogr,* 52(1):124–153.
3. JOHNSON, P. W., and FARRELL, M. J.: An experiment in improved medical and educational services for hard of hearing children at the Walter E. Fernald State School.
Amer J Ment Defic, 62(No. 2):230–237, 1957.
4. KARLIN, I. W., and KENNEDY, L.: Delay in the development of speech. *Amer J Dis Child,* 5(1):1138–1149, 1936.
5. O'NEILL, J. J.: An exploratory investigation of lipreading ability among normal hearing students. *Speech Monogr,* 18:309–311, 1951.
6. PINTNER, R.: Speech and speech-reading tests for the deaf. *J Appl Psychol,* 13:220–225, 1929.
7. RIGRODSKY, S., and STEER, M. D.: Mawrer's theory applied to speech habilitation of the mentally retarded. *J Speech Hearing Dis,* 26:237–243, 1961.
8. SCHLANGER, B., and GOTTSLEBEN, R. H.: Testing the hearing of the mentally retarded. *Train Sch Bull (Vineland),* 54(2):21–25, 1957.
9. SCHNEIDER, B., and VALLON, J.: The results of a speech therapy program for mentally retarded children. *Amer J Ment Defic,* 59:417–425, 1955.
10. SIMMONS, AUDREY ANN: Factors related to lipreading. *J Speech Hearing Res, 2:* 340–352, 1959.
11. SIRKIN, J., and LYONS, W. F.: A study of speech defects in mental deficiency. *Amer J Ment Defic,* 46:74–80, 1941.
12. STRAZZULLA, MILLICENT: A language guide for parents of retarded children. *Amer J Ment Defic,* 59:48–58, 1954.

USE OF THE "ODDITY PROBLEM" IN TEACHING MENTALLY RETARDED DEAF-MUTES TO READ: A PILOT PROJECT*

DOUGLAS K. CANDLAND AND DANIEL H. CONKLYN†

The purpose of this report is to describe the development and utility of a technique developed specifically to

* This study was supported by a grant from the National Institutes of Health, Public Health Service (M-5698 (A)) to the first author. The authors are grateful to Selinsgrove State School and Hospital, Selinsgrove, Pa., to Luther Craig Long, Ph.D., of the psychology department of

train congenital deaf-mutes with diagnosed mental retardation to read. The technique to be described is a modification of the "oddity problem"—a problem in discriminative learning which has been applied to various animals, including the rat (Wodinsky and Bitterman, 1953), cat (Boyd and Warren, 1957; Warren, 1960) and monkey (Moon and Harlow, 1955).

General Procedure

Method

The oddity problem consists of presenting the subject with several stimuli all but one of which are identical. The *S's* task is to respond to the stimuli by indicating the odd stimulus of the sample. When correct discrimination is made *S* is reinforced in a manner suitable to the species. For example, if the stimuli are X O X, *S* would select O. Similarly, if O O X were presented, the proper response would be X.

In working with retarded human *Ss*, four distinct phases of training were used. In Phase I three wood blocks, $4 \times 4 \times 4$ in., were presented to S. The blocks were painted with a different solid color; i.e., red, blue and yellow. Each trial consisted of presenting *S* with three blocks, two of which were identical in color. The *S* was taught to select one of the blocks by pushing it from the other. If the odd colored block was selected, S was given a small

that institution and to Daniel L. Kirk, M.D., superintendent, for their cooperation in providing subjects. This paper was presented at the Spring, 1962, meetings of the Central Pennsylvania Council for Research in Mental Retardation. The report is a reprint from *The Training School Bulletin,* official organ of The Training School Unit of the American Institute for Mental Studies, Vineland, N. J., Vol. 59, No. 2, August, 1962.

† Dr. Candland is assistant professor of psychology at Bucknell University. The junior author was at the time a graduate student at the same university, but is now with Armstrong Cork Company, Lancaster, Pa.

candy (M & M). A correction procedure was used so that if one of the identical blocks was selected, S was allowed to make another selection until the correct block was chosen. After each correct choice and reinforcement a new trial was begun.

In Phase II letters were substituted for the colors on the blocks. The color of the blocks was red and the letters were white and 3 in. high. The procedure of discriminating the odd block (letter) was used. The position of the blocks and the combinations of letters were altered randomly on each trial in order to avoid *S's* responding to the position of the block rather than to the letter.

When letters were discriminated successfully with consistently greater than chance accuracy, S was required to discriminate words by the same technique. In this phase (III), if the S had learned to discriminate the letters "B," "C," "A" and "T," three 5×8 in. cards containing the words "CAT," "BAT," and "BAT" were shown. Again, the task of the S was to select the odd card, in this case "CAT." Note that the three stimuli differ only in one letter—B or C.

The final phase of training (IV) consisted of presenting S with pictures of objects which corresponded to the words that had been discriminated successfully. In this phase, S was required to match the picture with the word. In addition to the common nouns which were taught by picture, simple action verbs were taught by the *E's* performing the action. In this manner such verbs as "run" and "sit" were matched with nouns by the S into simple sentences.

Subjects

A test was given to potential Ss in order to determine whether each had previous verbal or written experience with the words used in the experiment. A series of pictures; i.e., cat and dog, was given to the Ss. If S showed any indication of either verbal or written knowledge of the object the word was not used in the experiment.

The procedure reported here was evolved on four Ss. All Ss were congenital deaf-mutes; all were considered verbally uneducable; all were rated with IQ's between 41 and 60 (Leiter International Performance Scale). Since these Ss served primarily to allow refinement of the phases of the procedure, the results of the complete technique as applied to the fourth S will be described. This S was twelve years old at the onset of experimentation. The institutional diagnosis of this S was congenital deafness from natal brain damage; MA 5 years, 2 months. The S had been a resident of the institution for four years. From information available, S had never received any form of verbal training and was considered to be uneducable.

Results

PHASE I (ODDITY TRAINING). The S was able to discriminate the odd color from the sample with 70 per cent accuracy (chance = 33%) after five thirty-minute sessions of thirty trials each. A negatively accelerated learning curve resulted with S performing at chance accuracy during the first session and improving to the 70 per cent level by the third session. This plateau in performance was retained through the fifth session. Although it is likely that some Ss would reach a higher performance level, the S used in this study did not pass the 70 per cent level of accuracy within the number of sessions allowed for this phase.

PHASE II (TRANSFER TO LETTERS). In this phase, fourteen different letters were presented to S. They were A, B, C, D, G, I, L, M, N, O, R, S, T and U. After nine thirty-minute sessions of thirty trials each, the S was able to discriminate the letters from one another with 68 per cent accuracy. (chance = 33%).

PHASE III (WORD DISCRIMINATION). The S was able to discriminate seven words within twelve thirty-minute sessions. These nouns were cat, dog, man, girl, ball, and the verbs were sit and run. The criterion of discrimination was successful discrimination on at least 90 per cent of the presentations.

PHASE IV (ASSOCIATION WITH PICTURES). In the final stage of training S was able to associate all five nouns with the appropriate pictures and both verbs with the appropriate motions. This was accomplished in thirteen sessions of 30-minutes each.

Discussion

The significance of the results of this pilot work is the indication that the technique of the oddity-problem, adapted from research with animals, may be useful in teaching congenital deaf-mutes with presumed mental retardation to read. It is possible, of course, that the technique can be extended in some cases to teaching Ss to write by substituting the response of writing for that of choosing manually, as was done in this work. Similarly, this technique might be useful for Ss who are neither deaf-mute nor mentally retarded.

The technique described here can be instrumented easily in order to allow S continuous access to the stimuli. In this manner, S can work at the task when his motivation is high and several Ss may use the same machine, thus eliminating the cost in time and money of a trained operator. In this respect, the technique has the same technical advantages as many teaching-machines which may be adapted for use with deaf or retarded children (Porter, 1957). Indeed, several types of problem-solving apparatus are currently marketed which are modified easily to present the oddity problem.*

Several research questions suggest themselves regarding refinements in technique. Throughout the experiment a ratio of two similar stimuli to one dissimilar stimulus was used. This 2 : 1 ratio is, of course, the lowest possible ratio for the oddity problem. On the other hand, it is possible that a larger ratio (e.g., 4 : 1 or 5 : 1) would lead to more rapid learning.

Finally, in the studies reported here continuous reinforcement (FR 1 : 1)

---

* Foringer and Co., Inc., 312 Maple Drive, Rockville, Maryland, is able to modify its Osler-Foringer Discrimination Device to suit the requirements of this study.

was used. Although this type of reinforcement leads to rapid learning, it does not necessarily lead to strongest retention if extinction is taken as the criterion of retention. (Ferster and Skinner, 1957). It is possible that retention of the discriminations would be greater if a variable ratio schedule of reinforcement was employed when the response had become stable (i.e., Phase III).

Summary

A technique is reported for teaching congenital deaf-mutes with reported mental retardation to read. The technique is based on the "oddity-problem" —a problem of discriminative behavior used in animal research. The findings indicate that the technique may be applied successfully. Research problems concerned with refinement of the technique are discussed.

References

1. BOYD, B. O., and WARREN, J. M.: Solution of oddity problems by cats. *J Comp Physiol Psychol*, 50:258–260, 1957.
2. FERSTER, C. B., and SKINNER, B. F.: *Schedules of Reinforcement*. New York, Appleton, 1957.
3. MOON, L. E., and HARLOW, H. F.: Analysis of oddity learning by monkeys. *J Comp Physiol Psychol*, 48:188–194, 1955.
4. PORTER, D.: A critical review of a portion of the literature on teaching devices. *Harvard Educational Rev*, 27:126–147, 1957.
5. WARREN, J. M.: Oddity learning set in a cat. *J Comp Physiol Psychol*, 53:433–434, 1960.
6. WODINSKY, J., and BITTERMAN, M. E.: The solution of oddity-problems by the rat. *Amer J Psychol*, 66:137–140, 1953.

DEAF-BLIND CHILDREN—THEIR EDUCATIONAL OUTLOOK*

BYRON BERHOW

It is with a humble sense of appreciation that I accepted this spot on the program to speak to the convention of the AAWB on the educational outlook for deaf-blind children. It is a privilege and an honor to be here on the platform to share some thoughts with you, as well as to present the challenge we have before us in the matter of developing deaf-blind children to their maximum potential.

This small group of children (some 300 to 400 in the United States) is unknown and unheard of by most people. Until recently there were eight schools in the United States with operating departments staffed with teachers trained to teach this particular group of multiple handicapped children. I believe the Iowa School for the Deaf has closed its department, so there are now probably only seven. Six of the remaining departments are located in state residential schools for the blind and one in a state school for the deaf and the blind. I believe four schools—Perkins School for the Blind, the Michigan School for the Blind, the Alabama School for the Deaf and the Blind, and the Washington State School for the Blind—enroll out-of-state deaf-blind pupils at a non-profit fee.

Services for adult deaf-blind persons are usually given through state rehabilitation departments for the blind, or in the general rehabilitation programs. The Industrial Home for the Blind in Brooklyn perhaps does more in special services than any, or perhaps all other agencies together.

Education for deaf-blind children was nonexistent until Laura Bridgman entered Perkins School in 1837. Her success paved the way for others to receive an education. Upon the achievement of successful speech and higher education by Helen Keller, there followed national knowledge that deaf-blind children could learn and progress in our society.

Eventually, the American Foundation for the Blind entered the field, and with educational institutions for the deaf and the blind, organized the National Study Committee on Education of Deaf-Blind Children, which began active work in 1953. This committee is composed of representatives from the American Association of Instructors of the Blind, the Conference of Executives of American Schools for the Deaf, the schools having such departments, and the American Foundation for the Blind. Then an organized effort was made to search out the number of deaf-blind children. The known number of such children immediately increased considerably and the number of organized classes for them doubled. By 1960 the school population in these special de-

* An address, July 23, 1963, at the convention of the American Association of Workers for the Blind, held in Seattle, Washington. Reprinted from *The New Outlook for the Blind*, official journal of the American Foundation for the Blind, Inc., New York, December, 1963. The author is Superintendent of the Washington State School for the Blind.

partments had increased to eighty-seven. At that time there were 372 known deaf-blind persons under twenty years of age, and more than 3,300 who were twenty years and older. The report of October 1962 showed only seventy-eight such children in properly organized and staffed classes.

In 1954, in Paris, the World Council for the Welfare of the Blind created a Committee on Services for the Deaf-Blind. It was commissioned to study communication and minimum services for all deaf-blind persons. In 1959 it presented a lengthy and very helpful report to the Council during its meeting in Rome.

Psychological and psychiatric information on deaf-blind children is most difficult to obtain with any degree of reliability. Nevertheless, Perkins School for the Blind has created an evaluation team from its own staff which has traveled throughout this country and beyond our borders to study deaf-blind children. It has gone forward in this field with all of its unknowns and has given much good help to parents, state departments, schools and teachers. In time it will no doubt be able to make a reliable, significant and lasting contribution to this part of the work in addition to past good progressive efforts.

Deaf-blind children vary possibly in greater degree than any other group. There is variation in the remaining hearing, as well as residual sight. Due, no doubt, to disability in addition to deaf-blindness, we find a fairly large percentage are uneducable. Cerebral palsy, brain damage, emotional disturbance and other physical disabilities often accompany the loss of sight and hearing.

Recognition of a deaf-blind child for what he is is one of the most difficult of tasks. The first and most common diagnosis of such a child is that he is blind and severely mentally defective. In spite of the fact that this is often true, it is much more often true that the child has a potential ability that can be brought out and developed.

In order to bring out this development we must have a proper setting which includes good living conditions, learning and challenging situations from infancy, and finally, a qualified and patient teacher.

I would like to impress upon you the necessity of having a special department with teachers trained to teach deaf-blind children. A teacher of the blind or a teacher of the deaf is only partially trained for this work, and any combination of the two of them is not as satisfactory as one trained in this particular work to teach the child who is simultaneously deaf and blind. This has been recognized by national agencies, and a professional certificate for teachers of the deaf-blind child is available to qualified persons.

Of the two problems, deafness is the major one. However, departments for these children are usually found in schools for the blind. I believe that this is because these children probably integrate socially better with blind children. Perhaps blind and deaf-blind children have more of a common bond because both of them make much more educational use of the sense of touch and smell than do the deaf youngsters. However, deafness remains their greatest barrier to normal relationships and mental growth in areas of concepts, reasoning power, language and speech.

The education of the deaf-blind child should begin as soon as his handicap is known. The cornerstone of this "beginning" is "belonging." He should be a real member of the family and be included in every activity. The formative preschool years are, I believe, more important in the development of a deaf-blind child who has a positive potential than for any other who has a handicap. Self-reliance and physical independence are qualities that can and do grow during infancy, and parents must be encouraged to develop them at all times. This does call for good early counseling of parents and a follow-through by them. They must be imaginative and resourceful in finding ways to stimulate the child through his senses of smelling, tasting and feeling. Companionship of other children, too, is important in these early years.

Deaf-blindness is not a bar to achievement. The remaining senses and the latent mental capacity can make for educational advancement. Hence, such a child should be enrolled in a school with good personnel and equipment as early as possible.

A good school will subject the child to an intense and continuing sense training course which will develop from the simple to the complicated activity using both large and small muscles to do heavy, as well as fine or delicate type jobs. This is to train the remaining senses in as many ways

as possible to develop physical abilities to do the educational jobs that are to come.

When he is adjusted to a teacher and ready, communication should be introduced. This communication is called "vibration speech." Vibration is felt by the child as he places his thumb on the teacher's lips and the fingers on the cheek and jawbone. Vibration patterns of a few simple sounds can soon be recognized. He can learn to duplicate them with his own tongue and lips. Then he can learn to combine them into words and the teacher can physically demonstrate the meaning of each word. For example: the teacher can hold the child and jump with him each time the command word is given. This process takes great patience and gentleness on the part of the teacher, but when there is a carry-through to where the child responds correctly to two or three different commands one knows that speech communication is being achieved.

Teaching speech to a deaf-blind child is both a science and an art. The science may be learned because there are certain basics to be mastered. Not all teachers can become artists in this field even if they use much originality and initiative. I do not know how a teacher can get a deaf-blind child to speak voluntarily even if she knows all the basic principles, but an artist in the business will succeed and the child will develop in speech and language under her tutelage.

Good speech depends on a relaxed condition of the teacher-and-child combination, especially in giving vibration.

The production of vowels and consonants; pitch, quality and intensity; accenting, inflection and modulation, etc., are all dependent upon an easy, relaxed situation for proper learning.

Once the child has made a start on the road to speech, the second phase of language development may be begun. If the first step of speech is not mastered, language will not be developed. But when he does begin such development he is on the way to making educational progress. There is no known timetable or established rate of progress for a deaf-blind child. This depends so very much upon his attitude, personality and other qualities in addition to his innate mental ability.

The home life with houseparents, other children, the schedule, the disciplines, the responsibilities, the affection given, etc., are certainly important factors in the continuing development.

The total program of education for these children then is to help them adjust to their problems, to develop independence and habits of self-care, to acquire communication and language skills and to live as normally as possible according to our standards of good citizenship.

I hope you will read out of all this that deaf-blind children can make progress and can have a good future if we will but provide the opportunity for them. I feel that it is our duty to find them, recognize their problems and to provide good schools for them.

Are we able and will we meet the challenge of the education of the deaf-blind child? The answer lies with each and every one of us who works in this field of education and care—even if it is one of the smallest of the many groups we serve.

XVII. Considerations of Psychology

PSYCHOLOGICAL AND PSYCHIATRIC IMPLICATIONS OF DEAFNESS*

Helmer R. Myklebust

S ensory deprivation as a concept may include a wide variety of circumstances, actual or simulated.[6] Here we are referring only to the individual who has an actual impairment of a receptor. We are raising the question of impact, of psychological and psychiatric implications, when the ability to hear is permanently impaired or lacking. The clinical otolaryngologist often is confronted not only with the fact of deafness but with the ways in which it influences behavior.

Before considering the significance of deafness psychodynamically, it is important to weigh the nature of audition, especially in comparison to vision. The distance senses, hearing and vision, are the primary social and intellectual senses; taction, gustation, and olfaction are more primitive. However, the functions, the purposes, of hearing and of vision organismically are different. Vision is directional while hearing is nondirectional; hearing acts as an antenna

* Reprinted from the *Archives of Otolaryngology,* December, 1963, Volume 78, pp. 790–793. Copyright 1963, by American Medical Association. Dr. Myklebust is professor of language pathology and psychology, and director of the Institute for Language Disorders, The School of Speech, Northwestern University, Evanston, Illinois.

and scans the environment in all directions simultaneously. Moreover, hearing is mandatory. We cannot cease hearing even while asleep. Nature provided for one of the distance senses to be functioning constantly, and the advantage in self-preservation is obvious. Many other differences between hearing and vision relevant to the study of the psychological and psychiatric implications of deafness could be mentioned: we can hear in the dark, through walls, and around corners. From these facets of audition we conclude that hearing is the basic scanning, alerting, and contact sense in man, while vision is the primary foreground sense. When deafness ensues, the individual is deprived of his basic sense for environmental contact and exploration, so he must use vision for both foreground and background even though vision is not an efficient scanning sense. Each time the individual looks up to monitor his environment his attention to that which is of principal concern, to that which is foremost in the mind, is interrupted.

By nature man has input channels and monitoring systems which are highly efficient for maintaining homeostatic equilibrium. But when a sensory deprivation occurs, the means whereby the individual maintains this balance must be altered. He must modify the ways in which he attains knowledge of reality.

Although the human being is highly adaptable and can make compensatory adjustments, it is apparent that a sensory deprivation limits the world of experience. It deprives the individual of some of the material resources from which the mind develops. Because total experience is reduced, because reality is perceived less effectively, there is an imposition on the balance and equilibrium of all psychological processes; when one type of sensory information is lacking it alters the integration and function of all of the others. Experience itself is constituted differently. The world of perception, conception, imagery, and thought has an altered foundation, a new configuration. Such alteration occurs naturally and unknowingly because unless the individual is organized and attuned differently, survival itself may be jeopardized. Fortunately through evidence accruing from centers around the world some of these implications of a sensory deprivation are becoming clarified.[2] A fundamental task is to ascertain the ways in which learning and adjustment can be facilitated, although perceptual organization, the structure of the intellect, and the personality have been modified.

Most of our knowledge regarding the psychological and psychiatric implications of deafness derives from studies of persons whose sensory deprivation was sustained early in life and in whom the hearing loss was severe. We shall consider some of the ways in which deafness seems to alter psychological processes in those so handicapped.

Mental Development and Intellectual Capacities

Historically, one of the first questions raised in regard to the effects of deafness was whether lack of audition altered mental growth.[4] Although this question of effect on intellectual capacities remains with us, contemporarily our concern is more with the qualitative consequences. We are attempting to understand the relationships between early life deafness and cognition, thinking, memory, and conceptualization. It is evident that a deaf and hearing child might obtain the same quantitative score on a given mental test although employing highly different mental processes. Prediction from test results for the deaf, therefore, becomes even more difficult than for the hearing. These are the modifications which are so intriguing and basic to the question of psychological and psychiatric implications and which perhaps hold the key to many of the problems of learning and adjustment in the hearing-impaired.

The most clearly defined mental functions which have been shown to be modified by deafness are memory and conceptualization.[2] It seems that to remember experiences which are auditory, or readily lend themselves to making auditory associations, is more difficult when the experience must be perceived through vision, gustation, taction, or olfaction. However, while deficiencies in memory are manifested, memory in general is not impaired. Perhaps it is not surprising that when the input is different, not only the storing process but also that which is stored is different. Nevertheless, it is significant that experiences gained through vision and taction may be remembered more effectively when deafness is present, thus raising the issue of what and how anyone remembers. The study of this phenomenon is vital for better understanding the deaf and the hearing.

Social Maturity

One has attained social maturity to the extent that he is able to care for himself and to assist with the care of others.[1] The criterion is the factor of independence versus dependence. The human infant is highly dependent, and if he is not cared for properly he dies. Gradually he learns to feed and dress himself, to care for his toilet needs, to communicate, to direct himself, and to assist with the welfare of others. It is stimulating and provocative to apply this concept to all forms of animal life, phylogenetically and ontogenetically. What we see is that the species having no dependency at the time of birth, such as some types of fish, have the least complex nervous systems and attain only the simplest forms of behavior. In other words, the greater the dependency the higher the level of attainment to be expected; the less the organism is dependent on its parents at the time of birth, the more primitive it is phylogenetically.

The purpose of emphasizing this concept of social maturity is that it is highly relevant to study of the implications of sensory deprivation. Investigation has revealed that deafness increases dependency. Moreover, the increased dependency, this need for greater than average assistance from others, is most apparent in adulthood rather than in childhood; as the individual with deafness attains adulthood he is less able to fulfill the demands of his environment than when he was a child.

There are two aspects of this problem which need emphasis. All who deal with the emotionally immature are aware of the resentments that derive from being unduly dependent on others.[5] Individuals, perhaps even nations, do not have much tolerance for dependency, albeit their condition or circumstances might indicate that need for assistance from others is natural and to be expected. Likewise, those dealing with the guidance and psychotherapeutic needs of the sensorially deprived recognize that their greater dependency is the basis of many of their emotional conflicts.[3] Our task, it seems to me, is to help them accept those aspects which cannot be changed, such as being dependent on others to take telephone messages, but not to generalize from these aspects unduly. The need to be more dependent in certain respects may influence feelings of self-esteem and self-sufficiency in ways which are unwarranted and unnecessary if adequate assistance is provided.

This social maturity approach is useful also because it reflects the various ways that a deprivation leads to immaturity organismically. We have seen that when a distance sense is nonfunctional the individual is required to use the more primitive close senses in ways which are characteristic of less developed organisms. Studies of social maturity indicate similar circumstances. When deafness is present, the levels of self-help and self-direction are attained with good success, but the level of responsibility indicated by being able to assist with the care of others is less attainable; hence, the implication that the individual is less socially mature and more like one of a younger age.

Emotional Development and Adjustment

Studies of the emotional development of deaf children provide evidence of the importance of hearing in personality growth and structure and reveal that psychic stress ensues from this type of sensory deprivation. In one study we compared the self-perception of deaf and hearing children through their drawings of a man, of father, mother, and self. A number of differences occurred involving perceptual distortions of the head, hands, fingers, ears, limbs, lips, hair, feet, mood, and a factor which we referred to as maleness. The specific psychodynamics which were operating were not apparent, but the deaf child's body image and perception were not consistent with those for the normal.[2]

Psychologically and psychiatrically it is interesting to note that this study, as well as others, suggests that when deaf-

ness is present from early life it is more difficult to attain awareness of the characteristic roles by sex; masculineness and feminineness to some extent appear to be auditory in nature. Perhaps it is not strange, although revealing, that determination of and identification with the appropriate sex occurs most successfully when we can, consciously or unconsciously, monitor the world of sound. Stated differently, possibly the deaf child is more immature and confused in a psychosexual sense because he does not hear the taboos and innuendos regarding sex and because the process of internalizing the male or female role, a complex process for the normal, is even more intricate and ambiguous when hearing is lacking.

Implications such as these have been suggested also through studies of adults, both for the deaf and for the hard of hearing. While differences occur on the basis of age of onset, degree of hearing loss, and etiology, there are adjustment patterns which seem to characterize the impact of this sensory deprivation. The most noteworthy characteristic is the way in which the hearing-impaired feel aloof, disengaged, disassociated, and isolated with respect to other people. They are not behaving schizophrenically. They are outer-directed, almost extroverted, but feel they are watching a world rather than participating in it. They are seeking feedback, engaging in reality testing, but their lack of audition makes it difficult to interchange feelings and ideas with others. The studies on simulated sensory deprivation, likewise, emphasize the need of human beings to have constant feedback, constant sensory stimulation, in order to prevent distortion of reality to the extent that the consequences might entail actual mental illness. Simulated sensory deprivation as currently defined is not equivalent to actual sensory deprivation. In fact, the similarities remain to be ascertained. Nevertheless, if we were pressed to choose one way in which deafness most influences emotional development and personality structure we would say that it is the way in which it limits ability to sense the feelings, ideas, criticisms, and demeanors of others and hence restricts comparison with oneself.

The effect we are attempting to describe can best be thought of in terms of ego development. Deaf persons attempt to test reality and do not necessarily withdraw from it, but reality is difficult to perceive and apprehend when one has all of his senses; when one is deaf it is even more difficult.

When we asked deaf and hard-of-hearing adults to rate the extent to which deafness was a handicap, the hard of hearing rated it as being more of a hardship than did the deaf, and the males viewed it as being more of a deprivation than did the females. Although sex differences were significant, the greater the hearing loss the less it was considered a handicap.[2] This circumstance might be viewed as an advantage were it not for the fact that study of the emotional adjustment of this population showed that the greater the degree of the deafness the more emotional disturbances and immaturities were present. In other words, the more the individual lacked the experience of hearing the more he could not normally apprehend reality and the more immature he was, even being unable to be astutely aware of the significance of deafness as a handicap.

Trends and Needs

Knowledge concerning the psychological and psychiatric implications of deafness is accruing, making it possible to examine the trends and to evaluate the needs. Such observations, although inevitably based on assumptions, require that we define our objectives. Is our objective to have the sensorially impaired be as much like those who have normal sensory capacities as possible? Or is our emphasis to assist them in becoming self-reliant, self-actualized deaf people? These questions involve the norm of adjustment that serves as our guide, as our point of reference. We realize that if we persist in demanding that the deaf individual conform precisely to our norm for hearing persons he tends to develop emotional troubles that are essentially unrelated to his deafness. However, societies and culture assume norms of behavior which cannot be ignored. The implication is that the otolaryngologist must know the psychology and psychiatry of deafness and assist in alleviating its impact, especially its more pervasive effects, but at the same time recognize that there are features and attributes which must be accepted by the individual and by society. We are optimistic that some of the behavioral effect of this sensory deprivation can be modified. To some extent, our hope derives from the way in which new electronic techniques can be used to provide substitute monitoring systems. Another reason for hope, and an important one it is, is the increasing awareness of the needs of the sensorially deprived by otolaryngologists, psychologists, psychiatrists, and educators. More diagnostic, guidance, and treatment facilities are available than ever before. The needs continue to be great but there is advancement, and the outlook for the deaf is far from dismal; it could even be bright.

References

1. DOLL, E. A.: *The Measurement of Social Competence.* Minneapolis, Educational Test Bureau, 1953.
2. MYKLEBUST, H. R.: *Psychology of Deafness: Sensory Deprivation, Learning, and Adjustment.* New York, Grune, 1960.
3. ———; NEYHUS, A., and MULHOLLAND, A. M.: Guidance and counseling for the deaf. *Amer Ann Deaf,* 107:370–415, 1962.
4. PINTNER, R., *et al: Psychology of the Physically Handicapped.* New York, F. S. Crofts, 1946.
5. SAUL, L. J.: *Emotional Maturity,* Ed. 2. Philadelphia, Lippincott, 1960.
6. SOLOMON, P., *et al: Sensory Deprivation.* Cambridge, Harvard, 1961.

ADJUSTMENT PROBLEMS OF THE DEAF CHILD[*]

GRACE MOORE HEIDER

Human nature is socially acquired. The individual becomes a person only through social interaction. These two statements form the basis of our definition of personality: Personality is the person's concept of his role in certain groups. This concept determines his behavior within the group.
—FRANCIS J. BROWN in
Educational Sociology [†]

The adjustment of the deaf[‡] can only be considered in terms of what deafness involves, i.e., of the difficulties

[*] Reproduced from *The Nervous Child,* Vol. 7, No. 1, January, 1948, by courtesy of the copyright holder, Dr. Ernest Harms, now editor-in-chief of *Adolescence.* The author is with the Department of Psychology, University of Kansas.

[†] See THE RECENT BOOKS.

[‡] The question of nomenclature to distinguish, on the one hand, degrees of auditory deficiency and, on the other, age of onset, has received considerable attention.[2] For the purposes of this paper, in which we cannot take up the different aspects of the problem separately, we shall use

to which the deaf person must actually adjust beyond what is required of every human being. These may be thought of as representing at least two different levels. First, there is the sensory defect itself. The causes of deafness are many but their effect is more or less uniform in that it means a cutting off of auditory stimulation. Important variants in this situation are the degree of the handicap, the age of onset, whether the restriction of external stimuli is accompanied by internal head noises, and whether the onset of deafness was sudden or gradual. Profound deafness in some cases begins with little or no warning. Very significant is the fact that it is usually irrevocable. Less is known of the pathology of the ear than of the eye, for

the single term *deaf* and specify when we are restricting its meaning to special groups.

example, and the ear is less accessible to treatment. Hearing once lost is seldom regained.*

On a second level we may consider the fact that hearing is the basis of the means of communication used by the members of the nonhandicapped group among whom the deaf person lives. Because the deaf child does not hear, he does not spontaneously learn to speak or to understand others. Special training brings him some measure of facility in making himself understood and in understanding others but, as one educator of the deaf has said, what he gains is, at best, a crutch. The speech of the deaf is never so good that it can "pass" for that of a nondeaf person because the process of learning to talk and using speech is psychophysically different. When the deaf person speaks he is carrying out acts of which he cannot experience the full sensory effects. Similarly with lipreading, he must learn to understand a visual pattern of speech, and many of our common speech sounds are made with parts of the vocal apparatus that cannot be seen. The person who loses hearing later in life may retain perfect speech or speech that approximates that of the person with normal hearing, but he is equally handicapped in trying to understand others. Further, in the case of the deaf child the fact that he must begin to learn language later than the

normal child, perhaps at a time when the greatest readiness for language acquisition has already passed, and that he must learn it without the wealth of emotionally tinged auditory experience which comes to the normal child without effort on his own part, means that he is seriously retarded in this area over a period of years, if not permanently. And this broad handicap in communication in turn brings with it a series of consequences, educational, social and economic.

How far the primary handicap, i.e., the loss of sound as sensation, affects adjustment is a question that has been raised and not answered. Certainly sound plays a part in the structuring of the world of the person who hears. It has been suggested that sound sensations in themselves have an emotional or aesthetic value and that the deaf often try to secure greater stimulation in other ways to compensate for the relatively cold, lifeless media of the other senses.[1] There seems to be no direct evidence on this point. Deafness brings a certain amount of physical insecurity but it is interesting that deaf children on the whole seem, if anything, less prone to fears than normal children. This may be because there is less possibility of spreading tales of imaginary dangers, of witches and bogey men, in such a group and fewer accounts of accidents and fires.

Whatever the effects of the sensory deficiency itself, there is no doubt that the language handicap of the deaf and the consequences that follow in its train are much more important in determining their life situation. And what is most

---

* Cases in which radium treatment of adenoidal growth in the Eustachian tube brings a child with a serious hearing defect back to normal or near-normal hearing make an important exception to this generalization. The percentage of children whose deafness comes from this cause is small but the fact that they exist and can be helped is too little recognized.

significant about this aspect of the handicap is that still more than the sensory loss it brings the individual psychologically into regions of insecurity and conflict. Because the deaf are relatively few in number they may be said to occupy the position of a minority group in the world of the nondeaf and their situation involves many of the problems common to all minority groups. Some, especially among the deaf themselves, have suggested that they should escape some of their educational and social problems by giving up the effort to learn the means of communication developed by persons with normal hearing and that they should use a language of hand gestures for which they have full physical equipment. This would mean that they would live in groups of their own kind with whom communication would be as free and effortless as oral communication is among the nondeaf. These alternatives—living as handicapped members of the larger social group or living as fully privileged members of relatively segregated groups—represent very different social situations in which the problems of adjustment and personality integration are not the same. Actually both of these alternatives exist in our society and the individual deaf person, once he leaves school, is usually faced with the decision of choosing one or the other or an intermediate position. To many, the possibilities of the segregated group in which he may be a full member are enticing. At the same time there are many arguments against it which influence the decision of entering or remaining in such a group. First there is the linguistic fact,

that manual means of communication never remain complete translations of the spoken language from which they are derived.

The sensory data of the two differ and their inner dynamics follow different patterns which pull them further and further apart. The manual language of the deaf, even if it be taught in school as a direct translation of the spoken language, soon becomes colloquially different and grammatically less differentiated. Some educators insist that the language of the deaf should develop its own structure but the final result is that the individual who thinks in this language becomes less and less at home in either the written or spoken forms used by the "outside" group. In many cases it means that he finds it increasingly difficult to read the books and journals of the majority group and that he comes to live more and more exclusively in the thought of his own limited group. Some of the deaf discuss just this fact in regard to the decision whether to remain within the minority group or to take a position as near as possible to the larger group. For instance one deaf person said: "My contacts with deaf people have been very agreeable but as the years went by I grew tired of them because the greater group of deaf people talk about themselves. These are the ones who almost do not make contacts with hearing people."[6]

Another problem of segregation is that it is never complete. The deaf must remain economically part of the larger group whether they live among the nondeaf or in separate groups. Neither can the segregation have the continuity that a segregation based on race, for example, may have. While there is clear evidence that certain kinds of deafness are hereditary, possibly as recessive unit characters, the fact remains that most of the deaf have parents who hear and most of them have one or more nondeaf siblings. Many who marry have nondeaf children. And for many of the deaf the facts that are known of inheritance raise further conflict as to the wisdom of segregation. Alexander Graham Bell in 1884 published a treatise entitled "Upon the formation of a deaf variety of the human race" in regard to problems of intermarriage among the deaf and those having deaf relatives.[3] Recent research, while discounting the likelihood that the final outcome suggested by Bell would ever be realized, emphasizes the importance of heredity in showing that it probably plays a part in many cases of so-called acquired deafness with the onset in later childhood or adult life as well as in many congenital cases.

All this means that the deaf person is faced with a choice between using tools of communication for which he lacks the full physical equipment and living as a marginal member of the larger group, or immersing himself in a minority group which offers certain insulation from the tensions of the marginal status but at the same time no real separation or continuity. The decision is not an easy one and often involves guilt feelings built up by advocates of one form of education or the other during his formative years. Data from former pupils of schools for the deaf show that the insecurity and conflict involved in

this decision play an important part in their adult lives.[6]

Aside from these problems of group membership, the deaf person is faced with insecurity in all his personal relations with members of the nondeaf group. If he tries to use oral communication, with a stranger at least, he is never sure whether he will be able to understand or make himself understood. If he writes he is demanding that the other person take extra time and treat him as a special case. If he were wholly cut off the situation would not be so tantalizing as that in which he finds himself, where he can understand part of a conversation and then perhaps lose just the key word that explains everything. The boundaries between what he can and cannot do are not clearly defined and from this point of view his whole life situation is poorly structured. In other respects his situation is one that would be trying to anyone; plans are made and people move about him. He is expected to fall in and do what the group does. He is blamed and considered "stupid" if he does the wrong thing, yet a nuisance if he wants the activity in hand to be interrupted so that he can get a full explanation.

This question of being considered inferior by the members of the majority group whose standards he cannot fail to realize is one that is brought up frequently by the deaf themselves. Montague, for example, writes: "Yes, it would be helpful if one's friends would realize that it is deaf ears, not feeble minds, that make us slow on the uptake."[10] And the fact that the deaf are often socially and economically at a disadvantage in relation to the hearing world only confirms the feelings engendered by personal contacts in which their failure to understand the import of a situation puts them in the position of being less clever than others, and often in the position, as Montague says, of being moved around by them, "like a piece of furniture."

Another important factor in the lives of many children who are deaf from their early years is the fact that they are sent away from home for their education. No adequate evaluation of the effect of this kind of separation has been made for either deaf or hearing children. Burchard and Myklebust[4] have shown that the residential school deaf child measures as less mature on the Vineland Social Maturity Scale than the deaf child who lives at home and attends a dayschool but there are many deeper problems involved in taking a child of two or four or six away from his home. In many cases the fact that he is singled out from among his brothers and sisters to be sent away may easily be felt as rejection; the weakening of the early identifications and relationships must have some effect on the integration of the personality. Further, the amount of regimentation which can hardly be avoided and the relative impersonality of relationships in the ordinary residential school make the social climate very different from that of the average home. Whether it be for better or worse is not yet proved, but for many deaf children it seems to be educationally unavoidable. No other way has been found to

provide adequate specialized training for the one or two deaf children in a small community or even the number who might form an ungraded class in the community of moderate size. In the larger cities, schools in which the child may at least go home every weekend are becoming more and more the rule.

If we try to summarize the direction of difference between the life of the deaf and that of the nondeaf child which all these aspects of his handicap indicate we may say that each is such as to involve basic insecurities and conflict. What is the effect of this on the individual deaf person? So far there is no definite answer to this question. A number of studies have been made, many following the pioneer work of Pintner in using such means of evaluation as the Bernreuter Personality Inventory, the Rogers Test of Personality Adjustment, the Haggerty-Olson-Wickman Behavior Rating Scale, and the like. These studies attempted to answer the question whether the deaf were more or less introverted, more or less neurotic, more or less stable than the nondeaf. The more dynamic studies of personality have already shown the relative sterility of this approach with the normal groups for which these instruments were designed. They are still less fruitful for comparing the original groups with special groups for which their items may have entirely different significance. For example, a question such as: "At a reception or a tea do you feel reluctant to meet the most important person present?" may well indicate a feeling of insecurity or withdrawal on the part of a person with normal means of communication at his disposal, but for the person who is not sure whether he will understand what the other will say it need indicate nothing more than sound social expediency. This series of studies has given no decisive results even within the limits set by its measuring instruments. On the whole it has shown that the deaf are slightly more introverted, slightly more neurotic than the hearing but the differences found were so slight in comparison with the differences between the two groups in their life situation that they can only lead us to deny almost entirely the influence of environment on the formation of personality or to conclude that the measures used failed to touch the dimensions that should be studied. The latter alternative is certainly the more plausible.

Some exploratory studies have been made to resolve this situation. On the one hand there are studies which attempt to describe the psychological situation of the deaf in order to define more clearly the directions in which differences may be expected to occur.[6] Attempts have been made to use material such as the Rorschach or Thematic Apperception Test but with deaf children or adults who have been deaf since childhood the picture of the personality becomes confused with their language limitation and it is hard to know what significance the results may have.

In another study an analysis was made of language used by deaf and nondeaf children in describing a short motion picture story.[7] This analysis showed that the language retardation of the deaf involves not only the level which they may be expected to have reached at any given time in sentence structure and type of sentence used but also the dynamics of the thought structure. They used relatively rigid, unrelated language units which followed each other with little overlapping of structure or meaning. They constantly interrupted a narrative to explain "why" and rarely spoke of what was only a possibility rather than a realized fact. If we consider such a language task in any sense as a projective technique these differences may point to differences in personality structure as well as to differences in intellectual development.

An experimental study with preschool children has shown differences in personal relationships between deaf and nondeaf at early age levels.[8] In this study a game which only one child could use at a time was offered to pairs of children. Sixty-six pairs of hearing and forty-eight pairs of deaf children were observed in this situation and the results showed that with the hearing there was much more tendency for one to dominate the game than with the deaf. Further, when the descriptions of the games as they were played were classified in terms of degree of structurization, it was found that those of the hearing were again more highly organized and showed greater continuity of structure. These differences can be explained in part by the fact that the hearing had more effective tools of communication at their disposal. The ways in which language was used to enable one child to gain control of the situation without arousing either aggression or withdrawal on the part of the other gave fresh appreciation of its function in social relationships. At the same time these data brought into sharp focus the question of the effect of the more diffuse, less structured, less sharply oriented social relations of the younger deaf child on the development of his personality. It is hard to avoid the suggestion that there must be significant effects but so far no techniques have been tried which serve to evaluate them adequately. This task remains to be attacked, and only on the basis of a deeper understanding of the structure and dynamics of the personality of the deaf can there be built descriptions of the characteristic adjustments and directions which psychopathological developments may take within this group.

References

1. BALDWIN, M.: The road of silence. *Atlantic Monthly, 120:*730–738, 1917.
2. BARKER, R. G.; WRIGHT, B. A., and GONICK, M. R.: Somatopsychological significance of impaired hearing; in *Adjustment to Physical Handicap and Illness.* Social Science Research Council Bulletin 55, 1946.
3. BELL, A. G.: Upon the formation of a deaf variety of the human race. *Nat Acad Sci Memoirs, 2:*177–262, 1884.
4. BURCHARD, E. M. L., and MYKLEBUST, H. R.: A comparison of congenital and adventitious deafness with respect to its effect on intelligence, personality and social maturity. *Amer Ann Deaf, 87:*241–251, 1942.
5. GARDNER, W. H.: Report of the Committee on Hard of Hearing Children of the American Society for the Hard of Hearing (Proceedings), 1940, 103–111.
6. HEIDER, F., and HEIDER, G. M.: The adjustment of the adult deaf; in *Studies in the Psychology of the Deaf,* No. 2. *Psychological Monographs,* 53 (No. 5), 1941.
7. ———: A comparison of the sentence structure of deaf and hearing children, *in Studies in the Psychology of the Deaf,* No. 1. *Psychological Monographs,* 52 (No. 1) 1940.
8. ———: A comparison of the social behavior of deaf and hearing preschool children in an experimental play situation (not yet published).
9. ———: Deafness, in *Encyclopedia of Child Guidance,* New York, Philosophical Library, 1943.
10. MONTAGUE, M. P.: Pioneers of silence. *Atlantic Monthly, 154:*195–202, 1934.

HOW A DEAF CHILD THINKS*

IRVING S. FUSFELD

From the time society first turned to the need of education for deaf children a good deal of thought—perhaps we should say speculation—has been directed toward the manner of thinking in deaf children, the implication being

* This paper appeared first in *Deaf Welfare,* official organ of The National Council of Missioners and Welfare Officers to the Deaf, Birmingham, England, March, 1958.

that shut off from the experiences of sound they establish a modality of thought processes that is different and that by inference sets them apart. Much space was devoted to this point by early writers, mainly along lines of philosophical inquiry, and more recently by investigators of the perceptive and interpretive processes.

In the present discussion we are taking our subject literally, that is, conditions as they affect the child who for want of sensory power does not hear, the child who is deaf.

But before we enter this field of analysis, it may be helpful to consider a number of misconceptions which often cloud the horizon. Such misconceptions can be especially damaging if they form the background of ill-advised educational practice.

The first of these misconceptions is the belief that *only* by the instrumentality of verbal symbols is it possible for one to think. At a fairly recent meeting of educators of the deaf one speaker maintained that without language in the conventional sense, meaning verbal language, human thought is not possible. A number of veteran educators, long versed in the ways of the deaf child, took issue with him, contending that even without aid of verbal symbols deaf children do carry on a fertile form of mentalizing. It is true this manner of concept formation varies from that in which words are the common vehicle. But it is nonetheless a moving and stimulating exercise, by which thinking is promoted. It is here contended this nonverbal form of thinking, a *compound* of all the sensory possibilities in which only those dependent upon hearing are missing, provides a substantial base upon which the deaf child, when he has attained to a state of readiness for it, may build the formal manner of thinking which emanates from exposure to and experience with word-symbols. It is too often overlooked by those who conceive of the deaf child's preschool mind as a sort

of vacuum, that in one respect this precursor-state to verbalization, despite the minus quality in one sensory direction, is attuned more sharply in the nonverbal zone, if only out of the law of compensation. That is, compelled to rely more heavily on the nonauditory senses, the latter are re-enforced, or keyed, to a relatively greater degree than is the case with hearing children. A simple instance will illustrate. A deaf child on a railroad trip will of course be insensitive to the sounds and voices about him, but he is certain to be unusually sensitive to the vibratory effects, more so than is commonly the case. This accentuated awareness of nonauditory experience is in turn translated into a corresponding type of active thinking in which the concept components, by a chain of experiential associations, are nonverbal in character.

A second fallacy when one ponders on how the deaf child thinks refers to the matter of the greatly misunderstood psychological experience which goes by the term Imagination. Because the mental world of the deaf child is so largely bound by concrete experiences—visual, tactile, gustatory, olfactory, kinesthetic—it is sometimes mistakenly held that the abstract does not, can not, emerge from these experiences when they are nonverbal. Nothing can be farther from the fact. A nondeaf child, for instance, may gain the abstract notion of "sickness" from hearing the word employed on appropriate occasion, but by similar token the deaf child may gain an equally forceful concept from being in the presence of illness, the latter labeled with the highly expressive manual equivalent of the idea. For that matter it may be explained at this point that gesture language, both natural and formalized, is very much an imaginative experience in which the sign is a more or less abstract representation of the object, action or ideas, even when it supposedly outlines them by motions. If anything, employment of this form of communication enhances rather than inhibits the powers of imagination in the deaf child. Thus the imaginative experience may be here built in with a power equivalent to that in the hearing child, but it comes in via differing sensory avenues. An abstract idea is not a word-symbol; it may be experienced in the absence of the latter. A cartoon, for instance, may effectively convey a very subtle thought without benefit of a single word of script.

A third error that arises with respect to the mental processes in a deaf child is the idea that if he cannot acquire the skills of speech and lipreading to a working degree he must need be of subnormal intellectual capacity. The large number of very capable deaf persons in whom neither of these skills has attained more than rudimentary level, despite intense training effort, is adequate refutation of that concept.

We have the conviction that the good teacher is the one who can view the world through the eyes of the child. What he sees from that focus, if he has a sense of compassion for human nature, should enable him to produce an effective learning situation.

A shade of the same philosophy may apply if we wish to understand how a deaf child thinks. Let us note first the deaf child of an age prior to enrollment in school, for that is the area where the footings for the thought processes are laid. Denied the benefit of auditory experience, he must rely on the impressions that come to him via the sensory avenues which remain open to him. These do not occur in single or isolated fashion. They come tumbling in upon him in compounded occurrence, but in an order that is neither verbal nor grammatical. This is in marked contrast with the experience of his hearing brother or sister who from the start is exposed to both verbal and grammatical experience and which is unconsciously absorbed. The mass mixture of events that go on about the deaf child appears in no formalized sequence as is the case with lingual association absorbed via the ear. In the latter instance, it is of course a grammatical, or at least a near-grammatical or colloquial, experience, and thus a familiar language foundation is laid. For a deaf child this language pattern is absent, unless by dint of special effort speech and lipreading are imparted via the visual and kinesthetic senses, and then often with only questionable value.

But it must not be inferred that the mental experience of the deaf child otherwise, though failing in this grammatical acquirement, lacks the depth of thinking quality. On the contrary, it can be highly expressive in that respect. The channel is that of gesture which, following the cue of the sensory experiences borne in upon the cerebral theater, is disordered when judged by grammatical standards. But it is none-theless dramatically graphic. It has power and virility, even in the very young deaf child, with a deeply satis-fying emotional content that artificially acquired speech in his case could not possibly supply. It is a natural form of communicating since on the intake so much of his experience is of mass move-ment and gesture.

It is sometimes held that thinking is merely a form of subdued speech, that is with the outwardly manifest motor activity reduced to a point where it has become silent or inner speech. By this theory thinking is said to be only im-plicit speech. Let it not nevertheless be stated that if this is so the deaf child in whom speech beyond elementary vocal-ization is lacking does not have the power of thinking. On the contrary, if implicit speech is but greatly reduced motor activity, it would be perfectly logical to assume that implicit *manual* "speech," that is, also a greatly reduced motor activity, provides form for the thinking process in his case.

As has been suggested, the effect of the special nature of his early contact with a world in motion around the deaf child is to establish a mental outlook that is non-sequential when judged by grammatical rule, hence the propensity toward the type of language expression which is the despair of the teacher in the school for the deaf. When the deaf child comes to entrance age, he is then introduced to a language-minded dis-cipline. He is asked to trade for this new way of thinking his ancient and already deeply ingrained habit of ges-ture thinking which itself harmonizes

with the ever-moving panorama of the life around him. This transition is not easy for him. He finds it difficult to comprehend why expression, in speech, lipreading, writing and reading, must take on the to-him-odd characteristics which we know as "language princi-ples," when events about him in the real world do not occur according to the same principles. There is resistance, often with emotional support, making the task all the more difficult. We would lay much of the difficulty in language development for the deaf child to this condition, reflected of course in inner thought processes.

By benefit of skilled teaching the deaf child can learn to discard the old propensity and adapt to the new man-ner of interpreting, and making contact with, his environment. In this case he will take on a language-oriented, or-dered, verbal method as cue to his thinking processes.

The late Sir Richard A. S. Paget made this observation (The Origin of Language, chapter in *Science News*, 20, Middlesex, England): "It is through the invention of 'words' and 'names' and their corresponding 'units of thought' that man has acquired the power of logical thinking and the gifts of imagination and invention." But he did not say it had to be only via speech, for in that case it would mean a person without speech cannot think. For that matter he long was an advocate of the theory that speech, in the origins of language development, itself was founded on gesture. His later interests indicated clearly he recognized sym-bols for thinking could be fashioned also by manual means, for did he not propose a basic system of sign words by which the vocabulary of deaf children could be normalized? In the same sense, word-symbols expressed by deaf children by manual spelling, would serve the same purposes as implements for logical thinking.

How deafness acts as a modifying influence in the process of thinking is illustrated by the mechanics of that process. First, since thinking sharpens with an increase in quantity and quality of experience, that is, by an expansion and deepening of the stimulus-world, it follows that a sensory handicap is a limiting factor. Numbers of carefully controlled studies have shown that deprivation in environmental experience depresses attainment by the mental faculties, and there is no reason to deny a similar outcome results when a sensory source of acquiring experience is closed off.

Secondly, thinking to the best of our knowledge is a cerebral function, a finely coordinated action between reception-perception on the one hand and secondary associational reaction on the other. In this there is an exceedingly complex interplay of area upon area in the brain, analogous in a way to an intricate crisscrossing telephonic system, with specific exchange stations nominated as assigned centers for messages arriving from designated geographic zones. This analogy, however, is subject to an important exception. In the telephone system messages go in as physical vibration and are translated into electrical impulses, start on the way out as electrical impulses which

are in turn again manifest as physical vibration for the ear to sense at the other end. (In the human counterpart the electrical impulses assume the nature of neural energy release.) In no case in the mechanical electrical telephone engineering is the message stored during its in-and-out passage. Once delivered it is blotted out so far as the exchange machinery is concerned, unless by an attached device which mechanically records it for precise repetition at another time.

The brain operates on a similar principle of receipt and transmittal and by a sort of predesigned assignment by which a separate receiving center presides over messages coming in via each of the sensory pathways. This can be shown by a map of the brain. One of the distinguishing features of such an arrangement, however, is the method by which stimuli-registration is provided for in an outlying area immediately adjacent to the primary sensory receiving center. This outer or secondary sensory area has a unique dual role of registering the incoming impressions—in other words serving as a memory area—and of *relaying* them by associational pathways to other activating centers in the brain. This registering process results in a neural predisposition to respond in a previously activated, synaptic, manner when appropriate incoming stimulation occurs. The relative power of this neural reaction may well determine the basic nature of the phenomenon we call intelligence. Thus we have ready for such future use as occasion requires memory areas for sound stimuli, for visual experiences, and so on along the gamut of all the senses. A remarkably balanced arrangement along similar lines exists for the non-sensory, or motor, function, and in this way for instance does activation of speech or manipulation of manual communication originate in the brain.

With the deaf child not only is one of the cerebral receiving centers inoperative, that is, for incoming auditory stimuli, but its adjacent memory station for that medium remains inactive. The thinking process thus lacks full cognitive grasp within this field. Continuing to the end of the line, since ordinarily speech is a correlative of hearing, that power remains languid unless excited by the special methods devised by the school. It would add greatly to the understanding of the teacher's problem if these simple points were thoroughly realized. This realization should also include note of the likelihood the other cortical sensory areas may take up some of the lag by a greater and more meaningful enrichment of function. Thus the school may find assets of possibility beyond the usual in the remaining senses upon which to capitalize for the benefit of the deaf child.

A concluding point should be noted. No individual, deaf or otherwise, carries on the thinking process completely independent of other processes, the latter including the emotional states, sentiments, moods, and the feeling tones. An interlocking relationship prevails between and among these states. We may assume this holds true in the case of the deaf child—with an important qualification arising from the fact of his deafness. It is not difficult to realize that these processes markedly affect one another; thinking, for instance, may be profoundly influenced by one's emotional content, or one may be cast into certain moods by a train of thoughts. These influences may range from a very transitory duration to a long-drawn-out, even permanent, condition. It should be recalled, in this light, that the elements of frustration and tension may rise to unusual force in the deaf child, first from the fact of the shutting-out effects of the sensory handicap, secondly from the pressures involved in acquiring the means of communication demanded by the school, that is, speech and lipreading (and who is there to say these disciplines come easily?), and finally from the need of relinquishing a manner of communication which to him is both natural and facile and replacing it with a formalized, completely verbal language order of expression. These forces, we may add, do affect his thinking, and the extent to which they maintain a continuing effect is the measure of their influence upon that power. That they may hardly be salutary is an implication resting on the argument here outlined. It is the charge of the school to offset these effects, mainly by substituting for them a newer emotional satisfaction out of the powers that come from a developing competence in the conventional lingual forms of communication.

Note should be made also of the child upon whom deafness falls in the later developing years of childhood. It is difficult for the person in full possession of hearing to sense the inner turmoil of a child, or adult for that matter, who suddenly bereft of that power can still speak but cannot hear his own voice or the innumerable sounds previously so familiar. The feeling of having the floor on which one is standing suddenly collapse is a fair comparison. That this distress leaves an impression upon the thinking process should be apparent.

The educator, the missioner, the welfare worker, the rehabilitation officer, may well give heed to these considerations.

Summary

To sum up, we hold these considerations to be plausible in the light of our present understanding:

1. Command of word symbols does not alone provide the background for the power of thinking. In particular, in deaf children the concept elements may assume a nonverbal character.

2. The power of imagination is not a gift or faculty residing exclusively in those who hear.

3. Failure to acquire skill in speech or lipreading does not indict a deaf child as lacking in intelligence.

4. The preschool experience of deaf children, and indeed for much of their lives, is a culmination of compounded sensory activity in which only the sense of hearing is either seriously blunted or shut off. This mass nonauditory experience dictates their mode of thinking, that is, in an ideational, if not in the conventional grammatical, order. This tendency may in large part account for the difficulty they have in attaining satisfactory language expression in the usual verbal manner, and thus stands as the crux in their educational progress. The transition to the demands of an ordered grammatical language-learning discipline, by which word symbols become the chief vehicle for thinking, is the most difficult of the many steps they have to negotiate in the school situation.

5. Cortically the mental processes—the framework for thinking—involve an interplay of sensory-motor associational activity, both retentive and expressive. In these processes, the nonauditory experiences serve the same functional purposes, that is for thinking.

6. There is warrant for the suggestion that in the case of deaf children sign-symbols, either associated with or without their component word-symbols, are excitants to active thinking.

7. Thinking is not a compartmentalized phenomenon, and so in deaf children as with others it is clothed in feeling tones, moods and emotional content.

A GUIDE TO PSYCHOLOGICAL TESTS AND TESTING PROCEDURES IN THE EVALUATION OF DEAF AND HARD-OF-HEARING CHILDREN*

McCay Vernon and Donald W. Brown

It is the purpose of this article to provide psychologists, educators, and speech therapists with a usable guide to the basic intelligence and personality tests found to be most suitable for assessment of deaf children. The tests and procedures which will be described have been used by the authors in their positions as psychologists in schools, in rehabilitation settings, and in private clinical practice. The evaluations are made on the basis of this experience and on relevant findings from the literature of psychological testing.

Information about such tests and testing procedures is especially important today because of the rapid expansion of psychological services which should be utilized with deaf youngsters and which are being made available through school programs and speech and mental hygiene clinics. In many cases, however, the psychologists involved are not familiar with deaf children and are understandably unaware of the psychometric instruments which can be used with success. In like fashion the educators, audiologists, and speech therapists who do understand the ramifications of deaf-

ness in children are not always intimately familiar with the various intelligence and personality tests.

By describing and briefly evaluating the basic psychometric instruments, found to be applicable with deaf children, it is hoped that a useful reference will be provided for psychologists and others who are occasionally faced with the task of testing or interpreting test results of deaf children. At the same time, this information may enable personnel in schools for the deaf (or related agencies) who refer deaf subjects for psychological evaluation, to specify the basic tests they desire to have administered to the child. In this way, the probability of obtaining meaningful measurements of deaf youngsters will be substantially increased.

Intelligence Testing

Basic Considerations in the Intelligence Testing of Deaf and Hard-of-Hearing Children

A clear understanding of the following factors should precede any efforts to test or interpret test findings with deaf children:

1. To be valid as a measure of the intelligence of a deaf youngster an IQ test must be a nonverbal performance-type instrument (Burchard and Myklebust, 1942; Lane and Schneider, 1941). Verbal tests with deaf children are al-

* Reprinted with permission from the *Journal of Speech and Hearing Disorders,* official organ of the American Speech and Hearing Association, Washington, D. C., November, 1964, Vol. 29, No. 4, pp. 414–423. Dr. Vernon is Research Assistant Professor, DePaul Universty, and Donald W. Brown is a Fellow of the Institute for Research on Exceptional Children, University of Illinois.

most always inappropriate. They measure language deficiency due to hearing loss rather than intelligence (Brill, 1962; Heider, 1940; Levine, 1960, pp. 217–221; Myklebust, 1962; Myklebust, 1954, pp. 25, 237). An example of the tragic consequence of incorrect choice of tests is a student presently at the California School for the Deaf in Riverside who was given a Stanford Binet (verbal test) and received an IQ of 29 which led to her commitment to a hospital for the mentally retarded where she remained five years. Upon re-evaluation, using a performance IQ test, this girl was found to have an IQ of 113 which led to her dismissal from the hospital and her enrollment in a school for the deaf. In the California School for the Deaf at Riverside alone there are three deaf children previously misdiagnosed as mentally deficient who have been given performance tests yielding scores indicative of favorable academic potential, a finding subsequently demonstrated in the classroom.

It should be noted that all nonverbal tests are certainly not appropriate for use with deaf children. One main reason is that while many have nonlanguage items they may nevertheless require verbal directions (Heider, 1940; Lane and Schneider, 1941; Myklebust, 1960, p. 62; Wechsler, 1955, pp. 159–161; Zeckel, 1942; Zeckel and Kalb, 1937).

Hard-of-hearing children may give the impression of being able to understand verbal tests, but this is often an artifact (Levine, 1960, p. 265; Myklebust, 1962; Myklebust, 1954, pp. 241–242). In testing such children it is essential to begin with a performance measure and then, if desired, to try a verbal instrument. In cases where the score yielded by the former is appreciably higher, the probability is that it is the more valid, and further, that the lower score on the test involving language is due to the subject's hearing impairment and does not constitute a true measure of intelligence.

2. Even more than with hearing subjects, scores on preschool and early school deaf and hard-of-hearing children tend to be extremely unreliable (Heider, 1940; Hiskey, 1955). For this reason, low scores in particular should be viewed as questionable in the absence of other supporting data.

3. There is far more danger that a low IQ score is wrong than that a high one is inaccurate (Heider, 1940; Myklebust, 1954, p. 241; Wechsler, 1959). This is due to the many factors that can lead to a child's not performing to capacity; whereas, in contrast, there are almost no conditions that can lead to performance above capacity.

4. Tests given to deaf children by psychologists not experienced with the deaf or hard of hearing are subject to appreciably greater error than is the case when the service is rendered by one familiar with deaf youngsters. The atypical attentive set of the hearing-impaired child to testing which has been frequently cited in the literature is felt to be one of the reasons for this (Hiskey, 1955; Myklebust, 1954, p. 239; Zeckel, 1942).

5. It must be noted that the performance part of many conventional intelligence tests is only half or less of the test.

Therefore, to approach the validity of a full IQ test with a deaf child it is necessary to give at least two performance scales.

6. Intelligence tests for young deaf or hard-of-hearing children (age 12 or below) that emphasize time are not so valid in most cases as are other tests which do not stress time (Hiskey, 1955; Lane and Schneider, 1941). This is because these children often react to the factor of timing by either working in great haste and ignoring accuracy or else disregarding the time factor completely. In either instance, the result is not necessarily a reflection of intelligence.

7. Group testing of deaf and hard-of-hearing children is a highly questionable procedure that, at best, is of use only as a gross screening device (Hiskey, 1955; Lane and Schneider, 1941; Levine, 1960, p. 221; Myklebust, 1962).

Evaluation of Some Intelligence Tests Most Commonly Used with Deaf and Hard-of-Hearing Subjects

In order to evaluate these tests in a concise manner conducive to easy referral, a tabular form has been used. In fairness to both the tests and the reader it should be stated that these evaluations are based on the experience of the authors and the limited literature relevant to this area. For this reason, they are to a degree subjective and open to question. However, the tests described enjoy a wide acceptance and application by psychological personnel in schools and agencies working with hearing-impaired children (Brill, 1962; Levine,

1960, pp. 222–224; Myklebust, 1962; Myklebust, 1954, pp. 298–302; Myklebust, 1960, pp. 69–76, 161–177).

Personality Testing

General Considerations to Be Made in the Personality Testing of Deaf and Hard-of-Hearing Children

As in the case of intelligence testing it is important in the personality measurement of hearing-impaired children to take into consideration certain basic factors prior to evaluating specific tests. These factors are:

1. Personality evaluation is a far more complex task than is IQ testing, especially with deaf children. Because of this, test findings should be interpreted in light of case history data and personal experience with the child. In fact, it behooves educators of the deaf with long experience in the field to view with skepticism results reported by examiners who are unfamiliar with deaf children when these findings sharply contradict their own impressions of youngsters they know well.

2. Because of communication problems inherent in severe hearing loss, personality tests are more difficult to use with deaf subjects than with the general population (Graham and Kendall, 1960; Levine, 1960, pp. 225–226; Myklebust, 1962; Myklebust, 1954, p. 313; Myklebust, 1960, pp. 121–122; Zeckel, 1942; Zeckel, 1937). Not only do these tests depend on extensive verbal interchange or reading skill, but they also presuppose a rapport and confidence on the part of the subject that are difficult to achieve

when the person examined cannot understand what is being said or written. Paper and pencil personality measures are perhaps suitable for hearing-impaired children with well developed expressive and receptive language ability, but such youngsters are rare, and even with them the problems of test administration and interpretation make the meaningfulness of results highly fallible (Graham and Kendall, 1960; Levine, 1960, pp. 225–226, Myklebust, 1962; Myklebust, 1954, pp. 121–122). The need for fluency in manual communication by the examiner is especially evident in the area of projective testing.

3. There is some question as to whether the norms for the personality structure of hearing people are appropriate for deaf and hard-of-hearing subjects (Zeckel, 1942; Zeckel, 1937). Conceivably, deafness alters the perceived environment sufficiently to bring about an essentially different organization of personality in which normality would then differ from what it is in the case of a person with normal hearing (Bender, 1938; Hathaway and McKinley, 1951, p. 256; Myklebust, 1954, pp. 115–118, Zeckel, 1942). Although this is presently an unresolved problem, it is one that is frequently raised by scholars in the field of deafness and should be considered in any discussion of the personality of those with severe hearing loss.

4. The use of interpreters who express the psychologist's directions in finger-spelling and sign language is a questionable procedure. What is required is an interpreter, fluent not only in manual communication, but also in psychology and testing (Zeckel and Kalb, 1937).

Obviously such an individual would be doing the examining himself and not interpreting it for another. Therefore, results reported where an interpreter is involved are not likely to meet high standards of validity.

Evaluation of Personality Tests Commonly Used with Deaf and Hard-of-Hearing Children.

Because of the difficulties that have been pointed out above, few personality tests have had wide application with deaf or hard-of-hearing children. Four of the more commonly and successfully used are evaluated in Table II.

Screening Tests for Brain Injury

Because of the high incidence of brain injury among deaf children, especially those whom a teacher is likely to refer for psychological evaluation, it is appropriate to discuss some tests used to diagnose and measure this condition (Vernon, 1961). A thorough assessment of neurological impairment would generally include one or more of these psychological instruments plus neurological and audiological techniques of diagnosis (Vernon, 1961). A brief discussion of some tests and items from tests that are useful for detecting brain injury follows.

1. *Bender-Gestalt* (Bender, 1938). This is probably the most widely used screening instrument for the detection of gross neurological impairment. Standardization of norms is being continued; interpretation requires extensive training and experience. However, the Bender is a valuable part of a test bat-

TABLE I

EVALUATION OF SOME OF THE INTELLIGENCE TESTS MOST COMMONLY USED WITH DEAF AND HARD-OF-HEARING CHILDREN

Tests	Appropriate Age Range Covered by the Test	Evaluation of the Test
1. Wechsler Performance Scale for Children (1949)	9 years–16 years	The Wechsler Performance Scale is at present the best test for deaf children ages 9–16. It yields a relatively valid IQ score, and offers opportunities for qualitative interpretation of factors such as brain injury or emotional disturbance (Wechsler, 1955, pp. 80–81). It has good interest appeal and is relatively easy to administer and reasonable in cost
2. Wechsler Performance Scale for Adults (1955)	16 years–70 years	The rating of the Wechsler Performance Scale for Adults is the same as the rating on the Wechsler Performance Scale for children
3. Leiter International Performance Scale (1948 Revision)	4 years–12 years (also suitable for older mentally retarded deaf subjects)	This test has good interest appeal. It can be used to evaluate relatively disturbed deaf children who could not otherwise be tested. This test is expensive and lacking somewhat in validation. In general, however, it is an excellent test for young children. Timing is a minor factor in this test. One disadvantage is in the interpretation of the IQ scores because the mean of the test is 95 and the standard deviation is 20. This means that the absolute normal score on this test is 95 instead of 100 as on other intelligence tests. Scores of, for example, 50, therefore, do not indicate mental deficiency but correspond more to about a 70 on a test such as the Wechsler or Binet. Great care must be taken in interpreting Leiter IQ scores for these reasons
4. Progressive Matrices (Raven, 1948)	9 years–adulthood	Raven's Progressive Matrices are good as a second test to substantiate another more comprehensive intelligence test. The advantage of the Matrices is that it is extremely easy to administer and score, taking relatively little of the examiner's time and is very inexpensive. It yields invalid test scores of impulsive deaf children, who tend to respond randomly rather than with accuracy and care. For this reason, the examiner should observe the child carefully to assure that he is really trying
5. Ontario School Ability Examination (Amoss, 1949)	4 years–10 years	This is a reasonably good test for deaf children within these age ranges

6. Nebraska Test of Learning Aptitude (Heider, 1940; Hiskey, 1955)	4 years–12 years	A test comparable in value to the Ontario, and standardized for both hearing and deaf children
7. Chicago Non-Verbal Examination (Brown *et al.*, 1947)	7 years–12 years	This test rates fair if given as an individual test; very poor if given as a group test. The scoring is tedious and reliability is rather low
8. Grace Arthur Performance Scale (Arthur, 1947)	4.5 years–15.5 years	This is a test that is poor to fair due to the fact that timing is heavily emphasized; norms are not adequate, and directions are somewhat unsatisfactory. This test is especially unsatisfactory for emotionally disturbed children who are also deaf. With this type subject this test will sometimes yield a score indicating extreme retardation when the difficulty is actually one of maladjustment. It is also poor for young deaf children who are of below average intelligence because they often respond randomly instead of rationally
9. Merrill-Palmer Scale of Mental Tests (Sutsman, 1931)	2 years–4 years	The Merrill-Palmer is a fair test for young deaf children, but it must be adapted in order to be used and would require a skilled examiner with a thorough knowledge of deaf children
10. Goodenough Draw-A-Man Test (1926)	8.5 years–11 years	Directions are very difficult to give young children in a standardized manner. Scoring is less objective than would be desired, so this test is relatively unreliable. It does, however, have some projective value in terms of personality assessment
11. Randalls Island Performance Tests (1932)	2 years–5 years	This is one of the few nonverbal instruments available for measuring preschool children. It consists of a wide range of performance and manipulative tasks which, used by a competent examiner, provide diagnostic and and insightful information. This test is relatively expensive, but valuable

TABLE II

PERSONALITY TESTS USED WITH DEAF AND HARD-OF-HEARING CHILDREN

Tests	Appropriate Age Range Covered by the Test	Evaluation of the Test
1. Draw-A-Person (Machover, 1949)	9 years–adulthood	This is a good screening device for detecting very severe emotional problems. It is relatively nonverbal and is probably the most practical projective personality test for deaf children. Its interpretation is very subjective and in the hands of a poor psychologist it can result in rather extreme diagnostic statements about deaf children
2. Thematic Apperception Test (TAT) or Children's Apperception Test (CAT) (Stein, 1955)	Can be used with deaf subjects of school age through adulthood who can communicate well manually or can communicate very well in written language	This is a test of great potential, if the psychologist giving it and the deaf subject taking it can both communicate with fluency in manual communication. It is of very limited value otherwise unless the deaf subject has an exceptional command of the English language. This test could be given through an interpreter by an exceptionally perceptive psychologist, although it is more desirable if the psychologist can do his own communicating
3. Rorschach Ink Blot Test (Rorschach, 1942)	Can be given to deaf subjects as soon as they are able to communicate fluently manually or if they can communicate with exceptional skill orally	In order for the Rorschach to be used it is almost absolutely necessary that the psychologist giving it and the deaf subject taking it be fluent in manual communication. Even under these circumstances it is debatable if it yields much of value unless the subject is of above-average intelligence It would be possible with a very bright deaf subject, who had a remarkable proficiency in English, to give a Rorschach through writing, but this would not be very satisfactory
4. H. T. P. Technique (Buck, 1949)	School age through adulthood	This is a procedure similar to the Draw-A-Person test. It requires little verbal communication and affords the competent clinician some valuable insight into basic personality dynamics of the subject

tery for deaf subjects (Myklebust, 1962).

2. *Wechsler Performance Scale* (Wechsler, 1949; Wechsler, 1955). Quantitative pattern analysis of these scales is of controversial validity as a diagnostic tool for neurological dysfunction. There is fairly general agreement, however, that in the hands of a capable clinical psychologist, a partial qualitative type of diagnosis is possible (Levine, 1960, p. 228–229; Myklebust, 1954, p. 301).

3. *Memory-For-Designs Test* (Graham and Kendall, 1960). A relatively new test, this appears to have considerable value. Its precise scoring technique controls for variation in age, intelligence, and vocabulary level.

4. *Ellis Visual Designs Test* (Strauss and Kephart, 1955, pp. 149, 219). This test appears to have definite possibilities, but lacks validation (Levine, 1960, p. 229).

5. *Strauss-Werner Marble Board Test* (Strauss and Kephart, 1955, pp. 152, 215). This test is potentially excellent, but it is very hard to get. Scoring instructions are inadequate (Levine, 1960, p. 229).

6. *Hiskey Blocks* (Heider, 1940). This test requires a great deal of visualization and abstract ability and is of value for this reason (Heider, 1940; Myklebust, 1954, p. 300).

7. *Rorschach* (1942). The use of this test requires not only competency in administering the test, but also a fluency in the use of manual communication employed by the deaf. Results reported where these conditions are not met are of highly dubious validity.

8. *Kohs Blocks* (Kohs, 1923). These are similar to the block design subtest of the Wechsler Scales, but are more extensive. A qualitative diagnosis is possible, but norms are lacking for organic involvement.

9. *The Diamond Drawing from the Stanford Binet* (Terman and Merrill, 1937, p. 230). This test has good validity, is generally available, and can be easily administered.

10. Various measures of motor ability and development. Among these would be the railwalking test, tests of laterality, and certain items on the Vineland Social Maturity Scale that pertain to motor development.

Suggested Test Batteries for Deaf and Hard-of-Hearing School-Age Children

Because an adequate psychological assessment should properly be based on a series of tests rather than a single instrument, the following test batteries are suggested for the various age groups of a school population:

1. *Preschool.* Measurement of intelligence should be based on at least two of the following IQ tests: the Leiter International Performance Scale, the Merrill-Palmer Scale of Mental Tests, or the Randalls Island Performance Tests.

There are no suitable personality tests or tests for brain injury for deaf preschool children. Clinical judgment, medical, audiological, and case history data must be depended on exclusively for evaluation in these areas.

2. *Beginning School Age Through Age Nine.* IQ tests should include at least two of the following: the Leiter International Performance Scale, WISC Performance Scale, Nebraska Test of Learning Aptitude, Ontario Test of School Ability, Goodenough Draw-A-Man Test, or Progressive Matrices. Human figure drawing interpretation and Bender-Gestalt responses should be used to screen for personality deviations and organic brain damage.

3. *Ages Nine Through Fifteen.* The most appropriate measure of intelligence for this age range is the WISC Performance Scale. It can best be supplemented with Progressive Matrices, the Chicago Non-Verbal Test, or the Leiter International Performance Scale. Human figure drawings and the Bender-Gestalt become increasingly valid measures in this age range and are the best screening techniques for personality disturbance and brain damage.

4. *Age Sixteen Through School Graduation.* The WAIS Performance Scale stands out as the superior measure of intelligence for this age range. The second measure for intelligence found most valid is the Progressive Matrices. To the Bender-Gestalt and Draw-A-Person Test can be added or substituted the Memory-For-Designs Test as a screening measure for organic brain damage. Vocational tests should be added at this time. Their selection is a highly individual matter depending on the subject and available vocational educational facilities. For discussion of these tests, Helmer Myklebust's article is most helpful (1962).

Summary

It has been the purpose of this article to provide psychologists, educators, audiologists, and speech therapists with a useful reference for tests and procedures found helpful for the psychological evaluation of deaf and hard-of-hearing children.

Basic psychological tests of intelligence, personality, and brain damage have been evaluated and fundamental considerations regarding their use with deaf and hard-of-hearing children have been discussed. Recommended batteries for different age ranges of preschool and school-age hearing-impaired children are given.

References

1. AMOSS, H.: *Ontario School Ability Examination.* Toronto, Ryerson, 1949.
2. ARTHUR, G.: *A Point Scale of Performance Tests, Rev. Form II.* New York, Psychological Corp., 1947.
3. BENDER, LAURETTA: *A Visual Motor Gestalt Test and Its Clinical Use.* New York, The American Orthopsychiatric Association, 1938.
4. BRILL, R. G.: The relation of Wechsler IQs to academic achievement among deaf students. *Exceptional Child,* 28:315, 1962.
5. BRILL, T.: Mental hygiene and the deaf. *Amer Ann Deaf,* 79:279–285, 1934.
6. BROWN, A.; STEIN, S., and ROHRER, R.: *Chicago Non-Verbal Examination.* New York, Psychological Corp., 1947.
7. BUCK, J.: The H. T. P. Technique, a qualitative and quantitative scoring manual. *J Clin Psychol, Vol. IV,* 1948, and *Vol. V,* 1949.
8. BURCHARD, E. M., and MYKLEBUST, H. R.: A comparison of congenital and adventitious deafness with respect to its effect on intelligence, personality, and social ma-

turity (Part II, Social Maturity). *Amer Ann Deaf*, 87:241–250, 1942.

9. GESELL, A.: The psychological development of normal and deaf children in their preschool years. *Volta Rev*, 58:117–120, 1956.

10. GOODENOUGH, FLORENCE: *Measurement of Intelligence by Drawings*. Chicago, World Book, 1926.

11. GRAHAM, FRANCES K., and KENDALL, BARBARA S.: Memory-For-Designs Test: Revised General Manual. *Percept Motor Skills, Monograph Supplement 2-VII*, 1960.

12. HATHAWAY, S., and McKINLEY, J.: *Minnesota Multiphasic Personality Inventory Manual (Rev.)*. New York, Psychological Corp., 1951.

13. HEIDER, G. M.: The thinking of the deaf child. *Volta Rev*, 42:774–776, 804–808, 1940. (A review from an article in French by R. Pellet).

14. HISKEY, M. S.: Determining mental competence levels of children with impaired hearing. *Volta Rev*, 52:406–408, 430–432, 1950.

15. ———:*Nebraska Test of Learning Aptitude for Young Deaf Children*. Lincoln, U of Nebr, 1955.

16. KOHS, S.: *The Block Designs Test*. Chicago, Stoelting, 1923.

17. LANE, HELEN S., and SCHNEIDER, J. L.: A performance test for school-age deaf children. *Amer Ann Deaf*, 86:441, 1941.

18. LEITER, R.: *The Leiter International Performance Scale*. Chicago, Stoelting, 1948.

19. LEVINE, EDNA S.: *The Psychology of Deafness*. New York, Columbia, 1960.

20. MACHOVER, KAREN: *Personality Projection in the Drawing of the Human Figure*. Springfield, Ill., Thomas, 1949.

21. MYKLEBUST, H. R.: *Auditory Disorders in Children*. New York, Grune, 1954.

22. ———: *The Psychology of Deafness*. New York, Grune, 1960.

23. ———; NEYHUS, A., and MULHOLLAND, A. M.: Guidance and counseling for the deaf. *Amer Ann Deaf*, 107:370–415, 1962.

24. *The Randalls Island Performance Series (Manual)*. Chicago, Stoelting, 1932.

25. RAVEN, J.: *Progressive Matrices*. New York, Psychological Corp., 1948.

26. RORSCHACH, H.: *Psychodiagnostik*. Berne, Switzerland, Hans Huber, 1942.

27. STEIN, M. I.: *The Thematic Apperception Test*. Cambridge, Addison-Wesley, 1955.

28. STRAUSS, A., and KEPHART, N.: (in collaboration with L. E. Lentenen and S. Goldenberg.) *Psychopathology and Education of the Brain-Injured Child*. New York, Grune, 1955.

29. SUTSMAN, RACHEL: *Mental Measurement of Pre-School Children*. Yonkers-on-Hudson, World Book Co., 1931.

30. TERMAN, L. M., and MERRILL, M. A.: *Measuring Intelligence*. New York, Houghton-Mifflin, 1937.

31. VERNON, M.: The brain injured (neurologically impaired) deaf child: a discussion of the significance of the problem, its symptoms and causes in deaf children. *Amer Ann Deaf*, 106:239–250, 1961.

32. WECHSLER, D.: *Wechsler Intelligence Scale for Children*. New York, Psychological Corp., 1949.

33. ———: *Wechsler Adult Intelligence Scale*. New York, Psychological Corp., 1955.

34. ZECKEL, A.: Research possibilities with the deaf. *Amer Ann Deaf*, 87:173–191, 1942.

35. ———, and VAN DER Kolk, J. J.: A comparative intelligence test of groups of children born deaf and of good hearing, by means of the Porteus Test. *Amer Ann Deaf*, 84:114–123, 1939.

PSYCHOLOGICAL ASSESSMENT*

CORNELIUS P. GOETZINGER

The ability to communicate through speech and language is usually regarded as a strictly human accomplishment. Man by virtue of this ability has been able to raise himself above the level of all other terrestial creatures and, as a consequence, to reach his present eminence in the animal kingdom. It follows, therefore, that when an individual is deprived of the auditory channel, either congenitally or soon after birth, the primary avenue for language acquisition, an almost insurmountable barrier is placed on the normal communicative humanizing process. Thus it was that in the pre-Christian era the deaf were regarded as mentally incompetent and unlikely to profit from educational procedures. It was only through the vision of a few perceptive men during these early ages that the ignorance which enshrouded deafness was finally pierced, and the way opened for an eventual enlightened outlook.[1]

Prior to the development of standardized psychological tests after the turn of the present century, Greenberger,[2] a superintendent in a school for the deaf in this country, had sought a few game-like tests whereby he could screen school applicants for feeblemindedness. He proposed that picture books and a number test could be effectively

* A paper presented for the 50th Anniversary Program of Central Institute for the Deaf, St. Louis, Missouri, March 30, 1965. The author is Director of Audiology, University of Kansas Medical Center, Kansas City, Kansas.

employed for this purpose. In addition, he recommended that block building and tasks involving the perception of form and color could be used to advantage in attempting to get an index of a child's ability. To this end he wrote in 1889:

> Building with blocks, arranging with sticks so as to make certain forms, or any childish game can be made the means of finding out whether an applicant is capable of fixing his attention upon a subject, and whether he has any reasoning faculties.[2]

It is obvious from this statement that Greenberger had some insight as to the value of nonlanguage performance tasks in assessing the intellectual potential of language-deprived individuals.

Preceding the advent of the Goddard revision of the Binet Scale in this country, there were a few published accounts of studies which attempted to compare the mental abilities of deaf and hearing children. Taylor[3] in 1897 reported the results of a free-association spelling test which was administered to deaf and hearing students. Other studies around the turn of the century were conducted by Mott,[4] Smith[5] and MacMillan and Bruner.[6]

After the Goddard revision of the Binet, Kilpatrick[7] suggested that the scale or some modification of it be used for deaf children. Although he recommended that a commission be established to study the problem, Kilpatrick himself did not attempt a modification of the Binet.

It remained for Pintner and Paterson[8] to explore the usefulness of the Binet with the deaf. As a result of their experiment they concluded that the test as it stood was not suitable for use with the deaf. This finding triggered a series of investigations in schools for the deaf by Pintner and his associates which encompassed intelligence, language, educational achievement, etc. In addition, Pintner developed his non-language mental test, the Pintner Educational Achievement Test and a Performance Scale of Intelligence. In summarizing their research for the period 1914–1918 which was concerned principally with the measurement of intelligence using the Digit-Symbols, Symbols-Digit Test, the measurement of language ability with the Trabue Scales, and the measurement of memory span for digits, Pintner and Paterson[9] concluded:

1. That the Binet Scale, unmodified, was not suitable for use with the deaf;
2. That on the average orally taught pupils were superior to those taught manually because the bright students were chosen for oral instruction;
3. That on mental tests which did not depend on hearing the average deaf child was retarded from two to three years as compared to the hearing;
4. That on tests which involve hearing, as memory span for digits and the language scales, the deaf child on the average, regardless of age, was only equal to the hearing child of seven, eight or nine years;
5. That the deaf did not manifest a sex difference; and
6. That there did not appear to be a difference between the congenital and adventitious

deaf. However, on tests which were dependent on audition, those children who suffered hearing loss after four or five years of age seemed to benefit because of having once heard.

These conclusions which had been based on the results of tests which had been administered to several thousand deaf children appeared to offer strong evidence of mental retardation. Only one study, by Newlee[10] in 1919, offered contrary evidence. Using the same Digit-Symbols, Symbols-Digit Test which Pintner and Paterson had employed in most of their investigations, Newlee's eighty-five deaf subjects were found to be the equal of their hearing controls. Her findings, however, were criticized on the basis of small sample and selectivity of the same.

Subsequently, the Reamer and National Research Council Surveys[11,12] utilizing the Pintner Nonlanguage Mental Test and the Pintner Educational Achievement Test substantiated the previously reported mental and educational retardation of the deaf.

In 1928 Upshall[13] studied again the data from the National Research Council Survey. In an important substudy to the main investigation he equated day and residential school deaf children on the basis of chronological age, mental age, degree of deafness and onset of deafness. In addition, he controlled statistically years spent in school and age at school entrance. Furthermore, with the Barr Scale he rated the economic status of the homes from which the children came. Among other things Upshall concluded that the dayschool children were significantly superior to those from the residential schools. He attributed the superiority however to better teaching rather than to method of teaching.

About this same time in England, Drever and Collins[14] using their own Performance Scale found their deaf subjects to be equal or superior to their hearing controls. These findings, with the exception of the Newlee results, were in conflict with the previous research employing the Digit-Symbols, Symbols-Digit Test and the Pintner Nonlanguage Mental Test. As a consequence a series of studies comparing the deaf on performance and nonlanguage mental tests was initiated. Of particular note is the doctoral study of MacKane[15] in 1932. His deaf subjects who showed about a two-year retardation on the Pintner Nonlanguage Group Test were less than a year retarded on Performance Scales.

In the ensuing years an impressive amount of evidence has accumulated which indicates that the deaf are either normal or within normal limits when individual performance tests are employed to assess intelligence.[16,17,18] There are however, even yet, conflicting findings when the group-type nonlanguage mental tests are used.[19,20,21,11,12] In addition to the development of tests for assessing the mental capacities of the deaf, Pintner in conjunction with Brunschwig[22] developed personality tests for the deaf. They were questionnaires which used simple language in an attempt to circumvent the language problem of the deaf. The tests were standardized on hearing children. Although Pintner emphasized the similarities between deaf and hearing children, never-

theless in view of the fact that the deaf tended to show more unrealistic fears and were prone to choose immediate rewards rather than greater delayed rewards, Pintner concluded that emotional immaturity resulted from deafness.

Other studies by Springer,[23] Springer and Roslow,[24] Gregory,[25] Myklebust and Burchard,[26] and Lyon[27] showed deaf children to have more problems and to be more poorly adjusted than their hearing controls.

With reference to the adult deaf and hard of hearing as Barker, *et al.*,[16] pointed out in 1953 there had been many published opinions by experts in the field of deafness on the personality and adjustment of the hypacusic. However, at that time there was still a dearth of well-controlled studies. Welles[28] and Brunschwig[22] made surveys of such accounts. The former covered the severely hard of hearing who had suffered impairment in later life. The latter reported relative to subjects who had experienced severe early deafness. It also included statements from educators of the deaf relating to the psychological effects of deafness.

The results of the surveys showed that there was a considerable variation of opinion concerning the psychological effects of deafness. Some felt that the hearing impaired were uniquely different in personality. Others maintained that they did not differ from the hearing. Personality characteristics which were frequently attributed to the deaf and hard of hearing included introversion, despondency, sense of inferiority, hopelessness, suspicion, fear, supersen-

sitivity, brooding, bitterness, persecu-
tion complex, apathy and listlessness.
Cruelty, lack of sympathy, egocentrism
and selfishness were other characteristics according to Barker, which were
generally used to round out the personality.

With reference to the older research
three rather extensive studies used the
Bernreuter Personality Inventory. The
general conclusion reached as a result
of the investigations by Welles,[28] Pintner[29] and Pintner, *et al.*,[30] on hard-of-
hearing adults was that the latter were
slightly more neurotic, introverted and
submissive than the hearing. However,
the large overlap between groups was
more significant than the differences.

As might be inferred from the above
review, what might be termed the Pintner era in this country extended until
approximately the mid-forties. It was
chiefly characterized by the development of tests in order psychologically
to assess the hearing impaired, and also
to compare the hearing and hypacusic
on general indices of function. During
the Pintner era the principal tests for
the measurement of intelligence were
the Pintner Nonlanguage Test, the
Smedley Digit-Symbols, Symbols-Digit
test, the Pintner-Paterson Form Board
Scale, the Grace Arthur Performance
Test (Form 1) and the Chicago Non-
Verbal Examination which made its
debut in the early thirties. Another test
used somewhat in this era was the
Ontario School Ability Examination.

Following World War II there was a
tremendous industrial surge to supply
the wants which had been created as a
result of the war effort. Many of the
techniques which had been developed
in industry during the war for military
and defense efforts were either carried
over *in toto* or adapted to serve production during the recovery period. In
a similar manner, experts in the medical
and communication fields returned now
to civilian life with a fresh fund of
knowledge made possible by virtue of
the unlimited resources which had been
at their disposal during the crisis. Likewise, the interaction between various
disciplines which had coalesced during
the war was carried over into the recovery period. Insofar as the field of
deafness is concerned it could be said
that the science of audiology was con-
ceived during the war years. Included
in the term as used here are implied the
psychological, sociological, educational,
medical, rehabilitative, and communicative aspects of hearing and speech.

Of importance with reference to the
psychological assessment of the audito-
rily impaired was the development of
additional mental scales such as those
by Wechsler, Hiskey, Leiter, etc., and
tests to probe for organic brain damage
and aphasia by Halstead, Wepman,
Eisenson, etc. In addition, interest in
projective techniques and in electro-
physiological measurements has influenced psychological assessment.
With the Wechsler Scales it was now
possible to get a performance and verbal IQ and to investigate the significance of variation in test profile with
different etiological groups. In short,
differential diagnosis became a byword.
In conjunction with the interest of the
more minute features of mental functioning, there was a host of studies

dealing with visual perception of the deaf as compared to the hearing. More recently, the tide of interest has swung to the study of concept formation and linguistics, in an effort to unravel the perplexing problems which are engendered by deafness, and to provide a firmer basis for diagnosis. The incredible advances in electronics with the various types of computers have made possible the simultaneous recording of much physiological data during behavioral tests. Along with the aforementioned was the renewed interest in learning theory. Spurred on by the experimental work of Skinner we seemingly are verging on a methodological breakthrough in the education of the deaf through programed learning.

Irrespective of the advances which have been made, there are many problems associated with psychological assessment which in reality date back to the days of Pintner. One of fundamental importance pertains to the prediction of educational achievement in deaf children from psychological tests. As noted earlier, tests of the performance and nonlanguage type must be utilized with the deaf in order to get an index of their potential. However, Gates[31] more than forty years ago reported correlations between nonverbal tests and academic achievement for third-grade hearing children as being only .22. The correlation between verbal tests of intelligence and achievement for the same group was .65. Gates, furthermore, demonstrated that as intelligence tests became more verbal in content, the correlation with school achievement tended to rise. For example, the correlations between reading and IQ for grades four, five and six rose from .32 for the "most nonverbal" test to .76 for the "most verbal" test. In the same study the correlation between Binet mental age and a composite score from several reading comprehension tests was .49 for grades four, five and six. It should be pointed out, however, that the Binet is not the most verbal of tests, as it incorporates some performance type items.

A few correlation studies have been reported in the literature for deaf subjects. Upshall[13] in 1929 obtained a correlation of .53 between the Pintner Nonlanguage Mental Test and the Pintner Educational Achievement Test for 311 dayschool children; one of .675 for a total of 1,159 institutional children and one of .64 for 311 matched institutional children. He questioned, however, the appropriateness of using the product-moment correlation with the data because of the peculiar distribution of the achievement scores. Brown[32] computed correlations between total arithmetic and total reading scores and two intelligence tests (Grace Arthur Form 1 and the Pintner Nonlanguage) for ninety-eight subjects with chronological age held constant. The age range of the subjects was from 14 to 25. His findings were as follows: Pintner with total arithmetic was .45; with total reading .003; Grace Arthur with total arithmetic .37; with total reading —.06. Brown concluded that nonverbal tests do not measure educational achievement with the exception of arithmetic.

In an unpublished study some years ago the writer[33] undertook a correlation study between achievement test scores and scores from the Wechsler Performance Scale (Form 2) for 110 deaf students in the California School for the Deaf. The age range was from fourteen to twenty-one years. Suffice to say that correlations around .50 were obtained between the Performance Scale and achievement (Stanford Achievement Vocabulary, Paragraph Meaning and Arithmetic Reasoning). Of the subtests of the Wechsler only Digit-Symbols correlated as well with achievement as did the Wechsler Total Scale. When a five-variable partial correlation between Paragraph Meaning and the Wechsler Total Test was computed for forty-eight subjects with chronological age, years spent in school and age at school entrance statistically controlled, the correlation rose to .696.

More recently, Brill[34] reported that with the WISC and WAIS a mean IQ of 112 was required for an academic diploma, and an average IQ for a vocational certificate. As a result of the study he concluded that the tests are of value in predicting academic achievement.

Although, as Brill has pointed out, there is a relationship between academic accomplishment and the Wechsler Performance Scales, nevertheless, all too frequently in schools for the deaf there are children who do not measure up to expectations, even when such variables as age at school entrance, years spent in school, degree of deafness and age at onset are taken into consideration. For several years now, there has been much interest clinically in attempting to define patterns which

will provide clues for the poor progress of the aforementioned cases. In some instances there are rather clear-cut indications of specific defects such as aphasia, etc. Myklebust[35] has been particularly active in attempting to pinpoint specific disabilities which have been superimposed on deafness.

As mentioned previously, there is still much concern associated with the seeming retardation of the deaf on certain nonverbal tests of intelligence. Mac-Kane[15] years ago, after administering the Pintner nonlanguage test and the Grace Arthur performance scale (Form 1) to the same deaf subjects, concluded that the tests were measuring different abilities. Oleron[19] and Zeckel and Van der Kolk,[20] in consideration of their studies with the Progressive Matrices (1938 version) and the Porteus Mazes, respectively, concluded that the deaf are inferior in abstract ability. More recently, however, according to Levine,[36] Oleron, after summarizing experiments from his laboratory, associated with the role of language in puzzle box solving, and ". . . in the discrimination and utilization of relations in size, weight, speed and temporal or spatial-temporal events, . . ."[36] concluded that the role of language in problem solving and in relational learning was not so significant as previously supposed. Levine goes on to emphasize that there is still considerable discrepancy in the results of studies which are concerned with the perceptual-conceptual domain, and expressed the opinion that the divergencies are more associated with differences arising out of methodology rather than of fundamental disagreement *per se.* In connection with the foregoing Levine reviewed her own study of the Full-Scale Wechsler Test with deaf adolescent girls. The verbal portion of the scale was modified so as to facilitate a deeper probing into the thought processes of her subjects. In commenting on her findings Levine wrote the following:

> Analysis of the total results revealed that although the deaf subjects were quantitatively on an IQ par with the hearing, there were distinctive and significant deficiencies in patterns of thinking and reasoning, in conceptual maturation, and in level of abstractive ability. These deficiencies appeared to the investigator to resemble a picture of "underdevelopment" of mental potential, and the hypothesis was advanced that they are correctible through more effective educational procedures.[36]

Tantamount to the above discussion are the findings from two recent investigations at Kansas University which are now in preparation.[37,21] In the first study twenty-four deaf and an equal number of hearing adolescents (12 males and 12 females in each group) were compared on the Structured Objective Rorschach Test. The S.O. Rorschach Test (SORT) represents an attempt to develop an objective test of personality based upon the Rorschach scoring system and interpretative rationale. Its author, J. B. Stone, has published a preliminary version which may be obtained through the California Test Bureau.

The SORT is described in the test manual as

> . . . a radical modification of the traditional Rorschach Test. Although it uses the

same blots and basically the same scoring system and interpretative rationale, the SORT has no free responses and no inquiry. Instead it suggests responses and requires a fixed number of total responses. These features of the SORT permit (1) group administration and/or self-administration; (2) objective scoring; (3) objective standardization; (4) comprehensive norming, and (5) objective and simplified interpretation.[38]

As noted above responses are suggested in the SORT. For example, there are 10 triads of items for each Rorschach card. A triad consists of three short items such as "Airplane-Elks horns-Anvil." The subject is instructed to choose the item which, as he sees it, most nearly represents the card, or some part of it. Thus, he makes ten responses to each card, or one hundred responses to the complete series of ten cards. With reference to the deaf, spontaneous language in describing what is perceived is not required. Hence, the deaf are not severely penalized by virtue of a disability in language expression. Another apparent feature relative to the deaf is that the response items in a large measure are single words, or at most, short phrases relatively within the understanding of high school students.

Aside from the major objective of the test which is to measure personality, one also obtains a rating of mental function as in the original Rorschach. Of particular interest in this connection were our findings of poorer theoretical functioning and inferior inductive reasoning on the part of the deaf subjects as compared to the hearing controls. In contrast, the deaf were the equal of the hearing in practical intelligence and in deductive reasoning.

In conjunction with the SORT our deaf subjects had also been administered the full scale WAIS, as well as the Terman Nonlanguage Multimental Test. Unfortunately the hearing subjects had had only the latter test. For the deaf the mean WAIS IQ's were as follows: Full Scale, 94.67, Verbal Scale, 85.42, and Performance Scale, 108.13. For the Terman Test the mean IQ of the deaf was 95.84 and of the hearing, 105.17. One cannot of course, make strict comparisons between the SORT findings and those of the WAIS and of the Terman. However, it does not seem amiss to point out the similarity in results. Relatively speaking, below average scores were obtained in theoretical function and in inductive reasoning, presumably reflecting weakness in abstract ability or capacity to develop a principle from particulars. In a similar vein practical intelligence and deductive reasoning appear to be associated with ability to function mentally in concrete situations, and to go from the general to particulars. Insofar as the WAIS Verbal and Performance IQ's may be regarded as reflecting the aforementioned, it would appear that there is very good agreement in the two sets of data. Furthermore, it should be pointed out that the Full Scale WAIS IQ of 94.67 is practically identical to the Terman IQ of 95.84 which in turn is approximately 10 points poorer than the IQ of 105.17 for the hearing subjects. In short, the Terman, a nonverbal test, appears to be reflecting the language lag of the deaf.

Relative to the latter it was previously noted that the deaf manifest retardation on certain tests of the nonverbal type. Oleron,[19] it will be recalled, found the deaf to be retarded about two years on the 1938 Progressive Matrices test of Raven. In order to obtain additional data with the 1938 test we recently administered it along with the Chicago Nonverbal Examination and the Terman Multimental test to ninety-six children in the intermediate department of the Kansas School for the Deaf.[21] The reason for giving the Chicago Test was that research through the years has found the deaf to be within normal limits on this instrument. My own experience with the Terman Test, however, is that it gives ratings comparable to the 1938 Raven when used with the deaf. Another aspect of the study was to get an index of the test-retest improvement and reliability for the three measures.

To this end the three tests were administered to the subjects again after a three-months interval. The intermediate department was selected since we were reasonably sure that none of the children had previously been exposed to any of the tests. We were also concerned with other aspects of the tests which have not as yet been analyzed. Preliminary analysis of the data shows that for the first administration the group obtained average IQ's of about 80 for the Raven and the Terman tests, and about 97 for the Chicago Nonverbal. On the retest the group improved about 4–5 points on the former two tests and about 12 points on the latter. Hence, despite the apparent practice effects, the subjects still showed approximately a year-and-a-half retardation on the Raven and Terman Tests.

However, Myklebust,[35] citing Wright's dissertation, reported that deaf students at Gallaudet College were the equal of a control group of college students with normal hearing. In line with this finding were those of Schoeny[39] in 1964 at Kansas University. She administered the Full Scale WAIS, the Terman and the 1938 Raven Test to sixteen deaf subjects at the Kansas School for the Deaf. None of the subjects had been exposed previously to the tests. Schoeny did not find a significant difference either between the Matrices and the Performance Scale or between the Terman and the Performance Scale.

More recently, Gupta[47] administered the Raven (1938), the Terman and Paragraph Meaning of the Stanford Achievement Test to sixty students in the Advanced Department of the Kansas School. He compared the results with the data from the subjects of the Intermediate Department.[21] The mean CA of the Advanced Department subjects was eighteen and one half years as compared to thirteen and one half years for the Intermediate Department subjects. There was, therefore, an average age difference of five years.

Gupta found mean raw scores of 45 and 49, respectively, on the Raven and Terman tests for the Advanced Department subjects as compared to Intermediate Department scores of 33 and 37 (first testing of the subjects of Goetzinger *et al.*). The actual IQ improvement on the Terman Test was 27 points, or from 81 to 108. A Raven's average raw score of 45 represents normal intelligence at this age level. Hence, on

the one hand the younger subjects showed retardation, while on the other hand, the older subjects were normal. Both groups had been given reading tests with the older subjects (Advanced Department) showing less than a year's superiority. Additional statistical treatment of Gupta's data on the Advanced Department subjects (not included in thesis) involved a comparison of scores on the mental tests between the best and poorest achievers on the reading test. (The upper and lower 20 subjects were compared.) In short, the mental test scores between the groups were not significantly different.

Gupta computed Kendall Rank Correlations and Kendall Partial Rank Correlations with chronological age controlled between the variables. Insofar as reading ability (vocabulary and paragraph meaning) may be regarded as an index of the language ability of the deaf, the results strongly suggested that language level *per se* is only minimally associated with success on the mental tests.

The retardation of the Intermediate Department subjects on the Terman and Raven tests as contrasted to normal intelligence as rated by the Chicago Nonverbal (tests were rotated to counterbalance any order effects) may be related to inexperience with the type of problems of these tests rather than to actual deficiency. Seemingly, at some point from age thirteen and one-half to age eighteen and one-half experiences occurred which helped the advanced subjects of Gupta to obtain normal mental ratings on the two tests in question even though their gain in language as indirectly measured through reading was less than one year.

In view of the foregoing, the results appear to support the findings of Furth, whose research will be discussed subsequently.

Furth[40] and his associates compared deaf and hearing subjects on a number of nonverbal cognitive tasks which included reversal shift (reversing principle of action), conceptual control (choosing part and whole), conceptual discovery (sameness and symmetry and opposite), weight judgments (keeping weight judgments constant with changing shape), inferential reasoning (simultaneous procedure, sequential procedure and grasping procedure), extradimensional and intradimensional shift (shifting), similarity (discovering common attribute), conceptual transfer (level of conceptual attainment, verbalized shift), logical symbols (learning and using logical symbols), Gestalt laws, rote learning, memory for interfering colors (interfering and neutral colors), and memory span (nonsense figures and digits).

On all but four of the studies the deaf performed as well as the hearing. Furth stated on the basis of these findings:

> While we thus observe that in some instances the cognitive development of deaf children is retarded, we believe that the retardation is due to an experiential deficiency, only indirectly linked to language. This explanation is supported by a number of studies with deaf adolescents or adults where no differences between deaf and hearing subjects were observed. Apparently then this retardation is merely a temporary setback and is no longer apparent at an older age level.[40]

On four of the experiments, however, the deaf were inferior to the hearing. In the study concerned with the concepts of "sameness" and "opposite" the deaf were the equal of the hearing on the former but inferior on the latter. Again, on tests involving immediate recall of digits the deaf were poorer than the hearing. This finding has been consistent since the time of Pintner. However, from the clinical point of view we have consistently observed that children who have had preschool training in conjunction with an oral-auditory approach do better on the "memory for digits" subtest of the Nebraska Scale than those who have had no preschool training. Furth further reported that the deaf were not different from the hearing on "memory for nonsense figures." This finding also is consistent in the literature.

In connection with the above, Blair[41] studied memory for designs, tactual memory, memory for movement, object location, memory for dots and picture span and digit span. The deaf were inferior to the hearing on memory for dots, picture span and memory span. More recently, Goetzinger and Huber[42] compared thirty deaf and thirty-nine hearing adolescents on the Benton Visual Retention Test. These investigators studied immediate recall using exposure times of five and ten seconds. In the delayed condition the subjects were required to wait fifteen seconds, following a ten-second exposure, before responding. No differences between the groups were found in immediate recall. However, in delayed recall the deaf were significantly inferior to the hearing.

They speculated that the hearing subject, when instructed there will be a delay, essentially shifts his mode of remembering the designs, using perhaps subvocalizations (attaches names to the designs like triangle, square, etc.) to assist retention. However in the immediate recall condition the hearing and the deaf alike depend upon visual imagery. The deaf and hearing therefore are utilizing the same mechanism for recall and no differences are apparent.

Furth goes on to say that in another study although the deaf were the equal of the hearing in rote memory at ages seven to ten, they were inferior to the hearing at ages eleven and twelve. Finally, the adult deaf were inferior to college students with normal hearing "on transfer tasks where verbalized rules were of obvious help, but were equal on a transfer task where the kind of verbalization was not suitable."[40]

Rosenstein,[40] in a provocative discussion on concept formation, points out that there is still considerable disagreement among psychologists as to the nature of concepts, and that there is no precise explanation as to how they develop in hearing children, much less the deaf. In addition to the foregoing there is a problem of defining what is meant by the word concept. Apparently it means different things to different people. Rosenstein goes on to say:

> Let us explore this semantic difficulty a little further. Conceptual activity is one of the processes that are classified under the heading cognitive functioning, which is an encompassing term for all higher mental operations; in a word, knowing. In order to know, we must think; and often psychologists equate *conceptual activity* with the broader term *thinking*, when, in fact, conceptual activity is only one phase of the many activities and abilities involved in thinking. Problem solving and reasoning, for example, are cognitive activities which differ from concept formation, although it is true that old concepts may be used or grouped differently when one attempts to solve a problem.
>
> Not only do psychologists think of conceptual abilities in a very broad sense, but others use very limited definitions of concepts in their research on conceptual behavior. Still others take these limited definitions to explain *all* conceptual activity. Concept formation, for example, may be studied as an inductive process, or as a deductive process. Inductive concept formation is said to occur when a single summarizing statement (or thought) is the result of the combination of a number of hitherto unrelated experiences. To the young child *car* may mean only the family car. Soon he discovers that *car* applies also to the neighbor's automobile, which may be older and of a different color.
>
> Then he realizes that many different cars pass on the street, and comprehends *car* as a concept. Evidence that he has the concept of *car* is obtained when he points excitedly, as he notices a car he has never seen before (say, a Model-T Ford) and says, "car!"
>
> Deductive concept formation, on the other hand, does not result from successive encounters with objects that have certain aspects in common. The process in this case is reversed; the individual begins with a tentative summarizng or general statement, and applies it to objects or items that he successively encounters. He notes any conflicting information displayed by the items and compares it with the statement, thus sharpening and refining the idea (or concept) described by the statement.[40]

Rosenstein, furthermore, differentiates class concepts, or those which represent individuals or items, as for example, furniture for chair and table, etc., and concepts which are abstract ideas, such as roundness, which cannot be seen *per se*, but which can be recognized in objects which have it.

In view of Rosenstein's discussion it is clear that experimental results could have different outcomes. In conjunction with the above, he elaborated on the difficulty of measuring concepts in the deaf because of the language deficit, and discussed the current method used by many experimenters of structuring the task to circumvent the aforementioned. He commented further that the greatest problem in attempting to determine the nature of development of concepts in children is the overlap of factors, such as memory, images, imagination and association which contribute to concept formation.

As noted previously, the study of personality and adjustment of the hearing impaired during the Pintner era was largely accomplished with personality tests of the paper-and-pencil variety, inventories and behavior rating scales. Along with this type of approach was the method which relied upon the opinion of experts. In recent years there have been a number of studies in which projective techniques were employed. Several investigators have used the Rorschach, and other tests and techniques have been used such as Sentence Completion, the Mosaic Test, the Maps or Make-a-Picture Story, Human Figure Drawings, TAT, and Projective Play. Levine[36] has recently summarized the majority of such studies. In addition to the projective techniques there was the

comprehensive psychiatric study in New York.[43]

Although the Rorschach, TAT, MAPS and HTP have proved useful with the adolescent and the adult deaf, nevertheless for young deaf children, because of the language problem, there is virtually a void with the exception of projective play. While at times exceedingly pertinent information can be obtained from "Drawing the Human Figure," yet the paucity of the young child's language poses severe problems of interpretation.

The results of investigations with the Rorschach have, in general, been in agreement. As summarized by Levine[36] they have shown the deaf to have conceptual deficiencies, to manifest emotional immaturity, egocentrism and rigidity, to show a lack of social adaptability and to have constricting interests and motivation. With reference to the other test results, as a general statement, it can be said that the deaf show poorer adjustment than the hearing in most of the areas of comparison.

With reference to psychiatric interview, two studies during the last war were in agreement that depressive reactions were common among their hearing impaired patients. Ingalls[44] reported on 1,100 cases who had been admitted to the Borden General Hospital. He stated that 27 per cent were diagnosed as psychoneurotic and less than 5 per cent as psychotic. A majority of the psychotics were of the anxiety type. Also, those cases who had suffered hearing impairment in early childhood were said to feel injured, isolated, defective, hostile and depressed. Although audiological therapy was helpful to them it was no substitute for psychotherapy. The patients with recently acquired impairment responded more easily to audiological therapy which included lipreading, auditory training and the use of hearing aids. These measures were effective in relieving depressive states.

The second study by Knapp[45] involved 510 patients who had been admitted to the Deshon Army Hospital. The patients were studied psychiatrically and classified according to the relationship of their hearing loss to their psychiatric disability. In 82.3 per cent of the cases there was either no psychiatric disease or else the disease was unrelated to the hearing loss. Patients with more severe and chronic hearing loss (hearing loss for many years) reacted neurotically to the constricting effects of deafness by overcompensation in outgoing activities, by denial of hearing loss, by withdrawal from society or by exploitation of the disability. This group amounted to 5.5 per cent of the total. About 2.8 per cent classified as mixed cases, showed neurotic reactions to deafness plus psychogenic exaggeration of the deficit. Another 5 per cent manifested psychogenic loss superimposed upon minimal organic impairment. Knapp further noted that cases whose hearing impairment had persisted from childhood exhibited poorer adjustment. He concluded that the study showed "no one psychology of deafness." Furthermore, he disagrees with the opinion that deafness in early years favors better adjustment, and maintains that chronicity, or early deaf-

ness, although causing a less drastic sense of loss, nevertheless induces a more warping one.

Myklebust[35] recently compared deaf students from Gallaudet College with hard-of-hearing subjects from a hearing society. All subjects were administered the Minnesota Multiphasic Personality Inventory and in addition wrote an autobiographical account about "What my hearing loss means to me." Essentially he found a relationship between sensory deprivation and emotional adjustment which related to age at onset of deafness, degree of deafness, and sex. Those with profound deafness manifested the greatest emotional deviations. Males, irrespective of degree of hearing loss and age at onset, showed more personality disorder than females did. In addition, the deaf seemed unaware of deafness as a handicap. Hence they lacked insight into the significance of hearing loss. Although the hard of hearing estimated deafness to be a greater handicap, and showed more depression because of the hearing loss, nevertheless, the naivete of the deaf could not be regarded as an index of better adjustment. On the contrary, those deaf subjects who stated that deafness was no handicap were the very ones who were found to be most disturbed emotionally. Myklebust stated:

> . . . The primary conclusion to be drawn from this study, therefore, is that deafness, particularly when profound and from early life, imposes a characteristic restriction on personality but does not cause mental illness.[35]

Finally, with reference to mental illness of the deaf, Altshuler[46] reported that schizophrenia is the most common form of psychosis in those who were hospitalized. As with the hearing it accounts for slightly more than 50 per cent of the cases. However, the disease is no more severe in the deaf than in the hearing, but is characterized by impulsive aggressive acts which might be related to their orientation toward action. The most common reasons for referral to the outpatient clinic were acute psychiatric illness, homosexuality, poor work adjustment, social conflicts and family problems.

In the preceding paragraphs an attempt was made to contrast the psychological assessments of the Pintner era with those of the post-Pintner period. Of necessity much has remained unsaid and many excellent studies omitted from comment. However, it is hoped that at least a general idea has been conveyed of the breadth of psychological assessment then and now.

References

1. Davis, H., and Silverman, S. R.: *Hearing and Deafness*. New York, Holt, Rinehart and Winston, 1960.
2. Greenberger, D.: Doubtful cases. *Amer Ann Deaf*, 43:93–99, 1889.
3. Taylor, H.: A spelling test. *Amer Ann Deaf*, 42:364–369, 1897.
4. Mott, A. J.: A comparison of deaf and hearing children in their ninth year. *Amer Ann Deaf*, 44:401–412, 1899. Also, 45:33–39, 1900.
5. Smith, J. L.: Mental characteristics of pupils. *Amer Ann Deaf*, 48:248–268. 1903.
6. MacMillan, D. P., and Bruner, F. G.: Experimental Studies of Deaf Children. Special Report of the Dept. of Child Study and Pedagogical Investigation. Chicago, Chicago Public Schools, 1906.

7. Kilpatrick, W. M.: Comparative tests. *Amer Ann Deaf*, 57:427–428, 1912.
8. Pintner, R., and Paterson, D. G.: Some conclusions from psychological tests of the deaf. *Volta Rev*, 20:10–14, 1918.
9. ————: The Binet Scale and the deaf child. *J Educ Psychol*, 6:201–210, 1915.
10. Newlee, C.E.: A report of learning tests with deaf children. *Volta Rev*, 21:216–223, 1919.
11. Reamer, J. C.: *Mental and Educational Measurements of the Deaf*. Psychological Monographs, No. 132. Princeton, The Psychological Review Co., 1921.
12. Day, H. E.; Fusfeld, I. S., and Pintner, R.: *A Survey of American Schools for the Deaf*. Washington, The National Research Council, 1928.
13. Upshall, C. C.: *Day Schools vs Institutions for the Deaf*. Teachers College Contributions to Education, No. 389, New York, Teachers College, Columbia University, 1929.
14. Drever, J., and Collins, M.: *Performance Test of Intelligence*. London, Oliver and Boyd, 1936.
15. MacKane, K.: *A Comparison of the Intelligence of Deaf and Hearing Children*. Teachers College Contributions to Education, No. 585. New York, Teachers College, Columbia University, 1932.
16. Barker, R. G.; Wright, B. A.; Meyerson, L., and Gonick, M.: Adjustment to Physical Handicap and Illness: A Survey of the Social Psychology of Physique and Disability. Bulletin 55, Revised 1953, New York, Social Science Research Council, 1953.
17. Frampton, M. E., and Gall, E. D.: *Special Education for the Exceptional; Vol. II, The Physically Handicapped and Special Health Problems*. Boston, Porter Sargent Publisher, 1955.
18. Goetzinger, C. P., and Rousey, C. L.: A study of the Wechsler Performance Scale (Form II) and the Knox Cube Test with deaf adolescents. *Amer Ann Deaf*, 102:388–398, 1957.

19. OLERON, P. A.: A study of the intelligence of the deaf. *Amer Ann Deaf*, 95:179–195, 1950.

20. ZECKEL, A., and VAN DER KOLK, J. J.: A comparative intelligence test of groups of children born deaf and of good hearing, by means of the Porteus Test. *Amer Ann Deaf*, 84:114–123, 1939.

21. GOETZINGER, C. P.; WILLS, R., and CROUTER, L.: A comparison of three nonverbal IQ tests with deaf children. (in preparation.)

22. BRUNSCHWIG, L.: *A Study of Some Personality Aspects of Deaf Children.* Teachers College Contributions to Education, No. 687. New York, Teachers College, Columbia University, 1936.

23. SPRINGER, N.: A comparative study of the behavior traits of deaf and hearing children of New York City. *Amer Ann Deaf*, 83:255, 1938.

24. ———, and ROSLOW, S.: A further study of the psychoneurotic responses of deaf and hearing children. *J Educ Psychol*, 29:590, 1938.

25. GREGORY, I.: A comparison of certain personality traits and interests in deaf and hearing children. *Child Develop*, 9:277, 1938.

26. MYKLEBUST, H. R., and BURCHARD, E.: A study of the effects of congenital and adventitious deafness on intelligence, personality and social maturity of school children. *J Educ Psychol*, 34:321, 1945.

27. LYON, V.: The use of vocational and personality tests with the deaf. *J Appl Psychol*, 18:224, 1934.

28. WELLES, H.: *The Measurement of Certain Aspects of Personality Among Hard of Hearing Adults.* Teachers College Contributions to Education, No. 545, New York, Teachers College, Columbia University, 1932.

29. PINTNER, R.: Emotional stability of the hard of hearing. *J Genet Psychol*, 43:293–311, 1933.

30. ———; FUSFELD, I. S., and BRUNSCHWIG, L.: Personality tests of deaf adults. *J Genet Psychol*, 51:305–327, 1937.

31. GATES, A.: The correlation of achievement in school subjects with intelligence tests. *J Educ Psychol*, 13:129–139, 223–235, and 277–284, 1922.

32. BROWN, A. W.: The correlation of non-language tests with each other, with school achievement and with teachers' judgments of intelligence of children in a school for the deaf. *J Appl Psychol*, 14:371–375, 1930.

33. GOETZINGER, C. P.: Relationship Between School Achievement and Intelligence Test Data for Deaf Adolescents. Unpublished M. A. Thesis. Berkeley, University of California, 1950.

34. BRILL, R. G.: The relationship of Wechsler I.Q.s to academic achievement among deaf students. *Exceptional Child*, 28:315–321, 1962.

35. MYKLEBUST, H. R.: *The Psychology of Deafness. Sensory Deprivation, Learning, and Adjustment.* New York, Grune, 1960.

36. LEVINE, E. S.: Studies in psychological evaluation of the deaf. *Volta Rev*, 65:496–512, 1963.

37. GOETZINGER, C. P.: ORTIZ, J. D.; BELLEROSE, B., and BUCHAN, L. G.: A study of the S. O. Rorschach with deaf and hearing adolescents. *Amer Ann Deaf*, 111:510–542, 1966.

38. STONE, J. B.: *Manual of S. O. Rorschach Test*, Preliminary Edition. Los Angeles, California Test Bureau, 1958.

39. SCHOENY, L.: A Study of Deaf Adolescents with General Measurements of Intellectual Ability. Unpublished Master's Thesis. University of Kansas, 1964.

40. Report of the Proceedings of the International Congress on Education of the Deaf and of the 41st Meeting of the Convention of American Instructors of the Deaf. Washington, Gallaudet College, 1963.

41. BLAIR, F. X.: A study of the visual memory of deaf and hearing children. *Amer Ann Deaf*, 102:254–263, 1957.

42. GOETZINGER, C. P., and HUBER, T. G.: A study of immediate and delayed visual

retention with deaf and hearing adolescents. *Amer Ann Deaf*, 109:297–305, 1964.

43. RAINER, J. D.: *Family and Mental Health Problems of a Deaf Population.* New York, New York State Psychiatric Institute, 1963.

44. INGALLS, G. S.: Some psychiatric observations on patients with hearing defects. *Occup Therapy Rehab*, 25:62–66, 1946.

45. KNAPP, P. H.: in BARBARA, D. A.: *Psychological and Psychiatric Aspects of Speech and Hearing.* Springfield, Thomas, 1960.

46. ALTSHULER, K. Z.: Psychiatric considerations in the adult deaf. *Amer Ann Deaf*, 107:560–561, 1962.

47. GUPTA, KUNWAR PAL.: A Study of Two Non-Language Intelligence Tests with Deaf Subjects in the Intermediate and Advanced Departments of the Kansas School for the Deaf. Unpublished Master's Thesis. University of Kansas, 1965.

WANTED: A MEANINGFUL MENTAL HEALTH PROGRAM. APPLY ANY SCHOOL FOR THE DEAF*

TARAS B. DENIS

As stated by Arthur T. Jersild, professor of education at Columbia University:

> Every teacher is in his own way a psychologist. Everything he does, says, or teaches has or could have a psychological impact. What he offers helps children to discover their resources and their limitations. He is the central figure in countless situations which can help the learner to realize and accept himself or which may bring humiliation, shame, rejection and self-disparagement.[1]

In a way the foregoing serves to illustrate the nature of this paper, which was mainly inspired by Dr. Jersild's fine book, *In Search of Self*. And while his work deals with the application of psychological principles to the education of the normal child, there is no reason why it cannot be interpreted in the light of teaching the handicapped. Indeed, the challenge here is the implementa-

tion of Professor Jersild's words—actually and realistically—in a program with which I am on familiar terms: the education of the deaf child.

At the same time it is necessary to convey to the reader a general idea of the problems confronting deaf pupils, always remembering that the task of educating such children is enormous, to say nothing of adding psychological concepts to the school's curriculum. Yet, I stand convinced that unless mental health is given a much higher priority than it currently enjoys in schools for the deaf, for the majority of pupils progress will always remain a one-way street that inevitably terminates in a dead end.

Finally, it is not possible here to cover as many aspects of mental health applicable to the deaf as I would like. Rather, I must limit myself to a few random areas, namely, the problems of the deaf child in a residential school environment, as a blessing or a burden in his home, as an accepted or rejected

* Reprinted with consent from *The Fanwood Journal*, New York School for the Deaf, White Plains, April–May, 1963. The author is an instructor at the New York School for the Deaf.

playmate in his street—in brief, problems having to do with the mental well-
being of the deaf pupil as seen through
the eyes of one of his teachers, who is
also deaf and who, more than anything
else, now sees him from a psychological
viewpoint.

The School (Teacher) Environment

Many things that hold true in the
education of the normal hearing child
also hold true for the deaf child, and
one of these is teacher self-understanding.

> If teachers accept the concept that edu-
> cation should help each child to develop
> his real or potential self, it will be essential
> for the teachers to seek the kind of self-
> understanding which they are trying to help
> their pupils to achieve. If a person would
> help others to understand themselves he
> must strive to understand himself and he
> must be willing to accept help in the
> process.[1]

Obviously, teachers in schools for the
deaf are beset by a trio of problems:
(1) the education of the pupil, which as
I have mentioned before is an undertaking of great magnitude; (2) the psychological understanding of the child,
and (3) the psychological understanding of the teacher himself. Clearly then,
training centers for teachers of the deaf
should stress psychological as well as
educational techniques.

There are many teachers in schools
for the deaf who would sacrifice a deaf
child's mental health for a gain in overt
achievement, and often the latter is so
meager, so unessential, that the attempt
is all but wasted. By far it is better for
the teacher to understand the child's

psychological needs and to try to instill
in him some form of self-understanding
so that he may find use for this learning, even though the entire education
for some pupils may never amount to
more than a few grades. After all, nothing is lost since the child's education is
not terminated by the teacher's psychological insight, and indeed it may even
take a turn for better learning potential
should it succeed.

In the education of the deaf, subject
matter is not enough. The need here is
for teachers who understand both the
child and themselves. Until such teachers are available one-sided personalities
will continue to take one-sided places in
society and at best reap one-sided rewards.

The School (Child) Environment

Rather than openly siding with the
proponents of the residential school
program for deaf pupils or those who
favor dayschool curriculums, it is my
contention that the child and not the
school should be the decisive factor in
determining his or her educational environment.

While advocates of the latter type of
schooling often argue that theirs is a
program which affords pupils the
needed daily contact with parents and
siblings, in some instances the nature of
this contact is not always a happy one.
It may, in fact, prove detrimental to the
child's mental, and even physical, well-
being, especially if such a child is not
only rejected in his home, but is physically abused because as a deaf individual he is misunderstood or unwanted.

Many underprivileged children benefit from the care, understanding and social contact with their own kind that is provided in the residential school. Besides constructive outlets like trade skills, such a school also affords them a place to work off their energy through a variety of sports and supervised outdoor activities, free from the dangers inherent in crowded city conditions. Others may be spared the lethargic existence of rural out-of-the-way places. Certain aspects of culture, which would otherwise be unavailable to many of them, are within reach in the residential school. Finally, the school itself has the advantage of combining more efficiently the resources of its entire staff, including the direct services of both social worker and psychologist, for the good of its charges.

For other children, however, the residential school may product negative results. The child's limited contact with the world of sound, his confinement to a relatively fixed living area that tends to shield him from the realities—no matter how small—of day-to-day occurrences, and a somewhat stereotyped, regimented existence where most decisions are made for him may all but stifle his potential and growth as a separate individual. He may feel that his parents do not want him on their hands, that he is different—even guilty of some unknown offense—and is therefore being put away in a place that provides him with everything except that which he desires most, the love of his parents.

Ideally, before admitting a pupil, the residential school should thoroughly take into account the child's background and homelife. Residential status should never be awarded to a pupil whose homelife does not warrant it. The younger the child, the more care that is needed in exercising this judgment.

The Home (Parent) Environment

Like his normal hearing counterpart, being unwanted in the home may for the deaf child create problems far more serious than his inability to hear (and speak). Unhealthy mental attitudes, coupled with the loss of a valuable tool for learning, not only make his education more complicated for all concerned, but because in his particular case psychological assistance is slow, his mental situation may deteriorate beyond the point of correction. This is to say nothing of the cost of treatment and the time involved.

A deaf child, like all children, thrives best on love and a sense of security within the home. More than his hearing siblings, however, he needs to be understood by his parents. He needs help —not blame or shame—for his affliction, which should be viewed as a challenge that can be overcome. All too often parents are defeated at the initial impact, little realizing that this attitude is bound to permeate the child.

On the other hand, overprotection may contribute to the eventual problems of responsibility and adulthood. The deaf child who is brought up in a "sterilized" environment will very likely be unable to make his own decisions later on. Besides the possibility of such a child becoming the lifetime ward of his parents and relatives, he may foist his helplessness on others with whom he comes into contact—privately at first, then openly.

There are two kinds of ignorance on the part of some parents of deaf children. One kind is intentional and needs no elaboration here except that these parents, either through needless feelings of guilt or disgrace, ignore the child's needs for their own irresponsible, selfish ends.

The other kind stems from their natural inability to cope with the child's inner needs, more or less the result of the communication barrier. His external existence is provided for, indeed, but often with the expectation that he conform to the standards of the normal society surrounding him. All else, sometimes his desire to fraternize with other deaf children, but more important, his manner of communicating, is sacrificed for what the parents consider correct, or normal. Deviation brings disapproval, and whether or not the child understands why, he does have a difficult time trying to suppress that which for him is natural, i.e., self-expression through media other than the spoken word. And for some deaf children this is not just an educational catastrophe.

Much ignorance can be attributed to the fact that most parents are anxious to see their handicapped offspring become normal, and in their zealous pursuit of this overlook everything else. Such high hopes are understandable, of course, but at the same time they tend to make parents the gullible victims of publicity-minded academicians who paint rosy futures for all deaf children, not the actual few. Since their

advertising usually touches on the emotional rather than the realistic, who can resist? Indeed, it is not surprising to note the disappointment, the disbelief —and sometimes shock—of some parents once the pomp of graduataion has worn off. As for those parents, particularly the overconcerned, who may sense earlier that progress is not as promised, they are either successfully subdued by the verbal maneuvers on the part of the school personnel, or on their own behalf become resigned, even indifferent to the plight of their child.

Here some blame must be shouldered by the parents, many of whom fail to realize that putting their deaf child in the "right" school does not necessarily mean the problems posed by his handicap will be solved "in due time." On the contrary, miraculous results are the exception, not the rule; mediocre and even poor results are to be expected, if not accepted. Lest we forget, intelligence—as important as it is—is not an end in itself. A child's right to happiness and all other blessings that comprise what we call society cannot and should not be sacrificed to achieve but a part of the whole. Each individual is unique and should be respected as such; to deem otherwise is to attack the very foundation of our nation's educational structure—its strength, its heritage and its freedom.

Unless parents are prepared to lend themselves to unrelenting participation —realistically as well as enthusiastically —in the education of their handicapped child, the school cannot be held entirely at fault. For deaf children the home is the source of mental happiness which no school, no matter how advanced and equipped, is prepared to give.

The Home (Child) Environment

It is the rare child who does not care whether he is accepted by his playmates. Deaf children are no exception. However, more than just acceptance they need tolerance. Acceptance by children, we know, is one thing, but tolerance is a different matter, and particularly so when it has to do with a playmate, who in all outward respects appears normal, and yet is different. Here the dual nature of the problem makes it all the more difficult for the deaf child to enter into normal, equal relationships with hearing children.

To be unaccepted by his peers may for the deaf child—or for the matter, any handicapped individual—foster in him the problem of withdrawal as well as one of dislike toward the world of sound. He will be alone in more than one sense, at least until he is able to find companions, notably deaf ones like himself. Should he live in a community where there are none, or worse, in the suburbs or a small village, whatever the consequences accompanying his solitary existence, they are prolonged.

Even if he is accepted by his hearing peers, the deaf child is usually left to shift for himself in times of inaction, let alone conversation. If a class of leadership exists within the group, most likely he will occupy the last rung of the ladder. Usually, however, the handicapped individual accepts the inferior place that may be accorded him if only to remain a member of the group. Further, so long as physical abuse is not employed—and there are some who absorb it in stride—he tends to be resigned to whatever fun may be poked at him, having virtually become accustomed to it. Usually, his craving for identification with the normal or superior is much stronger than his desire to be recognized separately for what he is.

Obviously, the deaf child prefers the companionship of other deaf children because it is in his native element that he is best able to hold his own. Moreover, as he grows older, relationships with his own kind are bound to increase since intellectually he may be incapable of keeping pace with his hearing peers. The corresponding change in maturity is something else again. In brief, anxiety and other fears inherent in his participation in activities of the normal-hearing are heightened with the passage of time that brings with it new interests, situations and the like.

It is erroneous to suppose that only by association with hearing children can the deaf child ever hope to acquire normalcy, including increased powers of communication. It is here that mental happiness is overlooked by those who favor stronger integration. For instance, to expect a deaf individual to marry a hearing partner, while not unusual in itself, poses certain questions which can only be answered after the event, and even then strictly on an individual basis.

While the deaf child should be given the opportunity of associating with the normal as much as possible, he should not be deprived of similar privileges in regard to activities by and for the deaf. However, extremities in both directions should be avoided, and certainly the use of force.

Conclusion

Despite the phenomenal growth of new medical and clinical knowledge during the last two decades, it is comparatively recent that the deaf have benefited from its dissemination and application. This is especially true in the area of mental health which, owing to communication difficulties, merely adds to the problems of the psychologist and psychiatrist.

It is now well known that the nature of deafness gives rise to some forms of bizarre behavior, chiefly in the realm of social relationships. While it is true that steps have already been taken by different authorities to ameliorate the situation, they come at a late hour and, by comparison, are more token than technical.

In a normal society, where demand exceeds the supply of personnel needed to cope with the problems of mental health, it is only natural to expect a greater disproportion for a handicapped group that, numerically speaking, forms a smaller segment of the population. The deaf are no exception. Actually, however, they are in need of mental help most, but are getting it least.

Whether the State of New York has set a precedent in the field of psychological research for the deaf is not this paper's concern, but an excellent report[2] on the Mental Health Project for the Deaf, prepared by Dr. Kenneth Z. Altshuler of the New York State Psychiatric Institute, is available in a recent issue of the *American Annals of the Deaf*. (Incidentally, quite a number of other informative articles are included in the periodical. Besides another, which has to do with mental health and parents, topics covered are audiological, communicative, educational, vocational and counseling aspects of deafness, in addition to "national efforts relative to deafness," all by various authorities in the field.)

In the main, however, the interest in this absorbing volume is centered around deaf adolescents and adults. More effort perhaps will sooner or later be directed to a concerted attack at the roots of the mental problems of the deaf; the preschool and very young child.

While research is needed on the elementary school level, more direct steps can be taken by administrative authorities to improve the climate in many schools for the deaf. To list a few, parents—not only teachers—should receive training and advice in the recognition and control of emotional and behavioristic disorders in school children, including general, nontechnical information as available; less professional antagonism, more cooperation should exist between teachers and members of the clinical staffs; an in-the-classroom psychological service should be provided for those teachers wishing such assistance, and in schools having vocational training programs, the position occupied by a shop instructor should not be that of a skilled craftsman alone.

Finally, special consideration here must be given to an important problem regarding the residential school for the deaf. Houseparents and other personnel, who have long-time contact with the pupils, should not be selected at random; qualified persons, or at least those capable of being trained to the extent that they can add more knowledge as time progresses, should be given priority. Doubtless, such a proposal entails a rise in costs, but in the long run there is no denying that this preventive measure will repay itself many times over.

References

1. JERSILD, ARTHUR T.: *In Search of Self.* New York, T. C., 1952.
2. ALTSHULER, KENNETH Z.: Psychiatric considerations in the school age deaf. *Amer Ann Deaf, 107:*553–559, 1962.

XVIII. What Research Reveals

NEW INSIGHT INTO LIPREADING*

EDGAR L. LOWELL

Lipreading is an intriguing phenomenon. It has been the subject of many stories, television plays, and motion pictures. It is used in private investigation work, where its success depends in large measure upon lack of publicity. For many deaf people it is a major means of communication.

For the staff at the John Tracy Clinic lipreading is intriguing and challenging because there is so much about it we do not understand. It was to meet this challenge that we applied for and received an Office of Vocational Rehabilitation special project grant to study "factors associated with success in lipreading."

As an example of how little is known about lipreading: Do you know that you can read lips? Despite wide individual differences, almost everyone can lipread to some extent and a good many people can get most of a simple conversation by lipreading alone.

(If you don't believe it, try it out on your friends. Start with some easy sentences like "What time is it?" *or* "Do you have a piece of paper?" *Speak without voice and without exaggerating your lip movements—you'll be surprised at the results.)*

For the vocational rehabilitation counselor dealing with deaf clients, lipreading skill is more than intriguing —it can be a headache! Assessment of communication skills is inevitably one of his first tasks in dealing with a hearing-impaired client. Lipreading skills is one of the facets that must be explored. Then he must decide: "Would this client benefit from training in lipreading? Would improved lipreading skill increase his vocational potential?"

The counselor gets little help at this point because there are no commonly accepted tests for evaluation. He knows that extensive lipreading training is not only expensive but can be disheartening and frustrating if the client does not benefit from the experience—and he also knows, from experience, that some people do not.

Many deaf people lead busy, successful lives utilizing only oral communication. There are other deaf people who also lead busy, successful lives but who do not use oral communica-

* Reprinted from *Rehabilitation Record,* Office of Vocational Rehabilitation, U. S. Department of Health, Education, and Welfare, July–August, 1961, with consent of the author who is Administrator of the John Tracy Clinic, Los Angeles.

tion skills. The difference between these two groups does not seem to be attributable to any easily discernible factors.

Assessment of personality and intellectual characteristics associated with success in lipreading was the first problem undertaken in this research project. Previous research had not shown any consistent correlations between general intelligence and lipreading success. We hoped that some of the more recent tests of specific traits and abilities developed by factor analysis might give clues to some combination of personality characteristics and intellectual factors which might do the trick.

Our major task was development of a stable, objective measurement of lipreading skill. Despite some obvious drawbacks, slides seemed to be the only way of insuring the same lipreading task on each testing. A series of slides was prepared, consisting of thirty sentences which might occur in everyday conversation. They were presented one at a time, separated by an interval for writing down what was said. This test* proved to be very reliable, which was important for subsequent testing.

The everyday task of the deaf lipreader is somewhat different from the task required on this test. He can get a great deal of information and incidental clues from the face-to-face situation which is missing in the slides.

* We are indebted to Jacqueline Keaster for making the series available to us. It was taken from a larger one prepared by the Department of Otolaryngology, State University of Iowa.

Here only the head and shoulders of the speaker are presented. Our studies have shown that while people can do better when there are clues of context to help them, the ones who do best in the film test also do best when the clues are present.

These clues of context are so important that many people no longer speak of lipreading but rather of "visual speech reception."

One of the studies showed that not only are clues from the general situation helpful, but even the amount of the face you see in addition to the lips determines how much you can understand. In a study carried out by Dr. Louis Stone, the same sentences were presented under four different conditions. In three, the speaker was behind a plastic screen which partially obscured all parts of his face not exposed by a hole in the screen. In one, a hole allowed you to see just his lips; a second showed from the nose to the chin; a third disclosed eyebrows to chin; and in the fourth, the entire head and shoulders were visible. Sixteen carefully conducted tests under these four conditions showed that there were definite improvements in the lipreading scores as more of the face was visible.

Dr. Stone's study arrived at one unexpected conclusion: When the speaker maintained a severe or grim expression, he was easier to lipread than when he maintained a friendly smiling expression. An examination of the film suggests that the smiling face is more difficult to lipread because it is more difficult to tell when the message starts and when it stops. The smile exposes teeth and looks much like the image that is presented when certain sounds are being made. The unsmiling face, with lips firmly closed between sentences, definitely indicates the start and duration of the message.

Another indication of the importance of these small secondary cues comes from the fact that questions were more easily read than declarative sentences—probably due to the small movements of forehead and eyebrows that accompany questions.

In all, some sixty-five separate studies involving several thousand hearing and deaf people of all ages were carried out. On the basis of this work we have established a number of facts:

Ability to read lips varies widely from person to person. The usual distribution of test scores shows people of all levels. For our film test, with a maximum score of 188, the average score for the typical group of normally hearing subjects ranges between ninety and 100 words correct. One subject, a normally hearing college student who had no idea that she could read lips, made the nearly perfect score of 183.

On the average, women are better lipreaders than are men. In the absence of any definitive knowledge, it seems reasonable to attribute the superior lipreading proficiency of the average woman to native differences that are sex-linked, although our male readers may wish to draw their own conclusions.

Aptitude and personality tests of lipreaders are inconclusive. Several barely significant coefficients of correlation have been found between aptitude and personality tests and lipreading proficiency from the wide variety of aptitude and personality tests administered. Accounting for a substantial amount of lipreading success with psychological tests is still difficult. One conclusion holds that lipreading ability is relatively independent of other abilities, or that it is so complex that no test of a single trait or ability will explain very much of a person's lipreading success. The closest exception we have to this rule is language ability as measured by some of our school achievement tests. This is understandable, when we consider how much lipreading must depend upon guessing based on a person's previous experience with language. A person's fluency with the language and his ability to call up a wide variety of previous language experiences undoubtedly contribute to his success.

Since many speech sounds are made inside the mouth and are not particularly visible on the lips, Dr. Mary F. Woodward and Carroll Barber of our research staff investigated the visibility of initial consonant phonemes. Their results show that on the basis of visibility alone, there are really only about four distinctions which can be made, as opposed to the twenty-five distinctions that can be made on the basis of hearing.

The problem of expectancy involves the definite ideas humans have about the order in which words appear together. If someone asked you "What time is ——?" you would almost automatically supply the final "it." There are certain rules governing the order in which words are put together to form sentences, and while you may not be able to state these rules, you have "built-in expectancies." Success in lip-reading the word "you," for example, ranged from 11 per cent to 98 per cent, depending upon the surrounding words in the film test. Rules governing probabilities of sequences have been worked out, and although the computation becomes quite complex, it is possible to define the contribution of expectancy to success on the test.

Other factors also contribute to the ease with which a word can be understood by the lipreader. Pronouns appear to be the easiest to read; verbs, nouns, adverbs, adjectives, prepositions and conjunctions follow in that order. There also appears to be an optimum length, with three-letter words being the easiest. One- and two-letter words are about as difficult as four- and five-letter words. Longer words increase in difficulty as their length increases. One study even demonstrated that the ratio of vowels to consonants in a sentence influences the difficulty. The best ratio for successful lipreading appears to be that of an equal number of vowels to consonants.

These are just a few of the many interesting problems that have been studied. We realize, in the clarity of hindsight, that lipreading is a more complex phenomenon than we had ever dreamed. It remains as intriguing and as challenging as when we started.

To disseminate information about this project and the studies which had been carried out, a series of John Tracy Clinic Research Papers entitled "Studies in Visual Communication" have been published. Before our supply was exhausted we placed complete sets in 200 libraries. A monograph which summarizes all of our research in this area in detail is currently nearing completion.

THE ATTAINMENTS IN ENGLISH AND ARITHMETIC OF SECONDARY SCHOOL PUPILS WITH IMPAIRED HEARING*

D. C. WOLLMAN

This paper reports the findings of an investigation into the attainments in English and arithmetic of a representative sample of 14–16-year-old pupils with impaired hearing and considers factors which appear to influence such attainments.

Introduction

This study formed part of a survey of educational provision, curricula and methods of teaching for secondary pupils with impaired hearing (Wollman, 1961). Its aim was to explore a possible basis for an examination which

* A reprint from *The British Journal of Educational Psychology*, Vol. 34, November, 1964, and reproduced here by courtesy of that publication and the author, Dr. Wollman, who is in the Department of Audiology and Education of the Deaf at the University of Manchester.

would serve as a leaving certificate and as a means of assessing the comparative attainments in English and arithmetic of fourteen to sixteen-year-old pupils with impaired hearing.

Plan of the Investigation

It was difficult to find standardized English tests for pupils with impaired hearing who are likely to be retarded linguistically. Two tests were, therefore, specially designed. The first consisted of seventy items, including correct and incorrect sentences, prepositions, colloquial expressions, spelling, completion of compound and complex sentences and vocabulary. The second was a composition test in which pupils were asked to write three short passages: (1) describing some object or experience, i.e., my home, my favorite television program, (2) explaining some activity, i.e., lighting a fire, cleaning shoes, and (3) composing a formal letter, i.e., applying for a job. A choice of subject was allowed for each passage.

Two arithmetic tests were used. The Manchester Mechanical Arithmetic Test was considered specially suitable as it covered a wide range of processes including area, decimals and percentages which normally figure in the curriculum for older pupils. In the second test an attempt was made to provide arithmetical problems relating to familiar experiences.

In the first English test and the two arithmetic tests, one mark was given for each correct item. In the composition test a marking schedule was based on a five-letter scale (A–E) in which

the mark C was awarded if the material was intelligible and relevant even though there were mistakes in language structure. Using this schedule all papers were marked by the writer and two colleagues experienced in the assessment of the language development of pupils with impaired hearing. The product-moment correlations between markers were of the order of 0·9. The final mark awarded to each piece of work was the average of the marks given by each examiner.

The lower age limit of the experimental group was set at 14 years 0 months at the time of the test and the upper limit at 16+. It was not practicable to test the whole population of this age range. The aim was that the experimental group should be reasonably large and drawn from a representative selection of schools for children with different degrees of impaired hearing. The head teacher and staffs of thirteen schools for the deaf and/or partially hearing agreed to cooperate. The total number of pupils tested represented between a quarter and a third of pupils in these age groups educated in special schools (Min. of Education, 1959).

Hearing losses were assessed by finding the average of the hearing loss in the better ear in decibels (db) above normal threshold at the frequencies 500, 1,000 and 2,000 cycles per second. Pupils were divided on the basis of average hearing loss into two groups with a dividing line at 75 db. This level was chosen to separate those children who hear unamplified speech albeit imperfectly and those with more severe impairments who, in the main, have little or no experience of unamplified speech.

The two English tests were also given to 162 pupils (ninety-five boys and sixty-seven girls) at two secondary modern schools. Their ages ranged from 14 years 3 months to 15 years 6 months, with a mean of 14 years 9 months.

The Findings of the Investigation

1. In both English and arithmetic the pupils with impaired hearing were found to be retarded when compared with unhandicapped pupils. Their mean scores in the English tests were significantly lower than those of the secondary modern pupils. In the standardized arithmetic test they had a mean raw score of 14; this would represent a standard score of 85 for boys and 87 for girls (norm. 100, S.D. 15).

2. Amongst the deaf pupils, those with moderate impairments of hearing tended to obtain higher scores in English. Degree of hearing impairment did not appear to be a factor in performance in arithmetic.

3. Mean English scores for girls were higher than those for boys; but only amongst the severely deaf pupils was the difference large enough to be statistically significant. The superiority of the severely deaf girls was particularly marked in the composition test. Sex difference was not apparent in the results of the arithmetic tests.

4. The mean scores for the fourteen- and fifteen-year age groups were approximately equal. In other words,

there was no evidence of any increment of score through increase in age. The two age groups did not show variations in distribution of intelligence or hearing loss.

5. In the first English test the greatest success was achieved in those items where the emphasis was on comprehension rather than expression. Many pupils were successful with the questions about a prose passage which were worded in a straightforward manner but had difficulty with those in which the language structure was more involved. The pupils with impaired hearing scored as well as or better than the secondary modern pupils in the abbreviations, plural forms and spellings where reliance on a visual pattern may tend to produce greater accuracy.

In items requiring expression many pupils, especially the severely deaf, understood the idea required, but were not familiar with the conventional method of expression, i.e., "The ball went *break* the window." This was clearly demonstrated in those items where sentences had to be completed so as to make them intelligible and grammatically correct. All pupils, hearing and deaf, found sentences containing "across which" and "although" the most difficult and those with "and," "but" and "because," the easiest. The item with "although" was successfully completed by 39 per cent of secondary modern pupils, 12 per cent of partially hearing pupils and 4 per cent of the severely deaf; for the sentence containing "but" the comparable figures were 70 per cent, 48 per cent and 21 per cent. The differences between the percentages of pupils passing in the three groups gave some indication of the effect of hearing impairment on the understanding and expression of complex sentences patterns.

An analysis of answers in this section suggests that the difficulties encountered were of two main types: The sense of some conjunctions was not understood. Clauses of cause instead of concession were supplied after "although" and in many instances the word "because" was inserted. The use of a preposition with a relative pronoun caused confusion to many pupils, including a number from the secondary modern schools. Secondly, conventional language patterns were not known. The most frequent errors were: (1) the use of a single word to express an idea (The child was knocked down while *a car*). (2) errors in grammar, such as nonagreement of subject and verb, incorrect participles and wrong tenses.

6. The compositions in the second English test were analyzed to discover the average length of composition, average length of sentence and types of sentence used. The figures for length of composition are shown in Table I.

In all questions and amongst all pupils the average length of the girls' compositions was greater than that of the boys'. The tendency was for the deaf pupils to produce shorter compositions.

On the whole, the sentences were clearly enough marked off to make the count reliable and the classification straightforward, but there were instances of incomplete or unclassifiable expressions which had to be excluded from the analysis. The figures for length of sentence are given in Table II.

Variation in average length of sentence was seen to be related to degree of hearing impairment. Differences in sentence length between boys and girls were only apparent amongst severely deaf pupils where the girls' average was rather higher.

Four classes of sentences were distinguished—simple, compound, complex and compound-complex. Table III shows the proportion of different types of sentences used by pupils.

The analysis supported the finding in the first English test that degree of hearing impairment was an important factor in the complexity of written ex-

TABLE I

AVERAGE NUMBER OF WORDS PER COMPOSITION FOR BOYS AND GIRLS IN EACH HEARING LOSS GROUP

Question No.	Hearing Loss Greater Than 75 db.		Hearing Loss Less Than 75 db.		Secondary Modern	
	Boys	*Girls*	*Boys*	*Girls*	*Boys*	*Girls*
1	103.1	133.8	92.2	144.6	116.0	126.3
2	57.6	68.7	64.1	74.0	84.0	87.2
3	41.3	47.9	52.9	60.4	51.7	61.2

TABLE II

THE AVERAGE LENGTH OF SENTENCES FOR BOYS AND GIRLS IN EACH HEARING
LOSS GROUP

Question No.	Hearing Loss Greater Than 75 db.		Hearing Loss Less Than 75 db.		Secondary Modern Pupils	
	Boys	Girls	Boys	Girls	Boys	Girls
	Average number of words per sentence					
1	8.6	9.4	11.1	11.3	14.0	13.8
2	8.87	9.8	11.57	11.84	14.4	14.1
3	8.83	10.42	11.8	11.8	15.8	16.2

TABLE III

PROPORTION OF DIFFERENT TYPES OF SENTENCES USED

Type of Sentence	Hearing Loss Greater Than 75 db.	Hearing Loss Less Than 75 db.	Secondary Modern Pupils
	Percentage of each type of sentence		
Simple.....................	74	56	34
Compound...............	12	15	19
Complex..................	11	21	31
Compound-Complex........	3	8	16

pression. The pupils with impaired hearing used twice as many simple sentences as the secondary modern pupils. Three quarters of all sentences written by severely deaf pupils were simple sentences; approximately half the sentences produced by partially hearing pupils and a third of those produced by the secondary modern pupils were of this type. Pupils with losses less than 75 db used twice as many complex and compound-complex sentences as those in the other hearing loss group.

Enumeration was found to be a feature of many compositions produced by severely deaf pupils. It occurred even in some of the better ones, i.e., Girl, 16·4, 100 db. "My home have four windows and a door at the front of a house, three windows and a door at the right side, five windows at the back." In the worst there was merely a list of nouns or a string of echoic sentence patterns, i.e., Boy, 14·0, 105 db. "I have television, table, cat, bicycle, chair, flower and stool."

There was a tendency amongst the severely deaf pupils to describe or narrate in minute detail. In some instances, when beginning to write about "A day in my holiday," pupils would explain that they got up, washed, dressed, went downstairs, had breakfast, got in the car—a series of minor details which hearing pupils in the age range would take for granted.

Although some writers did not follow a recognizable pattern of English, it was usually possible, with a back-

ground of language experience, to interpret what the writers were trying to
say. In some compositions written by
severely deaf pupils confusion of
word order suggested translation from
a nonsyntactical sign language. Boy,
15·0, 85 db. "My bicycle from Christmas home at out play time pay shops
£18 19s. 6d. 36 week. Father by pay
bicycle shops."

Errors in grammar and construction
were found in the compositions of all
pupils but were more common amongst
the severely deaf. Articles and prepositions were omitted or were included
when they were not required. In some
sentences the wrong preposition was
used. It was apparent that the majority of pupils understood the function
and were able to use successfully, the
present, past and future tenses, but
there were many instances where incorrect forms of verbs were used. Irregular verbs, participles and the infinitive
were frequent sources of error.

Almost half the pupils with impaired
hearing were able to compose a letter
which was regarded as adequate. Of
the others, the main criticisms would
be social immaturity and lack of experience (practical or verbal) of the situations with which the letters dealt.

7. A large proportion of all the pupils showed a skill in the simple arithmetical processes (four rules); the majority gave no indication of ability in
more advanced work. Over half
showed little evidence of knowledge of
reduction and of tables of weight,
length, etc.; between two thirds and
three quarters were apparently unable
to deal with fractions, decimals and the

more difficult processes. There was little variation between the performance
of pupils in the two hearing loss groups
but such difference as existed was in
favor of the severely deaf pupils.

The majority of those tested were
able to deal successfully with simple
arithmetical problems. Far more errors were attributable to lack of understanding than to mistakes in calcu-
lation. In a problem about the cost of
fencing a plot of land, the length of
one side was given as the answer or
was multiplied by two or three; some
pupils multiplied the length by the
breadth, showing confusion between
this process and area.

8. Variation in test performance
among schools was investigated. The
results support K. P. Murphy's findings
(Murphy, 1956) of a wide scatter of
test scores from school to school and
his conclusion that these differences in
attainment cannot be explained entirely by variations in intelligence or
degree of hearing impairment. There
was little variation in performance between day and resident pupils. Those
with moderate impairments of hearing who were resident in schools catering for both deaf and partially hearing children tended to obtain lower
scores in English.

Discussion and Conclusions

1. The marked difference in English
attainments between severely deaf
girls and boys is confirmed by Myklebust (1960). The explanation may be
that, for the handicapped, the psychological changes of adolescence are

delayed and, therefore, boys remain linguistically inferior to girls until a later age.

2. The similarity of performance of the fourteen- and fifteen-year age groups may be partly accounted for by the organization of educational provision. Many schools are so small that it is not possible to arrange a system of streaming; brighter children may reach the top class at the age of twelve to fourteen years and complete their school career there. As they are working alongside older pupils with less ability and poorer attainments, they may lack the stimulus of competition and may accept the standards of their classmates. Unless they have a teacher enterprising enough to plan progressive schemes of work to suit individual requirements and to keep pupils interested and working to capacity, there will be the danger of educational stagnation.

It seems unlikely that secondary education for pupils with impaired hearing will be fully implemented until it is organized in separate schools for primary and secondary age ranges. This would make possible staffing ratios and scales of equipment appropriate to the secondary stage of education. It would encourage the use of methods appropriate to adolescents which would give reality to the work done in school and thus provide motivation to higher standards of attainment. One way would be to provide specialist courses of the type used in many secondary modern schools.

3. Results in arithmetic suggest that the elementary processes are receiving too much attention to the neglect of more advanced subjects which would be of greater interest to older pupils.*

Teachers are seeking to obtain perfection in fundamental processes before venturing further. Three points arise from this:

(a) The need for careful consideration about what is fundamental in arithmetic. A number of topics appear to owe their inclusion in the curriculum to the influence of tradition rather than to their intrinsic importance.

(b) Constant revision and consolidation of basic processes are likely to lead to frustration and lack of interest.

(c) Arithmetic at the secondary stage could be given a greater sense of purpose by being linked to other subjects of the curriculum.

4. Educational environment is an important factor in the standards of achievement of all children; it is of special consequence to those with impaired hearing. Normal children learn a great deal incidentally outside the school environment. Much of this incidental learning and especially that which is dependent on auditory clues are denied to the deaf child and the school has to make good the deficiency. It is to be expected, therefore, that differences between the quality of education provided will have greater effect in schools for hearing-impaired children. Some factors which may influence the quality of education are:

(a) Historically, most of the earlier schools were institutes for the deaf and dumb where the aim was to fit pupils to earn a living principally by semi-

* Min. of Ed. 1958.

skilled forms of labor. Some schools have inherited accommodation and physical conditions which are far from satisfactory.

(b) It was partly as a result of private effort that secondary education, in the first place for selected pupils, began to be developed. More recently nonselective secondary schools have been established but at the time of the investigation most pupils were not receiving a specific secondary education.

(c) The wide scatter of results amongst schools may reflect the lack of generally accepted standards for pupils with impaired hearing. Their attainments have been measured against norms for the unhandicapped. This has tended to emphasize retardation rather than to focus attention on positive achievements. It is hoped that the analysis of the results of the tests in the present investigation will serve to make more widely known the attainments of such pupils.

(d) Recent research (Ewing, 1957, 1960) has indicated the importance for pupils with impaired hearing of the provision of auditory experience in furthering linguistic development and general educational progress. At the time of this investigation there were considerable differences among schools both in the amount of electronic equipment available and in the efficiency with which such equipment was used.

It is not suggested that attainments in English and arithmetic—or indeed, in other subjects—are or ought to be the sole criteria of educational achievement. Modern thinking rightly stresses the importance of the school in providing for personality, social, physical and emotional development and for helping the handicapped to adjust to their disability; but, in a literate society, those with hearing impairments need to achieve adequate standards of communication (both spoken and written) if they are to integrate fully into that society.

References

1. Ewing, A. W. G. (Ed.): *Educational Guidance and the Deaf Child*. New York, Manchester Div., Barnes & Noble, 1957.
2. ——— (Ed.): *The Modern Educational Treatment of Deafness*. New York, Manchester Div., Barnes & Noble, 1960.
3. Ministry of Education: *Pamphlet No. 38– Teaching Mathematics in Secondary Schools*. London, H.M.S.O., 1958.
4. ———: *Education in 1958*. London, H.M.S.O., 1959.
5. Murphy, K. P.: A Survey of the Intelligence and Abilities of Twelve-year-old Deaf Children. Unpublished thesis, Manchester University, 1956.
6. Myklebust, H. R.: *The Psychology of Deafness*. New York, Grune, 1960.
7. Wollman, D. C.: Some Problems Involved in the Application of Secondary Modern Education for Deaf Pupils. Unpublished thesis, Manchester University, 1961.

EVALUATIONAL LANGUAGE PROCESSES IN THE DEAF*

RICHARD L. BLANTON AND JUM C. NUNNALLY

Concepts designating affective and evaluational processes are of special interest to students of the learning of language. The experiences designated by such terms usually lack precise external referents and should therefore present special difficulties in learning. It has been suggested that a child learns an evaluational term, i.e., *nice*, by having his own affective reactions identified and labelled by another person as well as by observing the expressive language of the other as he designates his own feeling states (Church, 1961). Since such learning would be very difficult for a deaf child, we would expect that deaf Ss would have a smaller vocabulary of evaluational and affective words and would have greater difficulty in employing them accurately than in using words by which observable objects and actions are designated. In support of this inference, the present authors found, in a study of some aspects of cognitive and language processes in the deaf

* Report of research partially supported by a grant (RD-846p) from Research and Demonstration Projects, Vocational Rehabilitation Administration. Reprinted by permission from *Psychological Reports*, Southern Universities Press, Missoula, Montana, 1964, 15: 891–894. The authors who are attached to the Department of Psychology, Vanderbilt University, are indebted to Carey Duncan and Margaret Trippe for aid in collection of the data, to Archer P. Bardes and W. Lloyd Graunke of the Tennessee School for the Deaf, and to W. C. Yates, Carl Owens, Milton Lillard, Barry Sutton, Virginia Hill, and Pearl English of the Williamson County Schools.

(Blanton and Nunnally, 1964), that deaf children choose fewer evaluational associations to words in a forced-choice measure of associational aspects of meaning, the Semantic Habits Test (Nunnally and Flaugher, 1963), than do control Ss. This technique requires S to choose the response he prefers to a stimulus word where two response alternatives of differing types are given. For example, *STAR:* —— *bright* —— *beautiful* pits a detail or property response against an evaluative or affective one. It was concluded that in comparison to hearing Ss, the deaf have weak tendencies to employ evaluative responses.

In the same study, a measure was obtained of Locus of Control, the tendency to attribute responsibility for the occurrence of events to other persons and external forces rather than personal action of the subject. This device was developed as a test for children by Bialer and Cromwell (Bialer, 1961). It consists of items such as: When nice things happen to you, is it only good luck? The deaf were found to attribute, to a significantly greater degree than controls, the responsibility for events to external, rather than personal or internal causes. Subsequent to this earlier research, an additional scale has been developed to measure attribution of evaluational responsibility. Miller (1963) has standardized a scale, which he calls the Locus of Evaluation Scale, as an adjunct to the Locus of Control measure. Illustrative items are: 1. Is it easy to decide who's right when you're umpire or referee? 2. Is it best to ask the other kids who does the best work in class? Credit would be given for a positive answer to the first question and a negative answer to the second, so that the higher the score, the more "internal" the locus of evaluation.

In summary, then, locus of evaluation is defined as the extent to which an individual has internalized a set of standards by which to judge actions or events or is dependent upon an external frame of reference. Locus of control is defined as the extent to which an individual perceives himself as being in control of environmental events or at the mercy of external forces. The scales have been standardized on children ten years through thirteen years of age (fourth through eighth grades.)

The present paper reports results from a readministration of the Locus of Control Scale and from the initial administration of the Locus of Evaluation Scale to deaf adolescents and controls. It was hypothesized that the relatively weak associative strength of evaluational terms in the deaf would be paralleled by tendencies to externalize responsibility for the evaluation of events.

Method

The Locus of Control and Evaluation Scales were administered without time limits to 137 deaf Ss at the Tennessee School for the Deaf at Knoxville and to 302 hearing control Ss obtained from the schools in Williamson County, Tennessee. There were fifty-six deaf males and eighty-one deaf females, no S being used who had less than an 80-db hearing loss in the best ear. Oral speech was not measured for these Ss nor was lipreading ability. Ss communicated principally by signing. Mean reading achievement was grade 4.56, $SD = .82$. Controls included 144 males and 158 females, a population judged to represent a cross section of Tennessee adolescents on socioeconomic and intellectual variables.

Academic achievement was comparable in the two groups, though the deaf were lower in reading and much more variable than the controls. Stanford Achievement test scores were available on the deaf Ss, with reading standard score mean $= 38.14$, $SD = 8.67$, battery $Mdn = 46.69$, $SD = 11.64$. Metropolitan Achievement test scores were available for the controls, with mean reading $= 51.82$, $SD = 6.81$, and battery $Mdn = 48.11$, $SD = 9.26$. Since the reading difficulty of the Locus of Control Scale is very low, it is felt that the differences in reading achievement would not bias the results of the testing in any serious way. The deaf were, however, older on the average. Mean age for the deaf was 16.77 and for the controls 14.72.

Results

Means, standard deviations, and values of t for all groups by sex are given in Table I. As can be seen, the deaf Ss do show a more external locus of evaluation, the difference being slightly greater for girls than for boys.

TABLE I
MEANS AND STANDARD DEVIATIONS

Groups	Deaf		Normal		t	p
	M	σ	M	σ		
			Males			
Evaluation	10.21	2.52	13.52	3.31	7.56	<.001
Control	12.61	2.16	15.72	3.55	7.48	<.001
			Females			
Evaluation	9.65	2.69	13.54	3.15	9.92	<.001
Control	12.72	2.10	17.27	3.65	12.17	<.001

The t for difference between the means of deaf and normal Ss without regard to sex is 12.47, a highly significant difference. The previous finding of an external locus of control in the deaf is confirmed by these data. There is apparent proportionality between the means and standard deviations in the case of the latter scale, and Bartlett's test for homogeneity of variance yields an F value of 2.98, which is significant at the .05 level. Even doubling the probability value, however, would not reduce the statistical significance of the difference obtained.

Discussion

Our results support the idea that the deaf not only have a weaker pool of evaluative terms and associations, but feel inadequate to make meaningful evaluative judgments and tend to rely on others for such discriminations. This is accompanied by the general pattern of behavioral dependency which is shown in the Locus of Control Scale and which has been commented upon by other writers. Perhaps the more important question concerns the relationship of the reservoir of evaluational terms and associations to actual evaluative behavior in daily life. Those who feel that normal evaluative discrimination may depend upon a well-developed reservoir of evaluational terms and network of associations by which they are related may find in our data possibilities for the further study of the problem.

Summary

Locus of Control and Evaluation Scales were administered to 137 deaf Ss at the Tennessee School for the Deaf and to 302 control Ss from the public schools of Williamson County, Tennessee. The results strongly supported the hypothesis that the deaf rely very heavily on others for evaluative judgments as well as behavioral decisions. The data were consistent with the frequently made observation that the deaf adolescent is more immature and dependent both in educational level and social-emotional growth. The problem of the importance of evaluational vocabulary for evaluational judgments was discussed.

References

1. BAILER, I.: Conceptualization of success and failure in mentally retarded and normal children. *J Personality,* 29:303–320, 1961.
2. BLANTON, R. L., and NUNNALLY, J. C.: Semantic habits and cognitive style processes in the deaf. *J Abnorm Soc Psychol,* 68:397–402, 1964.
3. CHURCH, J.: *Language and the Discovery of Reality.* New York, Random, 1961.
4. MILLER, O.: Role Perception and Reinforcement in Discriminating Learning among Culturally Deprived and Non-deprived Children. Unpublished doctoral dissertation, George Peabody College for Teachers, 1963.
5. NUNNALLY, J. C., and FLAUGHER, R. L.: Correlates of semantic habits. *J Personality,* 31:192–202, 1963.

SEMANTIC HABITS AND COGNITIVE STYLE PROCESSES IN THE DEAF*

RICHARD L. BLANTON AND JUM C. NUNNALLY

Several measures of associative patterns, cognitive styles, and attitudes toward self and others were obtained on 173 deaf adolescents and 178 normal controls. Results show reduced tendencies of the deaf to use evaluational concepts in association, but greater tendencies to devalue self and others. Deaf girls are much like deaf boys in associative and evaluational responses. Several possibilities for the study of implicit language processes in deaf and normal *S*s are suggested.

Since the mediation of symbolic functions is, at least initially for most subjects, principally auditory, we would expect that the deaf, because of differences in the cue patterns of symbolic responses, would have media-

* This research was supported by a research grant from the Office of Vocational Rehabilitation, Grant No. RD-846p-62.

The authors are indebted to: Margaret Aldridge for assistance in collection of the data; Archer P. Bardes and W. Lloyd Graunke of the Tennessee School for the Deaf; Isabelle Walker and R. T. Baughman of the Kentucky School for the Deaf; and W. C. Yates, Carl Owens, Milton Lillard, Barry Sutton, Virginia Hill, and others of the Williamson County Schools.

Reprinted with permission from the *Journal of Abnormal and Social Psychology,* Vol. 68, No. 4, April, 1964.

tional reactions which differ from those of normals. Hence, we might expect differences in thought and cognition to occur. Max (1937) showed that muscle tensions occur in the fingers rather than the throats of deaf subjects during implicit speech.

Some of the more interesting aspects of this problem have not been studied because of the lack of methods for studying language behavior in general. During the past ten years, however, a number of new techniques have emerged (Saporta, 1961) and have made possible some new approaches to the study of language and thinking in the deaf. The study reported here was an effort to explore the utility of some of these methods and develop some leads for further study.

Since the deaf do acquire language and frequently learn to read both printed words and speech movements, one may study associative patterns and preferences, the connotative meaning of relevant concepts, and other symbolic and cognitive processes. Patterns of differences obtained from such data may suggest interesting possibilities for the study of cognitive and social worlds of the deaf, and leads for the study of language in general.

Our purpose in the present study was to examine differences in the performance of deaf subjects on a series of tasks designed to measure associational and connotative aspects of language and cognitive processes in the hope that useful data might be obtained for designing more intensive studies of these phenomena in persons with other sensory and motor deficits as well as in normal subjects.

Method

Subjects

The deaf subjects were 173 children and adolescents from the Tennessee School for the Deaf, Knoxville, and the Kentucky School for the Deaf, Danville. There were eighty-one males and ninety-two females. Normal controls, eighty-three males and ninety-five females, were obtained from the Williamson County, Tennessee, schools, a population which represents reasonably well a cross section of Tennessee adolescents on socioeconomic and intellectual variables. Mean IQ of the deaf on the 130 subjects for whom data were available was 95.8 for males and 93.7 for females, the tests used almost exclusively were WAIS and WISC Performance scales. The IQ for the controls was 92.5 for males and 97.7 for females, estimated by the Lorge-Thorndike Test Level 5, Form A. Standard deviations were in all cases

slightly smaller than for the standardization population of the tests.

Hearing losses for the deaf subjects were in all cases severe, no subject being used who had less than an 80-decibel loss in the best ear, a common criterion for diagnosing total deafness.

Measures Obtained

SEMANTIC HABITS. Preliminary investigation has shown (Nunnally and Flaugher, 1963) that there are reliable individual differences in preferred patterns of association. Such preferences have been measured by several types of analysis of verbal materials, yielding typical forms of semantic relations among words. When subjects are asked to make responses that define, describe, categorize, or depict personal reactions to a named or exhibited object, they may respond with words indicating personal evaluation or dispositional relevance, i.e., "pretty," or "unpleasant." They may, instead of responding with positive or negative evaluations, give denotative or attributive responses, i.e., "blue," or "round," or categorical ones, i.e., "fruit," or "animal." These four types of responses, positive evaluations, negative evaluations, detail responses, and categorical responses, seem to be common types among normal adults. They have been studied by analysis of free verbal behavior, written material, and multiple-choice responses.

The method used in this study was a forced-choice one in which common responses are paired in a forced-choice item (Nunnally & Flaugher, 1963). When the subject is forced to choose between one association to the word and another, he may display consistency in his preference for evaluative associations, i.e., when these are paired with detail or conceptual associations. Illustrative items are:

     Knife: —— weapon —— dangerous

and

     Star: —— distant —— lovely

In these examples, categorical and detail responses, respectively, are compared with negative and positive evaluations. Scores based on such preferences are related to a number of other measures of individual differences (Nunnally and Flaugher, 1963) but are, in the present study, attempts to index preferred "routes" of silent language. The test consists of 143 items, and is scored for total positive evaluation (E+), total negative evaluation (E−), and for preference for detail over categorical associations (D/C).

SEMANTIC DIFFERENTIAL. The utility of the semantic differential in many forms for measurement of aspects of symbolic processes and meaning is well known. It is also useful in studying interpersonal judgments and attitudes (Nunnally, 1961). We used scales designed to measure Adjustment (A), Evaluation (E), Understandability (U), and Potency (P). The scales employed have been shown to vary systematically with personality variables as well as with objects scaled. Subjects in our study scaled five concepts: my parents, me, the future, deaf people, and blind people. The sample of concepts was intended to elicit a wide range of meaningful variations in

attitudes with respect to the self and others as well as typical differences in the connotative meanings assigned to concepts in general.

GOTTSCHALDT FIGURES. On the hypothesis that loss of one sensory dimension might result in compensatory development in another, we would expect an increase in some visual skills in the deaf, especially those involving exploration and detection in which skills of auditory monitoring are not important. On the other hand, conflicting or competing cues, resulting in tension in the subject, might lead to greater dependence on irrelevant information and possibly greater "field dependence" or "conformity" in judgment (Witkin, Lewis, Hertzman, Machover, Meissner, and Wapner, 1954). Since the Gottschaldt Figures (GF) test is positively correlated with measures of "field dependence" obtained by rod and frame, we included it in our battery. It might, however, because of the visual skill required, show whether the compensatory notion is more correct. The form used was developed by Thurstone (1944), contains seventy-two items and requires fifteen minutes of the subject's time. Score is total number of wrong choices.

LOCUS OF CONTROL. It might be expected that lack of an important source of behaviorally relevant cues would render the subject less able to interpret ambiguous situations and increase his uncertainty in choosing between alternatives. This would be expected to cause greater dependency on other persons or, by way of compensation, a greater tendency to externalize responsibility, attribute responsibility to "chance" occurrences, etc. The test used (Locus of Control—LC) was developed as an experimental form by Bialer (1961) and contains twenty-three items such as, "When nice things happen to you, is it only good luck?"

CATEGORY WIDTH. One of our concerns was to determine whether the deaf subject, as a result of the absence of auditory sense, shows any restriction in his conception of the range of events. Again, we may reason that absence of relevant sensory cues may result in differences in concept learning so that the subject's conception of the boundaries of categories or the score of concepts may be different. For this purpose, we used the Category Width (CW) test developed by Pettigrew (1958). Items measure the extent to which subjects attribute to common events a wide range or a narrow range of variability in size, frequency, etc. The test contains twenty items.

Testing Procedure

All tests were untimed, except for the GF for which fifteen minutes were allowed. The tests were administered to small groups, the deaf subjects being tested by workers skilled in communication with the deaf, and care was taken to see that each subject understood the task instructions.

Results

The data were examined by *t* test for differences between means and by correlational analysis. Since previous studies have shown sizable differences

between sexes on most of the measures used, the data were examined separately by sex. Means, standard deviations, and *p* values for the differences between means are given in Table I. It will be noted that standard deviations are quite comparable for all groups on all measures. It may, therefore, be assumed that our groups were able to perform the tasks so as to yield relatively homogeneous variation. This gives us some confidence in the generalizations we are able to make from the data.

TABLE I

MEANS AND STANDARD DEVIATIONS

	Deaf		Normal		
	$\overline{X}$	σ	$\overline{X}$	σ	t
Males					
D/C	15.56	3.80	14.95	4.67	.91
ΣE+	17.74	5.66	20.06	5.00	2.76*
ΣE−	19.69	3.93	19.78	4.29	.14
CW	97.90	17.76	102.90	18.57	1.75
LC	13.23	2.49	14.08	3.01	1.96*
GF	16.57	6.10	18.58	5.70	2.17*
Females					
D/C	14.10	3.91	16.51	4.87	3.70**
ΣE+	17.36	5.72	22.27	6.26	5.57**
ΣE−	20.22	3.87	21.62	4.93	2.15*
CW	96.67	18.95	92.92	17.24	1.40
LC	13.38	2.12	15.34	2.53	5.73**
GF	19.62	5.33	19.11	5.97	.61

Note.—D/C = detail/category, E+ = positive evaluations, E− = negative evaluations, CW = category width, LC = locus of control, GF = Gottschaldt Figures.
* $p < .05$.
** $p < .001$.

It will be noted that the means of the male and female control groups differ significantly on the Lorge-Thorndike Intelligence test, although in absolute terms, the difference is small (5.20).

Since it was conceivable that some of our measures might have such a large correlation with IQ as to produce artifactually significant differences between subjects, a partial correlation analysis was performed on all measures with both groups to remove the effects of correlation with IQ, and the means were estimated independently of their covariance with the IQ tests. The resulting means and correlation coefficients were not different in any noticeable or statistically significant way from those obtained by the original analysis, consequently the original means and standard deviations are presented in Table I.

SEMANTIC HABITS. In the comparison of deaf with normal subjects, we note that deaf boys choose fewer evaluative associations, preferring responses which refer to specific details associated with the stimulus. In their tendency to neglect the evaluative responses, however, it is only positive evaluations which are reduced.

Deaf girls show a similar tendency to neglect evaluative associations in favor of those which are more "objective." In this case, however, both positive and negative associations are significantly fewer.

Differences by sex are statistically significant for normals on all three scales, a finding which was expected (Table II). Deaf girls and boys, however, show similar patterns of performance on the measures of association, although there is a tendency for the deaf girls to prefer categorical associations to detail ones.

TABLE II

MEAN DIFFERENCE SCORES:
MALES MINUS FEMALES

| | *Difference* | | | |
	Deaf	*t*	*Normal*	*t*
D/C	1.46	2.47*	−1.56	2.15*
E+	.38	.44	−2.21	2.60*
E−	− .53	.89	−1.84	2.65*
CW	1.23	.44	9.98	3.68**
LC	− .15	.42	−1.26	2.98*
GF	−3.05	3.46**	− .53	.60

Note: D/C = detail/category, E+ = positive evaluations, E− = negative evaluations, CW = category width, LC = locus of control, GF = Gottschaldt Figures.
* $p < .05$.
** $p < .001$.

There not only is a markedly reduced preference for evaluative associations in the deaf, but this reduction is considerably greater for the deaf girls, normal girls being prone to react to stimulus words evaluatively to a much greater extent than boys (Nunnally and Flaugher, 1963).

LOCUS OF CONTROL. As we expected, locus of control for all female subjects is more internal, regardless of hearing status. The deaf subjects, as expected, show a more external locus of control than do the normals.

CATEGORY WIDTH. Again, our data are marked by large differences between sexes for normals, males having greater width, and an absence of such differences between sexes for the deaf. Comparing deaf with normal subjects, no differences are observed.

GOTTSCHALDT FIGURES. On this task our deaf boys show a marked superiority to normal subjects. Our deaf girls do not differ from the controls, nor do our normals differ between sexes.

SEMANTIC DIFFERENTIAL. These measures were included in order to measure attitudes toward the self and relevant social reference persons as well as attitudes toward the future. The scales were chosen to measure four factors: Adjustment, Evaluation, Understandability, and Potency (Nunnally, 1961). The data are summarized in Table III.

By comparison with normal boys, deaf boys rate almost all concepts less positively on all scales. They see themselves, their parents, and blind persons as less well adjusted and less good than do normal boys. While their view of the future is less optimistic, it is nevertheless seen as more understandable.

By comparison with normal girls, deaf girls, like deaf boys, see themselves and their parents as less good and themselves as less well adjusted. Their view of the future is less optimistic, but again they see it as more understandable. Other handicapped persons are viewed less positively, except that deaf people are seen as comparably well adjusted.

When sex differences are separately considered, we see that deaf girls are, in general, more positive in their ratings on all scales except for potency. Deaf boys rate person concepts as more powerful but as less well adjusted and less good. Between normal males and females, the principal differences occur in the more positive evaluation of parents, the future, and other handicapped persons by the girls. The self and other handicapped are seen as less powerful by normal girls also, a finding which was expected.

An overall finding is that both normal and deaf girls assign higher adjustment and evaluation ratings, normal and deaf boys higher understandability and potency ratings. These are response sets typically observed. The deaf, in general, rate the concepts less positively with the exception of the factor of understanding. To them the concepts rated are more clear and comprehensible, less healthy, and good than to normals.

Discussion

The finding that the deaf respond markedly less than normals to evaluative associations has several interesting implications. It may be due merely to the greater concreteness of the deaf in choosing among response alternatives generally. This would suggest that the deaf are no less interested than normals in the relevance of stimuli for personal well-being, but that *concepts* designating aspects of such relevance play a smaller role in the total repertory of concepts. This is supported by the semantic differential data, which suggest that evaluational behavior is not reduced. If it were only evaluative *concepts* which have lower response strength, we would expect proportionately fewer evaluative responses in a free-association task, a possibility now under study.

TABLE III
MEAN SCALE VALUES BY MEANING FACTORS ON SOCIALLY RELEVANT CONCEPTS FOR DEAF AND NORMAL SUBJECTS

Concept and Subjects	Adjustment	p	Evaluation	p	Understandability	p	Potency	p
My parents								
NM	6.68		7.05		5.59		5.89	
		<.001		<.001				
DM	6.07		6.10		5.40		5.68	
NF	6.96		7.48		5.51		6.07	
		<.001		<.001		<.001		<.001
DF	6.58		6.64		5.61		5.39	
Me								
NM	6.60		6.03		5.17		5.63	
		<.001		<.001				
DM	5.78		5.69		5.07		5.49	
NF	5.82		6.30		4.77		4.78	
		<.001		<.05		<.001		<.001
DF	6.09		5.86		5.47		5.00	
The future								
NM	6.39		6.56		3.75		5.58	
		<.05		<.001		<.001		<.001
DM	5.76		6.03		5.16		5.29	
NF	6.87		7.07		3.71		5.72	
				<.001		<.001		<.05
DF	6.64		6.50		5.34		5.33	
Deaf people								
NM	5.49		6.48		4.59		4.93	
				<.001				
DM	5.41		5.54		4.90		5.43	
NF	5.60		6.80		4.26		4.36	
		<.05		<.001		<.001		<.05
DF	6.13		5.95		5.11		5.14	

Blind people						
NM	5.48		6.34		4.79	4.89
		<.001		<.001		
DM	4.44		5.35		4.70	4.76
NF	5.42		6.61		4.61	4.25
		<.05		<.001		
DF	4.79		5.73		4.93	4.52

Note: NM = normal males, DM = deaf males, NF = normal females, DF = deaf females.

It is also possible that in normal subjects, auditory cues play a crucial role in establishing mediations between evaluative concepts and those denoting detail or categorical aspects of stimuli. Exclamations, ejaculations, expressions of satisfaction and dissatisfaction, approval and disapproval are important behavioral cues in spoken language, and hearing is a most important sensory mode in establishing the behavioral relevance of many other stimulus events. Attentional responses are more easily elicited by auditory than by visual cues, since receptor orientation is less complex and specific. This is especially true for social learning at the human level. It is possible that in the learning of concepts by the deaf, fewer links to the behavioral relevance of the original stimuli become established.

A third possibility is that there may be a correlation between the tendency to give evaluational responses and the age at which a concept is learned. Learning of concepts in early childhood may include proportionately more links to relevance, whereas detail and categorical links may be added later with frequency of use. If dispositional relevance were proportionally more important for a new concept than an old one, we would expect the deaf, for whom all verbal concepts are relatively newer, to show *more* evaluative associations rather than *fewer* ones unless the correlation were to age *per se* rather than recency. Studies of the acquisition of affective responses to objects by children of different ages may provide some evidence for or against this genetic hypothesis.

Our measures of cognitive style, while not intended to cover this area extensively, do provide us with some suggestive leads. If the variable of *field dependence* is validly measured by the Gottschaldt Figures test, then our data suggest that the absence of auditory cues does not make subjects more field dependent—indeed, our male deaf are significantly better at this kind of task due, perhaps, to the compensatory development of visual skills.

The deaf do show a greater tendency to localize responsibility for events externally. This may be due to greater negative feelings toward others generally, an observation supported by the semantic differential data. We note that deaf subjects rate themselves and other persons generally as more maladjusted and less good than do normals. Especially relevant is their perception of blind people as maladjusted and lacking in value. Normal subjects, on the other hand, while rating the deaf and blind as somewhat more maladjusted than themselves, nevertheless do not devalue either group. The tendency to devalue others is understandable in handicapped persons. The congenitally deaf child has great difficulties in social adjustment (Myklebust, 1954, p. 136) and it is understandable that such difficulties would result in a tendency to devalue others. That such tendencies are not completely directed externally is shown by the deaf adolescent's devaluation of self as well. An interesting finding from our scaling data is the security of the deaf child in his understandings. Other persons do not appear to him to be especially complex or confusing, difficulties which normals readily admit. The deaf adolescent has a rather pessimistic view of others and at the same time considerable confidence in its accuracy.

The finding that deaf girls are rather masculine in their cognitive style, semantic habits, and attitude scores also has a number of interesting implications. Normal girls are generally more concerned about social controls and are more passive and compliant. Aggressive behavior among girls is usually verbal rather than physical, and responses are more frequently dispositional than cognitive. It is possible that since these behavior patterns are frequently mediated through speech, deaf girls fail to acquire such patterns to the same extent that normal girls do. This may lead to inability of the mother of the deaf girl, unless she is also deaf, to establish the same pattern of identification with the feminine role, and, consequently, inhibition of masculine behavior tendencies. We are presently examining aspects of the relationship between deaf children and their parents for evidence concerning this possibility.

References

1. BAILER, I.: Conceptualization of success and failure in mentally retarded and normal children. *J Personality, 29*:303–320, 1961.
2. MAX, L. W.: An experimental study of the motor theory of consciousness. IV. Action-current responses in the deaf during awakening, kinesthetic imagery and abstract thinking. *J Comp Psychol, 24*:301–344, 1937.
3. MYKLEBUST, H. R.: *Auditory Disorders in Children.* New York, Grune, 1954.
4. NUNNALLY, J. C.: *Popular Conceptions of Mental Health: Their Development and Change.* New York, Holt, Rinehart, & Winston, 1961.
5. ———, and FLAUGHER, R. L.: Correlates of semantic habits. *J Personality, 31*:192–202, 1963.
6. PETTIGREW, T. F.: The measurements and correlates of category width as a cognitive variable. *J Personality, 26*:532–544, 1958.
7. SAPORTA, S.: *Psycholinguistics: A Book of Readings.* New York, Holt, Rinehart & Winston, 1961.
8. THURSTONE, L. L.: *A Factorial Study of Perception.* Chicago, U of Chicago, 1944.
9. WITKIN, H. A.; LEWIS, H. B.; HERTZMAN, M.; MACHOVER, K.; MEISSNER, P. B., and WAPNER, S.: *Personality Through Perception: An Experimental and Clinical Study.* New York, Harper, 1954.

XIX. Rehabilitation Background

SPECIAL FACTORS IN THE REHABILITATION OF THE DEAF*

JOHN B. RORABACK

One of the most basic needs of man is the ability to communicate with his fellow man. Without the ability to communicate, the individual is sentenced to little more than an animal existence. Without social intercourse, with its give and take, there is little or no opportunity to enrich the character and personality of the individual. The alternative is retreat into an inner citadel complete with moat and drawbridge. The bizarre behavior resulting from such an existence further compounds the problems and frustrations in adjusting to the demands of modern society.

The deaf child is no different from the hearing child in his needs and potentials; it is his environment that is deficient. The absence of the stimulation of sound in general and the sound of the voice in particular results in emotional flatness. One of the chief functions of sound in human life is the excitation of feelings and creation of moods. Without this stimulus, the deaf

* Reprint from the January–February, 1963 *Journal of Rehabilitation*, official publication of the National Rehabilitation Association, and with consent of the author who is Supervisor of Training, Division of Vocational Rehabilitation, Michigan State Department of Education.

child's identity with his surroundings is considerably lessened, with depression often resulting.

By contrast, the hearing child can gain a considerable part of the knowledge he needs for independent living simply by listening. In fact, he will learn much without any effort at all. His exchange of views, his insight into how others think and feel, and his understanding of the motives and behavior of his fellows, he owes almost entirely to his ability to communicate orally. To the hearing person, language is vibrant, colorful and alive. To the deaf, it is a cold, mechanical tool—at best devoid of the values derived from intonation, stress and inflection.

The hearing person is always identified with his environment through sound; he is never alone. He is part of the life around him. He belongs. The child born profoundly deaf misses all these blessings of communication with his environment and his fellow man. He is not a part of the world of sound which inspires poets to a lifetime of work and often sacrifice. He is not a part of the world which expends great effort, time, and money in support of our cultural heritage. The enrichment of the inner self derived from drama and music is denied him.

Academically, he is denied the basic tool with which to work—language. The deaf child does not learn that there are such things as words until he enters school. He laboriously learns that things and activities—and even he—have a name. With such a poverty of resources imagine, if you can, the frustration in learning the meanings of abstractions, and the time and patience demanded.

Reading, being based on "hearing" language, presents a particularly frustrating experience for the deaf person. The hearing person, as he learns to read, has already built up a substantial reservoir of knowledge of the world around him. He has learned in the normal course of events, quite effortlessly, many facts about his environment and about the behavior of his fellow man. He has learned something of the mores of his society. He has made adjustments and some beginnings in the development of his own character and personality. The major share of this he has learned without studied effort, through benefit of his hearing. His parents' warmth, acceptance, and disapproval he has realized primarily through his hearing organs. The cumulative effect of such an ongoing barrage on the mind is immeasurable. Certainly, we know that to be deprived of this advantage is a serious handicap.

Without benefit of normal everyday enrichment, the deaf child must laboriously pick away at the elements of language while attempting to grasp the continuity. It is almost impossible for hearing persons to appreciate the demands upon the deaf child's mind and spirit.

Consider the imposing mass of knowledge to be learned. Working at such a disadvantage, the profoundly deaf learner cannot keep pace with his hearing peers. Mentally, socially, and emotionally, an imposing lag exists between what the deaf pupil knows and has experienced, and what he should know and should be experiencing for his age. As he grows older, the gap will widen unless his language ability keeps pace with his needs.

As a result of the poverty of his background, the young deaf adult comes to the rehabilitation counselor underdeveloped, uninformed, misinformed, naive, sensitive, and sometimes bitter. His behavior is often strange and difficult to cope with. Without some appreciation of the reasons for his strangeness, the counselor has little prospect of understanding him and counseling him effectively.

Professionals who have devoted many years of their lives to the deaf find it difficult to cross the moat and they, too, often fail. How then can those less oriented hope to accomplish much? The only answer seems to lie in a humble attitude, a supreme effort at understanding the problems, dedication, patience, and acceptance of small gains. If we concern ourselves first with the difficulties experienced by the deaf in their interpersonal relationships, social adaptability, and job attitudes, we will be attacking the problem logically —since these are of far greater importance than the mere lack of vocational skills.

Social attitudes which operate to the detriment of the deaf do not all come from the limits of their ability to adjust to others. The attitudes of hearing co-workers and employers leave much to be desired. In some shops the deaf worker is still the court buffoon of the middle ages. Fellow workers sometimes lead the naive deaf worker into anti-social behavior which can result in loss of his job. His lack of information about social habits, customs, and usage can make him the victim of costly pranks. Such attitudes engender anger which can result in physical violence; the deaf cannot release their feelings through words and so strike out through unacceptable behavior.

In working with the young deaf adult the rehabilitation counselor is faced with a problem too often overlooked—disturbed parents. The deaf child frequently is rejected or perhaps overprotected and not allowed to develop his potential. The defensive attitudes of the parents of deaf children often seal the door to the latter's development. The deaf child perceives the truth through the surface display of concern and affection. He knows that he has not measured up. He then proceeds to build his own little world of egocentricity. His own needs become paramount. He seeks the emotional sustenance, denied by his parents, from others.

Throughout the entire rehabilitation counseling process, from initial interview to the ultimate end—satisfactory employment—runs the tenuous thread

of personal adjustment. Essential to personal adjustment are self-perception and the individual's attitude toward his disability, his family, his friends, and his society.

All this, of course, is intimately related to his family's attitude. In working with the family, the counselor must discover these attitudes. Are the parents overprotective, rejecting, hostile to society? Do they suspect exploitation when their son earns nothing in an on-the-job training situation? Do they realize the need for, and try to help their son develop, maturity, self-reliance, and the stamina to adjust to new situations? Can they and will they help him adjust to moving to a different area and living alone, apart from the family?

Realizing the limitations imposed by an impoverished command of language, the counselor can do much to help the client destroy the barriers created by society's lack of understanding of the problem.

First, the client must realize the implications of limited language in job and adjustment. A deaf worker must have enough understanding of language to comprehend directions and communicate intelligibly with his co-workers and employer. He must understand the terminology of his trade. He must understand the basic facts of job-holding with its responsibilities and benefits, and the need for flexibility in getting along with others; he must know what cooperation is.

In effect the counselor takes over where the educator leaves off. He must continue to cultivate in his client understanding and the development of acceptable attitudes so essential to vocational success.

As counselors, our basic aim is to learn to understand the client's thinking. In order to communicate, we must become familiar with the language usage of the deaf person and grasp the content and level of language regardless of its eccentricity. Such understanding will cue us on the language we must use to convey our own ideas. Authorities on Basic English have demonstrated that any idea outside the realm of science can be expressed in a vocabulary of 850 words. Why, then, not avoid words such as *employer, cooperation, social adjustment,* etc., when communicating with the deaf? Granted, we will be frustrated in gearing our language to a fourth-grade vocabulary, but with whose frustration are we concerned?

Finally, let's avoid questions that encourage a "yes" or "no" answer. Out of defensive pride, the deaf will often respond "yes" or "no" without really understanding the question. Questions that demand a statement or at least a phrasal answer will reveal whether or not the respondent has understood.

The counselor can further equip himself for the task of counseling if he has some knowledge of signing and manual spelling. The deaf person feels that here is someone interested enough to learn his language in order to communicate with him. The values in establishing rapport are prodigious. Even though the counselor may not have great proficiency, the impact remains, and confidence and cooperation are quickly heightened. Part of this, no

doubt, emerges from the fact that the deaf client gains a feeling of status in being able to manage his own interview without the need to lean on an interpreter.

One of the greatest and most frequently overlooked needs of a client who is detaching himself from his family is a deterrent to loneliness and homesickness; this is especially true of the deaf. This can be a definite threat to an away-from-home training program.

In this area of counseling, a more directive approach is often necessary. In addition, others can advantageously be brought into the picture to encourage the client in social mingling and participation in recreation and sports. This might be engineered with members of the local community or fellow workers at the place of employment. Its importance cannot be minimized as the feeling of belonging is so vital to stability and persistence on a new job with its demands for adjustment to the work environment. Surely everyone would agree that interpersonal relationships with fellow employees is basic to full acceptance of the job. It is incumbent, then, on the counselor to promote this in every way he can.

He can accomplish this by stimulating participation in company activities such as bowling and baseball teams, picnics, and Christmas parties. This goal can be realized most effectively working indirectly through the immediate supervisor and fellow workers. Such social mingling is invaluable in breaking down misunderstanding of the handicapped and can be an effective antidote to taunting, mockery, and buffoonery.

With the temptations of easy credit and installment planning, many people are faced with the problem of overextension of their resources. With personal bankruptcies on the increase in the general population, is it any wonder that proper evaluation and use of personal resources are a problem in counseling the deaf? The thorough counselor cannot ignore this aspect of personal adjustment, for the best rehabilitation plan can be wrecked on the shoals of oppressive indebtedness.

Unless one learns to live within his income, he cannot be happy no matter how suitable his employment may be. The frustration and anxiety growing out of incautious use of credit encouraged by ill-advised installment buying can result in garnishee and sometimes consequent loss of employment. Failing that, a projection of hostility can be directed toward one's job, fellow employees, and employer. This facet of guidance must be particularly well handled since it is so intimately related to the client's personal life.

Not the least important consideration in job adjustment is a full and clear understanding of the job demands. This must include a clear concept of how the individual worker has to work as a team member with his fellow men. What is his role? To whom does he answer? What are the lines of authority? With whom does he have to have good interpersonal relations? What are the attitudes of the other workers toward him? How can he improve these attitudes?

What habits and attitudes must the worker bring to the job? Is he aware of the following most essential qualities: promptness, steady attendance, good personal appearance, cheerful attitude, diligence, and productiveness (with a conscientious regard for both quality and quantity)?

Particularly troublesome for the deaf to understand are certain job elements which, when not adequately explained at the outset, can destroy the entire program. Knowledge of these elements comes easily to the average worker not acoustically handicapped, for he has the opportunity to learn much about them simply by listening from day to day. The major ones are: promotional policy, vacation policy, hours of work (especially when last-minute changes are made), pay fluctuations, change of duties, salary increases, and deductions (hospital and medical insurance, taxes, social security, Community Chest).

Probably the most simple and direct measures to overcome misunderstanding in these areas lie in: (1) assuring a full and complete review at the outset; (2) orienting the supervisor on the limits of communication; and (3) impressing the client with the importance of asking when he is not sure. Cooperation and understanding by fellow workers can be of inestimable value here.

Presuming that he has carefully evaluated the client's assets and determined his goals, the rehabilitation counselor's next task is to clarify with the client the immediate objective—formal training, on-the-job training, or special placement. In every case, the counselor will need to interpret the implications to both client and trainer. Work adjustment problems are many and varied and operate in all of these situations.

Particular emphasis must be placed on interpretation to the employer or trainer on the limitations of communication, the values of pantomime instruction, and the foreseeable misunderstandings which might evolve. If the employer is given some insight into these problems beforehand, they will not come as a shock. They will emerge as a challenge rather than an insurmountable obstacle.

In a larger shop, the foreman and fellow employees should also be oriented. This can forestall many problems of friction and unacceptable behavior.

If the employer and fellow workers are made aware of the fact that the deaf man has something to offer, that he is not unintelligent, and that his behavior results from a deprivation of opportunity, much can be done to smooth the way to mutual understanding.

ESTABLISHMENT OF REHABILITATION UNIT AT THE ARIZONA STATE SCHOOL FOR THE DEAF AND THE BLIND*

Thomas G. Tyrrell

In an effort to provide meaningful services to eligible deaf students so that they can qualify for regular, gainful employment the Arizona Division of Vocational Rehabilitation and the Arizona State School for the Deaf and the Blind have entered into a cooperative agreement.

Mutual concern by school and Division personnel has resulted in the desire to establish and maintain a rehabilitation facility within the school. For the past few years the Rehabilitation Counselor servicing the State School for the Deaf has mostly concerned himself with the senior students. By the time the

* Reprinted by consent from *The Arizona Cactus,* Arizona State School for the Deaf and the Blind, Tucson, December, 1965. The author is Coordinator, Rehabilitation of the Deaf, Vocational Rehabilitation Division, Arizona State Board of Vocational Education.

Rehabilitation Counselor opened the file on the older students they had already completed much of their training. Patterns including high dependency, in some cases on the sheltered environment, were well established and therefore very difficult to modify when adjusting to demands of a specific employer. This system relied heavily on the Rehabilitation Counselor's ability to appraise the individual's potential with some assistance from the evaluations done at the Rehabilitation Center at the University of Arizona. Since there are few tests specifically designed for the deaf, modified and "partial" measurements were utilized to understand something of the person's ability to function. It then depended upon the Counselor's skill to take that information and move toward an occupational objective with the student who was at that time, or shortly would be, moving out of a sheltered school setting into the competitive environment in the community.

By the establishment of the rehabilitation facility within the school, deaf students who are found eligible now get a much earlier evaluation; and school personnel assigned to this facility work under the Vocational Rehabilitation Coordinator to provide continuing evaluation and vocational adjustment to the individual. The concerted vocational rehabilitation program is utilizing the Division of Vocational Rehabilitation, school and community resources to raise the individual skills and functioning abilities to the highest levels in order to eliminate the too frequent under-employment of the deaf.

Of the two-hundred and twenty deaf students enrolled at the Arizona State School for the Deaf, approximately seventy are fifteen years of age and older. Each of these students is referred to the facility for possible services. Before a student can be accepted he must be determined to be eligible by criteria as set forth in the Vocational Rehabilitation State Plan. The eligibility determination is made by the Vocational Rehabilitation Coordinator of the Division of Vocational Rehabilitation who is assigned to this facility. Of thirty-three teachers of the deaf, ten have been selected from within the school to participate in the facility. During the time they are participating in the facility they come under the authority of the Vocational Rehabilitation Coordinator who is in charge of personnel and activities of the facility. Since teachers assigned to the Unit are, in effect, Vocational Rehabilitation personnel, during the time they participate within the facility, they are required to meet Vocational Rehabilitation standards, and as such personnel they are able to receive in-service training given to Vocational Rehabilitation personnel. This permits the facility teachers to receive training which enhances the rehabilitation program and provides curriculum currently not available at the State School.

The Vocational Rehabilitation Coordinator works closely with the Rehabilitation Center at the University of Arizona. This is done to insure maximal effectiveness of the evaluation procedure. By close coordination of evaluation and adjustment activities, the individual is receiving services of a new dimension individually selected and presented to develop his best potentials and thus preconditioning him for employment while still at the school.

A fifteen-year-old at the School for the Deaf has approximately four more years of training before graduation. The most salient advantage of this facility is an early and continuing evaluation and adjustment of the individual student by the Rehabilitation Staff using a total approach. We recognize that advanced medical knowledge has increased the number of survivors of multiple disabilities. Complex considerations and services are necessary. The Rehabilitation Facility provides medical services which the school alone cannot. Early medical evaluations are resulting in the provision of hearing aids and speech therapy which is most beneficial in training for, and maintaining, employment.

Regular staff meetings of all personnel assigned to the Rehabilitation Unit are conducted weekly. Written reports regarding each student's problems and/or progress are submitted to the Vocational Rehabilitation Coordinator to assure that the needs of the individual are being met. The Coordinator now spends whatever time is necessary with the students and teachers within the facility to coordinate the services, instruct personnel in rehabilitation procedure, and to insure the provision of services via the Vocational Rehabilitation Plan.

It is recognized that this Rehabilitation Facility is clearly a new approach and different from the curriculum now provided by the school. Selected teachers are providing Vocational Rehabilitation services under the direction of the Coordinator who is utilizing University and community resources to insure maximal development of skills and broader qualifications for employment. While the regular school program provides for the students' education, the Rehabilitation Facility provides for the vocational evaluation and treatment of their vocational adjustment problems as they occur, using all the facilities in the community to insure that each student upon graduation is as capable as possible of using his capabilities either in more training or in job placement. Upon referral to the Unit the student receives a vocational and psychological

evaluation at the University of Arizona Rehabilitation Center. The results of these evaluations are utilized for curriculum planning and counseling. This early effort initiates the continuing evaluation and adjustment conducted by the Rehabilitation Unit personnel. Early in the senior year the student again returns to the University Rehabilitation Center for more specific vocational evaluation. This latter evaluation permits focusing on specific vocational objectives and permits timely and coordinated rehabilitation services to qualify the student for employment. The new agreement permits the Vocational Rehabilitation Coordinator to spend whatever time is necessary to insure complete follow-up for the graduating student who returns to communities throughout the state. As Coordinator he functions on a state-wide basis, thus permitting him to continue working with persons after they leave the school. Counselors from other district offices receive instructions from the Coordinator and they are able to spend time at the school in order to familiarize themselves with the students who will be returning to various parts of the state upon graduation.

It is much too early to compile any statistical data which could be utilized by other schools and agencies; however, the feeling of enthusiasm on the part of students and faculty members is most encouraging. We believe that this new approach to the total rehabilitation of the deaf population will allow them to achieve a much higher level of vocational and social adjustment.

COMMUNICATION EVALUATION OF THE DEAF AND ITS IMPLICATIONS FOR JOB PLACEMENT*

Emil M. Zabell

From a pragmatic point of view it is assumed that any evaluation for vocational rehabilitation purposes should point to job objectives that are saleable. Depending upon the area in which the client lives, some vocational skills are in demand and others only lead to frustration and failure. Let us follow a typical communication evaluation of a profoundly deaf person and see what are the implications for job placement.

The client now age 29 became deaf when one year old due to the after effects of infantile paralysis. An audiometric examination, dated February 18, 1959, indicated a 95 db loss in the right ear and a 90 db loss in the left ear. He is unable to use an individual hearing aid. The client entered a school for the deaf at age 9 and graduated when he was 21.

The onset of deafness reveals to what extent a client has been exposed to the normal stimuli of sound. It is typical for the profoundly deaf rehabilitation client that he was either born deaf or became deaf prior to age six. Speech normally develops by the age of five or six, and since our profoundly deaf client did not hear or comprehend speech, his own speech did not develop normally. Unfortunately many of the orally trained deaf do not retain their speech and lipreading ability. The deaf

* Presented at the New York State Division of Vocational Rehabilitation Workshop on "Communication with the Deaf" in New York City, January 31, 1962. The author is Director of Psychological Services, The Jewish Society for the Deaf, New York, N. Y.

group seen by vocational rehabilitation counselors is a selective group in which the orally functioning deaf person is the exception.

Assuming we have an applicant who is a good lipreader, our field experiences reveal that this type of worker functions well enough where the questions and answers are routine but must resort to paper and pencil when the discussion becomes involved and technical. However, there is no doubt that the employer feels more at ease with this type of deaf worker.

The client's speech is typical of the deaf in that it lacks inflection and modulation and is nonfunctional with most hearing people. There is evidence of formal speech training but because of disuse, most of his speech is poorly articulated. However when his speech is combined with pantomime or sign language, it becomes useful in communicating with his normally hearing parents, siblings and friends. His lipreading is poor.

Thus we are faced with the problem of training and placing our client in an occupation that does not require speech or hearing. There are many occupations that do not require speech or hearing. However, many of these occupations are denied to the deaf because we have been unable to break down the barriers set up by employers and the public. In some occupations the barriers have been surmounted to some extent. In New York City, the deaf fill many jobs in the printing and garment industries. They operate business machines and many types of power machines, all of which require manual dexterity. On the other hand, large industrial firms will use plant safety rules as an excuse to bar the deaf from any of their jobs. Yet the safety record of the deaf is especially good in plants that have a long history of employment of deaf workers.

Hotels and restaurants also bar the deaf from many jobs because the employer is afraid to expose the public to a deaf employee's inadequate communication. Yet here too there are many jobs in hotels and restaurants that do not require oral communication. More realistically, because of the lack of communication skills, the deaf seldom establish their own commercial and mercantile businesses.

Unfortunately some vocational counselors who lack technical knowledge about the deaf and their vocational qualifications regard the deaf as unemployable and hence only go through the motions of promoting jobs for this type of client. There is still not enough promotion work being done in selling vocational skills of the deaf to employers and until it is done many of the deaf remain unemployable.

Client communicates best with hearing people in writing and with deaf people in sign language. He reads and writes on a fourth grade level.

This means that the client must take training in a vocational skill that does not require intensive textbook work or lectures. Since the average reading level of a deaf adult is between the 3rd and 5th grade, we must assume that the client who has a lower reading level is either mentally retarded or has been denied adequate education. Certainly early deafness is one of the most serious of educational handicaps. The deaf client must learn speech and language primarily through visual clues. He does not think in grammatical sequence and usually writes in a confusing manner, using a sign-language type of grammar which leaves out words he considers nonessential. There is no consistency in the use of syntax.

The education of a deaf person requires additional years of schooling, and in many states the deaf student does not graduate from an institution for the deaf until he is twenty or twenty-one. If he has unusual scholastic abilities, he can, by taking a qualifying examination, continue his education at Gallaudet College for the deaf in Washington, D. C. A few highly-gifted deaf individuals have also attended and graduated from other colleges and universities.

In some cases where the client has not been properly educated, although he has a normal intellectual potential, tutorial assistance in basic English is indicated. This is also true for the foreign-born deaf who must learn how to read and write English. It is unreasonable to expect a foreman to be comfortable about an employee with whom he has little or no means of communication, or must call on a third person to act as an interpreter. The foreman who can use sign language is too rare a person to be counted upon to solve the problem of illiteracy.

There seems to be undue optimism on the part of otologists and vocational counselors as to the significance of residual hearing. Although no cutoff point has been established to determine when residual hearing can be exploited, it is unrealistic to insist that the deaf must wear hearing aids when they cannot hear adequately through amplification. An individual who has residual hearing that was not put to use at an early age will rarely, if ever, in his adult years have the right combination of gross intelligence and motivation that may enable him to endure the long hours of auditory training and speech work necessary to rehabilitate his residual hearing. The degree of deafness is apparently of less consequence than the factors of intelligence, personality and overall aptitude. Too often hearing aids have been given to the deaf but were not used because the aid was not useful or wanted. Too often speech therapy and lipreading lessons have been authorized and the deaf client has wondered why. If a deaf client has not been able to learn to speak and lipread while in school for a period of ten to sixteen years, how much can be expected in thirty lessons given once or twice a week? It has also been the writer's experience that the deaf adult resists this kind of adult education training because he feels he has been in school long enough and is now ready to go to work.

Some of our less literate deaf may be very difficult to place because they make a very poor impression when first seen by the employer. Frequently the client needs to be helped to enter competitive industry by either arranging for an "on the job" training program, or by convincing the employer that the best way to evaluate the deaf applicant is to try him out on the job after a short period of orientation. The foreman who uses written instructions during the breaking-in period is often rewarded by finding that he has a valuable worker on his staff. The foreman must also understand that a deaf worker's language deficit is not a true measure of his intelligence and ability. Mental ability as demonstrated by his use of sign language often far exceeds his limitations in the use of the English language.

The deaf person's educational retardation is primarily due to the slow and difficult task of teaching language. Should this process ever be speeded up, the average deaf person will be able to achieve educational and vocational goals now denied him.

The low reading level of the average deaf client has been an obstinate barrier for the deaf in obtaining Civil Service jobs which they are quite capable of doing. The general written examination given by many Civil Service Commissions has screened out both the inferior and the capable deaf applicants. The Federal Civil Service Test Development Unit is interested in finding suitable tests for deaf applicants to replace the difficult language tests. State and local Civil Service Commissions are also beginning to examine their deaf applicants more realistically.

Language achievement must be considered by the counselors in terms of the language comprehension required by the job. It is poor planning to train a deaf person in a skill for which he shows aptitudes but is at the same time, not saleable. For example, the employer may tell you that he cannot hire your applicant who was trained in camera repair work because "We get many types of cameras for repair and must explain each job order to the worker." If the deaf applicant functions on an adequate language level, then he can handle the job. If he has a low level of language achievement, then time, money and effort have been wasted.

The reading and writing level of the client must also guide the counselor in the kind of language he will use in communicating with the client. Frequently, rather than admit ignorance, your deaf client will agree with you in a stereotype way or will pick a key word out of your question or statement and respond to it as though it was a word-association test. This too has implications in terms of an employer-employee relationship. Many of these clients do quite well on a job providing there is a more literate deaf person working in the same department. Any other job placement will frequently fail to hold up.

Follow-up on job placement of the deaf is important. A deaf person will sometimes leave his job because no one helped him understand his role as a worker. Because he misses the shop talk, he can misunderstand changes that are taking place in the shop. He gives the appearance of being temperamental and uncooperative. Counseling in the shop for the worker can save many a placement from falling apart.

In some instances a deaf worker will not notify his employer when he is ill. It doesn't occur to him to do so because he was not told that this was the right thing to do. Once he understands that this is his responsibility, there is not further trouble on this score.

In the rural areas farming would seem to be a desirable occupation for the deaf. However, there are both social and communicative limitations. The social limitation is the more serious. The deaf person has a need to live and work in the large cities where he can become a member of a deaf society. Thus he is able to marry and live a more normal life among his friends.

The communicative disadvantage for the deaf in farming occupations is simply that they cannot hear the cries of livestock. However, this has not prevented many of the deaf from going into this line of work.

Statistics on the occupations of the deaf can be misleading if you do not look into the subgroups. For example, the professional group when studied closely will reveal only rare examples of professors, doctors, lawyers, dentists, etc. It will show a high per cent of teachers of the deaf. Statistics on the deaf can also be difficult to interpret because it is often difficult to know how to classify various acoustically handicapped individuals. Are they deaf, hard of hearing or progressively deafened?

Despite the limitations which bar the deaf from many jobs, the deaf occasionally succeed in occupations usually denied them. For example, deaf persons have on occasion won distinction as business men, artists and professors. This speaks well for their adaptiveness and perseverance. Finally we must conclude that the deaf are able to compete successfully with hearing workers in those occupations where communication is not a major factor.

XX. The Postschool Prospect

OCCUPATIONS OF THE DEAF*

STANLEY K. BIGMAN

What kind of jobs are held by the deaf? What is their contribution to the nation's economy? What are the conditions of their life and work? How satisfied are they with their economic position?

Questions such as these have received little systematic study. When plans for research on such matters were first broached in 1955, almost twenty years had elapsed since the last previous attempt at large-scale study of the deaf population. In the interim a great many practical questions had arisen to create day-to-day problems for teachers of the deaf, vocational counselors, rehabilitation workers, and welfare agencies, as well as organizations of the deaf themselves. The immediate concerns of these groups furnished the impetus for research.

In April 1956, support was made available by the Office of Vocational Rehabilitation, the National Association of the Deaf, and Gallaudet College.

Obtaining a sample of the adult deaf population was the major technical problem of the survey. Concerning the size and characteristics of that population there is no accurate information. Up to 1959, estimates of the prevalence of deafness were still being made on the basis of figures obtained from the National Health Survey of 1935–36.

Data were gathered by personal interview, using deaf interviewers. The surveyed group was intended to include only the deaf, and to exclude the hard of hearing. This objective was sought without the formulation of a verbal definition or tests. Instead, the deaf field representatives were instructed to interview only persons who were known as deaf by other than deaf persons or who considered themselves deaf. The group obtained was thus defined in sociopsychological, rather than

* This study was supported in part by an OVR Grant. A version of this paper was read at the meeting of the Eastern Sociological Society, Boston, Mass., April, 1960. It may be identified as Publication A-1 of the Office of Social and Environment Research, Gallaudet College, Washington, D. C. It is here reprinted from *Rehabilitation Record*, official publication of the U. S. Vocational Rehabilitation Administration, November–December, 1960.

The author is chief, social studies section, division of occupational health, Public Health Service, U. S. Department of Health, Education, and Welfare. At the time of this study he was director, office of social and environmental research, Gallaudet College, Washington, D. C.

in biological terms; it represents what we may call the deaf community.

In all, 10,101 deaf persons were interviewed during the survey period of 1956–57. Close scrutiny of the procedures and comparison of the survey findings with Census data suggest that the survey respondents were not completely representative of the total deaf population. In all likelihood the survey undersampled the age groups under twenty and over sixty, women, Negroes, and persons at the lowest economic level.

Of the persons interviewed, two thirds were men and most (86%) were between twenty and fifty-nine years of age. Almost all (97%) were white; the few non-whites were mostly (nine out of ten) Negroes. This paper thus deals essentially with white deaf people in the productive period of their lives. Nearly four fifths of the group (7,920 persons) were employed at the time of the survey. About 90 per cent of the men were currently employed; among the women, most of the remainder being housewives.

All respondents reported some schooling. More than 90 per cent had attended state residential schools for the deaf, at which nearly 70 per cent of them had received all of their formal education. About 9 per cent claimed at least one year of college training (compared to 14 per cent of the total population), among white respondents of both sexes. Virtually none of the non-whites reported even one year of college. The number of years of schooling was lowest among the oldest respondents and highest among those in their twenties. As in the population as a whole, the educational level of the deaf has been rising in recent decades.

The deaf community, as identified in this study, turns out to include some persons who are not completely deaf. In the survey group, only half said that they were totally deaf, while one in ten claimed to be able to hear (though not necessarily to understand) some conversation. On the other hand, the deaf community apparently does not include many people who became deaf relatively late in life. Only one per cent of those in the survey reported having become deaf at the age of fourteen or later, while 80 per cent were deaf before the age of six.

To aid in communication at work with hearing supervisors and fellow-employees, the deaf make use of writing, speech, lipreading, and manual techniques of signing and fingerspelling. Over half of the respondents reported that they used two or more of these communication techniques. Writing is apparently relied on most widely; it was used exclusively by about 30 per cent of those in the survey, and in combination with other techniques by over two third. Speech and lipreading were each reported by one in three, signing and fingerspelling by one in six.

Only about 40 per cent claimed that their skill in the difficult technique of lipreading was "enough to understand conversation" or "excellent." These estimates of ability were higher among women than among men, and increased with the age at which deafness occurred.

Mechanical hearing aids were reported used, whether at work or elsewhere, by only about 10 per cent of the respondents.

The deaf were concentrated heavily in skilled and semiskilled manual occupations. Thirty-six per cent of the respondents were classified as craftsmen, foremen and related workers, and a similar proportion as operatives and related workers. These two groups included three fourths of the men (mostly skilled craftsmen) and three fifths of the women (mostly semiskilled operatives.) These figures contrast sharply with those for the total population; about two fifths of all men and one fifth of all women are found at those two occupational levels. As would be expected, relatively few deaf persons occupy professional or technical, clerical or sales positions, in which a premium is placed on communication skills. The lack of such skills may also account for the comparatively small number of deaf persons in service jobs.

Despite the marked concentration just noted, small numbers of deaf people were found in a wide range of occupations. About 400 distinct occupational titles were reported. Relatively large numbers were working as printing craftsmen, teachers, farmers, machine operators, assemblyline workers, and dressmakers and seamstresses.

More than 50 per cent of the employed deaf were in manufacturing industries (contrasted with 25 per cent of the total population.) The industrial strongholds of the deaf were the printing and publishing industries (both newspaper and job shops) and the schools for the deaf.

Individual earnings from wages and salaries were relatively high in survey group: their median of $3,465 was considerably above the national figure of $2,818.

Undoubtedly, the occupational position of the deaf is influenced by the condition of their hearing impairment and the skills they acquire to offset it. There was some evidence to suggest that the age of deafness was highest among farmers and among unskilled laborers, and lowest, among those in professional and technical occupations. On the other hand, those who had become deaf at the age of six or later were relatively twice as numerous among the professionals and the nonfarm owners and managers as among other occupational groups.

Degree of deafness showed only a slight relationship to occupation.

The means of communication used at work showed some variation with occupational level. More methods were reported in use by those in professional and technical positions, and fewer in the less skilled occupations. Professionals used speech more than any other method, and more than any other occupational group. Lipreading was also used by over half of the professional workers, and writing by a similar proportion of professionals. All other groups relied most heavily on writing; for example, more than 70 per cent of craftsmen and of operatives. Manual signs were least often used by clerical and sales workers, most often by service workers and laborers.

Those estimating their own lipreading ability as "good enough to understand conversation" or better varied from a high of 60 per cent among professionals to lows of 30 per cent among laborers and 25 per cent among farmers. These proportions parallel the percentages reporting use of lipreading in communicating at work.

Stability as opposed to mobility in employment was measured crudely by the longest period in a single job during the preceding ten years. It should be emphasized that no value judgment is intended by the use of the terms "stability" and "mobility"; it is not assumed that staying long in a job is either "better" or "worse" than moving from one job to another.

The survey findings suggest that neither age of becoming deaf nor degree of deafness is strongly related to job stability. Those born deaf seem to have moved slightly more than others from job to job, perhaps because relatively many of these persons were in less-skilled occupations. On the other hand, the totally deaf were apparently somewhat more stable in their jobs than those with some residual hearing—which might be due to "better adjustment," or to greater uncertainty about obtaining another job and consequent unwillingness to leave a position. Those who had the least lipreading ability and were able to profit by the use of a hearing aid had a feeling of relative security and a willingness to risk a move from one job to another—feelings perhaps not shared by other deaf persons.

The respondents apparently feel that the hearing persons with whom they come in contact through their jobs are not unfriendly. Asked why they left each of the last three jobs they held, only sixteen out of 8,744 employed during the previous ten years gave prejudice against the deaf as the reason. To a question on the attitude of hearing workers toward them, little more than one per cent replied, "Unfriendly." Less than one per cent of the 7,920 employed reported that they had applied for union membership and been rejected. About a tenth of the 3,225 who were union members claimed that there had been "some difficulty" in admission, though not necessarily because of their deafness.

Opinions of the respondents were solicited on their working conditions, earnings and opportunities for promotion. Conditions and earnings were rated as "Good," "Fair," or "Not Good." Promotion was similarly rated, but there was a fourth alternative, "No promotions in this kind of work." The proportion of respondents answering "Good" were:

Working conditions—about 85 per cent of each sex.

Earnings—about 70 per cent of men, but 60 per cent of women.

Promotion—about 30 per cent of men, but 20 per cent of women.

This dissatisfaction with chances for advancement should be considered together with the minute percentage who left jobs because of prejudice against the deaf.

The general satisfaction of the deaf with the conditions of their employment may be seen from a composite Index of Job Satisfaction constructed from the three items above. On the Index, 70 per cent of the respondents were rated

Very High or High, 16 per cent Medium, and 8 per cent Low or Very Low (the remaining 6 per cent had given incomplete answers). A small but clear relation was shown to exist between a high degree of satisfaction (as measured by the Index) and less than complete hearing loss, lipreading ability described as enough to understand "conversation" or "excellent," and the use of a mechanical hearing aid.

It was possible to compare the occupation which 3,900 respondents had held longest during the preceding ten years with the kind of work for which they would have liked to be trained "if starting all over again." Over half indicated that they would prefer the same job or some other at the same level of skill and status; that is, professionals would like to be trained for professions, craftsmen for skilled crafts, and so on. This was especially true of persons in higher level jobs. Those in the lower prestige and lower-paying occupations expressed a desire for training in crafts, clerical work, or professions.

A collective evaluation of each occupation by those who had worked at it longest was provided by a "Stay vs. Leave" Index—a measure taking into account the numbers desiring to remain and those desiring training in other fields instead. On this Index, which would range from plus 100 (all desiring to stay) to minus 100 (all desiring to leave) the average for all respondents was minus 9.6 showing the prevailing wish to change. Only two groups of occupations showed any real holding power—the printing trade and all the professions except teaching. Marked

contrasts were noted between what the respondents considered the mild attractiveness of the other professions, and the unattractive character of teaching; between, in their opinion, the mild attractiveness of clerical work in general, and the unattractiveness of typing and sales jobs.

A somewhat different perspective is gained by comparing, for the 2,400 who expressed desire for training in a new occupation, the number who would like to leave each field with the number who would like to enter it. Examination of occupational ratings derived from this and the preceding measure shows three groups of occupations:

1. Some attractive both to deaf persons in the field and to those outside (printing trades, and professions other than teaching).

2. Some similarly unattractive (laundry and drycleaning work, sales, miscellaneous operative work, common labor).

3. Some seemingly more attractive to those outside than to those who had worked longest at them (business ownership, typing).

The great magnetism of the printing trade for the deaf may be seen from this statistic: more than 80 per cent of those whose longest job was in that field would enter it again if given a choice. Significantly enough, the occupational group chosen by the largest number of teachers, after teaching itself, was the printing trades.

The survey on which we have reported here was in many respects exploratory. Answering many questions about the experiences and the situation of the deaf, it has raised a great many more. Some of these can and will be resolved through further, more detailed analysis of the survey data. Others will require further research, some of which is projected at the present time.

CASEWORK WITH THE DEAF: A PROBLEM IN COMMUNICATION*

STEVEN K. CHOUGH

The caseworker dealing with the deaf client faces a frustrating problem regardless of the agency with which he is affiliated. The difficulty in communication is a paramount problem in any social work service for the deaf. In practice, the caseworker as well as the psychiatrist, psychologist, physician, rehabilitation counselor, or other professional is faced with the problem of communication and its distortion at every step in his work with the deaf client. The natural result is difficulty in understanding the client as a person, his problems, his feelings, and his potential strengths. The importance of communication cannot be overemphasized. Without communication the client-worker relationship cannot be established and help cannot be given.

It is difficult to discuss or describe the "typical" deaf person, because people who are termed deaf may vary widely in the degree of hearing loss, methods of communication used, their attitudes toward their deafness, and many other factors. They experience and interpret culturally engendered

* Reprinted, with permission of the National Association of Social Workers, from *Social Work*, Vol. 9, No. 4 (October, 1964), pp. 76–82. The author is Senior Psychiatric Social Worker, Mental Health Services for the Deaf, Department of Medical Genetics of the New York State Psychiatric Institute, Columbia University.

frustrations or gratifications according to their own personality and developmental history. It is, therefore, not advisable to assume that all deaf persons face the same kind of problems or respond to these problems in the same way. Perhaps emphasis should be placed on the principle that deaf persons are just people and, as such, are subject to the same problems as the unhandicapped.

Keeping this variability in mind, one can note certain general characteristics in terms of "deafness." There is, perhaps, a communicative difference among those who are deaf at birth or become deaf in early childhood, those who become progressively deaf because of gradual loss of hearing in later life, and those who become deaf suddenly in adulthood. The distinction in communicative ability in these three categories of the deaf is too complex to discuss here. For the purposes of this paper the term "deaf persons" is used to describe both those totally deaf from birth or early childhood and those partially deaf or hard of hearing who are unable to understand normal conversation.

It is estimated that today there are approximately 250,000 deaf children and adults in this country. "In a representative crowd of 700 Americans, we find no more than one who is deaf."[1] The deaf pass unnoticed and are pretty much lost in the general mass of people. "They have no *visible* characteristics that set them apart. They generally become known only as communication demands reveal their severe disability."[2]

In social work literature, authors discussing work with the deaf usually have focused on persons with partial hearing loss and on communication through the use of a hearing aid; the communication problem in work with severely deaf clients and the need for skills in communicating with them have received little attention. There is a possibility that much is missed with the deaf client in any social agency or health facility when communication is limited. It is hoped that this article, dealing with the effect of communication obstacles, various methods of communication used by the deaf, and the need for skills in communication, will be of some help to social workers in recognizing and dealing with the communication problem in order that the casework method may be utilized with the deaf. When a caseworker is mentioned in this paper, reference is being made to one who himself is a hearing person.

Effect of Communication Obstacles

One of the most basic needs of human beings is to communicate with others.[3] Each of us is aware of the fact that communication is not only the key to intellectual comprehension but also a medium for the expression of feelings and emotions. Dr. Rose Spiegel states:

> Communication is a dynamic process—experience in itself and also the gateway to other experience. Communication not only is a psychobiologic means, it is also an end—a process whose fulfillment brings its own gratification.[4]

She continues by saying that communication is a process that has, in a sense, some of the quality of growth and maturation, because a person has been shaped as a personality by his specific life experience in communication with others. Of significance, too, is the statement of Dr. Jurgen Ruesch, an outstanding authority on communication in psychiatry, to the effect that

> Since man needs a certain amount of gratifying communication in his life in order to learn, to grow, and to function in a group, all events that significantly curtail communication eventually will produce serious disturbances.[5]

Helmer R. Myklebust, a psychologist specializing in work with the deaf at Northwestern University, explains that

> Man is highly dependent on his senses. Through his senses come the sensations

[1] Williams, Boyce R., and Chase, Elizabeth A., Deafness: New Approaches, *Rehabilitation Record*, November–December, 1960, p. 17.

[2] *Ibid.*

[3] Sharoff, Robert L., Enforced Restriction of Communication: Its Implications for the Emotional and Intellectual Development of the Deaf Child, *American Journal of Psychiatry*, Vol. 116, November, 1959, p. 445.

[4] Specific Problems of Communication in Psychiatric Conditions, in Silvano Arietti, ed., *American Handbook of Psychiatry*, Vol. 1. New York, Basic Books, 1960, p. 910.

[5] Ruesch, Jurgen, General Theory of Communication in Psychiatry, in Silvano Arietti, ed., *ibid*, p. 903.

which constitute his experience. Upon the information he receives from his senses he builds his world, his world of perception and conception; of memory, imagination, thought, and reason.[6]

The ordinary infant does not first learn how to read but learns to comprehend and use the spoken word; he acquires auditory language. Dr. Edna S. Levine, an authority on psychology of the deaf with rich experience in working with deaf children and their parents, mentions Sigmund Freud as having acknowledged the importance of hearing in the metaphor "ego wears an auditory lobe."[7] Language, depending to a large extent on hearing, is the form that conveys ideas or messages, especially in interpersonal relations. "The existence of speech and language for all human beings seems to be bound to the human propensity for symbol-making."[8] Many scholars have long declared that without language human nature almost ceases to exist. Language is, it is seen clearly, the symbolic reservoir of the feelings, emotions, ideas, attitudes, and motives that are involved in the expression and perception of human experience and behavior.

The emotional development of the deaf, then, can scarcely remain unaffected by the barrier to comprehension. When a deaf child attempts to learn all aspects of language, an auditory sense deprivation limits to a large extent the world of experience. Since learning language, including reading, is initially a matter of hearing, the deaf child in school must work much harder than the hearing child to remember and memorize. Because of the language deficiency created by this sense of deprivation, the deaf child is faced with difficulty in understanding what is put before him and has trouble expressing himself. His vocabulary is built slowly and may be limited. It can be concluded that the lack of language is a great obstacle to thinking itself and to psychosocial maturation. It is, however, a serious mistake to assume that the imperfect language used by a deaf person means defective mental ability.

> An inability to communicate creates barriers to the satisfaction of basic needs. Since the individual's well-being depends in large part on his ability to satisfy his own needs harmoniously with the needs of others, the deafened person may experience considerable frustration both from inner, emotional sources and from outer, social situations.[9]

The majority of deaf persons have learned from experience that they cannot avoid meeting further frustration in communication. Because of difficulty in, or in some instances lack of, means of communication there can be nothing for some but a life of deprivation, loneliness, and dissatisfaction. It is difficult for the deaf to communicate their problems, their frustrations, their needs, and their hopes.

> In addition, they are apt to be sensitively aware of their own shortcomings, and even more so of the indifference and misconcep-

[6] *The Psychology of Deafness.* New York, Grune & Stratton, 1960, p. 1.

[7] *The Psychology of Deafness.* New York, Columbia University Press, 1960, p. 25.

[8] Spiegel, *op. cit.*, p. 917.

[9] Fibush, Esther W., The Problem of Hearing Loss, *Social Casework,* Vol. 36, No. 3, March, 1955, p. 125.

tions of the hearing world about the needs and problems of the deaf.[10]

Sharoff warns parents of deaf children not to restrict them from expressing themselves through natural communication, because such restriction can affect their ability to grow to emotional and social maturity.[11]

When deaf persons' communication with hearing persons becomes extremely frustrating, they are apt to seek ways of defending themselves by withdrawing or aggressively controlling the exchange of conversation. However, for them the real problem is not deafness in itself but the fact of living in a hearing world. Actually they live in mental isolation and suffer the lack of healthy socialization. Most of them are uninformed and misinformed about many things pertaining to the hearing world and even to the deaf world.

Methods of Communication

The communication methods used widely by the deaf in this country are speech, lipreading, writing, fingerspelling, and sign language. Speech and lipreading are referred to as "oral communication," sign language and fingerspelling as "manual communication."

Fingerspelling or the manual alphabet is defined as "the regular letters of the alphabet are formed by standard positions of the fingers of one or both hands . . . and words and sentences are thus spelled out in straight language."[12] Sign language refers to "an ideographic method of expression in which words and ideas are graphically formulated through codified gestures of the arms, hands, and body aided by facial expression."[13] While the characteristics of the sign language are more colorful, lively, and dramatic than other means of communication, it has some disadvantages, especially those of grammatical disorder, illogical systems, difficult expression of abstract ideas, and linguistic confusion.

The combination of oral and manual communication is referred to as "the simultaneous method" or "multiple communication." This is characterized by the use of the sign language and fingerspelling, with the individuals at the same time speaking. By "speaking" is meant either vocalization or movement of the lips without actual speech. In practice, when a hearing person, while using manual communication, speaks, the deaf person to whom he is talking can read his lip movements while watching his hands as well. When the latter speaks aloud while using manual communication, the hearing person can listen to him. If the deaf person speaks inaccurately or unclearly, the hearing person can move his eyes quickly to the other's hands, picking up his meaning from the sign language and fingerspelling. Understanding the deaf individual's speech depends upon both his ability to speak and the hearing person's familiarity with the speech of the deaf; it is probably best for the latter to watch the manual communication as well.

Fingerspelling has some advantages

---

[10] Levine, *op. cit.*, p. 40.
[11] Sharoff, *op. cit.*, pp. 443–446.
[12] Levine, *op. cit.*, p. 321.
[13] *Ibid.*

over sign language, especially in that it permits use of the names of people and places, technical or abstract words, and certain words that cannot be expressed by sign language. Its major values are accuracy and exactness. To many deaf persons, however, telling a story or listening to it through the manual alphabet only is slow, dull, colorless, and emotionless. They prefer a combination of sign language and fingerspelling to any one of the other methods. A number of the deaf, as well as the hard of hearing, can read lips and speech with amazing skill. The oral method is a desirable medium for those who can understand normal conversation. Unfortunately, though, the majority of the deaf are poor in speech and lipreading. Just as many people do not have a natural ability in music, many deaf persons do not have a natural talent in the art of lipreading.

Casework services with the deaf through written communication can be successful but are available to a limited number of highly intelligent deaf persons. Many deaf people confess a difficulty in comprehension when this method is used, admitting that they usually guess at meanings on the basis of familiar words. Just as hearing people prefer oral or spoken communication to written communication, so do almost all deaf people prefer manual communication. The written method seldom can express the emotional tones the worker needs to grasp, and the slowness of this method may affect the flow of ideas and feelings. The less formal education the deaf client has received, the more difficulty the worker

may have in communicating with him through the written method alone.

The author agrees with Levine's statement:

. . . manual conversation eases the strain of lipreading and talking in prolonged interview and enables the subject to relax somewhat while still continuing to converse. This is a particularly important consideration in cases of emotional disturbance, in which the writer has noted a preference for manual communication even on the part of habitual oralists.[14]

In the simultaneous method, if a deaf person misses a word or a statement on the lips, he always has the manual method to fall back on, because manual communication is perceived more adequately than lip movements.

Even the most expert lipreader is grateful for the larger visual area presented by the hands when used along with speech. . . . the average deaf person finds himself watching the lips, with his peripheral vision getting assurance from the hands that he is not missing anything. In this manner we have a communication procedure that is exact and free from guesswork.[15]

In addition, multiple communication can be of great value in developing speech and improving skills in lipreading.

Need for Communication Skills

Few social workers are trained in the skills necessary for social service to the deaf; still fewer know how to cope with

[14] Levine, *op. cit.*, p. 165.
[15] Garretson, Mervin D., The Need for Multiple Communication Skills in the Educative Process of the Deaf, *The Banner*, North Dakota School for the Deaf, Vol. 72. March, 1963, p. 3.

the communication problem in actual practice. Also, hearing workers frequently encounter a feeling of uselessness and hopelessness when assigned to help deaf clients with whom they feel they cannot communicate. Because of the unusual communication skills necessary, the social worker with the deaf has been limited in utilizing his usual knowledge and skill. He cannot talk with the client.

Because of lack of adequate communication, few deaf clients and patients are able to describe themselves or their needs adequately. How can the caseworker encourage the essential dignity and self-worth of these deaf clients? How can they be helped to develop and utilize their strengths? How can they be helped to feel like useful and adequate citizens in the community? How may they be assured of a worker who has both an understanding of and appreciation for the problems of the deaf? If communication is recognized as a prime factor in the caseworker-client relationship, how, then, can the simultaneous method be used by a worker to help the deaf improve their social functioning?

The following is an example of how deaf clients suffer because of communication obstacles and of how they can be helped through use of multiple communication with the caseworker.

Mrs. A was a congenitally deaf woman with two children. Because the father had been out of the home for some time she had received Aid to Families with Dependent Children for six years. An earlier caseworker, unable to communicate with her even through writing because of her limited education, had obtained the sparse social information in her case record from her children and other relatives. Little or nothing was known about Mrs. A's feelings or her perception of her situation. She had been severely isolated much of her life, and limited social and educational experience had followed a traumatic childhood.

Early work with Mrs. A was educational, not traditional casework. She was helped to understand the standardized sign language, improve her knowledge of English and of basic mathematics, and learn to tell time with the aid of a special type of clock. She was encouraged to go out of the house, to use public transportation, and to adjust in socialization with other deaf people. Eventually she was able to move into a rehabilitation program, learn a trade, and accept employment in competitive industry. Communication with this client was not easy, but the use of the sign language combined with fingerspelling permitted the exchange of thoughts and ideas necessary in the educative and casework process.

Some of the general psychosocial factors prevailing among the deaf should be considered. After leaving a school for the deaf, a great number of deaf persons tend to maintain association with other deaf people through various organizations of the deaf. Their tendency to seek social satisfaction from other deaf persons rather than from hearing people has given rise to a complicated social system. Many deaf persons, although desiring to seek out other deaf people, may for various reasons be unable to do so, leaving them no choice but to withdraw and live in a world of loneliness.

Some clients seem to feel ashamed or uncomfortable in asking help from social agencies, especially the public welfare agency, because they regard their need for public assistance and case-work help as an indication of failure. Since deaf people constitute a small group in any given city, they may know almost every other deaf individual, and are likely to feel uncomfortable in the presence of other deaf people if they are known as recipients of public assistance. Capable deaf people have great pride in their own achievements and abilities. More specifically, as a class they are proud of their economic independence. Consequently, many of them are highly critical of deaf recipients of public assistance or have little respect for them. Such facts discourage economically deprived deaf clients from seeking out other deaf people socially. The social worker needs to be sharply aware of this psychology of the deaf in relation to their stereotyped concepts of social work.

Suggestions for Caseworkers

In work with hearing-impaired clients, as well as all hearing clients, the caseworker endeavors to help them lead a useful and satisfying life. The worker should remind himself that he is not treating a deaf client as a disabled person but as a human being whose disability is an integral part of his personality.

The caseworker should accept the deaf client as he is and help him maintain his self-respect and personal dignity. He needs to be able to "give and take" freely with all types of deaf clients in order to establish rapport. He then will be able to enable them to bring out the important feelings, their hopes, and

the significant aspects of their lives that they may have had difficulty sharing with others.

Caseworkers can help hearing-impaired clients a great deal through arranging for medical examinations, the purchase of hearing aids, and planning for auditory and speech training. However, it is an erroneous conclusion that a hearing aid and remedial training will soon put everything to rights. Those who are hard of hearing or have a speech defect may need much more help than a hearing aid can give them. What is important in considering any casework service are:

1. Assessing the factors in the deaf client's personal and social development.
2. Assisting him, on the basis of this assessment, in coming to grips with the reality of his problem and in helping him work toward personally acceptable and realistic goals.
3. Helping him in locating and using various resources in the community.
4. Assisting, when necessary, in co-ordinating the various services available to him in his rehabilitation program.

When the hearing caseworker begins working with the deaf, he is apt to seek a third person who is capable of interpreting for the deaf client. It is not easy, however, for the worker to gain rapport with the client with a third person present. When the interpreter is a parent or other relative, it may be especially difficult for the worker, because the person may perform the role of collaborator by talking *about* rather than *for* the deaf client. In such interviews there is always the danger of the interview becoming a conversation between the worker and the interpreter. It should be kept in mind that the caseworker is responsible for maintaining the focus on the deaf client, not on the interpreter. When the hearing-impaired client gains confidence in the worker through skilled communication, he will often prove to be a highly cooperative interviewee.

The manual alphabet is the unified, standardized method all over this country, but in the sign language there are many "dialects" in different areas, just as in oral communication used by hearing people. In addition to mastering the sign language together with finger-spelling, the worker may need to master dialects as much as possible. When he is faced with unfamiliar gestures used by the deaf interviewee, he may ask him what is meant. The deaf client will usually be glad to explain, for he can thereby feel useful. Too much help requested of the client by the worker may, however, affect the role expectations of each and alter the relationship.

When the caseworker needs to obtain information about a deaf client from other persons, the deaf client must know why the worker wishes to see others, and what purpose will be served. The client should participate to the extent that he gives the worker permission to obtain the information and the worker discusses with him how important other people can be in relation to a better understanding of his situation.

In the case of a joint or family interview while the deaf interviewee is present, the caseworker should continuously let him know precisely what is being discussed. If the client wants to say something, the interviewer should break off his discussions with the other persons and listen to him or explain as well as he can exactly what they are discussing. It should be realized that the deaf client has learned in the most heartbreaking way how to wait. Keeping him involved in the caseworker's thinking and planning will help greatly in breaking down his isolation and impassiveness and enable him to develop more desire to participate in the casework plan.

Summary

The most significant need in the successful practice application of social work with the deaf is the recognition that the great barrier in communication is the first problem encountered by hearing caseworkers new to work with the deaf. In the usual interview situation, the client has a chance to tell his own story in his own way and the worker has an opportunity to hear his problems, needs, and feelings as the client expresses them. On the other hand, there seems to be an inability or natural reluctance on the part of a hearing caseworker unfamiliar with the deaf to overcome the communication obstacles that exist. There is apparently an equal inability on the part of deaf clients to tell their story to the uneasy and awkward interviewer.

As the casework relationship with

the deaf client is developed, the worker learns how he feels about his hearing loss and his unsolved problems and finds the range of his motivations, capacities, and opportunities in the process of the social diagnosis and treatment. Deaf people usually place their confidence in a hearing worker who is skillful in multiple communication and who has acquired an understanding and appreciation of the general problems of the deaf. The caseworker, therefore, is urged to learn these communication skills so that he can talk with the deaf in the most relaxing way. As Ruesch has stated:

> If we attempt to explore the secrets of psychotherapy, we invariably fall back upon its first and most important requirement— that, in addition to the patient, there must be another person present who is accessible and visible, who can be talked to, and who is ready to understand and to respond. Once interpersonal feedback is established, the exchange elicits in the patient the sensation of pleasure. To be acknowledged is pleasant; to be understood is gratifying; to be understood and to agree is exciting. This gratification becomes the driving force which induces the patient to seek further improvement.[16]

Caseworkers who work directly with deaf clients or patients are much in need of preliminary preparation, as are

[16] Ruesch, *op. cit.*, p. 904.

any professionals who specialize in new fields. It is suggested that there should be at least one caseworker trained to communicate with the deaf in a large agency or hospital in which deaf recipients are helped or are designed to be helped. Where can he learn the sign language and fingerspelling? There are many available sign language facilities provided by schools for the deaf and by city clubs, state associations, religious organizations, and fraternal orders for the deaf. The period of learning manual communication depends to a great extent upon the individual's ability and motives, ranging from several months to several years. It must be realized that learning manual communication is an art, just as is learning any foreign language.

It is hoped that the hearing social worker who is confronted with the problem of communicating with deaf clients will use his skills and make a real effort to help the clients achieve mutually acceptable and realistic goals. While skill in communication is but one phase of the casework process, it is an extremely important one, basic to the application of other aspects of the casework method. If the significance of adequate communication with the deaf is realized by social workers, more deaf clients may accomplish the reality and gratification of full citizenship.

"TRULY REMARKABLE PEOPLE"*

Edgar L. Lowell

I want to talk to you about some ideas, some impressions, and some of the knowledge that has been accumulated that might contribute to our understanding of people who are deaf.

First of all, we must distinguish between the various degrees of deafness. Much misunderstanding about deaf people arises from confusion on this point.

We should not judge the deaf person on the basis of what a hard-of-hearing person can do, even though both have hearing problems, and both, especially if they wear hearing aids, may be put in the same category by the general public.

The next and equally important distinction must be made on the basis of age at onset of deafness. In other words, did the individual have any opportunity to acquire language and speech through hearing, or did he have to rely primarily on vision? This is the distinction between the deaf and the deafened person. In general, the language, speech, voice quality of the deafened person can be expected to be better than those of the person who has never heard.

Another major topic traditionally included in a talk on the "psychology of the deaf" has to do with mental development. This is a particularly thorny

issue for two reasons. The first is that most intelligence tests are verbal tests and depend on the individual's language ability, the very area in which many deaf people are deficient, for the measurement of their intelligence. The second problem is that the factors which cause deafness may also cause mild brain damage. When the brain damage is severe, it is fairly easy to pick up, but there is a considerable amount of mild brain damage, or what it has become fashionable to call "neurological involvements," among the deaf. These are subtle involvements which interfere with the perception and utilization of information, yet are not severe enough to rate a clear-cut diagnosis of brain damage. Our tests for detecting this condition are wholly inadequate, but it is certainly not inconceivable that the factors that would cause damage to the auditory system *in utero* may also cause damage to other parts of the central nervous system. We must always consider the possibility that in any reporting of intelligence test data involving the deaf we may be including a significant number of people suffering mild brain damage, thus confusing the true picture.

Impaired language development really poses a classical "chicken or the egg" problem in assessing the intelligence of the deaf. We are not in a position to know whether the deaf person we are testing has poor language because he has low intelligence, or

* Reprinted from *Rehabilitation Record*, a publication of the U. S. Vocational Rehabilitation Administration, Department of Health, Education, and Welfare, Washington, D. C., May–June, 1962.

whether his inability to realize his full mental potential is due to his limited language. Given these cautions, let us look briefly at a few of the studies that have been done to evaluate the intelligence of people who are deaf.

The early classic study by Pintner and Reamer in 1920 covered more than 2,000 children in schools for the deaf. In general, their conclusions were that the deaf children were approximately two years behind their hearing comparison groups on intelligence tests, and five years behind them educationally. In the forty or so years since this early study, there have been literally hundreds of similar studies. As we became more sophisticated, it became possible to construct tests made of subtests, each aimed at measuring a single factor or facet of intelligence. The important finding on many of these tests was that, although the deaf were inferior in some areas, in others they did better than the hearing comparison groups. These tests have shown, for example, that deaf people have superior memory for design and movement, while their ability to recall digits is inferior to that of people with normal hearing.

These findings are important because they emphasize the fact that although deafness has some effect on intellectual development, it is clearly not a general one.

How well deaf students can perform on today's nonverbal intelligence tests is indicated in a recent study by Quigley and Frisina of 240 selected deaf students in schools all over the United States. They found that the mean score on the Chicago Nonverbal Performance Scale was 102, slightly better than the average of 100. When it came to educational achievement, as measured by the Stanford Achievement Test, this group, with an average age of fourteen years, had an average achievement grade-level of slightly below the fourth grade. At fourteen we might expect them to be at the eighth-grade level, indicating a retardation of four years.

We must remember that the educational achievement was measured on the Stanford Achievement Test, a test designed for administration to normal hearing children with normal language ability. Again, we must return to the conclusion that although deafness undoubtedly influences mental development, our ability to evaluate the extent of the influence is hampered by the language-oriented tests that are available. Further confirmation of this viewpoint is contained in an interesting study by Eva Stunkel, a psychologist from the United States Civil Service Commission, who studied the performance of deaf and hard-of-hearing college students on verbal and nonverbal tests used in the selection of Federal Civil Service employees. She found that deaf people have above-average ability on a nonverbal reasoning test, yet showed weakness in handling tests of a verbal nature.

Another major heading traditionally included in talks about the psychology of the deaf is personality development. When they say "personality," psychologists generally mean the scores that people get on personality tests. These, again, are strongly dependent on language and are of questionable value for use with deaf people. For example, on the widely used Minnesota Multiphasic Personality Inventory, there are a number of questions such as "I am easily awakened by noise," "I would like to be a singer," or even, "At times I hear so well it bothers me," which clearly are inappropriate for the deaf population. I will not labor this point other than to say that those tests which are more appropriately used with the deaf suggest that there are some differences in test score results. Not all deaf people are free from personality problems any more than all hearing people are.

The personality organization of a deaf person is understandably different. His relationships with others, his relationship to the world, are inevitably altered by deafness, but we must look to other sources than personality tests for an understandable picture of these consequences.

Where are we to look? We might expect that if the personality and social development of the deaf were uniquely altered by deafness, it would show up in their occupational adjustment. Here we fortunately have the very fine study on occupational conditions among the deaf by Lunde and Bigman, which is a sampling of more than 10,000 deaf people. A few of the highlights from this report may help to answer our question. Two out of three deaf people in this sample were married, which is about the same ratio we find in the general population. This certainly speaks well for their personal and social adjustment. Of the married ones, approxi-

mately 95 per cent were married to other deaf or hard-of-hearing people. About 9 per cent claimed at least one year of college as compared with approximately 14 per cent in the general population, but it is encouraging to note that the number of years of schooling was lowest in the older-age groups in this study, and highest in the younger groups, suggesting that this condition is improving.

But what of the actual satisfaction on the job? Of those employed during the ten years of this survey, almost two thirds had held a job for five years or more, and 40 per cent had been on the same job for ten years or more. This, it seems to me, is an excellent record, and one which would argue strongly against deafness having any universal or overall unfavorable influence on the personality or social adjustment of deaf people, at least as it is reflected in job stability. On an index of job satisfaction constructed from questions concerning working conditions, earnings, and promotions, more than 70 per cent of the respondents were rated as having very high or high job satisfaction, and only 8 per cent as having low or very low job satisfaction.

Lest this picture appear too rosy, it is important to add that there is evidence of underemployment of the deaf in this study.

In the general population, approximately 40 per cent are engaged in professional, technical, managerial and white collar and clerical occupations as compared with 17 per cent among the deaf, while 52 per cent of the general population are engaged in manual jobs as compared with 83 per cent of the deaf. In view of the other favorable factors that have been pointed out, this would be rather clear evidence of underemployment.*

By this time I hope that many of you are beginning to be a little disturbed about what I have been saying. The truth is that I am, too. But this is the traditional approach to what is commonly called, "the psychology of the deaf," namely, a listing of facts that have been accumulated about the measurable attributes of people who do not hear. This description is flat and colorless. There is not too much fault you can find with the figures I have reported, but I rather imagine they don't satisfy you. I believe that the solution to this problem lies in the fact that understanding other people is not a one-way or one-sided process. To know, to understand, to appreciate persons who are deaf must involve a consideration of the impact of their deafness on those who can hear.

Facts re Deafness

Let us turn our attention to people who hear. Let us try to schematize the relationship between the deaf and the hearing person. It will be necessary greatly to oversimplify the situation,

---

* It may be fair to qualify this interpretation by the fact that in so many areas of "professional, technical, managerial and white collar and clerical occupations," ease of communication via speech (including use of telephone and intercommunication facilities) is an important consideration, and hence the fact of "underemployment" may in most instances be regarded as an inevitable sequel.—I.S.F.

and I am afraid that when we are through we will only have "elaborated the obvious"—but perhaps that is the role of psychology. Let us start with five facts that most psychologists use. I will only highlight those concepts essential for my arguments—concepts I believe most of us would agree upon.

The first is the undeniable fact that most people who are deaf have a communication handicap. The second is that we all have "expectations" about how things should go in the world, and whether we realize it or not, we are quite dependent on these expectations. The third is that we all carry around with us an appraisal of ourselves or a self-concept. The fourth and fifth are related: our behavior is influenced by learning and our learning is facilitated and influenced by our satisfactions.

Let us first consider "expectation." We all have expectations about how human behavior will, or should, take place, and when these expectations are not fulfilled, we are apt to be upset. If, for example, instead of talking to you about the "psychology of deafness," I had pulled some balls out of my pocket and done a juggling act, your initial amusement would soon have given way to uneasiness and concern. You might not even have been aware of why you felt uneasy, but you would have. That is an extreme example, but my point is that if I had not behaved as you had expected, you would have been disturbed.

Now let's take the case of the person with normal hearing who has not had previous experience with the deaf—

and I am afraid this represents the vast majority of the population. He may have some difficulty in understanding deaf speech, and his own communication with the deaf person may be slow and limited. He has some normal expectations about how communication will take place between himself and his fellow man. When it does not work out that way he is disturbed. And what happens then? We can imagine he will try to eliminate the cause of his uneasiness or distress as soon as possible by terminating the conversation.

I remember vividly, for example, my own withdrawal when attempting to buy a bottle of cleaning fluid in a French department store. My communication ability in French is definitely deficient. After about fifteen minutes of futile gesturing, mumbling poor French, I finally gave up, and feeling very foolish and inadequate, walked out of the store wearing my conspicuously stained tie.

Depending upon his self-concept, the failure of the hearing person to understand or to communicate effectively with the person who is deaf may also create uneasiness. With other hearing people he can communicate easily, but when dealing with the person who is deaf, the all-important communication process is suddenly not working well. "Whose fault is it? His, or could it be mine?" This can cause feelings of concern and may lead to avoidance or withdrawal.

Let us now consider the last two factors, the influence of learning on behavior, and the influence of satisfaction on learning. The point here is that we tend to learn those things which give us pleasure and satisfaction, and this learning determines our future behavior. In a new situation we tend to do the things that we have learned in the past that brought us pleasure or satisfaction. We also learn to avoid those situations which cause us pain or unpleasantness.

If we attempt to apply these two factors to our hypothetical situation involving attempts at communication between a hearing and a deaf person, and if we accept the possibilities described earlier, we can see that those two factors will only reinforce withdrawal or avoidance. If the hearing person is distressed or disturbed by the lack of confirmation of his expectations, or if he withdraws from the situation because his failure to communicate arouses within him feelings of inadequacy, then learning will only reinforce the situation and increase the likelihood that when he is again confronted with an opportunity to communicate with the deaf person, he will avoid it.

The conclusion is rather grim. And while this is an obviously oversimplified analysis, I believe it does point to the inevitable conclusion that the psychology of the deaf person is shaped in large part by the reaction of the hearing people with whom he comes in contact.

I would like to take this analysis a step further because I am sure that by this time many of you have noticed that I have talked only about the reactions of the hearing person. What about the expectation and self-concept of the person who is deaf? What about his learning?

The general laws of psychology apply to people who are deaf as well. They too find their behavior shaped by past learning and their learning facilitated by the satisfactions they receive. What are the expectations the deaf person builds up? If our previous analysis is right, he must learn from experience that the withdrawal or avoidance reaction is an expected behavior of the average hearing person. Can we expect that the deaf person will derive much satisfaction from these encounters? Not likely. We can predict that he will learn to interact primarily with those people with whom he can communicate effectively. Some incidental evidence that this may be the case was given in the earlier report that 95 per cent of the married people in the Lunde and Bigman study were married to other deaf or hard-of-hearing people.

The remarkable and surprising thing is that the deaf do not limit themselves to communicating only with other deaf people. Instead, they make the extra effort and get along in the world very successfully, as the Lunde and Bigman study also demonstrated.

If you have followed my reasoning this far, I think we are led to an inevitable conclusion which was the purpose of this analysis. That is that the deaf are truly remarkable people. Despite a communication handicap, it is clear that they have that extra something—call it what you will, intelligence, motivation, personality, desire—which enables them to persist in their efforts to interact with people with normal hearing. Those who succeed must do so at the cost of greater effort and greater understanding than are required of most of us.

The other conclusion which follows from this analysis is that the success of the deaf person also depends in large part on the understanding of the hearing person. If a new and more realistic image of the deaf is to be created, it must come from increased understanding and awareness on the part of the general public. The responsibility and the challenge are squarely up to us.